A NASTY LITTLE WAR

Also by Anna Reid

The Shaman's Coat: A Native History of Siberia
Leningrad: Tragedy of a City Under Siege, 1941–44
Borderland: A Journey Through the History of Ukraine

A NASTY LITTLE WAR

THE WESTERN INTERVENTION
INTO THE RUSSIAN CIVIL WAR

ANNA REID

BASIC BOOKS

NEW YORK

Basic Books
Hachette Book Group
1290 Avenue of the Americas, New York, NY 10104
www.basicbooks.com

Printed in the United States of America

Originally published in 2023 by John Murray in Great Britain
First US Edition: February 2024

Published by Basic Books, an imprint of Hachette Book Group, Inc. The Basic Books name and logo is a registered trademark of the Hachette Book Group.

The Hachette Speakers Bureau provides a wide range of authors for speaking events. To find out more, go to hachettespeakersbureau.com or email HachetteSpeakers@hbgusa.com.

Basic books may be purchased in bulk for business, educational, or promotional use. For more information, please contact your local bookseller or the Hachette Book Group Special Markets Department at special.markets@hbgusa.com.

The publisher is not responsible for websites (or their content) that are not owned by the publisher.

Maps drawn by Barking Dog Art

Typeset in Bembo MT by Hewer Text UK Ltd, Edinburgh

Library of Congress Control Number: 2023945260

ISBNs: 9781541619661 (hardcover), 9781541619654 (ebook)

LSC-C

Printing 1, 2023

For my father, Alex Reid

Contents

PART III
White Advances, April–September 1919

PART IV
White Retreats, September 1919–March 1920

PART V
The End, 1920

Illustrations follow page 170.

Maps

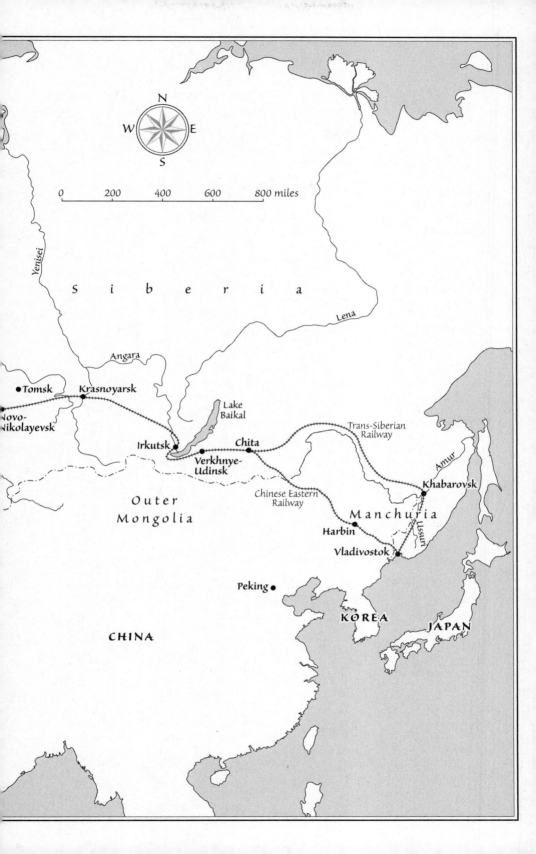

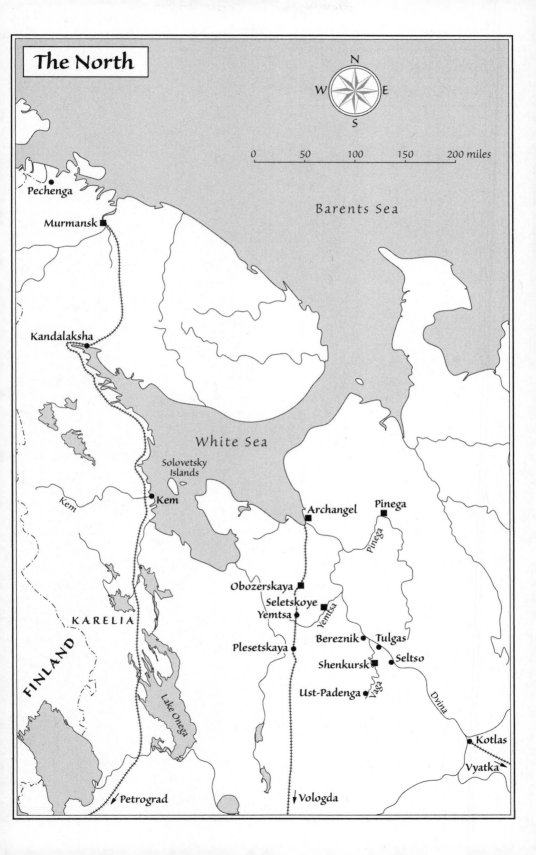

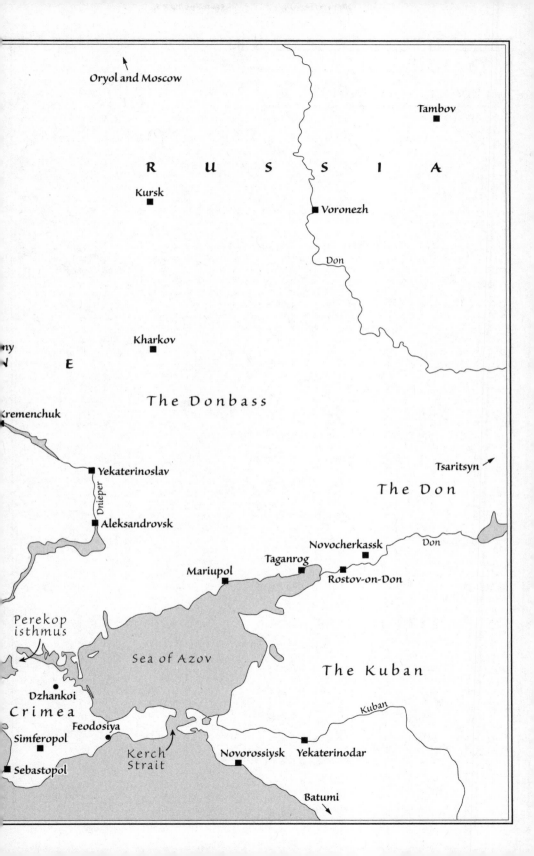

The Baltics
(Borders as settled 1920–2)

FINLAND

Vyborg

Lake Ladoga

Biorko Sound

Helsingfors

Kronstadt

Terijoki

Petrograd

Krasnaya Gorka fort

Neva

Gulf of Finland

Baltic Sea

Reval

Narva

Gatchina

ESTONIA

Lake Peipus

Dorpat

Walk

Pskov

Wenden

Courland

Riga

LATVIA

Lettgallen

RUSSIA

Libau

Mitau

Daugava

LITHUANIA

Kaunas

Vilnius

N
W   E
S

EAST PRUSSIA

POLAND

0   120   140   160   180 miles

Note on Place Names

Most of the cities mentioned in this book have gone through one if not two name changes since the Intervention. To avoid anachronism I have used the names of the period, hence Petrograd rather than St Petersburg, Reval rather than Tallinn and – reluctantly – Russian Kiev rather than Ukrainian Kyiv. Today's names are flagged in the text. Where applicable, I have also used the anglicisations of the time – so Archangel instead of Arkhangelsk, Sebastopol instead of Sevastopol, and the Dnieper river rather than the Dnipro or Dnyepr.

A NASTY LITTLE WAR

Introduction

O N A BEACH at the mouth of the river Dvina on a windless midsummer day, the sky is a great bright dome, the woods the piercing green of the Arctic's fast-forward growing season, the sea the steely blue that tells you it was ice not long ago and will be again soon. Overhead, terns wheel and screech: the nicely onomatopoeic Russian word for them, my companion tells me, is *krachki*. Along a curve of sand, a tall black building – a wooden lighthouse. Behind, marram grass, a gap-toothed boardwalk and a mound topped by a pink obelisk. Close to, the monument is falling to pieces, stone facing coming away in chunks, iron railings twisted and rusting. Still in place, in bronze, are a hammer and sickle and the words: 'Glory to the patriots, tortured by the Interventionists on the island of Mudyug, 1918–20.'

The Mudyug obelisk commemorates one of the most quixotic and, for the millions of civilians affected, tragic Western military adventures of the twentieth century: Britain, France and America's attempt to reverse the 1917 Russian Revolution. Known as the 'Intervention', it started out as a sideshow to the war against Germany, its chief aim to secure Allied supplies after Russia's extraordinary new leaders, the Bolsheviks, made peace with Berlin. After Germany's defeat it expanded, morphing into an explicit drive to replace the Bolsheviks with one of the conservative – nicknamed 'White' – regimes setting themselves up around the old empire's periphery.

The operation was substantial. Some 180,000 Allied troops from sixteen countries (Britain, France, America, Japan, Italy, Greece, Poland, Romania, Czechoslovakia and Serbia, plus colonial troops from Canada, Australia, New Zealand, India, Morocco and Senegal) took part, in half a dozen theatres ranging from the Caspian Sea to

I

the Arctic, and from Poland to the Pacific. With them came guns, tanks, aircraft, uniforms, food and medical supplies, as well as over £100 million in loans. It ended two years later with fewer than two thousand Allied lives lost and one not insignificant gain – independence for the Latvians and Estonians. But as to overthrowing the Bolsheviks, it comprehensively failed. In port after port, as the Red Army advanced and the White ones collapsed, Allied troops destroyed equipment, filed back onto their ships and sailed away. Typically, the last they saw of Russia was smoke rising from burning warehouses, and quaysides packed with desperate, left-behind refugees.

It was a humiliation, and given all the Allied promises, a shameful one – best forgotten, or conveniently elided with the Great War. The willed forgetting persisted. Richard Nixon, delivering a Message of Friendship in Moscow in 1972, and Margaret Thatcher, receiving Mikhail Gorbachev at Chequers in 1984, both stated that their countries and Russia had never been at war. They were put right, but given its uniqueness – the only time America has sent troops to Russia, and the only time since the Crimean War that Britain and France have – it is surprising how little discussed the Intervention still is today.

Civil conflicts are always messy, but the Russian Civil War – more accurately Wars, with 'Russian' in inverted commas – was especially so. By the time the Allies arrived in force, in the summer of 1918, two dozen different so-called governments functioned on the territory of the former Russian Empire. ('Dictators', joked a British aide, were received 'from 7 to 10; Supreme Rulers between 10 and 1; prime ministers could be admitted between 2 and 5.'[1]) Though by end the Allies concentrated their support on a spin-off from the old tsarist army, initially they were happy to partner with whatever forces came to hand. At different times and places, Intervention troops fought alongside Red Russians against White Finns; with Germans, White Russians and national Balts against Red Russians and Red Balts; with Armenian socialists against Turks and Azeris; with White Russians against national Ukrainians; and with Poles against national Ukrainians and Red Russians – and this far from exhausts the list. The fighting itself was equally confusing. All the armies involved were small and weak, so that towns changed hands with dizzying frequency. Troops deserted en masse to the enemy and back again; civilians were indistinguishable from fighters; and individuals and propaganda materials freely crossed vague, ever-changing front lines. A recurrent theme of Intervention accounts is Russia's disconcerting formlessness. The country is variously compared to a 'half-cooked plum pudding', to butter and to quicksand – all easy to cut into, but hard to get free of. Propping her up was 'like trying to get a feather-bed to stand on end'.[2]

Into this chaotic scene stepped an intensely conventional figure – the British regular army officer. Unmistakeable in neat moustache, jodphurs and wide-skirted belted jacket, he had been born into a middle-class family somewhere in the counties, been sent to prep and public school, to the Sandhurst or Woolwich military academies, and then to the Western Front. Institutionalised from early childhood, untravelled except with the army, ignorant of women save for his mother and sisters (and perhaps prostitutes), he was to the modern eye both extraordinarily experienced – in responsibility, discomfort, fear and death – and extraordinarily innocent. Though he had grown up in the age of Freud and Joyce, Gandhi and the Suffragettes, they touched his world-view not at all. Son of the most powerful nation of the day, his touchstones were Empire – an *a priori* Good Thing; country – foreigners were by definition funny; and faith – sincere, though best kept to oneself. His style – its understatement intended to convey natural superiority – was modelled on the heroes of John Buchan: decent, anti-intellectual, self-deprecating and eternally stiff of upper lip.

Responses to being sent to Russia varied. Pre Germany's defeat, career soldiers were usually disappointed at being diverted from the main action. Non-regulars, however, were only too delighted to escape it. 'As most people on board had come back from a considerable amount of service in France', a subaltern remembered of the cheerful mood on his Arctic-bound troopship, 'the Expedition was looked upon as a picnic.'[3] Americans and Canadians often felt tricked. Told they were going to Europe to fight the Kaiser, they now learned that they would be restoring, as they saw it, the equally despotic Tsar. The second, post-Armistice wave of troops was officered by volunteers. Some signed up just because demobilisation left them at a loose end, but more than a few – sometimes reluctant, later, to admit it – out of genuine conviction. An Old Etonian felt himself 'committed to a crusade' and 'could not wait to go' – a stance his London friends thought 'quite mad'.[4]

Disembarking from their ships, all found themselves on wildly unfamiliar ground. Around far-northern Murmansk, stony tundra – grey boulders, stunted birches, bleak little tarns – stretched as far as the eye could see. Even in midsummer it was piebald with snow, and in the twenty-four-hour winter darkness temperatures dropped to forty degrees below freezing – so cold that sentries had to be relieved every half hour, lest they die from exposure. Further south tundra gave way to the different endless sameness of the *taiga*. 'Trees trees, trees', remembered a Lambeth-bred private; 'That's all you saw, all day long . . . If you put your small kit down by a tree and you went twelve yards away, you'd have a hell of a time finding it again.'[5] Two thousand miles away on the desert-bound Caspian, the Silk Road city of Baku backed onto dun hills, its swallowtail battlements enclosing mosques and camel-trains and all the exotic nationalities of the Caucasus and Central Asia – more Persia than Russia. To the west, on the Black Sea steppe, green-gold grasslands rippled to the horizon. 'There was nothing to see', a dreamily disoriented Scot wrote of a refuelling halt, 'except grass and flowers, and an occasional partridge, and nothing to hear except the slow escape of steam over the singing of larks . . . It was the biggest place I had ever seen.'[6] To cope, he and others groped for what they knew, likening bits of Siberia to 'the Simla hill districts', Burmese 'scrub jungle', Switzerland, Northumberland and the English Lakes.

As well as disorientation, Russia meant a crazy patchwork of experiences, as different as possible from the grim monotony of the trenches. Interventionists rode on sleds and steam trains, slept in log cabins and luxury hotels, improvised river gunboats and the world's first air-dropped chemical weapons, distributed food aid, addressed striking railway workers, took tea with warlords and princesses, got swept up in epic retreats, organised several coups and at least one assassination. During not infrequent periods of downtime, they also strenuously enjoyed themselves; their private papers overflow with

early morning rides ('just like going cub hunting'), fishing ('mosquitoes in good fighting form'), swimming ('top-hole'), church-visiting
('tawdry Ikons . . . no seats'), mule-racing, ice-yachting, and most of
all with extraordinarily unpleasant-sounding shooting expeditions.
('The marsh was very marshy indeed', a midshipman wrote to his
mother of a midwinter expedition after snipe.) The minimisation of
suffering and violence was in the style of the times, and helped gloss
over impending defeat. But much of the time the enjoyment feels
genuine. In the archives, the photographs that slip from the folders are
not of heaped typhus victims, but of cheerful young men, sporting
comic shaggy hats, grinning into the sun from wayside railway platforms or rustic verandahs.

What did these men make of the Russians, and what did the Russians
make of them? Characteristic of the Intervention – and another
contrast with the war in France – were daily interactions between
soldiers and civilians. Since Allied troops were few, they relied on the
local population for transport, labour and accommodation. Billeted
on village families, they squashed with them into earth-floored, bug-
infested cottages of one or two rooms. Despite the language barrier,
communication often flourished. Old people were taken for their
first-ever rides in motor cars; crowds gathered to wonder at wind-up
gramophones; children were given sweets and shown the workings of
torches and binoculars. In the back of his notebook an American
private wrote down the names Anna and Alexandra – girlfriends?
children? – and the Russian words, phonetically spelt, for 'pencil',
'shirt', 'face', 'hair', 'hand', 'baby', 'trouser', 'key', 'cup', 'pipe', 'chair'
and 'hat'.[7] Others sketched ingenious novelties that caught their eye:
samovars, a rope-and-pulley cradle-rocking device, pole-boats and
different designs of sled.

It was not, of course, an equal relationship. The first words of
Russian a British supply sergeant learned were *loshad* and *seichas* –
'Horse' and 'Now'. 'We didn't ask to stay the night, as far as I remember. We just took our gear inside and it was taken for granted that we
would do. Very pleasant people.' The words Russians most often
addressed to him were *Daitye tsigaret* – 'Give a cigarette': 'They really
were a nation of scroungers. One can understand, of course – the

poor folks didn't have *anything*.'[8] But as well as pitying their poverty, he also admired their resourcefulness and craftsmanship: it was amazing that with axes alone they could build a bridge strong enough to take a tank. And often they gave as good as they got. One woman gave a soldier a spectacular scolding when she caught him milking her cow – 'she took the milk off him; he was trembling!'[9] Another chased a naked group out of her *banya*, coming after them with scoopfuls of hot ash. Probably the commonest Allied–Russian interaction was '*skolko*-ing' – from the Russian for 'how much?' – as soldiers bartered army-issue food and clothing for eggs, milk and souvenirs.

In the refugee-crowded provincial cities where the military missions made their headquarters, officer Interventionists enjoyed a positively hectic social life. Viewed as potential saviours – or, if the worst came to the worst, tickets out of the country – by the local middle classes, they were treated to a whirl of concerts, dances, tea-parties and amateur dramatics. 'Such flirtations with the pretty *barishnas*!' wrote the handsome heir to a Milwaukee meat-packing fortune of his time in the North; 'Such whispered gossip and intrigue and scandal in light-hearted Archangel!'[10] A Yorkshire signals sergeant was thrilled to be invited to the ballet by his unit's telephonist, a refugee baroness:

> When I went into the box the whole audience stood up and shouted in Russian 'How d'ye do! Welcome!' And all the Russian troops that were in there, they all saluted. I didn't know what to do – I saluted back, and knew the Russian for 'thankyou', and they were delighted . . . It was a marvellous show.[11]

Much trickier were relations between the Interventionists and their counterparts in the various counter-revolutionary Russian armies. Though individual friendships were made, overall the relationship was one of mutual incomprehension and exasperation – shading, as the White cause began to founder, into vituperation and dislike. 'Our Russian allies', a British artilleryman remembered of his time teaching gunnery in Western Siberia, were

> generous to absurdity at times, laughter-loving frequently, devoted comrades at odd moments, delightful hosts and good talkers. [But]

from a military or business point of view they were a flop . . . They could not get things done, they were lazy, untidy, pessimistic, boastful, ignorant, untruthful and dishonest. They had no patriotism, though they wept over Holy Russia. They bragged, but were incompetent and often cowardly. They were cruel. They hated the Allies for not sending enormous armies to settle their troubles, while the only people who could clean up the mess were themselves.[12]

The Etonian who 'could not wait to go' – Major Hudleston Williamson – was almost as disparaging about his opposite numbers in the South: an 'extraordinary crowd' sporting 'epaulettes like great tea-trays' and spurs that 'jingled like marbles in a tin', they were friendly enough, but 'apart from swearing frightful oaths of revenge on the Bolsheviks', not much use.[13] French forces in the Black Sea port of Odessa were equally dismissive, reporting to Paris that White command gambled, drank and installed their mistresses in luxurious staff trains – *bordels roulants* – while all around starved. The more perceptive Interventionists grasped the reasons for the Russians' disorganisation and apathy. They had lost families and friends, homes, wealth, a war and their country. They were not just stuck in the past, but in shock. Though angered by persistent black-marketeering of British supplies, Williamson turned a blind eye on the grounds that it would be 'the worst possible form' to criticise people who had 'suffered so severely' – especially since plenty of British officers were 'doing pretty well, thank you, with the whisky.'[14] The Whites' worst psychological handicap, he thought, was the memory of the 1917 mass mutinies within the Imperial Army. 'When one's own men have turned against one, it can always happen again. And I have often wondered since – had I been in their shoes, would I have been any better?' Williamson's empathy, though, was unusual. Messing separately from their Russian colleagues, most Allied officers got to know them only superficially and saw only their failings.

The disillusion was reciprocated. Especially after Germany's defeat, there was great bitterness amongst educated Russians in general that the Allies were not coming in overwhelming strength to Russia's aid. Instead she was being fobbed off with token forces, sub-standard army surplus, and mid-ranking officers who thought they knew best despite never having set foot in the country before.

'The English responded to any Russian views', a White general remembered, with

> back-slapping, and that typical English joviality that makes interlocutors wonder if they are dealing with a very clever and cunning person, or a complete simpleton. The outcome . . . was always the same. The English always did everything their own way, and always met with failure.

Things would not improve, he thought, until they stopped treating Russians like some 'small, savage tribe' of Indians or Malays.[15] An encounter between an embedded British officer-journalist (the *Daily Express*'s John Hodgson) and a Prince Obolensky, attached to the Military Mission in the South, was the kind of thing he meant. Truthfully but tactlessly, Hodgson observed to Obolensky that the White government was failing because it was hopeless at administration. Obolensky – bearer of one of the grandest names in the country – retorted that an English one in the same circumstances would do no better. 'I told him', Hodgson relates,

> that he was mistaken, because [in England] the sense of civic responsibility was so high . . . that at any given time the Corporation of any sizeable city could tackle without grave risk of disaster the task of governing the whole Empire.[16]

Condescension, in the circumstances, was inevitable, but it would not have been the first time that the prince had to bite his tongue.

The blackest mark against the Interventionists – some Americans honourably excepted – is their connivance in White war crimes. Militarily, the Civil War was not very bloody. The armies involved were small, and set-piece battles few. Off the battlefield, though, it was extraordinarily violent, characterised by mass executions of civilians and prisoners of war, rape, torture, hostage-taking, village-burning and looting. The single group who suffered most were Jews. All sides, including the Red Army, committed pogroms. (The word derives from the Russian verb *gromit*: to smash or destroy.) But the Whites, in the South in the second half of 1919, were amongst the worst. Britain, by then the Whites' last remaining active backer, could have threatened to withdraw support if the massacres did not cease – and done so. Instead, she turned a blind eye. In Westminster and on the ground, reports of White violence against Jews were denied or downplayed, and protests and petitions brushed aside. The various British military missions also used the Whites' 'Jew-equals-Bolshevik' smear in their own Russian-language propaganda, many if not most mission members believing it themselves. One of the most jolting aspects of researching this book, even taking into account the prejudices of the day, was discovering how even the most likeable officer diarists – in other respects fair-minded, commonsensical men – littered their private writing with witless antisemitic jibes.

The Intervention was a pointer to the future. Overlapping with the close of the Great War proper, it was the victors' response to state failure in their own backyard and to a fanatical, fast-spreading new ideology. It was where Britain began to lose her imperialist swagger, and America her foreign-policy idealism. In France and Germany it fractured and radicalised, pushing Europe down the road towards another world war. The dilemmas it raised – when to step into other countries' civil conflicts; how to deal with regimes that reject international norms; how to counter radicalism; whether to ignore allies' human-rights abuses – echo down the decades. The political noise of the time is familiar too: the mixture of good intentions and self-delusion, the flag-waving and empty promises, the cover-ups, exaggerations and downright lies. And afterwards, when the soldiers have skedaddled and the lies been exposed, the shame, the shiftiness, the calls to move on.

At the time of writing (spring 2023) Intervention place-names – Kyiv, Kharkiv, Odesa, Kherson – are in the news again, as Putin's Russia attempts to reconquer its thirty-years independent neighbour, Ukraine. Hideous telescoper of time are the pictures from the ground: burned-out buildings, railway stations packed with refugee women and children, civilians lying dead on the streets where murderous soldiers have been through. Appalled, the West is sending Ukraine money and arms, which have allowed her to start pushing Russia back. Ukrainians hope for a quick victory, and for NATO membership to make them safe in the future. The Kremlin hopes that the West will lose interest, and cut Ukraine loose. Likeliest perhaps, unless Putin falls from power, is a battlefield stalemate followed by a frozen conflict – better than today's daily carnage, but still grim for Ukraine and destabilising for the rest of the world.

There is no simple read-across from the Intervention. Today's war is not a civil one, and the impressive and staunchly democratic Ukrainians are not the inept, revanchist Whites. The lazy lesson from 1918–20 – that Western meddling in the region failed then, and will again now – is completely mistaken. If the Intervention does have something to teach, it is that Putin will fail for the same reason that the Whites did: because he underestimates the desire for freedom of the non-Russian nations, and because for his own people, he has no programme beyond the empty assertion of Russia's greatness and right to rule. A century ago, the West pulled out after barely two years and should have done so sooner, since all it was doing was prolonging the Civil War. This time, the cause is both good and viable, and *pace* America's Republicans, resolve seems set to stay strong. Perhaps history's most useful reminder is that outsiders, and indeed Russians themselves, often get Russia spectacularly wrong. Hope that conventional wisdom is wrong again now – that Ukraine wins quickly and decisively, that Putin goes, and that Russia recovers her sanity and intervention a good name.

PART I

After the Revolution,
February 1917–August 1918

I

Unerhört!

In the years before the Revolution, Russians had a favourite story about their ambassador to Washington, a 'grand seigneur of the old school' called Yuriy Bakhmetev. Called to the Secretary of State's office, he was surprised when the American, having greeted him politely, lounged back in his chair and crossed his feet on his desk. Sitting on the other side of the desk, Bakhmetev followed suit. The Secretary of State removed one foot; Bakhmetev did the same. And after a slight pause, the American removed the other.[1]

It was symptomatic. European in culture but Asian in size, Russia had always been difficult. For Western liberals in general, she was Europe's last, bloodstained autocracy – especially so after the original 1905 'Bloody Sunday', when Tsar Nicholas shot down peaceful protestors outside the Winter Palace. For Britain, she was also an imperial competitor, jostling for influence in the Near East. Naturally scratchy relations with Pacific neighbour America were made worse by her panoply of legal restrictions on Jews. The roller-coaster of events that upended Russian policy and led to the Intervention got underway with the outbreak of the First World War. Abruptly, Britain as well as Russia's established ally France found herself on Russia's side. Great hopes were placed on the Russian 'steamroller', which cartoonists drew puffing – 'Toot tootsky!' – over rows of pointy German helmets, with a bearded *muzhik* at the wheel. Disappointment followed almost immediately, with a stunning defeat at Tannenberg, in East Prussia. More ground, including Warsaw, was lost the following summer, and a 1916 offensive into Austrian-ruled western Ukraine, though successful, was horribly costly. Far from squashing the enemy, the steamroller had proved antiquated, expensive and liable to go into reverse. The Russian public too had had enough, and in early 1917 anger boiled over in the

13

mass demonstrations and naval mutinies known as the February Revolution. Nicholas abdicated, and power went to a coalition Provisional Government, which promised to revive the war effort and create an elected assembly to draw up a new constitution.

Thrilled at the prospect of democracy and a rebooted Eastern Front, the Allies greeted the transition with overwhelming enthusiasm. From London Lloyd George sent a sonorous telegram, expressing Britain's 'profound satisfaction' that Russia now practised 'responsible government'. From Paris, prime minister Clemenceau welcomed her to the family of republics. The end of tsarism was especially welcome in Washington, where President Woodrow Wilson was about to break election promises by entering the war. Secretary of State Robert Lansing immediately sent the Provisional Government a letter of recognition, getting it off a few hours before Paris and London did the same, and in a speech to Congress Wilson was able to talk of 'wonderful and heartening events', and of how the 'great, generous Russian people' had always been 'democratic at heart'.[2] No-one was sorry when Bakhmetev refused to represent the Provisional Government and resigned. Underneath his courtly manners, thought Lansing, there had always been 'something barbaric about him' – his indifference to the slaughter on the battlefield 'heartless and savage', and his devotion to the ruling family 'medieval'.[3]

The congratulations, though, were to a government that barely deserved the name. From the outset the Provisional Government had little authority, running in parallel with a network of radical, informally elected grass-roots committees known as soviets. These soon permeated every workplace, most pertinently the Petrograd and Moscow garrisons. In the resulting confusion, Russia's state apparatus began to fall apart. In the cities, police stood aside as a crime wave broke. In the countryside peasants drove out their landowners, and the railways, increasingly, swarmed with deserters. The general breakdown was egged on by the obscure revolutionary Vladimir Lenin, a small balding man in a three-piece suit who had returned from exile in April, his slogans 'Power to the Soviets' and 'Loot the looters'.

Focused heart and soul on the great struggle with Germany, the Allies refused to see what was happening. Prime example of the British government's blindness was its failure to give asylum to the Russian royal family. A week after Nicholas abdicated, Lloyd George proposed, and the War Cabinet approved, an asylum offer, duly passed on by the British ambassador to Petrograd. But before Nicholas had time to reply, the government withdrew it again – under pressure, it was revealed over sixty years later, from King George V. The Tsar and the King were first cousins and uncannily similar in appearance: in pre-war photographs of royal visits to Osborne or Balmoral they look like twins. By 1917, however, George no longer wanted to be associated with 'Nicky' – still a bogeyman to the British public – and even less so with his neurotic German wife. He was in the process of dropping his own triple-barrelled German surname in favour of penny-plain Windsor, and did not want the rebranding undone by unpopular, has-been relatives, especially ones that would need to be expensively put up. Over the next few weeks a barrage of letters from his private secretary persuaded Cabinet to change its mind, amidst vague talk of the Romanovs moving instead to the south of France.

After a Bolshevik firing squad murdered the whole Romanov family the following year, the episode was hushed up. When the British ambassador concerned wrote his memoirs in the early 1920s, the Foreign Office threatened prosecution and withdrawal of his pension if he did not pretend that the asylum offer had always stood. When Lloyd George later wrote his own memoirs he was also induced to self-censor, crossly rewriting a chapter titled 'Czar's Future Residence'. Ironically, the consensus amongst historians is that the Romanovs could not have taken up the offer anyway, since the soviets, who controlled their guard, would never have let them leave the country.[4]

Washington's brand of willful blindness was exemplified by the Root Mission, sent to Russia in July 1917 to fact-find and encourage renewed prosecution of the war. Headed by retired senator and foreign-policy sage Elihu Root, its membership was distinguished and imaginatively chosen, including the vice-president of the American Federation of Labor, the president of the Harvester Company (a big exporter), the campaigning journalist Charles Edward Russell and the evangelical YMCA founder John Mott, as well as the Army Chief of Staff and various Russia experts. How it nonetheless utterly misjudged things and rubbed Russians up the wrong way is related by Dmitri Fyedotov, a twenty-five-year-old naval lieutenant tasked with accompanying Admiral James Glennon on a tour of naval bases. Fyedotov knew America well, having spent two years in an arms-purchasing job in Washington. Playing host with Russia in disarray was nonetheless agonising. Embarrassed, at a welcoming reception, by the Provisional Government's scruffiness ('never a well-shined pair of shoes between them'), he vented in his diary. Root and Glennon, he wrote, were useless old men, and the other Mission members ignorant and patronising, assuming that a modern arms factory they were shown was foreign-run, and that every society woman had slept with Rasputin. Their general attitude was that of missionaries 'descending upon a tribe of benighted savages', and time and again he had to remind himself that they were his country's guests, and that he must keep his temper.[5]

The first stop on Glennon's naval tour was Sebastopol, headquarters of the Black Sea Fleet. On arrival, Fyedotov was appalled to find it in the throes of a bloodless but large-scale mutiny, the sailors on strike and the flagship's officers disarmed. Faced with a foreign visitor, however, the sailors' soviet itself put on a show, treating Glennon to 'turret drill' on the Fleet's newest battleship and to lunch at the officers' club. In the afternoon Glennon gamely addressed a mass meeting – the sailors should return to their duties and start building democracy. And in the evening – having made frantic arrangements for the Mission carriage to be attached to the next train out – Fyedotov was able to take away the Fleet commander, Admiral Aleksandr Kolchak, later to lead the White armies in Siberia. Though Glennon was oblivious, it was a close shave – as Fyedotov knew from personal experience, mutinies could easily turn violent. Back in Petrograd, waving the Americans off, he felt acute envy. They would 'sail in their ships, serve in their regiments, work in their offices, respected and honoured', while he and his colleagues faced an 'utterly uncertain future'.[6]

He had done his work too well, for on its return to Washington the Mission reported that the Provisional Government was firmly in control, and the general situation stabilising. Lansing told Wilson that he was 'astounded at their optimism . . . I hope that they are right, and I presume they know more about it than I do.' His own instinct was that the Russian Revolution would be like the French one, getting 'worse and worse until some dominant personality arises to end it all.'[7] But while the Provisional Government had a chance, it should be supported, and American aid duly kept flowing, to the tune of $188 million ($3.4 billion in today's money) by the end of the year.

The money, though, was beside the point. What fatally undermined the Provisional Government was the Allies' insistence that Russia keep fighting. A summer offensive, launched in mid-June and aimed at pushing the German and Austrian armies out of Ukraine, flopped disastrously, and when the Germans counter-attacked nearly two hundred thousand Russian troops were killed or wounded. In September a right-wing general attempted a coup. It failed, but from then on it was obvious that the government's days were numbered, and on 7 November 1917 it was put out of its misery when Bolshevik militias took over the Winter Palace and declared Soviet rule.

The Provisional Government's fall was not unexpected: even Washington, by November, could see it was doomed. But that it was Lenin and Leon Trotsky who took over was. Exiled pamphleteers and café-haunters for years, they had been back in Russia for only a few months and led one of a swarm of ever-mutating small revolutionary parties. Though Lenin drew crowds with his dry but oddly compelling speeches, he and his sidekick were hardly known in the West, and the diplomats in Petrograd had had no contact with them at all. In the resulting ferment of rumour, sorting fact from fiction was extremely difficult. 'Committees are formed', wrote young French attaché Louis de Robien, 'and so are committee Councils, and council Committees: they all claim to be saving the country and the world . . . it is impossible to make head or tail of it.'[8] The one thing everyone agreed on was that the extraordinary new regime could not last for long – the American ambassador cabling, on the morning after the takeover, that it would 'collapse within a few days'.[9]

In the capitals, the politicians wondered how to respond. Lansing canvassed mutiple views but emerged none the wiser, admitting to the President that he couldn't hazard 'even a guess' as to how things might develop. Definitely, America should not recognise the Bolsheviks – it would only make them 'more insolent and impossible'. But otherwise, his advice was to 'sit tight and wait and see.'[10] In London – shaking to Zeppelin raids – foreign affairs were in the hands of a very different figure, Arthur Balfour. A Tory former prime minister and grandee of the high Victorian old school, he was one of the largest landowners in Scotland and resembled a dishevelled stork. Brainy and idle, he was also the opposite of a conviction politician, his most-quoted saying, 'Few things matter very much, and most things don't matter at all.' Lansing – sixteen years younger and a neat-featured, precisely dressed ex-lawyer – found him exasperating: hopeless on detail and prone to windy philosophising. But Balfour agreed with Lansing's 'wait and see' policy, summing up his own position in a presentation to the War Cabinet. The vital thing was not to push Russia into the arms of Germany, and to that end the government should neither give in to pressure from the right to denounce the Bolsheviks, nor rise to Trotsky's anti-imperial goading. Given that Trotsky was already calling for a general peace – albeit with 'no annexations, no indemnities' – it was probably too late to prevent the westward transfer of German divisions. But if Britain could avoid an open breach it might be possible to stop Germany accessing Russian coal, oil and wheat. Accusations of indecisiveness should be ignored: 'If this be drifting, then I am a drifter by deliberate policy.'[11]

Bad signs, however, were already piling up. First, it was becoming obvious that the Bolsheviks were at least as authoritarian as the tsars. One of Lenin's first acts after he took power was to close down opposition newspapers, including those on the left. Another, hidden in a flurry of legislative cant on freedom of religion and rights for women, was a decree creating an internal security agency, the Extraordinary Commission for Combating Counter-Revolution, the initials of which – Ch K or Cheka – quickly became the most frightening word in the language. In early December, elections were held to a Constituent Assembly, as promised by the Provisional Government. But there would be no transition to democracy. Most votes having gone to the Bolsheviks' rivals the Socialist Revolutionaries (SRs), the Assembly was closed down by militiamen on its opening day. Second, the new regime was as radical as promised on the economy. Land and most businesses, it was announced, would be nationalised, and private homes made subject to confiscation. Tsarist-era government debt would be repudiated – a serious blow to France, millions of whose small savers had invested in Russian bonds.

Third – and worst by far – were the Bolsheviks' moves towards peace with Germany. Peace was central to their propaganda message – 'Peace, Land, Bread' a key slogan – and Lenin knew that to escape the fate of the Provisional Government he had to make the promise real. But since Germany occupied a large slice of the country, the price would be painful territorial concessions. Three weeks after taking power he took the first step, applying to German High Command for an armistice, and on 1 December 1917 talks began at German headquarters in Brest-Litovsk, a war-torn town on today's border between Poland and Belarus.

Proceedings opened with one of history's great bad dinner-parties. General Max Hoffman, German commander in the east, was seated opposite a long-haired peasant who the Bolshevik delegation, feeling themselves too bourgeois, had picked up off the street on the way to the station. A Prince Ernst von Hohenlohe-Langenburg, there to lend presence, was placed next to Madame Bichkova, a celebrated Socialist Revolutionary terrorist just home from eleven years in a Siberian prison. The peasant, asked whether he would prefer white wine or red, enquired which was stronger and lost no time in getting extremely drunk.

Lenin's plan was to drag out the talks for as long as possible, in hope of revolution in Germany and the country's military collapse. Champion talker Trotsky was sent to lead them, and three weeks in, having treated the Germans to a short course on Marxism, asked for an adjournment so that he could return to Petrograd and consult. In exchange for a formal peace settlement, he reported, Germany demanded all the territory it currently occupied – Poland, western Ukraine, and the southern Baltics. The offer rent the Party's Central Committee, with Lenin passionately in favour of acceptance, and most other members furiously against. With no mandate either way, Trotsky returned to the negotiating table with a novel formula: 'No peace no war.' It would delay things a little longer, and if Germany went on the offensive, demonstrate that Russia was not the aggressor. But the German side now laid down an ultimatum: unless Russia accepted its terms by 9 February, they would resume their advance. The deadline passed, and again Trotsky bafflingly declared that Russia was not making peace, but also leaving the war. At the end of the meeting Hoffman leapt from his chair with a spluttered '*Unerhört!*' – Unheard of! – and a week later the German armies started moving east again, virtually unopposed.

With the panicked public fleeing the capital, Lenin was at last able to force the issue through the Central Committee. Politically it was one of his finest moments. Germany's demands were now even more punitive: the whole of Ukraine and the Baltics, and heavy indemnities, payable in gold. Opposition was furious and personal. At one point it looked as though the party must split and the government fall. At another Lenin threatened to resign. He won the climactic midnight vote by only seven to five, after Trotsky swopped sides, and at the subsequent meeting of soviet representatives there were shouts of 'Traitor!' and 'Judas!' But by risking his regime Lenin had saved it; grasping the nettle – the need for peace no matter how high the cost – that neither Nicholas nor the Provisional Government had had the guts to tackle. On 23 February he sent an acceptance telegram to Berlin, and a formal treaty was signed in Brest-Litovsk on 3 March. Over the previous two years, the Allies had been surprised and disappointed by Russia several times over: when the 'steamroller' failed; when the Provisional Government crumbled; when *outré* revolutionaries took over; and now, by her outrageous deal with the Kaiser. At each swerve they had hoped for the best, and each time, the country had taken another dive. There were plenty more to come.

2

'A lot of impossible folks'

BREST-LITOVSK WAS A turning-point. For the next several
months, the Bolsheviks tried to keep the Allies dangling, hinting
that they might renege on the treaty and reopen the Eastern Front. It
was nonetheless the point at which the Allied governments began to
convince themselves that something had to be tried in Russia. What
that ought to be was not yet clear, but 'wait and see' no longer sufficed.

The treaty came at a critical moment in the war. Eighteen days
later, on 21 March 1918, a massive German artillery bombardment
heralded the first of the 'Ludendorff' offensives, designed to knock
out France before the Americans arrived. Under-manned and under-
supplied, the opposing British Fifth Army fell to pieces, retreating
four miles on the assault's opening day. Shells hit Paris for the first
time, one destroying a church full of Good Friday worshippers. Fear
and anger fastened on Russia: Brest-Litovsk was a heinous betrayal
and the Bolsheviks traitors in German pay. And what about Germany's
extraordinary territorial gains? She had already transferred thirty-five
divisions west. With her new eastern empire how many more would
she be able raise? Would her warehouses fill with Ukrainian coal and
grain, Baltic flax and timber?

The Allies' first military reaction to Brest-Litovsk was to secure two
Russian ports: Murmansk, 650 miles north of Petrograd on the Barents
Sea, and Vladivostok, 6,000 miles to the east on the Pacific. Though
in retrospect the move was the Intervention's first step, its immediate
aim was limited and practical – to prevent stocks of Allied war material, originally meant for the tsarist armies, from falling via the
Bolsheviks into German hands. Of the two ports, the easier by far to
dominate was Murmansk; a tiny place, halfway up a barely inhabited
fjord, built at the start of the war to receive British supplies. PoWs had

been used to construct a single-track line connecting it to the railway network, an estimated twenty-five thousand of them dying of starvation and privation in the process. Present in harbour, in uneasy co-habitation, were the HMS *Glory*, under Rear Admiral Thomas Kemp, and two Russian battleships, the *Chesma* and the *Askold*, both of which had thrown out their officers and declared for the Revolution. Ashore, power was in the hands of a soviet, headed by a three-man group consisting, unusually, of a revolutionary but non-Bolshevik ship's stoker called Aleksei Yuryev, a naval adjutant, and a former officer in the Imperial Guards. In mid-February Kemp asked them if he could land marines to help keep order, and they telegraphed to Trotsky for instructions. The British being for the moment a lesser danger than the Germans, Trotsky told them to cooperate. The *Glory* and the Red Flag-flying *Chesma* exchanged salutes, and for the next few months Kemp and the soviet worked together quite amicably.

Vladivostok – 'Lord of the East' – was a much bigger challenge. A colonial city of over one hundred thousand people, the majority Chinese or Korean, it had sprung up in the past twenty years, its architecture as assertively incongruous as that of Calcutta or Hong Kong. Terminus of the Trans-Siberian Railway – the great engineering feat of Nicholas's reign – it had been the main disembarkation point for American wartime aid, and several hundred thousand tons' worth – munitions, metals, cotton, rubber, food and vehicles – still waited there for onward transportation. In January 1918 London announced that the HMS *Suffolk* was being despatched from Hong Kong to keep an eye on the situation. Japan immediately sent two ships of her own – so quickly that they arrived a day earlier than the *Suffolk* – and America followed suit in February, with the USS *Brooklyn*.

As in Murmansk, the decision to put troops ashore was taken by a naval man on the spot, Japan's Admiral Kato. The city was becoming increasingly lawless, and his pretext came on 4 April, when robbers burst into a Japanese-owned shop and shot three staff. Overnight Kato informed his British and American counterparts that he was about to land 500 marines to protect Japanese nationals and property. The *Suffolk*'s captain was enthusiastic, chipping in with another fifty to guard the British consulate. The American, however, stood pat, sensing that landings were diplomatically premature. He was right: the subsequent rumpus forced Japan's foreign minister to resign, and at the end of April the Japanese and British marines were withdrawn and the Vladivostok soviet declared workers' rule.

While on the peripheries the navies itched for action, at the centre, responsibility for maintaining relations with the Russian government had switched from the diplomatic corps to a new set of semi-official representatives. Barred by their governments' non-recognition of the new regime from direct contact with the Bolsheviks, the Allied ambassadors had been more or less irrelevant since November. In February 1918, fearing German occupation of Petrograd, they decamped with their staff 350 miles east to Vologda, a postcard-pretty country town that possessed no restive urban proletariat and sat hand-ily on the railway line north to the White Sea port of Archangel, where British warships sat reassuringly in the offing. The doyen of the corps was David Francis, a sixty-eight-year-old six-times gov-ernor of Missouri who loved women, whisky and poker, and went everywhere with a pedal-operated travelling spittoon. ('When he wished to emphasise a point', wrote a Brit, 'bang would go the pedal, followed by a well-aimed expectoration.')Equally fat and jovial was French ambassador Joseph Noulens, a centre-left former minister who had been in post for less than a year. The Americans complained that he talked too much, and the Russians thought that he looked like a prosperous grocer. There was no British ambassador – he had retired and not been replaced.

Installed in buildings allocated to them by Vologda's welcoming town council – the Americans in the local Nobles' Club, the French in a girls' school – the diplomats settled down to provincial life. Francis played cards and golf; Noulens kept busy meeting the trains full of Allied nationals – English governesses, French and Belgian coal-miners – passing through on their way to Archangel and home. The social highlight of each week was Francis's Saturday afternoon tea-party, to which he shrewdly invited not only the whole diplomatic corps – Italian, Belgian, Portuguese, Romanian, Serb, Japanese, Chinese, Siamese and Brazilian – but also the local station master and mayor. (The latter blushing with pride every time Francis referred to

Vologda as Russia's 'diplomatic capital'.) French attaché de Robien spent his evenings with a pair of scholarly and mildly eccentric grand dukes, distant Romanov cousins who had until recently bicycled along the corridors of their palace, and now lodged in two rooms at the back of a yard. On 1 May, which happened to fall on Orthodoxy's Maundy Thursday, he was pleased to see communicants at the cathedral outnumbering attendees at a May Day rally.

While the ambassadors rusticated, in the capital the job of maintaining relations with the Russian government passed to four diplomatically inexperienced and, it turned out, impressionable men. France's liaison with the Bolsheviks – by far the most left-wing of the four – was thirty-seven-year-old Jacques Sadoul. A leading member of the French section of the Workers' International, he was a protégé of the Socialist minister for armaments, Albert Thomas, who had sent him to join France's military mission to Petrograd the previous October. America's representative was a family connection of Francis, thirty-three-year-old DeWitt Clinton Poole. Like Sadoul, he had been posted to Russia only the year before, and been promoted to consul after his boss died of a stroke. (Brought on, Poole thought, by the 'laments and demands' of his Russian wife's many relations.) In competition with Poole on the American side was Raymond Robins, a flamboyant figure who had made money in the Klondike gold rush before turning evangelical campaigner. A member of the rose-tinted Root Mission, he was now with a notionally 'Red Cross' delegation, funded by a Montana copper magnate, that had supported the Provisional Government's pro-war propaganda effort, and since switched to information-gathering.

Britain's point man with the Bolsheviks, in Russia much the longest of the four and the only one who spoke the language, was thirty-year-old Robert Bruce Lockhart. Vice-consul in Moscow since 1912, he had established himself as a 'cheerful young man' and a 'good mixer', with a professionally useful taste for gypsy bands and dancing. When the Bolsheviks took over in November 1917 he was at home in Scotland, despatched there to 'rest' after failing to break off an affair with a married Russian aristocrat. It was a piece of luck, because when Russia hit the news he was called in for emergency briefings by half the War Cabinet – most of whom turned out to be almost entirely ignorant of the country's geography. Just before Christmas the summons came from Downing Street. Charmingly pretending amazement at Lockhart's youth – '*The* Mr Lockhart?' – Lloyd George questioned him closely, then told him to go back to Russia, get in touch with Lenin and Trotsky, and if rapprochement with Germany threatened, put as many spokes into its wheels as possible.

In this limbo period before the Allies landed in Russia in force, both sides were playing a double game. As well as keeping a line open to the new regime, the Allied governments also wanted to look at the alternatives. Though the Bolshevik regime had defied predictions that it would die at birth, it was still extremely fragile, its hold on Petrograd and Moscow dependent on the loyalty of their garrisons, and particularly on revolutionary Latvian regiments known as the Latvian Riflemen. And outside central Russia, round the old empire's peripheries, rival governments were declaring themselves and form-ing their own militias. In the first months of 1918, French and British military intelligence made tentative contact with two of the largest – the centre-left Ukrainian Rada government, based in Kiev, and the Don Cossack 'Host', headquartered in the southern steppe town of Novocherkassk. Novocherkassk also hosted the Volunteer Army, a small force, long on officers and short on soldiers, created by the cabal of tsarist generals who had tried to overthrow the Provisional Government the previous September. Allied contacts with these organisations did not, at this stage, go anywhere, the judgement being that they were not as strong as they pretended to be and too close to Berlin.

The Bolsheviks, for their part, on the one hand feared Germany, whose occupation of the Baltics put it only a stone's throw from Petrograd, and, on the other, Allied invasions from Vladivostok or Murmansk. Their tactic was to butter up both sides, giving Allied representatives as well as German ones full diplomatic privileges and quantities of leadership face-time. When the government moved from Petrograd to Moscow in March 1918, Trotsky personally escorted the Allied missions to their new quarters, and flattering requests were made for more American railway engineers, to add to a corps already sent to help the Provisional Government. The buttering-up failed to work on DeWitt Poole, but did the trick with Sadoul, Robins and Lockhart. Committed to the Revolution from the start, Sadoul quickly became Trotsky's close confidant, dropping in to his rooms almost every evening for late-night chats. In his reports to Thomas he argued passionately that France should recognise the Bolshevik government and work for an alliance. 'In twenty-four hours an agreement would be reached. Thus we would save Russia. Thus we save the Revolution.'[2] Later in the year he went completely over to the cause, leaving French government service to work for the regime as a propagandist. Robins was strung along with promises of a Russian–American trade deal, and in May – declaring Trotsky 'a four kind son of a bitch, but the greatest Jew since Christ' – took a draft agreement to Washington. He also took with him a hyper-romantic pamphlet, *The Truth About Russia*, written by his friend the British newspaper correspondent Arthur Ransome (who in carefree defiance of journalistic ethics had not only moved in with the vice-commissar for foreign affairs, Karl Radek, but fallen in love with Trotsky's private secretary). Writing to his daughter around the same time, Ransome added a comic drawing. One man grips another by the shoulder and points at the word SENSE, written in giant letters on the side of a building: 'This is meant to be as much like a barn door as possible. But the Imperialists won't see it . . . Politics is what keeps Dor dor in Russia and makes him SICK.'[3]

Lockhart, though no socialist, was seduced too. Meeting Trotsky for the first time – for a whole two hours – he was star-struck. With his 'wonderfully quick mind and a rich deep voice . . . his broad chest, his huge forehead, his strong fierce eyes', Trotsky was 'the very incarnation of the revolutionary.' And his 'belligerent fury' against Germany seemed entirely genuine: 'If the Bosche bought Trotsky, they bought a lemon.'[4] Two days before the signing ceremony at Brest-Litovsk, Lockhart had his first meeting with Lenin, who assured him that the treaty was a temporary expedient – 'a robber peace' – and that 'passive resistance' would force Germany to maintain more, not fewer, troops in the east.[5] If only Britain could dissuade Japan from invading the Russian Pacific, the Soviet government might invite her to land her own troops, in a new joint effort against their common enemy. Along with Sadoul and Robins, Lockhart lapped up this line, advising the Foreign Office that the Bolsheviks were there to stay, and could and should be done business with.

'What a shame', Sadoul wrote to Thomas on 31 May 1918, 'that Clemenceau, Lloyd George and Wilson . . . have not been able, in six months, to spend eight days in Petrograd! Without a doubt, a few conversations with Lenin and Trotsky would have opened their eyes.'[6]

It was an intriguing thought. Though not without faults, all three Allied chiefs were remarkable men, amongst their countries' great twentieth-century leaders. Most strongly in favour of overthrowing the Bolsheviks was 'the Tiger' – French premier Georges Clemenceau. Seventy-seven years old, he was a pugnacious veteran of the left, coming to the end of a career in the course of which he had practised as a doctor, done time in gaol for organising anti-government protests, taught riding at a Connecticut girls' school, fought two duels and, most of all, campaigned for social justice, writing countless articles, founding five censor-defying newspapers and helping publish Zola's *J'accuse*. His loathing of the Bolsheviks stemmed from a hatred of violent radicalism, the bloody results of which he had witnessed during the 1871 Paris Commune. Elected prime minister in November 1917, a time of dangerous discontent in the army, he was also the Frenchman doing the most to win the war. Visiting the front with him on the eve of the first Ludendorff offensive, British junior minister Winston Churchill found him a man after his own heart. 'In the highest spirits and as irresponsible as schoolboys on holiday',[7] they went right up to the firing line, standing on a hillock to watch the flash of guns hidden in a nearby wood. On the drive back a shell-burst panicked a string of horses on the road ahead and Clemenceau leapt out of the car and caught one by the bridle. The old man, Churchill thought, was wonderful, the embodiment of France.

Least in favour of getting involved in Russia was President Wilson. Tall and thin, with a narrow, cleanshaven face – the kind of man who looks good in a top hat – he was inclined against militarism by both personality and experience. The clever, devout son of a Presbyterian minister, he had grown up in the South, amid painful memories of the Civil War. His first career was in academia, as a professor of government and history, and his first presidency that of Princeton, where he might have stayed had it not been for a row with the university's trustees. Instead he had plunged with stunning success into politics, entering the White House two years after his first election to public office. Distracting from a landmark programme of trust-busting and tax reform, foreign policy immediately became a bugbear. During his first term military incursions into revolutionary Mexico ended in embarrassment, and he had stayed out of the European war for as long as possible, trying to broker peace talks and resisting pressure to retaliate after German submarines started sinking passenger ships with Americans aboard.

Somewhere between Clemenceau and Wilson on the Russia question was Britain's consummate persuader, David Lloyd George. From a genuinely humble background – in a remote part of Wales, his schooling paid for by a cobbler uncle – brains, charm, energy and good looks had taken him from a firm of country solicitors to the House of Commons and thence to the chancellorship, where like Wilson he had pushed through landmark social and economic reforms. Since 1916 he had deftly held together a three-party National Government, not to mention a marriage and a long-term, semi-public relationship with his private secretary. A sceptic by nature and no big-picture imperialist (he had condemned the Boer War), for him Russia was an irritation. Urged to caution by most of his Cabinet, but to action by the War Office (and not helped either way by serenely detached Foreign Secretary Balfour), he tended to take the line of least resistance, changing his mind as events swayed this way and that.

Even 'Tiger' Clemenceau, though, accepted that no large-scale intervention in Russia was possible without American agreement. The first official suggestion that more be done than just discreetly funding anti-Bolshevik groups came on 7 January 1918, when the French ambassador to Washington submitted a proposal for a joint expedition from Manchuria, aimed at taking control of the Far Eastern section of the Trans-Siberian Railway. His timing was bad – the day before Wilson made his visionary 'Fourteen Points' speech to Congress sketching out a new world order. When the war was won, the President declared, the map should be redrawn according to the principle of 'self-determination' – in other words according to the wishes of the peoples concerned, expressed where necessary in plebiscites. Peace would be guaranteed by a League of Nations, to which members would refer disputes, and back militarily if adjudication broke down. Russia had the whole of Point VI to herself – promised 'unhampered and unembarrassed opportunity' to take her own political path.[8]

'Unembarrassed opportunity' did not, however, preclude a finger on the scales. Secretary of State Lansing had quickly abandoned his initial 'wait and see' stance and was now ardently anti-Bolshevik – a cold warrior before his time. Though the Secretary of War, Newton Baker, was sceptical, Wilson allowed Lansing to start sending money to the Volunteer Army, via a tortuous route that avoided the need for Congressional approvals. He also ignored Raymond Robins's draft trade deal with Moscow, correctly judging that Robins was being played. But this did not mean that Wilson wanted to send troops. Russia was still a mess – 'a lot of impossible folks'. And as he had learned in Mexico, trying to reverse a revolution by force was like 'using a broom to sweep back the sea.' He was also worried about the Japanese. No Siberian intervention, Tokyo had made it clear, was going to happen without them, and it was obvious that they had eyes on northern Manchuria and the southern branch of the Trans-Siberian. A Japanese landing also risked backlash, since Russians still smarted from their defeat in the 1905 Russo-Japanese War.

Wilson accordingly turned the French proposal down. It was not, however, the end of the matter. From January to April, as the Brest-Litovsk Treaty was sealed and the German armies rolled into Ukraine and the Baltics, London and Paris continued to push him on Russia, the issue looping between the capitals in a tangle of notes, declarations and memoranda. Refusing, despite Lansing's urgings, even to make a clear anti-Bolshevik public statement, Wilson turned down six separate diplomatic appeals for military action in the period. It was a missed chance, for as the Intervention's military men were soon to put it, Allied forces could at that stage have marched on Moscow 'like a knife through butter' – though what they would have done when they got there was another question. Instead the debate went nowhere, stumbling about in a fog of misapprehension (Russia is sending PoWs to reinforce the German army!), wishful thinking (Japan will march across the Urals!) and war-porn rumour (Chinese torturers are teaching their unspeakable arts to the Cheka!). In Washington, reports of growing warlordism failed to discourage airy talk of humanitarian missions and trade initiatives. In London, reports of those same warlords' brutalities failed to discourage quiet funding of them. Angry Russian émigrés gave their views; so did businessmen back from forays into the chaos to find out what was happening to their mines and factories. Nothing was made any clearer by Paris's despatch to Washington of the philosopher Henri Bergson.

Entirely against the trend of Russia policy in the Allied capitals – though in line with the approach being pushed by Lockhart, Sadoul and Robins – was the situation in Murmansk. Here, the British navy had not only reached an amicable agreement with the settlement's soviet, but was actually fighting on its behalf. Behind the paradox was Finland. A Russian possession since the beginning of the nineteenth century, its national movement had long simmered. But it was split between right and left, and after the Bolshevik coup both sides separately declared Finnish independence. Each formed its own army, and they clashed for the first time in January 1918. The conflict then turned into a proxy war, Moscow backing the Finnish Socialist Workers' Republic, Berlin the Government of White Finland. In March and April Germany landed divisions, and within six weeks controlled the whole country. Hence a German-Finnish threat to Murmansk.

Swept up in the action – and completely unbothered by the political contortions involved – was twenty-one-year-old Charles Drage, a lieutenant on the HMS *Cochrane*. Since arriving in Murmansk in early March, he had been combining fun – billiards ('riotous'), debagging ('left most of my pyjamas in the mess'), shooting and eating a gull ('quite good') – with drilling his sailors, setting up a rifle range and creating observation posts on nearby hills. There was a brief flurry of excitement on May Day, when he was ordered to ready a landing party in case of trouble. 'Immense jubilation on the part of my company, coupled with complete indifference as to whether they were going to fight Red Guards or White Guards, Huns or Finns or Bolsheviks.'[9] Things stayed quiet, and they handed back their weapons in a grump.

They got their action soon after, at the tundra-bound inlet of Pechenga, seventy-five miles to Murmansk's northwest. Responding to rumours of a Finnish expedition, the *Cochrane* entered the inlet on 3 May 1918, butting her way through sea ice until she could move no further. Met by Saami fur-traders on reindeer-sleds, the landing party – a mixture of British marines and sailors, British-officered Red Guards and Russian sailors from the revolutionary *Askold* – loaded their gear onto the Saamis' sleds and marched further on up the inlet. Drage's company set up camp in the visitors' hostel of a monastery; further on the *Askold* sailors occupied the monastery itself; and the marines and Red Guards stationed themselves on the road to the nearest town, just over the Russo-Finnish border. In Drage's unflaggingly can-do diary, nervousness shows through. It was his first command ashore. Would his sailors, many even younger than him, remember their orders? Would their boots – 'the shoddiest purser's crabs' – hold together, and would their rifles work in the cold? The tundra – an endless, flattish, backdropless vista of snow and leafless knee-high bushes – was disconcerting. Though apparently clear and open, it was astonishingly easy to get lost in it, even with one's men spaced only ten paces apart. 'However', Drage wrote, 'the great thing is that we are ashore, and ought to see some fun.'[10]

It began on 10 May, when the outpost on the road was attacked and almost encircled by about two hundred Finns on skis. Gathered at the main camp, the little force strengthened its defences. A field gun was taken to pieces and reassembled on top of an overlooking hill. Permafrost foiled attempts to dig a gun-pit, but Drage was intrigued to come across a broken sundial, marked for the whole twenty-four hours. 'Of course in these latitudes it would be, but somehow one can never get used to the idea of the sun going round in a circle above the horizon.' The following morning a breathless messenger arrived from a nearby fishing settlement: soldiers had arrived half an hour ago, and claimed it for the White Government of Finland. The ensuing Anglo-Soviet counter-attack was a near-disaster. Positioned on a low ridge above a frozen river, Drage's company mistook attacking Red Guards for Finns and fired on them, and the gun on the hill loosed one round and fell over. Presently the whole force retired to

a very convenient ravine, from which a further advance did not look
promising . . . The country in front was bare of cover (and nothing
looks quite as bare as snow), we were running short of ammunition
and at the same time firing began to be heard in our rear, in the direction of the camp.

The officer of marines tried to 'stalk' one of the Finnish machine-
guns, but was 'shot through the shoulder for his pains.' At this last-
redoubt moment the Finns' fire slackened and it became clear that
they were moving off. To thank, it later turned out, was an unseen
shell from the *Cochrane*, which hit the road behind them. 'This
finished the scrap and we spent the rest of the day trying to dig
ourselves in, in four feet of snow and with two stoker's shovels to a
company.'[11]

As Drage said, it was only a scrap. (Though Finnish snipers lurked,
the main force did not return.) But it also pointed to the future. Sent
back to the *Cochrane* to recuperate from snow-blindness, Drage shared
its sickbay with a small Saami girl who had lost a hand after picking
up a discarded detonator. She was the Intervention's first recorded
civilian casualty. There were other omens too. One day the twenty
sailors from the *Askold*, supposed to be stationed at the monastery, left
their post and walked without warning into camp, drinking and
shooting up telegraph poles on the way. It was good riddance, Drage
wrote on seeing them sent under guard to Murmansk: they were
useless and had been 'behaving like brutes to the monks.' His next
diary entry notes without comment that a captured Finn has been
'killed by the Russians'. Civilian suffering, desertions, a prisoner-
killing: in topsy-turvy form – Britain fighting with Reds against
Whites – the Intervention was beginning to take shape.

3

Brother Czecho

TWO DAYS AFTER the skirmish at Pechenga, a minor incident at a small Siberian railway station set off the chain of events that nudged America into Russia, and with her the rest of the Allies. The station stood just outside Chelyabinsk, a pleasant, unimportant town on the eastern edge of the Urals. Early in the morning on 14 May 1918 a train steamed in packed with Austrian and Hungarian PoWs, heading home as agreed under Brest-Litovsk. On the neighbouring line, across the platform, stood several trains belonging to two regiments of Czechs, part of a sizeable national force that had fought in the war on the Russian side, against Austro-Hungary. To the Czechs, the Austrians and Hungarians were imperial oppressors. To the Austrians and Hungarians, the Czechs were traitors, fellow-citizens who had gone over to the enemy. There were shouts and cat-calls, and as the Austrian train began to move off a man in one of its last trucks picked up part of a cast-iron stove and flung it at a group of Czech soldiers standing on the platform below. One of the Czechs was hit and fell to the ground; the others ran after the still slow-moving train, brought it to a halt, forced the occupants of its last three trucks to get out and demanded that they identify the miscreant. The Austrians, who were unarmed, complied, and the Czechs lynched the man on the spot – their officers, as Czech accounts have it, powerless to intervene.

What were trains full of Czechs doing in the Urals in the first place? Recruited from expatriates, deserters and PoWs, a Czech Brigade had fought alongside the tsarist armies since the start of the war, and in summer 1917 helped win a famous victory at Zborow, in present-day western Ukraine. When the Bolsheviks took power in November, the Brigade was being expanded into a Legion, and it subsequently adopted a stance of armed neutrality, defending railway junctions only so that its own regiments could move east, away from the advancing Germans. With the Eastern Front in tatters, the Czechs' new aim was to rejoin the war on the Western one, in time to help liberate their nation as per President Wilson's Fourteen Points. The short route home being blocked by the enemy, they would have to take the long way round, eastward via Vladivostok. By spring 1918, therefore, dozens of trains carrying about fifty thousand Czech troops were strung out along the five thousand miles of the Trans-Siberian Railway.

They were in a parlous position, because all along the route towns were being contested by rival militias, with whom they had to negotiate safe passage. Twenty-three-year-old Legion captain Gustav Becvar, a round-faced, middle-class boy from Brno whose regiment had gone over to the Russians back in 1915, recounts his first encounter with Red Guards. The meeting took place in the upstairs drawing-room of a fine townhouse, now resembling 'a carelessly kept armoury' with revolvers and daggers scattered over tables, windowsills and mantlepiece. Becvar's CO, a Prague barrister in civilian life and 'always very anxious to be within the law and regulations', was conciliatory, declaring that the Legion had no interest in Russia's internal affairs and wanted only to leave the country as soon as it could.

> For a time our hosts looked as though they might cause trouble. But at length they . . . surlily gave us their decision. 'All right. We will delay our attack on the station. But don't fail to go quickly. We can't have you here.' As if we wanted to stay!¹

In Moscow, over the heads of the soldiers on their trains, the nation's political figurehead, future president Tomas Masaryk, came to an agreement with the Bolsheviks that the Legion could go on its way in exchange for surrendering its weapons. The Legionaries themselves had other ideas. Arriving at Penza, still on the wrong side of the Volga, on 18 April, Becvar's men grudgingly stacked a few rifles on the platform, but hid the rest between the double walls of their reinforced carriages. Across the river at Samara, however, a heavy-jawed commissar demanded thirty rifles in exchange for a locomotive, and the same happened at Ufa and at Zlatoust. 'Argument was always useless, and we realised that we were being subjected to a kind of danegeld.'[2] Station by station the Reds became more obstructive, so that by the end of the month all the Czech trains, still strung out along thousands of miles of railway, had more or less come to a halt.

Becvar arrived at Chelyabinsk a few days after the 14 May lynching, to represent his regiment at a Legion conference. He found the town already under *de facto* Legion control, the Czech train commander having marched in his men and forced the local soviet to release ten Legionaries detained for questioning. In the station's waiting-room, delegates furiously debated whether to stand by the Moscow agreement, as urged by Masaryk's National Council, or repudiate it and carry on to Vladivostok by force. On the conference's third day, 23 May, a messenger burst in and handed a paper to the chairman, 'whispering excitedly the while'.[3] It was an intercepted directive from Moscow to all Siberian soviets, telling them to disarm the Legion, break up its regiments and conscript its soldiers into the Red Army. Furious, the Czechs immediately voted to reject the Moscow agreement and defend themselves. Trotsky's response, in another order to the Siberian soviets, was a declaration of war: 'Every armed Czechoslovak found on the railway is to be shot on the spot.'

It was an empty threat, because to the world's amazement, over the next two months the Czechs knocked the Red militias over, taking control of almost the whole Trans-Siberian. Penza was captured on 28 May, Tomsk on the 31st, Omsk on 6 June, and Samara on 8 June. It was not a walkover: Becvar records a night march through seventeen miles of dense forest, mosquito bites so bad they squeezed your eyes shut, black bogs, no campfires, a friend ambushed and killed. And as he and other Legionaries later preferred to forget, they also fought the 'Internationalists' – fellow-Czech and Slovak former PoWs who had joined the Revolution rather than the national cause. (One was Jaroslav Hašek, future author of *The Good Soldier Švejk*.) But the Legion's discipline and cohesion told, as did the charisma and tactical brilliance of the jug-eared young colonel in charge of central Siberian forces, a former medical orderly called Radola Gajda. The Czechs' string of victories culminated with the seizure of Vladivostok, whose Bolshevik soviet was given a taste of its own medicine in a swift and ruthless coup. As related by an expatriate businessman, the 15,000 Legionaries already in the city 'got up early one morning and surrounded the Bolshevik headquarters [so that] a good many were peacefully snaffled.' Other soviet members tried to escape on torpedo boats, but were foiled by the British and Japanese cruisers still anchored in the bay. When a diehard rump barricaded themselves into a print-works, grenades were used to set fire to its paper store and 'as they emerged they were either shot down or knocked on the head.'⁴ The dirty work done for them, the Allies – including the Americans this time – landed small detachments of marines to help keep order. On 12 July Becvar's regiment rolled into proud little Irkutsk, central Siberia's oldest city and the gateway to Lake Baikal, and shortly after the American consul there reported 'perfect order along the line, a few Czechs being left at each town to look after policing.'⁵

The Czechs' victory was astonishing. A tiny, stateless nation of 10 million had taken control of northern Asia's great geo-strategic communications artery, from the Volga to the Pacific, and had done so on its own initiative and using its own resources, without any help from the Great Powers. It was a stunning debut.

Russian reactions varied. The Bolsheviks, of course, accused the Czechs of being creatures of the imperialists. Their nickname for them was 'Tcheko-sobaki', from *sobaka*, the Russian for dog. The Socialist Revolutionaries, who had their own Siberian army, huffed that they themselves had done the heavy lifting before the Czechs arrived on the scene. Even non-revolutionaries had mixed feelings. Making a speech to local dignitaries in Irkutsk, Becvar saw their smiles evaporate when he explained that the Legion was not inter-ested in Russian affairs, and only wanted to get home as fast as possi-ble. Upper-class refugees from the capitals were disconcerted by the Czechs' self-assurance. Baroness Sophie Buxhoeveden, an elderly former lady-in-waiting to the Tsarina, spent two days sharing a railway carriage with Czech soldiers while on her way to Omsk. They were 'fine men', extremely friendly and polite, and generous with their envy-makingly ample supplies of coffee and sausage. But they were also startlingly outspoken, volubly discussing the 'political questions of the moment . . . with a wonderful knowledge of the subject', and 'very democratic in their views'.[6] An intelligent, look-on-the-bright-side woman, she didn't exactly disapprove, but it wasn't what she had been used to at court. No matter that the Czechs had made Siberia safe, other old-guard figures frankly loathed them. Writing from embittered exile later on, the ultra-conservative White general Konstantin Sakharov described Legion troops as 'self-important', like 'a troop of liveried servants'. Their famous revolt had been nothing but 'a chain of small meaningless clashes' and Czechoslovakia itself was a fake 'mosaic state'.[7]

For the pro-Interventionists in the Allied capitals, the Legion's triumph was manna from heaven. Without consulting the Legionaries' preferences (or indeed the maps), the boldest spirits started dreaming up plans to send them north to bolster Allied forces at Murmansk, or south to join the Volunteer Army. More immediately, they could be used to bring round still-cautious President Wilson. One of the small, self-determining nations of his Fourteen Points speech, the Czechs already appealed to his sympathy, and an American expedition to Siberia could now be framed as a rescue mission, a helping hand for a brave little nation in peril. Japan's inevitable involvement, it could also be argued, would be less bitter to Russians if given a fellow-Slav coating.

None of this made sense. The Czechs needed no help, and Russians resented them. But boosted by Masaryk's tireless lobbying, the rescue narrative played excellently with the American public. Sixty-eight years old and an academic philosopher by profession, the National Council leader was no romantic firebrand. His nose for publicity, however, was second to none. During a whirlwind tour of America in spring 1918 he packed out Carnegie Hall in a joint event with Polish celebrity pianist and prime-minster-to-be Ignacy Paderewski, and at the close of a four-day Central European gathering in Philadelphia, rang the Liberty Bell and signed a 'Declaration of Common Aims' using the same ink-well used in 1776. When the Legion took up arms in defiance of his safe-passage deal at the end of May he made the best of it, painting the rising in epic colours. The press followed his lead. Bound together by unshakeable esprit de corps, the Legionaries personified their newborn nation. Their trains were a 'rolling republic'; their trek through a war-torn land another

'Anabasis' – Xenophon's march home with his Ten Thousand. With the German army crouched just outside Paris, it was a welcome good-news story. Jarring reports of Czech violence against Austrians and Hungarians in Siberia's enormous PoW camps, wired in by far-flung Red Cross workers, were ignored.

Behind the scenes Masaryk was also willing to use the Legion as a bargaining chip. If America recognised Czechoslovak independence, maybe it would be willing to stay on for a while in Russia and carry on opposing the Bolsheviks. In Washington he lunched with Lansing and with Wilson's confidant Edward House, impressing both, and was received by Wilson at the White House on 18 June. The President did not immediately recognise Czech independence. (That came in September 1918, by which time the Austro-Hungarian Empire was patently on its death-bed.) Instead their main topic of conversation was intervention in Russia and what role the Czechs might play.

Over the next fortnight, while far away the Legion skirmished with ragamuffin Reds through sleepy Siberian towns, pressure within the American government for intervention mounted. House wanted a humanitarian mission plus small security force; the belligerent Postmaster General a massive multi-national expedition of tens of thousands; Lansing something in between. The evangelical YMCA founder John Mott played on Wilson's faith. The Russians were 'a dark people groping after larger light.' If the President could only '*believe* in Russia', Providence would guide him.[8] On 2 July came the news that the Czechs had taken Vladivostok. It materially changed the military calculus: any American forces landing there would now be sure of a welcome. The next day a sixth formal request for troops arrived from the Supreme War Council in Paris, and, on a sweltering Fourth of July cruise up the Potomac, Lansing bearded Wilson with yet another memo stressing the opportunities offered by the Czechs. They introduced a 'sentimental element' into the argument: giving 'protection and assistance' was a very different thing from sending troops to 'save the Russians from themselves'.[9]

Two days later Wilson buckled. Summoning Lansing, Secretary for War Baker and the army and navy chiefs to the White House, he presented them with a Russia plan. Seven thousand American and an equal number of Japanese troops would be landed at Vladivostok.

They would help the Czechs wipe out the last pockets of Bolshevik resistance around the southern shores of Lake Baikal, then assist them in guarding the Trans-Siberian, but without venturing west of Irkutsk. It would be announced that the expedition was helping the Legion defend itself against armed German PoWs, and that America had no intention of interfering in Russia's internal affairs or impinging on her sovereignty. The administration would await developments before taking any further steps. Everyone around the table nodded assent except for the army chief of staff, General Peyton March. Wilson turned to him: 'Why are you shaking your head, General?' March, who saw no point in going to Russia but also that Wilson had made his decision, observed only that he had already outlined the military risks. 'Well', replied Wilson, 'we will have to take that chance.'[10] It was a gamble he would regret almost as soon as the dice rattled from the cup.

4

Aide Memoire

WHILE THE CZECHS took matters into their own hands across Siberia, the same pattern – military action first, political acquiescence later – was being followed by the British in the North.

Since the winter, Admiral Kemp had kept up good relations with the Murmansk soviet and cool but working ones with the authorities at Archangel, the historic timber port a day's sail to the southeast. The cruiser HMS *Attentive* kept watch there, and a sizeable expatriate business community as well as French, British and American consuls remained in place. In spring 1918, with substantial numbers of marines already ashore at Murmansk and Pechenga, the War Office decided to send a small military force to take over northern operations. Its commander was Major-General Frederick Poole, a fifty-eight-year-old Indian Army man who had earlier been in charge of the supply mission to Russia. Not a brilliant soldier – up to the war he had only made the rank of major – he was shortly to prove a worse politician. He arrived in Murmansk on 24 May, and a month later his deputy, Major-General Charles Maynard, joined him with the force itself.

As related by Maynard in his memoirs, the expedition (code-name 'Elope') was supposed to be secret. Home on sick-leave, he had bumped into an old army friend at his club. Now with the War Office, the friend said he might have a job for him but declined to give details, 'saying that he could make no further reference to it till he got behind the closed doors of his own room.' Hope swelling of a division in France, Maynard accompanied him to his office, where he waved at a wall map and asked, 'Ever heard of a place called Murmansk?'

A mixed force of 1,160, Maynard heard, made up mostly of men rated unfit for the trenches, was being sent to the Russian Arctic. Half would help the 400 Royal Marines already in Murmansk continue to defend it against the Finns and Germans. The other half would occupy Archangel, 'equip and train such Czecho-Slovaks as should find their way to that port', and organise 'a local Russian contingent, which it was confidently anticipated would reach a strength of at least 30,000.' When ready, the new army would 'join hands with the pro-Ally forces in Siberia', and after that, 'assist in opening up a new front against Germany.' The whole enterprise, the friend conceded, was 'somewhat in the nature of a gamble', but would Maynard take charge of its Murmansk element? Judging the scheme full of 'alluring uncertainty' but 'undoubtedly sound', Maynard agreed.[1] That not every government department was as enthusiastic was apparent at the Treasury, when he went to apply for sterling with which to pay for local labour. Rather than pay cash, he was told, he should make use of 'an immense number of barrels of salted herrings', bought by the army some time ago and currently in Norway. 'The Russians', the official said, 'would certainly be short of food; so why should I not feed them herrings, instead of giving them any money?'[2] (The fish were duly transported to Archangel, where they sat in front of the cathedral, getting smellier and smellier, until they were thrown away.)

On 18 June Maynard's North Russia Expeditionary Force set sail from Newcastle, on the troopship *City of Marseilles*. The onboard briefing for officers was even more ambitious than his own at the War Office. Twenty thousand Czechs were expected at Archangel, and another four Russian divisions would be raised before winter, enabling a 350-mile advance by rail on Vologda. There were also lines to be taken in conversation with locals. 'We are to rub it in', wrote a cynical lieutenant colonel, 'that England, and not Germany, is Russia's friend, and the stunt to be played for all it is worth is "Russia for the Russians".'[3] Orders to give nothing away in letters home he thought absurd, since even the girl at the tea-stall at York station had known where the Expeditionary Force was bound.

In the twenty-four-hour daylight of midsummer's day, after a crossing slowed by an outbreak of Spanish 'flu amongst its Indian stokers, the *City of Marseilles* docked at Murmansk. Rounding the final rocky headland Maynard was disappointed; the town was nothing but a collection of what looked like workmen's huts, with rubbish everywhere and fir logs, half-shaped for building, lying about like giant spillikins. On board the *Glory* he was introduced to General Poole – as he carefully put it, 'one of the most confirmed optimists it has ever been my fortune to meet.' A few weeks previously, Poole explained, a Bolshevik envoy – 'quite a good old bird' – had arrived from Petrograd with an ultimatum: unless Britain recognised the Bolshevik government, two Red Guard divisions would shortly be on their way. The friendly Murmansk soviet had also received telegrams from Lenin and Trotsky ordering it to eject the British by force. In response Poole had sent 250 Royal Marines, plus a French mobile battery and assorted Serbs and refugee Red Finns, eighty miles down the railway to guard the next two towns along, Kandalaksha and Kem.

Poole also introduced Maynard to the Murmansk soviet's improbable spokesmen, Lieutenant Commander Georgi Veselago and Major-General Nikolai Zveginstev (once of the achingly smart Preobrazhensky Guards). As Maynard quickly realised, they were in an extremely delicate position, caught between British demands and Moscow's, and between their own natural sympathies and the hungry, sullen dockworkers and railway men who made up Murmansk's small civilian population. Poole's treatment of them nonetheless gave him 'considerable amusement':

> They were his pals Sviggens and Vessels . . . Taking Veselago by the arm, he would say, 'Now, Vessels, when are you going to fix up that agreement with us?', or to Zvegintzoff, 'Hullo, Sviggens, what do those old Red Guards of yours intend doing?' He treated them rather as a house-master might treat a couple of his prefects; giving them to understand that they must realise their responsibilities and act for the good of the house, yet determined . . . that no action taken by them should run contrary to his own preconcerted plans.[4]

Four days later, on 27 June, Maynard set off down the railway to take a look at Kandalaksha and Kem, accompanied by a forty-man platoon armed with two Lewis guns, and by Colonel Cudbert Thornhill, former head of military intelligence at the Petrograd embassy, and in Lockhart's words a 'rabid' anti-Bolshevik.[5] The journey was slow –

the line so rickety that the train rocked alarmingly at anything above thirty miles an hour – and the scenery 'monotonous in the extreme. Twenty miles through pine forests – then a small clearing, with a siding and rough station buildings. Thirty more miles of forest – and then another similar clearing. And so it goes on.' The view opened up only when the train crept over a bridge across a river, sending Maynard back to 'glorious hours luring hard-fighting trout from some Scottish stream.'[6]

At a wayside halt fifty miles short of Kandalaksha they encountered their first obstacle, when a 'rascally-looking' crowd gathered round the train, preventing it from moving. Thornhill went to talk to the stationmaster, an 'abusive swine' whose obstructiveness suggested that the threatened Red Guard divisions had already set off from Petrograd. Realising that if the divisions got through to Kandalaksha he would not be able to stop them carrying on all the way to Murmansk, Maynard took drastic action. 'A revolver at the head of the still-cursing station-master' cleared the line, and an officer and NCO on the footplate lent 'needed encouragement' to the train's driver and stoker.[7]

They were only just in time, because standing at Kandalaksha station, when they drew in a couple of hours later, was a train full of Russian soldiers, with engine attached and steam up. To prevent it setting off before the French and Serb units stationed in the town could come up, Maynard drew up his platoon as if on parade on the track in front of the Red Guard train, while he went to parley with its commander. The commander and two others appeared at a carriage door extremely drunk, and a 'heated discussion' followed, Thornhill translating with deliberate slowness. Twenty minutes later the Serbs and French arrived, and Maynard was able to leave the Russian train under their guard and carry on to Kem. There he found another two Red Guard trains, but also a company of Poole's Royal Marines. This time the Red commander agreed 'almost amicably' that his men be 'detained pending further developments', and while Maynard returned to Murmansk to report, all three trains were disarmed without resistance and sent back south. 'Without a single life being lost', he wrote with justifiable pride, 'some seven hundred to eight hundred of the advanced troops of what was intended to be an attacking force had been turned back to their base minus machine-guns, rifles, and ammunition.'[8]

What he skated over was the fate of Kem's soviet. Like Murmansk's, it was theoretically Bolshevik but acquiescent. As a junior officer present put it, 'Nobody seemed to know whether we were at war with the inhabitants or not; nor were the inhabitants themselves any better informed.'[9] Despite there having been no trouble in the area, Maynard ordered a house-to-house weapons search, to be carried out by the Royal Marines and a detachment of Serbs. During the sweep, on the night of 4/5 July, the soviet's president, vice-president and secretary were all shot dead. Exactly what happened is unclear. Maynard's version, given in a cable to Poole two months later, was that on being disturbed by the Serbs the men drew revolvers and threw a bomb, and were shot in the ensuing struggle.[10] The American consul in Archangel picked up different versions. One was that the soviet members had been unarmed, and were executed by firing squad on a nearby beach. Another was that two had resisted arrest and died in a fire-fight, but the third had given himself up and been killed by his Serb guard. The British consul, Douglas Young, thought the whole incident an 'unwarrantable outrage', and the subsequent so-called investigation, ordered by Kemp, a cover-up. When the Archangel soviet sent its own investigators, he noted, they were not allowed to leave their train.[11]

Today's memorial to the Intervention's first three Bolshevik dead is only a few years old, a recent addition to a dandelion-invaded plaza overlooking the swirling Kem river. An engraved plaque shows their faces in three-quarter profile; eyes blank, collars stiff, hair rigidly parted. In line with the Civil War's general intractability in Putin's Russia – how to fit it into the glorious national narrative? Which side, losers or revolutionaries, to back? – the only information given is their names and dates. No wilting carnations or weathered wreaths sit beneath, and small children eddy round on bicycles, disturbing the siesta of a group of wolf-like but peaceable stray dogs.

Murmansk's soviet, meanwhile, had been persuaded to throw in its lot with the Allies. It had little choice, because with rail transport cut, it was now wholly dependent on ship-borne Allied food aid. But it also resented Moscow's imperiousness. Though earlier Trotsky had approved cooperation, with the Czech revolt the wind changed, and on 7 June he wired that it should not be 'conniving with foreigners'. The commissar for foreign affairs, Georgiy Chicherin, went further, demanding that it take 'belligerent action' to make the Allies leave. The soviet's president, ship's stoker Yuryev, was cutting in reply. The British and French, he pointed out, were defending Murmansk against imperialist Germans and White Finns, and since without troops it was impossible to expel them anyway, such demands only 'got people excited'. On the 28th Lenin himself came on the line with a veiled threat: 'If you still refuse to understand Soviet policy . . . you have only yourself to blame.' Yuryev snapped back: 'It's all very well for you to talk like that, sitting in Moscow.' Three days later *Izvestiya* published a decree, signed by Lenin and Trotsky, proclaiming him an enemy of the people. In a final altercation with Chicherin the same evening Yuryev got in a parting shot. Chicherin opened by telling him that he could expect to be denounced as a traitor. 'Comrade,' Yuryev riposted,

> why can't you look at things soberly? You're always coming up with fine words, but never tell us how to put them into practice. Can you supply the region with food . . . and send us a big enough force to carry out your instructions? If not, there's no point in lecturing us.

Chicherin spluttered back that he should tell 'the [Allied] admirals who put you up to this' to expect a rising. 'Comrade Chicherin', Yuryev replied, 'I have the impression that Count Mirbach [Wilhelm von Mirbach, the new German ambassador to Moscow] is standing behind *your* back' – upon which Chicherin ordered that the line to Murmansk be cut.[12] On 6 July – encouraged, presumably, by news of the Kem killings two nights before – the Murmansk soviet signed a formal defence pact, and shortly afterwards Poole made his hold on the port secure by disarming the *Askold*. Some of her sailors tried to row to shore, but there was no more resistance after they were machine-gunned from the quayside, and one killed.

For Lockhart, still *de facto* representative to the Bolsheviks in Moscow, this June–July curtain-up period was purgatory. Once so generous with his time, Trotsky would no longer see him, and his meetings with Chicherin were short and formal. His stock had fallen in London too, thanks to a *volte face* in favour of Intervention in his despatches home. As he admitted later he was not really convinced, but had sensed the way opinion was swinging and lacked the courage to resign. It had discredited him across the board. For anti-Interventionists he was a careerist turncoat, for pro-Interventionists an 'obstinate young mule' who had finally seen sense and could now be disregarded. His updated advice – to send large forces and expect little help from '"loyal" Russians' – went unheard. Instead the tide ran with 'a clamjamfrey of military experts ... who regarded the Bolsheviks as a rabble to be swept away with a whiff of grapeshot.'[13]

In sleepy Vologda, the ambassadors too began to feel the chill wind of Moscow's displeasure. Through May and early June, relations had been relaxed. Ambassador Francis received a Bolshevik representative – 'a shrewd Jew with the cheek of a government mule' – who tried to pump him on the likelihood of Allied landings. Francis teased: 'I told him that sometimes I thought Allied intervention would take place, and at other times thought otherwise, sometimes changing opinion several times ... during these long Russian days.'[14] Shortly afterwards he even made a trip back to Petrograd, mainly to see his mistress but also to rehoist the Stars and Stripes over the American embassy. The Bolsheviks ignored it.

But at the end of the month, as the Czech Legion took Vladivostok, the mood changed. A fanatical Chekist (and soon-to-be founding father of the Gulag), Mikhail Kedrov, arrived with a guard of Latvian Riflemen and threw out Vologda's friendly mayor. De Robien's gentle grand dukes were sent to the local prison, whose governor – 'a nice man' – at least let them stroll about the prison garden. Bolshevik soldiers started passing through the station in large numbers, 'comfortably installed in first-class carriages with their tarts.' The diplomats also got their first glimpse of an armoured train – metal coal trucks lined with timber and sandbags, with loopholes cut in the sides.[15]

The chill turned to outright hostility when the Bolsheviks' rivals the Socialist Revolutionaries launched three separate but simultaneous risings. The revolutionary party of the countryside rather than the city, the SRs had split with the Bolsheviks over Brest-Litovsk and over Lenin's 'Food Army', thuggishly requisitioning in the villages. The day after SR leader Mariya Spiridonova denounced Lenin at an All-Russian Congress of Soviets, two SR Chekists talked their way into the German ambassador's office and killed him with a grenade before escaping through a window. When Felix Dzerzhinsky, the weasel-faced psychopath in charge of the Cheka, went to their barracks to arrest them he was arrested himself, and the rebellious unit also seized the telegraph exchange and the Cheka's own head-quarters, in what had been the offices of an insurance company on Lubyanka Square. The Bolsheviks' guard-dog Latvians being out of town, the SRs could at this point have arrested the Bolshevik leader-ship and seized power. But they muffed it. As Lockhart put it, 'their imagination failed them', and apart from 'sending telegrams all over the country to announce the success of their coup d'état, they did nothing.'[16] On the day of Mirbach's assassination a charismatic former terrorist, Boris Savinkov, also launched an officers' uprising in Yaroslavl, halfway between the capital and Vologda; and four days later, on 10 July, the commander of Bolshevik forces on the Volga, a former lieutenant colonel in the Imperial Army, defected with a thousand men to the new SR-led Consitutent Assembly ('Komuch') government at Samara.

The risings were only loosely coordinated, if at all, and all three quickly came to nothing. Trotsky recalled the Latvian Riflemen to Moscow, and by the end of the next day they had recaptured the barracks, the Lubyanka and the telegraph office, and arrested the SR leaders. Mirbach's assassination did not provoke Germany to declare war, Yaroslavl was recaptured within a fortnight, and the poor Komuch – moderate, and the only government in the country with a claim to democratic legitimacy – lasted only a few months. The lieutenant colonel was taken captive by his own men and committed suicide. To the Bolsheviks, though, it looked like an Entente-backed conspiracy, and they reacted accordingly. On 12 July the deputy commissar for foreign affairs, Karl Radek, arrived in Vologda with his friend Arthur Ransome in tow. An odd-looking man – tiny, with a large head – Radek was a virtuoso satirical journalist and had been a favourite with the diplomatic contingent in Moscow. Lockhart describes him as 'a cross between a professor and a bandit', with a cap 'stuck jauntily on his head, his pipe puffing fiercely, a bundle of books under his arm and a huge revolver strapped to his side.'[17] With a cartridge belt added to the outfit, he now walked in on the ambassadors' morning meeting. Given the unrest in Yaroslavl, he said, they must move back to the capital, where comfortable villas had been prepared for them. They refused, pointing out that Mirbach's fate was a bad advertisement for Moscow and that they felt safe where they were. More demands, more refusals, until Radek said that he would put guards on the embassies and that, without a permit, nobody would be allowed to come or go.

In Washington, meanwhile, President Wilson was making public his reluctant decision to send troops to Siberia. On 8 and 9 July Lansing individually called in the British, French and Italian ambassadors, and outlined Wilson's plan. Despite having been pressing for intervention for months, they were disappointed – 7,000 American troops were far too few. ('Really preposterous!' Lloyd George exclaimed on hearing the news; 'Another Khartoum!') The War Office, however, was delighted – a foot was in the door, and it might open further – and immediately despatched a second battalion to Vladivostok from Hong Kong.

Alone in his study and without input from advisors, Wilson next drew up a four-page statement of American Russia policy, known as his 'July 17 Aide Memoire'. Characteristically, it combined high-mindedness with evasion. 'The clear and fixed judgement of the Government of the United States,' it opened, was that military intervention would 'add to the present sad confusion in Russia rather than cure it.' The US could not, therefore, 'take part in any such intervention or sanction it in principle.' However, action was permissible 'to help the Czecho-Slovaks . . . get into successful cooperation with their Slavic kinsmen', and to 'steady any efforts at self-government or self-defence', and the US government was happy to contribute a small Siberian force to that end. The government was also happy to send a small force to Murmansk, 'to make it safe for Russian bodies to come together in organized bodies in the north.' In the meantime the Russian people were assured 'in the most public and solemn manner' that no 'interference of any kind' with their country's sovereignty was contemplated, nor any 'impairment of her territorial integrity'. Nowhere did the document explain exactly *who*, besides the Czechs, America would be supporting, nor did it make any mention of the Bolshevik regime.[18] The Aide Memoire was not as meaningless as some critics pretend: its clear gist was that America was sending the smallest possible forces for the shortest possible time, and that the Allies should not ask for more. But its contradictions did reflect Wilson's continuing uneasiness. As he confided to his friend and advisor Edward House, 'I have been sweating blood over what is right and feasible to do in Russia . . . It goes to pieces like quicksilver under my hand.'[19]

The day before Wilson wrote his Aide Memoire the Bolsheviks took another step towards a final breach with the execution, on Lenin's orders, of Nicholas II and his family. They were likely doomed anyway – the wave of exemplary killings known as the Red Terror was beginning – but the decision was precipitated by the prospect of their rescue by the Czechs. After taking control of the Trans-Siberian the Legion had rolled through the Volga cities, and was now approaching Yekaterinburg, the industrial centre in the southern Urals to which the family had been moved two and a half months earlier. On the night of 16 July the Tsar, Tsarina and their five children were ordered down to the basement of the house in which they were held, and shot at point-blank range by a locally organised firing squad. A clumsy attempt was made to anonymise the bodies using sulphuric acid, and they were dumped in nearby mineshafts. Nine days later Yekaterinburg fell to the Czechs, and with the news about to get out anyway the government announced the Tsar's execution, but gave no information on the rest of the family.

In Vologda the diplomats put on mourning, and when de Robien's grand dukes were taken away to Petrograd, waved them off at the station to show support. The Russian public, though, seemed little moved. On the Petrograd trams there was smirking and mockery, and in Moscow Lockhart saw 'amazing indifference' – people were too exhausted and concerned with their own upturned lives, he thought, to care. American consul DeWitt Poole got a startlingly workaday take on events from a Harvester Company representative still resident in Yekaterinburg. The local commissar, informed gossip had it, had gone ahead in a 'burst of pride . . . After all you don't get any chances in the course of an ordinary life to shoot an imperial family, and quite seriously that was probably a motivation.'[20] When the news reached Buckingham Palace, George V was advised not to attend a memorial service at the Russian church in Marylebone, but did so anyway.

Semi-imprisoned in their embassies and itching for news from the Western Front – where the Germans had just been pushed back across the Marne – the ambassadors decided it was time to leave Vologda for Archangel. On the morning of 23 July a threatening telegram from Chicherin hurried them up, and by ten that evening the whole corps – 140 people including servants – were installed in railway carriages, ready and waiting. The exception was Francis, who carried on with a poker game, saying that he would come when everything was ready. He had plenty of time, because although the ambassadors are usually described as 'escaping' to Archangel, in reality they were deliberately let go, with power-play delays for emphasis. Two days later the diplomats' carriages were finally made up into a train, with a Red Guard wagon attached to the back, and at one o'clock in the morning of 25 July it set off, Vologda's clutch of onion domes sliding out of sight against a mauve midsummer-night sky. Halfway to Archangel the train was met by Kedrov, checking on progress, but the diciest moment was at Bakaritsa, the terminus and port across from the town on the opposite bank of the Dvina. Knowing that Poole intended to land, and not wanting to be caught up in fighting or taken hostage, the ambassadors insisted on a boat direct to Kandalaksha, on the other side of the White Sea and securely held by the Royal Marines. For a tense three days the Archangel soviet made them sweat, with fusses about visas and diplomatic seals. Finally, at four o'clock in the morning of 29 July, they were given clearance to leave. Poole made his move four days later.

5

'We are not here to conquer'

U NLIKE MURMANSK, ARCHANGEL was a proper place, its foundation dating back to the chance arrival of an English merchant
adventurer, who finding that he had taken the wrong turning for
China, stopped and made a trade deal with Ivan the Terrible instead.
Though British and American soldiers exoticised it absurdly in their
letters home, pre-revolutionary photos breathe provincial pride and
prosperity. At the Society of River Pilots' 300th anniversary banquet
garlands loop and wineglasses twinkle; the trustees of the Olginsky
Gymnasium stand in front of a big new brick building; awnings shade
trestle-tables at the consecration of a church. Today its painted cathedral is no more, demolished under Stalin. But a bastioned merchant's
yard, home to the city museum, survives, and on a bright June morning the light still bounces off the mile-wide Dvina. A sea wall bears
faded Soviet-era murals: 'Be ready!' and 'Take up bicycling!' There
are no Putin posters to be seen, and when his name is mentioned
people sniff slightly: '*My sever*' – 'We are *the North*.'

Poole's landing, on 2 August 1918, met little opposition. Politically
as well as militarily it was well-prepared. A cross-party group of
centrist tsarist-era politicians and former Constituent Assembly
members, approved and financed by the ambassadors at Vologda, was
set to form a new government. Lined up to head it was one of the
elder statesmen of Russian democratic socialism, Nikolai Chaikovsky.
A sage-like figure with a long white beard – and one-time leader of a
utopian farming community in Kansas – he did not actually know
Russia very well, having spent half his adult life in exile in London.
But he was respected internationally and across the political spectrum, thanks largely to his wartime fundraising for the Russian Red
Cross.

The ouster of Archangel's Bolshevik soviet was managed by a young Russian naval officer, Georgiy Chaplin. He already had British links, having served on a British submarine raiding German shipping in the Baltic early in the war. The submarine's captain, Francis Cromie, was later made naval attaché, and running into 'Charley' again after the Revolution, organised for him to go to Archangel to prepare the ground. It was a relatively easy task, Archangel's political class being small and moderate, and the Bolsheviks popular only in its lumber-yards. Chaplin found plenty of recruits from amongst tsarist officers who had drifted north, and a local councillor and newspaper-owner brought the business establishment on board. When the new government was announced on the morning of 1 August there was some shooting in the centre, but by afternoon the tsarist tricolor flew again over the town hall, and the soviet was being chased upriver on paddle-steamers – pursuit encouraged by its prior emptying of the town treasury.

The Allied flotilla sailed in on the evening of the 2nd, unopposed except by a battery on Mudyug Island, which was soon silenced by seaplanes from HMS *Nairana* (the first combined sea–air action in British naval history). The twelve-year-old daughter of a Russo-Scottish timber-trading family, Yevgeniya Gherman, watched from the balcony of her home. Townspeople packed the street and shore-line, perching on the boulders where usually women did their laundry. From up a telegraph pole, a boy shouted that he could see a mast, and,

> as if entering the stage from the wings of a theatre, the first ship of the flotilla came into view. The others followed. They were all there – Russian, British, French, American. They sailed serenely, majestically, one after the other, in perfect formation, against the pink glow of the setting sun. There was a breathless hush followed by tremendous cheering.[1]

Yevgeniya had a rose-tinted viewpoint and fuzzy recall. (For one thing America's USS *Olympia*, at Murmansk since March, did not take part, though the flotilla did carry a detachment of the *Olympia*'s sailors.) But Poole's landing was indeed broadly welcomed, as a return to stability and moderate, non-arbitrary government. Chaikovsky arrived – in the steam yacht HMS *Salvator* – the same evening, to steam whistles and more cheering crowds.

News of the Archangel takeover struck Moscow like a thunderbolt. Coinciding with the arrival of the British battalion from Hong Kong at Vladivostok, and of another British force at Baku, to defend its oil-wells from the Turks, it seemed as though the counter-revolution was finally underway. For several days, Lockhart wrote, rumours swirled:

> The Allies had landed in strong force. Some put the figure at 100,000. No estimate was lower than two divisions . . . For forty-eight hours I deluded myself with the thought that the intervention might prove a brilliant success. I was not quite sure what we should be able to do when we reached Moscow . . . but I had no doubt of our being able to reach the Russian capital.[2]

When the real numbers came through – 1,500 troops, only 600 of them combatant – he was appalled. It was a blunder, he thought, 'comparable with the worst mistakes of the Crimean War.'

The Bolsheviks' response was serious and immediate, but carefully calibrated. The British consulate was put under armed guard, Chekists sitting in the lobby while upstairs consular staff burned documents in the fireplaces. Lockhart's request that they be allowed to leave for Archangel was refused, but they were not arrested. The French were briefly detained while their offices were searched, and Sadoul's pro-Bolshevik reports, embarrassingly, published in *Izvestiya*. Left alone were DeWitt Poole and the other Americans, who the Bolsheviks still hoped to woo. The British spies in town – none of them remotely effective – were allowed to go amateurishly into hiding.

Able only to wait and see what the Kremlin had planned for them, for the next four weeks the British and French representatives marked time. In the mornings they gathered at the American consulate, and in the afternoons played football (Sadoul in goal). In between games, they may also have tried to organise an anti-Bolshevik coup. Lockhart's version of events is that on 15 August two officers from the crucial Latvian Riflemen knocked on his door with a letter of recommendation from British naval attaché (and Chaplin's former sub captain) Francis Cromie. In exchange for Allied support for Latvian independence, they suggested, the Riflemen might be willing to defect to the Allied force in the North. Lockhart immediately consulted with French attaché General Jean Lavergne, and they decided that the Latvians' proposal was plausible, and that they should be given a laissez-passer to Poole and funds. Negotiations were put in the hands of a local agent, the many-aliased Odessan Sidney Reilly, who two days later reported that talks were proceeding well and put forward a much bolder plan: for an anti-Bolshevik rising in Moscow itself.

In Lockhart's account he and Lavergne categorically turned the idea down, warning Reilly to have 'nothing to do with so dangerous and doubtful a move.'[3] There may have been more to it than that, but in the event the 'Lockhart Plot' was superseded by new attacks by the Socialist Revolutionaries. On the morning of 30 August a young SR poet bicycled up to the headquarters of the Petrograd Cheka and shot dead its head as he was getting into his car. (Amazingly, the poet was able to pedal away, but was picked up the following morning.) The same evening Lenin made an anti-Entente speech at a metal-working factory, and as he was leaving the building, a woman stepped out from the crowd with a revolver and hit him three times in the neck and shoulder. She was Fanny Kaplan, only twenty-eight but already a veteran of eleven years in prison for bomb-making under the tsars.

Now the Bolsheviks' gloves came off. Lockhart, his lover Moura von Benckendorff (the same married woman who had got him into trouble the previous year) and his deputy, Captain William Hicks, were all arrested at gunpoint in the small hours, and the men taken to the Lubyanka. Lockhart was questioned by the Cheka's deputy head, a baby-faced Latvian called Yakov Peters, who showed him the safe-passage letter Lockhart had given the Latvian officers. Belatedly realising that they had probably been *agents provocateurs*, Lockhart refused to answer, and was locked in a cell with Hicks. At 6 a.m. a woman was brought in:

> Her hair was black, and her eyes, set in a fixed stare, had great black rings under them. Her face was colourless . . . We guessed it was

Kaplan. Doubtless the Bolsheviks hoped that she would give us some sign of recognition. Her composure was unnatural. She went to the window and leaning her chin on her hand, looked out into the daylight. And there she remained, motionless, speechless, apparently resigned to her fate, until the sentries took her away.[4]

At 9 a.m. Lockhart and Hicks were released and caught a droshky home through streets that were oddly quiet even for a rainy Sunday morning. At the (neutral and thus still-functioning) Dutch legation they were given dreadful news: Chekists had burst into the old British embassy in Petrograd and shot Cromie dead on the stairs. It was the regime's first killing of a diplomatic representative. The Monday was Lockhart's thirty-first birthday, which he spent pleading at Chicherin's offices for the release of Moura, still being held in the women's prison, before a supper of black bread and sardines with Hicks. On Tuesday the newspapers trumpeted an Anglo-French 'bandit plot', and on Wednesday Lockhart was arrested again, together with most French and British officials in the capitals. That night, though he did not know it, Kaplan was executed in a garage in one of the Kremlin courtyards, with a car engine running to drown the noise.

It is not clear whether Kaplan acted alone, as she claimed during her interrogation, or was part of a wider SR plot. Either way, the regime reacted with an orgy of violence. Though Lenin was back at his desk within three weeks, in prisons everywhere 'bourgeois hostages' were executed wholesale, and lists of the victims published in the papers. In the two months after Kaplan's attack over six thousand death sentences were issued, but the actual number of killings was much higher. 'Whole blocks', an Anglo-Russian intelligence man still at large remembered,

> would be surrounded by the Cheka troops, and everybody systematically examined . . . Ex-officers, bankers and merchants [were] taken even if their documents were perfectly in order. Other people they would arrest on suspicion, and woe betide him who had no papers.[5]

He disbanded his own couriers to Archangel, but not before eighteen of them were caught and shot.[6]

For five days Lockhart was held in the Lubyanka again, hardly sleeping and praying that Lenin would recover and the executions abate. Peters came several times to interrogate him, and was polite and even confidential, reminiscing about his jewel-heisting, policeman-murdering days in London's revolutionary underground, and showing where tsarist torturers had pulled out his nails. Once, as he and Lockhart stood talking at a window, a van drew up in the yard below:

> A squad of men, armed with rifles and bandoliers, got out and took up their places in the yard. Presently, a door opened just below us, and three men with bowed heads walked slowly forward to the van. I recognised them instantly . . . three ex-ministers of the Tsarist regime, who had been in prison since the revolution. There was a pause, followed by a scream. Then through the door the fat figure of a priest was half-pushed, half-carried . . . I felt sick and turned away. 'Where are they going?' I asked. 'They are going to another world,' said Peters drily.[7]

Transfer to windowless but comfortable rooms in the Kremlin did not reassure, since they had previously been occupied by one of the executed ministers.

Meanwhile, neutral Sweden brokered negotiations for a prisoner swop, the opposing pawn Maksim Litvinov, the Bolsheviks' representative in London. (And charming, longtime Hampstead-resident language teacher to half the Foreign Office's Russia desk.) Probably of greater moment to Lenin and Trotsky was the fact that the Allies were now obviously going to win the war. Ludendorff's spring offensives had failed, 1.5 million American troops had arrived in Europe, and the Entente's counter-attack, launched near Amiens on 8 August, was steadily pushing the Germans back. On 28 September Peters reappeared in Lockhart's rooms, with a Mauser strapped to his side and a 'broad grin on his face': Lockhart would be released on Tuesday. On bidding goodbye he 'rather sheepishly put his hand into his pocket and pulled out a packet.'[8] Would Lockhart be kind enough carry a letter and signed photograph to Peters's English wife?

Lockhart spent his final days in Russia with Moura, packing his few remaining possessions – his flat had been ransacked – and trying not to think about the fact that he was leaving her behind. On 2 October the released mission members gathered, and after the usual unexplained wait, at two in the morning their train finally steamed out of Moscow station. There was another, three-day holdup at the Finnish border crossing, while Litvinov made his way from London. In a Kipling-esque show of nonchalance, Lockhart and Lavergne organised a tournament of pitch-and-toss, the soldiers and station officials, according to Lockhart, gathering to watch and becoming 'almost as excited as we did.'

On arrival home he was called in by dreamy Balfour, who showed more interest in theoretical Leninism than in the actual situation on the ground ('Such matters as the relative strengths of the Bolshevik and White armies were not mentioned') but asked him to write a report for the War Cabinet. In it, Lockhart recommended that the government either abandon intervention altogether, or else intervene at 'proper scale', with at least a hundred thousand troops. Small forces would attract the same odium but only prolong the conflict.[9] It was good advice, but that the government ignored him was not surprising: he was bumptious, had flip-flopped, and generally caused a lot of trouble. And despite everything he was also still rather dazzled by the Bolsheviks. Mass murderer Peters's letter was delivered as promised: 'Politics apart, I bore him no grudge.'

Prey to wishful thinking and the Moscow–Petrograd bubble, for the past eighteen months the Allied diplomats had repeatedly been wrong-footed by events. They had foreseen the popular revolution of February 1917, but not the Provisional Government's collapse, the Bolsheviks' coup or their survival in power. Though he was right on the Intervention overall, Lockhart's self-deluding streak conformed to a pattern – one to be repeated by the soldiers now taking centre-stage.

PART II

The Intervention Begins,
August 1918–April 1919

6

Charley Chaplin's coup

THE PRELIMINARIES OVER — initial landings made, diplomats whisked home — the Intervention proper began. In the North, things got underway with the arrival — Stars and Stripes fluttering, band playing 'Teasing the Cat' — of the 4,800 men of the 339th Infantry Regiment of the United States Army. Nearly all from Michigan, they were physically fit but inexperienced — essentially civilians, called up and given a few weeks' basic training over the summer. Though allotted to Russia on the assumption that as Midwesterners they would be used to extreme cold, they were also mostly city-bred — clerks and factory workers from Detroit and Milwaukee. Some were recent immigrants from Russia or Poland — told to drop 'wop lingo' and 'Talk United States!' by the rest. But for many, the journey to New York for embarkation was their first time out of their home state. In Britain they received another few weeks' training ('Rain, drill and mutton'), and set sail for Archangel on 26 August, on the troopships *Nagoya* and *Somali*.

The voyage took eleven days, during which a deadlier enemy than Huns or Bolos struck: Spanish 'flu. First recorded in an army camp in Kansas in the spring, it was entering its second, more virulent wave. 'All the bunks', wrote medical orderly Godfrey Anderson on the *Somali*, 'were occupied by soldiers desperately ill, with raging fevers. Others lay on stretchers, the breathing of all a rasping wheeze.'[1] By mistake most of the regiment's medical supplies had been stowed on the *Nagoya*, so that soon all he could prescribe was 'No. 9s', the infamous laxative pill doled out for every ailment. Three 'hindoo crew' were the first to die, their bodies tipped into the sea off Norway's North Cape.

On 4 September – a grey, windy day – the ships entered the Dvina estuary. For Anderson the landscape was a 'godforsaken wilderness . . . Here and there some wretched settlement of a few squalid shacks; an occasional stack of swamp hay piled along the shore, or some decrepit fishing schooner lying befouled and waterlogged.' The channel narrowed, and sand-spits coalesced into willow-filled islands; there were sawmills, and in the backwaters, moored rafts of logs. But still buildings were few, and the inhabitants did not look pleased to see them. 'Whenever we passed people on shore they stared back at us, listlessly and apathetically, making no sign of greeting or friendliness whatsover.' Archangel itself, Anderson admitted when they dropped anchor opposite the town, seemed like a decent-enough place, with churches and a 'majestic' cathedral topped with 'half a dozen bulbous spires'. But again, men in nearby fishing boats 'ignored us completely, and we got the impression that we were not welcome here.' His spirits were raised by the sound of the *Nagoya*'s band and by the sight of her snapping flag, 'lovely as a wind-whipped rose . . . We had never realised before how beautiful those stars and stripes were, and how much that flag meant to us, here in this hostile land.'[2]

The Americans arrived just in time for a coup. Soviet historians accused the Interventionists of waging a colonial war. This was anachronistic – the hey-day of imperialism was over – and untrue insofar as the Allies had no ambition permanently to annex Russian territory. But they did use the techniques of empire: raising local levies, picking local leaders and deposing them if they stepped out of line.

This General Poole now proceeded to do with Chaikovsky's Northern Government – first of several centre-left administrations to be ousted by the right with Interventionist help. Though Poole's landing and Chaikovsky's installation four weeks earlier had gone smoothly, relations between the two had been bad from the start. The fault was not all on one side. Chaikovsky was stubborn and politically naïve, insisting on his right to fly the Red Flag, and appointing as ministers a narrow slate of young, politically inexperienced SRs, none of them local. But Poole was worse, overriding the new government with military decrees that turned Archangel into a mini dictatorship. Influenced by the officers around Chaplin, he banned public meetings, censored newspapers, threatened capital punishment for Bolshevik propaganda, and arrested and gaoled dozens of 'politicals'. Matters came to a head on 3 September, when Chaikovsky dismissed a French colonel who Poole had appointed military governor. In the small hours two nights later Chaplin's men broke into the government's living quarters, which were situated across the street from Poole's office for military intelligence. Without the British opposite stirring – the usual patrol outside their building mysteriously absent – they marched Chaikovsky and four of his ministers onto a boat and took them to the Solovetsky Islands, on the far side of the White Sea and home to a thick-walled fortress monastery.

Later the same morning the newly arrived American troops paraded through the centre of town, reviewed by Poole and the Allied ambassadors. The ceremony was coming to an end, remembered Ambassador Francis, when Poole 'turned to me and said "There was a revolution here last night." I said "The hell you say! Who pulled it off?" He replied "Chaplin".' Chaplin was standing nearby, and Francis called him over. 'I said "Chaplin, who pulled off this revolution here last night?" He said: "I did . . . The ministers were in General Poole's way . . . I see no use for any government here anyway."' His manner, Francis noted, indicated that he was 'proud of the deed' and 'expected commendation'.[3]

The ambassadors were furious. Though Chaikovsky was irritating, they had been putting a good deal of effort into mending bridges between him and Poole, and had not wanted to see him ousted. Particularly presumptuous was Chaplin's timing, which was obviously designed to make it look as though he had American backing. That he had Poole's support was obvious too. During the parade, wrote French attaché de Robien, 'General Poole and his headquarters staff had radiant faces . . . Even if they took no part in last night's little operation, they cannot have done much to prevent it.'[4] Everybody knew that the head of British military intelligence, Colonel Thornhill, was a close friend of Chaplin's, and according to US naval intelligence it was commonly assumed that he had not only known of the plot, but 'had a hand in getting it up.'[5]

Angry meetings followed. Francis dressed Poole down, and together with the British chargé d'affaires, Francis Lindley, demanded that he arrest Chaplin and his accomplices. Poole refused. Chaplin, when called in and upbraided, retorted that he was 'a Russian officer, on Russian territory, and not in the employ of President Wilson.'[6] A note was nonetheless sent to Maynard's base at Kem (the closest port to the Solovetskys), ordering the immediate release of Chaikovsky and his ministers. The next morning the town woke to rival proclamations pasted up on the lamp-posts: one from Chaplin announcing that 'the time of party struggles' was over and a 'mighty wave of reconstruction' beginning; another from the ambassadors, naming no names but deploring the kidnapping and promising no more 'regrettable incidents'. The *Arkhangelski* responded with a general strike, and for twenty-four hours Detroit motormen manned the town's pride and joy, its electric tram. (Tickets not being required, the poor crowded aboard and rode rowdily up and down the long main street.) The following evening Chaikovsky and his ministers returned, and President Wilson formally notified London that if Poole tried anything of the sort again, American forces would be withdrawn.

The newly arrived Americans themselves made out the situation as best they could from an information sheet handed out by British command. The Bolsheviks, it explained, were mostly criminals, whose 'natural, vicious brutality' had enabled them to take power. They were also puppets of the Kaiser: their government was 'entirely in the hands of the Germans', and their army officered by Germans in Russian uniform, 'impossible to distinguish'. In brief, the 339th were not there to fight 'Russia nor honest Russians', and in letters home they should be careful not to give ammunition to wilfully ignorant 'peacemongers'. A section headed 'Russian Character' gave tips on dealing with the locals:

> Generally speaking, the Russian is exactly like a child – inquisitive, easily gulled, easily offended . . . Consequently two golden rules for dealing with Russians are: 1. Treat him very kindly, absolutely justly, but absolutely firmly. 2. Never believe him when he says 'It is done' . . . Go and see for yourself.[7]

Thus briefed, two out of three American battalions were immediately sent to the fighting line, to join the start of an extraordinarily ambitious offensive. Poole now had at his disposal 4,800 American troops, 2,420 British, 900 French and 350 Serbs. Potentially most useful as well as most numerous were the Americans – green but young and on the whole keen, and if not down with Spanish 'flu, fit. The British, conversely, were all too experienced – mostly wounded, gassed or otherwise unhealthy 'Category B' men, officially rated strong enough only for garrison duty. As agreed with Washington, the whole force came under British command. With it, Poole planned to advance on four different fronts: south along the railway line, southeast along the river Dvina and its tributary the Vaga, east along another Dvina tributary, the Pinega, and southwest to the small port of Onega, on the White Sea. His targets were Vologda, where the ambassadors had spent the spring, and Vyatka, a town on the east–west railway line from Petrograd to the northern Urals. Vologda would be reached by rail, and Vyatka via the Dvina riverport of Kotlas, terminus for a branch line. Vologda was 350 miles away from Archangel, Kotlas 300 miles away, and Vyatka another 200 miles beyond that.

For the Americans, just the journey to the front was an adventure. Private Clarence Scheu, of Company B, 1st Battalion of the 339th, marched straight from the *Nagoya* onto a coal barge, and the following morning tugs started pulling it and another upriver. 'Suffering Sea Cooks', Scheu wrote in his diary, 'what a rotten hole they have dumped us into now, coal dust 2 inches thick, damp filthy dungeon . . . no light, ventilation or anything.'[8] The scenery, when they were allowed on deck, was pretty, the river twisting through woods touched with autumn colour. But they continued to be dogged by 'flu, three men dying in four days and the barges pausing at village cemeteries to bury them. In the evenings the company's best singer warbled sentimental ballads: 'Memories', 'Poor Daddy He Is Reckless', 'Dreaming' and 'Will the Angels Guard My Daddy Over There?'

On 12 September, now 130 miles south of Archangel, the battalion arrived at the prosperous riverport of Bereznik, where Poole had already established a field base. Forty 'flu sufferers were transferred to a British field hospital and the rest kept going. Three days' journey on they finally reached the fighting line, their first action a dawn raid on a Bolshevik-held village. Scheu's company combed an island for escapees: 'Find one dead Bolo. Others escape thru the flats to mainland. I fired 40 rounds.'[9] On 20 September – now off their barges, hiking through woods by day and sleeping in peasant cottages by night – they met proper resistance for the first time, at the enemy-held village of Seltso. 'Bolo artillery opens up heavily. We spend night on hill, no shelter. Rain falling . . . no eats and no sleep for 24 hours.' The next day two platoons were ordered out 'to feel the Bolos' position':

> We run into a nest of machine-guns, we retire. Bolos still shelling heavily. Perry and Adamson of my squad wounded, bullet clips my shoulder on both sides. On rejoining lines we are immediately ordered out again with the assistance of C and D companies, at all costs to take Seltso that night. We attack, enter Seltso and find it evacuated by the Bolos an hour before. Am terribly tired, hungry and all in, so are the rest of the boys. Casualties in this attack 4 killed and 10 wounded.[10]

Another brand-new soldier, Private Edwin Arkins of Company C, was in the same action, part of a group ordered to attack the village with fixed bayonets:

> Come upon one of our men killed and one wounded. The sight of that first casualty I'll never forget; the lower part of face a bloody mess; the eyelids swollen and blue and the head resting on the inside of the upturned helmet. Later came across a wounded bolshevik artilleryman who has leg shattered. As Sergeant and I stop beside him, he utters one word, 'Comrade', in German. Sergeant suggests we put bayonet through him for fear he rise up and shoot at us.

Instead they took the man's rifle, and carried on into the village, where civilians who had taken shelter in a cellar were being 'routed out screaming by the loud commands of a sergeant, who fires his pistol into ground to emphasize his orders.'[11]

Then as now Seltso was a tiny place – a row of log-built farm-houses, each with its big vegetable patch, on a high sandy bank overlooking the leafy green wetland that is the sprawling Dvina. The road through it is a bumpy earth track, and on a spring day the loudest sound is the back and forth of cuckoos. But over the next few months it became a front-line redoubt, deemed, with the odd randomness of war, to be worth many American and Russian lives. The inhabitants themselves, of course, had no say in the matter. Scheu's main contact with them was when he went out 'foraging', using gestures to barter sugar for vegetables. 'The natives', he thought, 'seem hostile, but not openly. They seem to take us as a necessary evil.'[12]

While Scheu fought on the upper Dvina, medical orderly Anderson arrived by 'sidewheeler' at Shenkursk, on its tributary the Vaga. Though remote – even today, road access is over a floating bridge in summer, and river ice in winter – Shenkursk had a population of two thousand, making it the second-biggest town in the province after Archangel. A white-painted wooden cathedral (burned down under Stalin) dominated the waterside, and a large walled convent, famous for icon-painting and goldwork, the town centre. It was also surprisingly gentrified, thanks to summer holiday-makers and to the tsarist penal system, which exiled many Petersburg liberals there. (The Americans were surprised to see people 'fashionably dressed', some 'carrying walking sticks, similar to the English fash-ion.'[13]) With no shipyard or railway it was even less of a natural Bolshevik stronghold than Archangel, and when Poole made his landing the town council sent a deputation to ask him for support. An initial two American platoons duly arrived in Shenkursk mid-September, and a trio of settlements fifteen miles upriver were occupied to act as forward outposts. By the time Anderson arrived in the second half of October the town was in the process of being turned into an army base, with Headquarters in one of its largest private houses, the 310th Engineers in a brewery, and the officers' hospital in part of the convent. Anderson's first job was to help convert the local high school – blue and white, with wooden half-columns and fretwork – into a soldiers' hospital. Collapsible iron bunk-beds were set up in the classrooms, and the assembly hall – artificial palm, grand piano – became the main ward. One of the schoolmasters came in every day to check a rain gauge in the front yard, and an 'energetic little gray-haired woman' saw to the stoves and the oil lamps. The soldiers called her 'Mamma' and treated her to tots of rum.

The Americans treated their hosts with a degree of casual disrespect. Out strolling one day, Anderson and friends saw that the Engineers had run a trench through a church graveyard and unearthed some human remains. A skull was 'lying conveniently to hand, its eye sockets full of frozen mud', and with 'the compulsion of schoolboys to idly kick a tin can' they booted it ahead of them down the main street, before losing interest and abandoning it by the side of the road.[14] Far, far more serious was the fact that they brought Spanish 'flu with them. In the first month after their arrival in Russia about eighty Americans had died of it in Archangel alone, and with 'appalling virulence' the disease now hit Shenkursk. The locals, wrote Anderson,

> seemed to have no resistance whatsoever. By the 11th of November we had around 100 patients on our hands. Both our hospitals were filled, so was the Russian civilian hospital. The small stone hut at the rear of our barracks was full of corpses awaiting coffins, of which there was a shortage. It was the same in the outlands – people dying by the hundreds. Funeral processions were constantly wailing through the streets.[15]

The battalion's medical detachment did what it described in its end-of-mission report as 'considerable good work', visiting 'most of' the villages nearby and helping the sick 'as much as possible'.[16] How much difference this made is impossible to say. The 1918 mortality rate for the Archangel region as a whole was 30 per cent higher than normal, mostly due not to hunger, though that was severe too, but to the American-imported virus.[17]

While the 1st Battalion of the 339th took control of the upper Dvina and Vaga, the 3rd Battalion was fighting on the railway – the Interventionists' first taste of armoured train warfare. The term 'armoured train' is misleading. Though they got more sophisticated later on, in 1918 they were still ramshackle affairs: ordinary trains, armed with whatever guns were available and reinforced with sand-bags and logs. Used by all sides and wherever there were railways during the Civil War, they came into their own in the open country of the South, where they could operate in cooperation with cavalry units, sweeping to a depth of several miles each side of the line. In the North they were penned in by forests, hard even for infantry to penetrate, and, except where bogs thinned the pines, they never had clear views, making targeting hard and observation of line of fire near-impossible.

Improbably in command of Archangel's example was a wealthy, Bloomsbury-connected journalist and Liberal MP, Hilton Young. Thirty-nine years old, he had joined the Navy when war broke out, and only just recovered from the loss of his right arm during April 1918's Zeebrugge Raid. He was also in mourning for the love of his life, a young airman called Miles Day, shot down over the Channel. (Judging by his funny, flying-elated letters Day was well worth loving. In one he describes wallpapering his Camel's cockpit, in a pattern resembling 'a mixture between two pepper-mints and a lobster.') Convalescence back with his parents had been a 'hopelessly restless and strained affair',[18] and Young was delighted when on reporting fit to the Admiralty he got orders to catch a train the next day for Invergordon, and thence take ship to Russia.

Poole's offer, on Young's arrival in Archangel, of the armoured train command was startling – made, it turned out, because he had once been in charge of a theoretically mobile siege gun in Belgium. Hesitating to believe his luck, Young tried to look as if he

> had been born and bred in an armoured train. After all, had I not been in charge of 'Mother' in Flanders? It was true that she had never been fired or even moved in my time, but still she was a gun on a train, and that was something.

Poole went on to explain his campaign plan. 'Our forces were to dash ahead as fast as trains and steamers could carry them, and well before winter they would be securely installed at Vologda and Vyatka.' His staff too appeared to think that it 'was all quite possible', though to

Young it 'seemed a little bad for the theory that we should already be hearing of severe fighting only forty miles down the line.'[19]

Over the next ten days Young raced to put together his train. Out in front were two sacrificial flat-cars in case of mines, with brushes attached to sweep detonators off the rails. Next, 'in the bows', came No. 1 armoured car with a 3-inch howitzer, then the engine, then No. 2 car with a 2½-inch Vickers gun. An infantry car carried the 'landing party'; then came three cars with more howitzers and two 30-inch naval guns, and lastly the ammunition wagons and sleeping carriages. With eight Royal Marines Light Infantry, two British artillery sergeants, and a Russian driver, stoker and carpenter on board, the imposing assemblage left Bakaritsa on 18 August. At once the forest swallowed it up, identical pines ranged in 'endless perspective on each side', so that it felt as though the train were at the bottom of a cutting, its walls 'made not of earth but of the boughs of trees.'[20] As darkness fell campfires twinkled up ahead, and two large troop trains appeared, parked in sidings. This was the headquarters of 'Vologda Force', led by a Colonel Guard of the Royal Scots. Made up of men rejected as unfit for France (one in three wore glasses), it had arrived in Archangel shortly before the Americans.

For the next fortnight Young's train had 'quite a hot time'. It first went into action on 22 August, reconnoitering a Bolshevik position behind a burned bridge eleven miles to the south. With eighty French infantry on board, Poles to man the naval guns, and twenty Russians with lightweight Lewis guns under a teenage cadet, it puffed quickly past the last Allied outposts and into no-man's-land. There it slowed to walking pace, following the blue-uniformed *poilus* as they swept the undergrowth each side of the track. Members of a colonial regiment used to guerrilla war in West Africa, they had 'a most comfortable and reassuring air', and coming on woodpiles ideal for a sniper worked through them 'like hounds in covert.' A little further on, past a double bend, the enemy position came into sight, the burned bridge a dark break in the metallic sheen of the lines. A Frenchman came running with the news that an enemy armoured train had been sighted. A tense wait, a puff of white steam above the trees, then a black square loomed dimly, coming slowly out from amongst the trunks. There was a flash of light from the black square, and at the same instant I gave the word to fire and [our] howitzer cracked in my ear. A shell screamed close overhead and burst with a thud in the forest behind. I could not see ours burst.

Four more shells were exchanged, none making a hit, and both trains retreated.[21]

The attack proper began on 31 August. The whole of Vologda Force – the armoured train in front, then the engineering corps to repair track and bridges, then the two troop trains – set off at 10 p.m. on a moonless night, drawing up as quietly as possible just beyond 'Woodpile Station'. Waiting for the dawn and for the French infantry to get into position, Young smoked a pipe and listened to the owls in the tops of the trees. It would be an equal fight, he thought. He had eleven guns, compared to what he guessed was the enemy's four, but they had at least twice as many men. Feeling it was 'hardly right for a vessel to go into action nameless' he decided to christen his train Miles, and chalked the name on its 'bows'.

At 4 a.m. the train set off, Young warning the driver 'that if he made the slightest clank, or puff or feather of steam, his cab would at once be struck by many large shells.' Counting off telegraph poles it reached its firing-point, and the big guns were swivelled into position. When the uproar began it was indeed a fair fight: previously 'ridiculously bad', the Bolsheviks' gunnery was now 'quite business-like'. (Young wrongly putting the improvement down to the arrival of a German artillery officer.) The firing slowed as up ahead, the poilus launched their attack. Young edged his train forward to see what was happening, to find that beyond the double bend the Bolsheviks had taken up the rails. But before long, 'little knots of blue men' appeared on the line: the battle was won. Amazingly, the French had managed to get through the forest without being observed, and when they appeared to the side of the Bolsheviks' defences, the enemy fled.

For the next seven rainy days both forces were continuously on the move. The Bolshevik train slowly retreated, demolishing bridges and pulling up rails as it went. 'HM Armoured Train Miles Day' and its crew followed, rebuilding and mending. As they travelled the two trains fought a 'long slow duel . . . each side firing backwards and forwards along the line wherever he guessed that his adversary might be.'[22] For the soldiers it meant cold rations, boiled water from pools and snatched naps under the trucks – making Young nervous, every time they moved off, that not everyone had been rousted out. The officers took turns riding in the driver's cab, where one could sit on warm pipes. On 7 September, across yet another burned bridge, they finally entered Obozerskaya – not just railwaymens' huts, but a sizeable village with station, church, water-tower and ring of rushy fields.

There, on any sane calculation, Vologda Force should have stopped. In the past five days it had advanced only twenty-two miles. Vologda was still nearly three hundred miles away, and there was no hope of getting there before the first snowfalls. What Young did not know at the time was that the prospect of forming a joint front with the Czechs had also vanished: the Legion's summer push into the Urals had come to an end and it was in retreat. The best course, Young thought in retrospect, would have been to withdraw Vologda Force for the winter to Archangel. Second best, if it had to stay 'out in the air', would have been to dig in at Obozerskaya. 'The course with least to recommend it was to go on advancing, and that was the course upon which the authorities decided.'[23]

After a three-week pause, 'Armoured Train Miles Day' duly set off again, with in place of the *poilus* the Americans of the 3rd Battalion, who had arrived at Obozerskaya just as it was being captured. (Three had been killed in a small Bolshevik counter-attack, the Intervention's first American deaths in battle.) The Bolsheviks had used the time to build strong new positions nine miles away, the other side of a half-mile-wide bog. The first attempt to take them, on 28 September, was a disaster, after two American columns, supposed to circuit the bog in the dark and cut the railway line to the Bolsheviks' rear, got lost and returned to their starting-points. A simultaneous direct attack up the line also failed, with the assault party outgunned and Young's shells failing to clear the crowding trees. Several detachments were

> surrounded and wiped out; the rest, with many casualties, made their
> way back to the bridge and to the woods on our side of the marsh . . .

Gallant work was done by some of the young American officers and NCOs in rallying their men and in fighting their way clear after they had been surrounded.[24]

What Young left out was that two Americans were killed by friendly fire, after Colonel Guard mistakenly ordered the shelling of a bridge which they were still defending.

A second 'Battle of Big Marsh' six weeks later succeeded, thanks to more training and the arrival of twenty skilled and aggressive Canadian gunners. (They were members of a volunteer force of 375, armed with twelve 18-pounders, and were to get Allied forces out of tight spots time and again in the winter to come.) When Vologda Force steamed through the Bolsheviks' abandoned positions the remains were rather pathetic: dead bodies, muddy trenches and a listening apparatus made out of wire and biscuit tins. After another three days and nights of 'constant alarms, shooting, advancing, stopping, mending the line and advancing again', orders finally came that Vologda Force was to go no further, and in a forest clearing the 310th Engineers began digging trenches and building blockhouses.

The Dvina front also saw hard autumn fighting. After a short break in Shenkursk, Private Scheu's B Company was sent into the thick of it – to the front-line village of Seltso, to reinforce embattled units of Royal Scots. Disembarking from their barge on the night of 10 October, three platoons were ordered to go forward on foot. 'We have difficulty finding our way', Scheu wrote in his diary, 'men floundering here and there in swamp; we almost stumble into enemy's lines . . . Repulse infantry attack on our right.' His next entry is also headed 'In Woods': 'Battle still going on, change our position slightly, enemy infantry attack repulsed, their shells keeping the sky light at night . . . Bolos must have received reinforcements, they practically have us surrounded.' For another three days the Americans held their ground, outgunned because a Canadian field-piece mounted on a raft was unable to get within range. 'Shell exploded near me today', Scheu wrote on the 13th. 'Was floored by the concussion but not hurt. Myself and 11 others ordered out tonight on listening post patrol, outside our lines. We are in a tight hole.' The following day they were spotted and 'all hell broke loose':

> They had discovered listening post and were circling in our rear, hordes of them. We gave them several volleys apiece and retired to our lines . . . I roll sideways down hill and land in small creek bottom, lie low 'til darkness, Bolos shouting and searching 20 or 30 feet away.

When he reached the rest of the company he found it already preparing to leave, and after dark the whole group slipped away through a bog, abandoning all their kit except for rifles and ammunition. Scheu worked out that he had had six hours' sleep in the past eighty-four: 'Ye Gods, what a night.'[25]

They dug in, rather randomly, at Tulgas, a village ten miles downstream. Like Seltso it stood on sandy bluffs above the sprawling Dvina, at a point where a small tributary entered the main river. The Bolsheviks held the upriver half of the village, to the south of the tributary, the Allies the downriver half, to the north. Between, dominated by a massively timbered eighteenth-century church, was a small wooden bridge. On 22 October a Bolshevik attack was repulsed, and two nights later a bold American counter-attack – circling through the woods to attack the upper village from the rear – succeeded: the Bolsheviks were gone. Now, as on the railway front, it was time to dig in for the winter. 'Got the russkis helping us, hauling logs and sand', Scheu wrote.[26] How loyal they were he could not tell: 'We cannot distinguish between a Bolo and a native; they may all be Bolos as much as we know.' Try to get any information out of them, and 'they shut up like a clam.'[27]

A month earlier, on 26 September, the American government had sent a formal note to the other Allies. 'All military effort' in the North, it said, 'should be given up except the guarding of the ports themselves, and as much of the country round them as may develop threatening conditions.'[28] Instead, as the first snow began to fall, about ten thousand American, British and French soldiers found themselves spread out in four different directions up to two hundred miles south and east of Archangel, their furthest outposts tiny villages surrounded by wilderness. Maps showing a continuous, horseshoe-shaped front misled. In reality it was a spread hand, with no lateral communication between the fingers. The nearest navigable port, through the winter ahead, would be Murmansk, and the only way to reach it a 200-mile cross-country trek west to the Murmansk–Petrograd railway. Poole's always absurd plan to take Vyatka and Vologda had come to nothing. Nor had any back-up plan been followed: troops had simply been ordered to dig in wherever they happened to be when the offensive's failure became impossible to ignore.

7

The Hush-hush Brigade

Two days after Poole occupied Archangel, the advance party of another British expeditionary force landed at a radically different Russian outpost: Baku, on the western shore of the Caspian. From the vertiginous windows of one of the flame-shaped glass towers that dominate its modern skyline, its history is in the view. Straight ahead, on the mid-curve of a great bay, the walled old town, with bubble domes and a plump minaret. Beyond it, mansard roofs and knuckle-fisted plane trees: a Belle-Epoque *arrondissement* set down in the desert. And on the hills and at the water's edge, the fantasy palaces of the twenty-first century: a pleated fan of a sports stadium, a water-lily shopping centre, an art gallery that resembles a resting manta ray. The old Persian city was on a branch of the Silk Road. The Parisian quarter was built in the 1880s and 1890s, when an oil boom made Baku, by then under Russian rule, one of the richest places in the world. The modern drilling platforms that paid for the manta ray and water-lily are offshore, invisible in the morning haze. But look south, and herds of Soviet-era nodding donkeys are still there, arrhythmically grazing on a buff-coloured, black-splotched plain. In 1918 the oilfields resembled a giant Native American encampment, the derricks wigwam-shaped and built of wood.

The oil, of course, was what mattered. Up to the Russian Revolution, Britain had been quite successful at keeping it out of Germany's hands. A naval blockade prevented imports from overseas, and when Germany invaded oil-rich Romania, a team of engineers got in ahead and dynamited the country's wells and refineries. After the Revolution, the fear was that the Turks would capture Baku, and that Caspian oil, pumped across the neck of the Caucasus to the Black

Sea, would take its place. Worse, a Turko-German army might pour through the 'Caucasus Gap' into Central Asia, threatening British India. With all this in mind, the War Cabinet decided that a force should be assembled at Baghdad, march north through neutral Persia, and sail from the Persian fishing port of Enzeli across the Caspian to Baku, if possible at the invitation of whatever authorities were in charge there at the time.

Chosen to head this second 'hush-hush' expedition of the Intervention was Major-General Lionel Dunsterville of the Indian Army, a likeable, boyish man, devoted to his wife, who travelled everywhere with an illustrated Bible. At boarding-school with Kipling, he was the original for prankish, Empire-destined Stalky, and received his instructions, in early January 1918, with suitably Stalky-ish gusto: 'I am on a Special Mission, vastly important and interesting. God give me strength, courage and intelligence to carry it through.'[1] Nothing happened very quickly, and for the next five months he sculled about the ancient towns of northern Persia in a convoy of Ford cars, with no troops to speak of but showing the flag and administering a little light famine relief. Gradually the various elements of 'Dunsterforce' made their way up from Iraq: 1,120 infantry, including Punjabis and Gurkhas; 200 officers and NCOs, including large contingents of Australians, New Zealanders, Canadians and South Africans; three aeroplanes and fourteen armoured cars. At the beginning of June it went into action for the first time, to push a German-backed Persian revolutionary, Mirza Kuchak Khan, off the road to the coast. Fighting continued for several weeks, but on 5 August Dunsterville drove down through ricefields to Enzeli, where a revolutionary committee with which he had negotiated earlier in the year ('all very pleasant and "comrade-y"'[2]) had just been arrested and sent to Baghdad.

Baku itself was a tinderbox. With a multi-ethnic population of three hundred thousand – Shia Azeris and Christian Armenians, plus Russians, Jews and Greeks – it was perennially combustible, and had seen four days of bloody rioting in March, after its Russo-Armenian soviet arrested an Azeri general. (About twelve thousand people, mostly Azeri, had been killed.) Britain's representative in the city was consul Ranald MacDonell. In oil before joining the Foreign Office, for sixteen years he had lived an even-tenored ex-pat life, raising a family, collecting carpets and using the luxurious sleeper train to Moscow as a retreat from mail and callers. Now his wife and children were back in England, and it was his job to persuade the Baku soviet's leader, an Armenian Bolshevik and fellow former oil executive called Stepan Shaumyan, to invite Dunsterforce to help defend Baku from the Turks; specifically, from the 'Islamic Army of the Caucasus', made up of regular Ottoman units and Azeri cavalry and approaching from the south.

Like Lockhart and Trotsky in Moscow, for several months the consul and the revolutionary both played a double game. MacDonell assiduously cultivated Shaumyan, visiting his flat in the evenings and playing trains on the floor with his ten-year-old son. ('I was usually the deposed Grand Duke who had become a shunter . . . once I was executed for having hidden my mistress in a sack of grain.'³) But he was also in contact with the numerous counter-revolutionary plotters in town – mostly, he could see, hopelessly amateur: 'Every tsarist captain had gazetted himself Colonel or General, and the whole thing was rather like a comic opera.'⁴ Shaumyan was in a tricky position similar to Yuryev's in Murmansk. He desperately needed military support against the Turks, and his mostly non-Bolshevik soviet was pressuring him to apply for it to Dunsterville. But Moscow had neither come up with troops of its own, nor given him permission to make an approach. Caught between the soviet and the capital, he therefore tolerated MacDonell's buttering-up, but kept him at arm's length.

Under pressure from his superiors, in late June MacDonell reluctantly became involved in a farcical coup plot. Its leaders were a priest and a former Privy Councillor, who with no notion of discretion called one day at his flat, flourishing 'a visiting card the size of an invitation to the Lord Mayor's Banquet.' Fifteen hundred Russian officers, the Councillor promised, were in hiding in the city, ready to rise, and as soon as they did so the '"better elements" would join us and everything in the garden would be lovely . . . All that was required was vast sums of money from me.'⁵ Wistfully, MacDonell furnished him with a large quantity of paper roubles, which he carried away in MacDonell's favourite and nearly new pigskin briefcase. Communication with the priest was via a girl typist at Bolshevik headquarters, who slipped notes into his hand during mass.

The conspiracy was soon discovered, the Councillor escaping in suspiciously good time with his bulging briefcase. MacDonell was arrested and interrogated by Shaumyan, but let go after a few hours. It was all by the by, because on 31 July Shaumyan was overthrown by his soviet, which had voted to defy Moscow and request help from Dunsterville. A new five-man Centro-Caspian Dictatorship was declared, combining Russian SRs and Armenian nationalists, all in their late twenties. Shaumyan and his commissars tried to flee by boat, but were caught a few miles offshore and gaoled. For once, it was a coup the British did not engineer.

Still not wholly in control of Enzeli, Dunsterville did not sail immediately. Instead he sent ahead his political officer, Colonel Claude Stokes, to assess whether Baku was defensible. Arriving on 4 August, Stokes initially assumed that it wasn't. The Islamic Army already had the city under semi-siege, and the Dictatorship was insecure, liable to be overthrown by a Bolshevik artillery unit just arrived from Red-held Astrakhan. Orders that if there was nothing doing he should destroy Baku's oil-wells were unrealistic too. 'Someone in the War Office', he wrote later,

> had a picture in his mind of an officer landing secretly from a boat with a box of matches . . . and hastily rowing away leaving them in flames. As it happens the oilfields covered several square miles and gave employment to 120,000 men, all of whom had rifles.[6]

He would have advised Dunsterville that Baku was already lost, if the following day, to general astonishment, the Islamic Army had not abandoned its positions in the city outskirts and pulled back four miles into the hills. (It had run out of ammunition.) Instead, he telegraphed that Dunsterforce should come on, and about thirteen hundred men were despatched over the following fortnight. (The piecemeal landings sparking the rumour, believed to this day, that to give the impression of greater numbers the same soldiers were marched off the boats each morning, and back onto them each night.)

Leaving behind a skeleton force spread between Persian hot-spots, Dunsterville himself set sail on 16 August, on a once well-appointed passenger steamer called the *President Kruger*. Its Russian crew were a taste of things to come, refusing to fly the tsarist tricolor (Dunsterville compromised by flying it upside down, turning it into the Serbian one) and insisting on bringing their wives (according to a British rating, 'handy for doing our washing'). Landing the following day, Dunsterville found Baku again closely besieged, the forward Turkish batteries within shelling range of the main harbour. Its defences, he quickly discovered, were feeble. The 'Baku Army' – a nine thousand-strong scratch combination of Russian oil workers and Armenian peasants – held good positions on the hills around the city, but was not big enough to man a proper defensive line. It was also completely undisciplined, soldiers coming and going as they pleased. Paralysing as well as dumbfounding was its system of committees. Each battalion had one, as did each company within each battalion, and they held meetings while actions were actually in progress, so that if orders were carried out at all, it was after the relevant moment had passed.

Disaster struck on 26 August, while Dunsterville was briefly back at Enzeli. At 10.30 a.m. the Turks attacked 'Mud Volcano', a sulphurous outlying hill held by a 150-strong company of the North Staffordshire Regiment. Heavily outnumbered, the North Staffs hung on for three hours, before being rushed and overwhelmed. Seventy men and three officers were killed in the engagement, and another thirty-five men and eleven officers wounded. '[We] were four to one', Dunsterville wrote on his return to Baku, 'and the Armenian infantry sent to support refused to go. As it is, the risk of the town being taken is so great that I dare not keep this Diary by me any more.'[7] With 119 casualties in total, he had lost almost a tenth of his force. Five days later the Turks resumed their attack, taking two more hills and ninety Royal Warwickshires prisoner after a Baku Army battalion to the Warwicks' left fled. It was enough, Dunsterville wrote, 'to fill one with despair', and that Baku still held out was a 'prolonged miracle'.[8] The question now was how to save the civilian population from the Islamic Army's inevitable revenge massacre: 'all these women and children . . . promenading every evening on the boulevards by the electric light and quite unconscious that in any hour's time they may be having their throats slit.'[9]

The next morning Dunsterville tackled the Dictators – a 'curious collection' of two ex-tsarist junior officers, an able seaman 'whose name I forget but whom we nicknamed "the Pirate"', 'a Jew and not at all a bad fellow' and an Armenian lawyer, 'quite the best of them [and] full of pluck.'[10] Summoning them to his headquarters – in the once-plutocratic Hôtel d'Europe – he let rip. When a small counter-attack would have succeeded, he told them, he had found the entire Baku Army loafing back into the city 'with their hands in their pockets and their backs to the enemy.' Their military planning was worthless. Why bother studying the map or discussing positions, when 'you know from experience that your troops, when ordered to attack, inevitably retire?' That being so, he would no longer throw away the lives of his own brave men. They should send envoys under a flag of truce to the Islamic Army, and negotiate surrender in exchange for forty-eight hours in which to evacuate civilians. On his own intentions he was furiously incoherent, simultaneously vowing to fight on to the bitter end, to evacuate immediately come what may, and to cross the Caspian and set up a 'fresh and more useful movement' in Turkestan.[11] The Dictators responded in kind, accusing Dunsterville of betrayal and of not having provided as many troops as promised. At one point, MacDonell remembered, one of them abruptly rose and left the room. Dunsterville signalled to MacDonell to follow, and when he caught up with the man on the stairs he turned 'like a tiger at bay, and shaking his open hands in my face cried "I will blow you dogs into the sea."'[12] Most adamantly against surrender were the captains of three Russian-manned gunboats, who threatened to fire on the British ships if they tried to leave, and to bombard the Armenian quarter of town if the Dictatorship gave way.

For the next fortnight Dunsterville and the Dictators stood toe to toe, waiting for the Turks to launch their final assault, but also ready at any moment to turn on each other. Dunsterville contemplated deposing them and setting up his own government, but though 'very much tempted', decided that he lacked the necessary officers. He also suspected, probably correctly, that they were in secret communication with the Turks, and meant to use Dunsterforce as a bargaining chip. The Turks' gunnery, meanwhile, was becoming so accurate that it was obvious they had spotters in the city. Shells regularly hit the Europe, and followed when Dunsterville transferred to the Metropole. During the last days, as the tension mounted and the Baku Army melted away, he somewhat lost his head, carrying on a charade of normalcy − a banquet for an Armenian bishop, meetings about food supply and a textile mill − and defying repeated War Office orders to evacuate. No attempt was made to sabotage the all-important oilfields.

At four in the morning of 14 September the Turks launched their attack. Taking a ration van up to the firing line, a Canadian colonel found 'a hopeless situation. Everyone falling back and many running away.' British-trained artillery were 'doing nothing', in 'very poor positions' with 'nobody to tell or show them where to shoot.' The Dunsterforce senior officers who should have been taking charge were sitting at the Metropole − a 'conceited outfit and not worth a pinch of snuff.'[13] Russian headquarters was chaotic, packed with people all shouting at once, while the C-in-C dashed between continuously ringing telephones. By mid-afternoon the Islamic Army held all the high ground around the city, and Dunsterville ordered that when darkness fell, evacuation should begin. As the sun set and firing died down, dusty, sweat-soaked British units filed through derricks and shanty-towns to an inconspicuous suburban wharf, where the *Kruger* and three smaller steamers lay waiting. Two took on wounded and left for Enzeli; the *Kruger* and the third waited for the remainder.

The last hurdle was the Dictators, two of whom came aboard the *Kruger* and demanded that Dunsterville send his men back to their positions. Dunsterville said that he was sailing immediately; the Dictators that if he did so their gunboats would fire on him. To which, according to his memoir, Dunsterville replied,

'I hope not' and bowed them off the ship. A staff officer whispered in my ear 'Why not arrest them and take them along?' − a useful suggestion, but I felt we could accomplish what we wanted without introducing any complications.[14]

At midnight, with 870 men aboard, her lights out and her bridge padded with conveniently-to-hand bales of cotton, the *Kruger* cast off. The last small steamer followed, loaded with as much ammunition as she could carry from the nearby city arsenal. As Dunsterville had guessed, the Dictators had been bluffing about the gunboats, which were nowhere to be seen. But as the *Kruger* crept past the guardship at the harbour entrance, somebody – a revolutionary crew-member, Dunsterville assumed – turned on her lights, and the guardship opened fire. Three 'pom-poms' came over the *Kruger*'s bridge, but she was soon out of range and carried on at full speed for Enzeli, arriving there without further incident the following evening. Twenty-four hours later the slow, explosives-laden steamer behind, by then given up for lost, came in too, the two officers on board explaining that to get her past the guardship they had had to take a crewmember hostage, and stand with revolvers drawn over her captain and stokers. Hit six times, it was a miracle that she had not blown up.

In Baku, the Azeris perpetrated their massacre – no mention of which mars Dunsterville's cheery memoir. For three days the Islamic Army's regular Turkish units paused outside the city while Azeri ir-regulars broke into Armenian houses, pulled out their inhabitants and murdered them on the streets. An Armenian organisation counted 8,988 bodies; the total number of deaths was probably around ten thousand.[15] About thirty thousand people fled by sea to already over-crowded Enzeli, where they crowded into warehouses or built them-selves shelters out of planks and metal sheeting. Housed in tents on the beach, Dunsterforce turned to relief work. MacDonell, who like many had left Baku with nothing except the clothes he stood up in, was in charge of refugee organisation – heartbreaking work, especially once Spanish 'flu and typhus hit. Getting sick children to hospital was almost impossible – parents hid them rather than let them go – as was turning away new refugee boats. The day after instructions were issued that they be directed elsewhere, an oil tanker dropped anchor with three hundred rain-soaked figures huddled on its open deck, so emaciated that 'their clothes clung to them like cobwebs on a stick.'[16] They were the survivors, the tanker captain explained, of six hundred he had set out with ten days earlier. Torn between bursting into tears and losing his temper, MacDonell did the latter. The captain declared that he would not lift anchor again even if the British blew him to pieces; the refugees stayed.

Almost as excrutiating was the job of formally disarming an Armenian general, Jacques Bagratuni. Formerly of the Imperial Army and the Dictatorship's minister for war, he was one of the few people, MacDonell thought, who had given his all to defending Baku, despite constant pain from the recent amputation of a leg. MacDonell had worked with him often, talking 'much about our sympathy for Armenian aspirations, and hopes of an eventual Armenian National Home.' Now Bagratuni steamed into Enzeli with a few hundred still-loyal troops, to be met with a British demand that he give up his weapons. Briefly it looked as though he might refuse – 'They had lost everything; British aid had failed them; this was the last straw' – but wiser counsels prevailed, and MacDonell was landed with performing the requisite ceremonial:

> It was a pathetic moment when the General laid his sword, hilt fore-most, on the cabin table. I had no instructions about the General's sword, but I felt sure he would not run amok with it, so I said I thought he should keep it. He replied, with great dignity, that I must then hand the sword back to him. This I did, hilt first; nevertheless I was conscious of doing it all wrong – rather as one would hand an umbrella to a friend on a rainy night.[17]

From the point of view of the wider war the Dunsterforce expedition may have been worth it. By putting up, in Stokes's words, 'a very fine bluff for six weeks', it prevented a new flow of oil to Germany at a critical moment, which Ludendorff himself judged a 'serious blow'.[18] At the time, though, it looked like a fiasco, and the press were unsparing. Young lives had been thrown away to no purpose; the whole venture was abortive, quixotic, rash. Having sent what he himself admitted were insulting telegrams to the War Office when ordered to evacuate, Dunsterville was in disgrace. Everyone was being 'very nice', he wrote on return to HQ at Baghdad, but there was 'a general sort of feeling that I have been a naughty boy and ought to be put in a corner.'[19] Fears of court-martial receded, but he was relieved of his command, and Dunsterforce broken up.

★

The coda to the Dunsterforce story is what happened to the Armenian Bolshevik Shaumyan and his colleagues. Imprisoned by the Dictatorship when it took power at the beginning of August, they had been able to negotiate release and a ship during its last days. Dunsterville had given their departure his blessing, and before they sailed, MacDonell had even gone on board to bid Shaumyan farewell and split a bottle of sweet champagne. The obvious destination for them would have been Bolshevik-held Astrakhan, the Volga-mouth port on the Caspian's northern shore. In fact they ended up – whether by mistake, or on the intiative of the ship's crew, or at British behest is unclear – at British-garrisoned Krasnovodsk (today's Turkmenbashi), on its eastern one. If it was a mistake it was a fatal one, because soon after their arrival the local authorities – subordinate to a British-backed government known as the 'Trans-Caspian Committee', 300 miles away up the railway to Tashkent – took them at dead of night to an empty stretch of desert and executed them.

The news took a while to leak out, but when it did, the 'Twenty-Six Baku Commissars' were immediately inscribed in the roll of Soviet martyrs – brave faithful, foully slain by wicked imperialists. A famous 1926 painting by Isaak Brodsky – Soviet Russia's Norman Rockwell – depicts the scene: the condemned men lit by the dawn atop a railway embankment, shaking their fists in proud defiance; down below, lurking behind the firing party, three sinister figures in British khaki. They remained a *cause célèbre* throughout the Soviet period, so much so that Reginald Teague-Jones, the young intelligence officer who had liaised with the Trans-Caspian Committee, spent the rest of his life under an alias for fear of assassination.

Scoffed at by Western historians for decades, the Soviet version of events gained credibility with the publication of Teague-Jones's own diaries, after his death in 1988. When Shaumyan and his colleagues were first detained, the diaries revealed, the Trans-Caspian Committee, led by a former train driver, had wanted to send them to General Wilfred Malleson, over the Persian border at Meshed. Citing a shortage of manpower Malleson had demurred, and suggested that the Trans-Caspians 'find some other way of disposing of them.'[20] Teague-Jones attended the subsequent meeting at which the Trans-Caspians decided on execution, but claimed to have left before they made up their minds. Perhaps that was true, but since Punjabi sepoys were all that stood between them and a Bolshevik advance from Tashkent, the idea that he could not have prevented the killings is laughable. Soviet propaganda around the Intervention was crude, hypocritical and exaggerated – but did not always have to be untrue.

8

'Eggs loaded with dynamite'

W HILE THE INTERVENTION met its first repulse in dusty Baku, in the farmlands of Flanders and northern France, the grim slog against Germany was finally drawing to an end. In the second week of August the Allied armies had launched their 'Hundred Days' offensive at Amiens, and in a series of battles at the end of September and beginning of October they broke through the Hindenburg Line. The German government petitioned for a cessation of hostilities, and at five o'clock in the morning of 11 November, in a railway carriage drawn up in a royal hunting forest northeast of Paris, the Armistice was signed.

To the far-flung Interventionists, it did not immediately feel very relevant. In northern Persia a lieutenant with Dunsterforce rode over to his German opposite number under a white flag, to tell him that the war was over. The German did not believe him, but 'it all seemed pretty unreal out here anyway, [so] we agreed to differ over a bottle of quite palatable Caucasian wine.'[1] On Archangel's railway front, Hilton Young spent Armistice Day fighting the second 'Battle of Big Marsh', and on hearing the news felt curiously unmoored, as if shot forward into a future in which he 'had no business and no place.'[2] In a village in western Siberia, Czech Legionary Gustav Becvar was waiting with his company for a Bolshevik attack to begin when a soldier came running with a slip of paper. '"Gentlemen", his CO announced, "This message says that an Armistice has been signed in France." We listened politely . . . and went on shuffling about to keep warm.'[3]

With no inkling of the Armistice for another eight weeks, amazingly, was Private Scheu of the US Army's 339th, who spent 11 and 12 November fighting off an attack on the Dvina village of Tulgas. The first day's barrage lasted from dawn to dusk. The village was vulnerable because the British had prematurely withdrawn their gunboats, and Scheu's platoon occupied one of its most exposed positions, a forward blockhouse next to the creek and church. At 1 p.m. the platoon's machine-gunner was killed by a sniper's bullet as Scheu helped him reload, and soon afterwards a second man fell dead while crouching at a loophole. A third well-aimed round hit Scheu's own rifle, breaking it in two, and shells started landing so close that thrown-up earth had to be pushed out of the loopholes before the Americans could return fire. As dusk fell the enemy tried to rush the bridge across the creek: 'Above the din', Scheu scribbled in his diary, 'we could hear the Bolo officers shouting orders to cross, even when they knew it was plain suicide. My hat is off to some Bolo soldiers.' Through the night they stayed quiet except for 'low murmurings' from the other side of the stream – either out after their dead and wounded, or preparing 'a big surprise for us in the morning.'[4]

As Scheu feared, when the bombardment recommenced the Bolshevik guns included a new battery of howitzers, brought up in the darkness. With high-explosive shells landing every fifteen seconds, it was heavy even by Western Front standards. By 10 a.m. the enemy had their range: 'Shells were just raining about . . . and we knew we were in for a hit.' When it came an hour and a half later three men were killed instantly and Scheu wounded in the hand and shoulder.

We crawl out, bullets thick outside. A shell buried its nose in the ground 10 feet away – but luck was with me, it was a dud. Finally reached priest's house, about 20 yards from blockhouse. 'Twas a sad sight inside. The priest was decapitated and the entire family killed outside of a little girl.[5]

The men dressed each other's and the child's wounds and lay huddled together until dark, when they were able to move to a first-aid station at the other end of the village.

On the tug ferrying the wounded to hospital at Bereznik, Scheu discovered that thanks to a Canadian battery, the fight was actually swinging the Allies' way. Seventy-nine enemy dead had been counted inside American wires, against their own fourteen dead and twenty-eight wounded. 'Battle still raging. Hope the boys give 'em hell . . .

Feel dizzy as a loon.'[6] By the time he finally heard that the war with Germany was over, in the second week of January, he had recovered from his wounds and was having not too bad a time in the rear. ('Went to a Russkie party tonight; had 3 Barishnas (girls); one is all you can handle; they are buxom lassies, good and strong.'[7]) The news came just as his company was ordered back to Tulgas. 'The Armistice', he wrote angrily, 'doesn't mean a damn thing over here . . . "Under British Command" is the title of this fiasco.'[8] Had the US government forgotten his and the 339th's existence?

Elsewhere, the Armistice changed everything, the combatant nations staggering to their feet in a fundamentally altered world. Though not occupied, Germany was fragile and humiliated, and where the Hapsburgs and Ottomans had ruled, new countries waited to be born. The victors had the challenge of higher expectations. Press censorship was lifting and party politics resuming. Soldiers wanted immediate demobilisation; trades unions better pay; women the vote; Indians, Irish and Egyptians independence. It was a moment of hope and celebration, but also of entry into a new and demanding age.

As far as Russia policy was concerned, victory destroyed the Intervention's original *raison d'être*. There was no longer any need to worry about Germany getting hold of Allied military supplies, or to try to rebuild the Eastern Front. On the other hand, it also created new opportunities. The Black and Baltic Seas were suddenly open to the Allied navies, and hundreds of thousands of fighting men in France theoretically free for deployment elsewhere. Russians both White and Red assumed that large armies would immediately be sent east. Interviewing Lenin in the Kremlin a few days before the Armistice, the *Manchester Guardian*'s correspondent found him curiously unmoved by the revolutions roiling Germany and Hungary, and anxious at the prospect of the Allies coming through the Dardanelles: 'What can we put up against these, if they really send them, and if the Allied soldiers really obey their rulers and march?'[9] British and French expatriates in German-held Kharkov (today's Kharkiv, a commercial city near the present-day Russia–Ukraine border) similarly awaited Allied occupation, collecting funds for a welcoming presentation flag.

Some new forces did indeed immediately set sail. The day after the Armistice, as Lenin feared, an Allied naval squadron passed through the Dardanelles. And a few days later a remodelled version of Dunsterforce – dubbed North Persia Force or Norperforce – landed back in Baku to take it over from the defeated Turks. Headed by a Scottish general, William Thomson, it stayed until the following summer, supporting, and on important matters such as oil dictating to the ministers of a new Azerbaijan Democratic Republic (ADR). Though short-lived – the Red Army marched in a few months after Norperforce left – the collaboration was rather successful. Colonial policemen bicycled the streets, food aid was organised, and the opera house, casino and brothels reopened. Though the British censored the press, the ADR could boast of being the world's first-ever Muslim parliamentary democracy, and the ninth country in the world to give women the vote. Azeris continued to massacre Armenians and vice versa, but on a smaller scale, up in the hills.

These power-vacuum-filling moves did not mean, however, that Britain felt compelled to race to Russia's rescue immediately. The country's disgraced, second-order status was rubbed in by its exclusion from the official victory celebrations, the tsarist-hangover Russian ambassador to London bitterly noting that though the city was draped with every sort of flag, only the War Office – 'staunch friend, endowed with [a] better memory than the rest of Whitehall' – flew the Russian tricolor.[10] Behind the scenes a series of memos and meetings resulted in the same sort of 'wait and see' policy with which the Allies had initially responded to the Bolshevik takeover twelve months before. Though the main argument for intervention had evaporated, Bolshevism itself remained a threat, and Allied troops in the North could not be withdrawn before spring anyway. There was also the question of national prestige. As Lloyd George put it to the House of Commons, for Britain to say to her Russian proxies 'we are exceedingly obliged to you, you have served our purpose . . . Now let the Bolsheviks cut your throats' would be mean and unworthy.[11] On 30 November the military missions in Archangel and Vladivostok were accordingly told to carry on as before and that nothing would change for the present.

The first post-war Anglo-French summit was held at Downing Street on 3 December 1918, revealing differences that persisted throughout the Intervention. The immediate Russia-related question on the agenda was whether Russian representatives should be invited to attend the upcoming Peace Conference in Paris, and if so, which. Clemenceau was adamantly against any sort of dealings with the Soviet government: it had betrayed the Allies, and the Conference was none of its business. He was also against inviting representatives from Finland, Latvia or Estonia, all of which had declared though not yet actually won independence. Lloyd George took the opposite line. One could not pretend 'there were no Russia'. The Bolsheviks, 'whatever might be thought of them', held most of the country, and 'facts could not be neglected because they were unpalatable.' But he was more thinking aloud than making an argument, and a decision would anyway depend on President Wilson.[12]

A secondary but significant Allied player was Canada. Her Dominion status meant she did not have her own ambassadors, nor, in theory, her own foreign policy. But the war, during which she had lost over sixty thousand men for the old country, had already severely strained this arrangement, and now the Intervention was doing the same. Shortly before the Armistice, the Canadian prime minister, Robert Borden, had been flattered into sending a first batch of 680 troops to Vladivostok, and a second, larger group was now waiting out its quarantine period in Victoria, British Columbia. Mid-Atlantic when the Armistice was signed, he arrived in London to a pile of telegrams from his deputy in Ottawa, begging him to cancel the expedition. Public feeling against it was running high, and it would be rash to force soldiers to go against their will. Wanting to keep his place at the top table in London, Borden compromised. The troops would go, but not venture into the Siberian hinterland, and return home in the spring. The War Office sniffed that in that case they might as well leave straight away; offended Ottawa riposted that London did not seem to know what her own policy was in Russia, and no more did Washington or Tokyo.

While in the capitals heads still rang with the mighty reverberations of the Armistice, in Siberia a British general was promoting another military coup. The background was characteristically complicated. By late summer 1918 between ten and nineteen separate governments

– depending on what you counted as one – had declared themselves east of the Volga, the biggest of them the Socialist Revolutionary Komuch government in Samara, and a reactionary 'Duma' government in Omsk. Urged to unify by the Allies, in early September some two hundred representatives from ten different organisations came together and, in the course of a two-week conference brokered by Britain's donnish High Commissioner, Sir Charles Eliot, agreed to merge into an 'All-Russian Provisional Government', to be led by a five-man, SR-dominated Directory. Samara being on the point of being retaken by the Bolsheviks, the new body moved across the Urals to Omsk, where it uncomfortably shared power with the hostile Duma government, which though officially subordinate never stepped down.

Into this fraught scene stepped the Allied military. By far the biggest contingent, aside from the already present Czech Legion, were the Japanese. Earlier in the year, Japan and America had agreed to send 7,000 troops each to Vladivostok, later upped to 12,000. With the opportunity wide open to tighten its grip on Manchuria, Tokyo ignored the agreement, and landed 72,000, under General Otani Kikuzo, a veteran of the Russo-Japanese war. It also made a protégé of a twenty-seven-year-old half-Buryat former tsarist officer, Grigoriy Semyonov, who had rallied a small, ultra-violent force in the Russo-Chinese borderlands and until the Czech rising been the only military figure in Siberia successfully fighting the Bolsheviks. For a while Britain and France had funded him, and with much larger-scale Japanese support, his Special Manchurian Detachment now numbered 5,000, made up mostly of Mongols and Chinese but also including Japanese, Koreans and a company of Serb cavalry. An old army colleague of Semyonov, the pale-eyed Baltic-German psychopath Baron Roman von Ungern-Sternberg, operated more flamboyantly (Buddhism, opium, knick-knacks made of human skin) over the Chinese border.

The next largest Allied contingent were 9,000 Americans, the first batch of whom – 1,590 men of the Philippines-based 27th Infantry – landed at Vladivostok on 16 August 1918. Their commander – and as things turned out, wisest of Intervention generals – was Major-General William Graves. The earnest, spectacled son of a Southern

Baptist minister, he had been flung into the job very much against his will. In the midst of eager preparations to take command of a division in France, a telegram had arrived from the army chief of staff, ordering him to catch the first available train to Kansas City, for a meeting with Secretary of War Newton Baker. Arriving post-haste at Kansas City railway station the same evening, he found Baker in the waiting-room, about to leave. In the few minutes available Baker apologetically told him that his French command was cancelled, and that he was being sent instead to Siberia. The whys and wherefores were in a sealed envelope: 'This contains the policy of the United States in Russia, which you are to follow. Watch your step; you will be walking on eggs loaded with dynamite. God bless you and goodbye.'[13] In the envelope, all Graves found was President Wilson's vague July Aide Memoire. No more specific instructions followed, and in his telling he arrived in Vladivostok on 1 September with 'no information as to the military, political, social, economic or financial situation in Russia', nor any clear idea as to who if anybody he was supposed to be fighting.[14] His subsequent interpretation of his non-orders, backed by Baker but vigorously contested by the pro-Intervention State Department, was that American forces should stay neutral and disengaged. He did not manage to stick to this entirely: under a later agreement, American troops took control of part of the Trans-Siberian, which meant occasional skirmishes and ambushes. But on the whole he stood his ground, putting himself furiously at odds with the other Allies as well as with White Russians.

Present from early August but in much smaller numbers were the British and French. Britain's contribution was an 800-strong battalion of the Middlesex Regiment, an elderly, B-rated unit, armed with equally elderly Maxim guns, previously on garrison duty in Hong Kong. Traditionally nicknamed 'the Die-Hards', they were known behind their backs as 'the Hernias'. Full of go, however, was their fifty-one-year-old colonel, John Ward, possessor of one of the army's most remarkable biographies. He had started working life aged twelve, as an itinerant labourer on the canals. At nineteen he had joined the army and built railways in the Sudan, at twenty-three he had founded the Navvies and Bricklayers' Union, and at forty, been elected for the Liberals to the House of Commons. When war with Germany broke out he signed up again, this time as an officer, and recruited several 'navvies' battalions' before getting his Middlesex command.

He itched for action, and two days after landing in Vladivostok, entrained the Middlesexes for the Ussuri river, where Red units – in his terminology 'the Terrorist Army' or 'German-Magyar forces' – were fighting the Czechs and Japanese. After three weeks of discovering that Siberian mosquitoes can bite through blankets, the Middlesexes got to use their Maxims from 22 to 28 August, when two armoured trains equipped with guns and crews from one of the British ships at Vladivostok helped put the Reds to flight. 'It was just ding-dong open fighting' wrote thrilled Ward, 'wonderfully spectacular in character.' On one occasion the Japanese cavalry swept up a slope 'in a beautiful line, forward over all resistance, white flag and all', and on another they overwhelmed a Red train, bayoneting Russians overboard 'with the same motion as if they were shovelling coal.'[15] The battle was the end of organised Bolshevik resistance in the Russian Far East.

In overall command of the British military mission to Siberia was General Alfred Knox. An Ulsterman of impressive, even terrifying appearance – hooded eyes, beak of a nose, implacable chin – he knew Russia, or at least a slice of it, well, having been military attaché at the Petrograd embassy through the war. (Solzhenitsyn gave him a walk-on part in *August 1914*, in which he plagues an overburdened Russian general with questions and 'artificial European smiles'.) In London he had lobbied hard against Lockhart, damning his advice to make a deal with Lenin as 'criminally misleading'. (Ransome, he thought, 'should be shot.' No *Swallows and Amazons*!)[16] Establishment Russians adored him, and so did most young British officers. 'Physically fine' and 'not too damned clever', wrote one, Knox made 'one proud to belong to the same race.'[17]

Arriving in Vladivostok a few days after Graves, Knox assembled a mostly Anglo-Russian staff after his own conservative mind. The odd man out – periodically debagged by the rest – was twenty-four-year-old William Gerhardie, son of a wealthy Petersburg business family and an aspiring aesthete and playwright. Immune to the Knox charisma, he later made fun of him in a fictionalised memoir, titled *Futility*. The general, he wrote, 'divided the world into two big camps: the humanity he called "good fellows", and the humanity that he called "rotters".' In one scene a cynic suggests to Knox that 'whenever you come to examine very carefully a Russian officer's scheme for the salvation of his country, it invariably boils down to giving him a job.' 'At a glance', wrote Gerhardie, 'I could see that [Knox] had classed the fellow as a "rotter."'[18]

Also in the rotter camp was Omsk's new All-Russian Government, led by its five-man Directory. Squabbly and impractical, it was not much more than a talking shop. But it lobbied hard for diplomatic recognition, and would have got it had it not been for the ambition of Admiral Aleksandr Kolchak. Forty-three years old, dark-eyed and intense, Kolchak was one of the tsarist navy's stars – a polar explorer, an expert in mine warfare and, from 1916, commander of the Black Sea Fleet. Whisked away from mutinous Sebastopol by the Root Mission, he had gone with it to Washington, and the Bolshevik coup had found him in Tokyo, where he approached the British embassy to volunteer his services. After a couple of false starts Knox met him there in August 1918 and was impressed, writing to the director of military intelligence that the admiral was 'the best Russian for our purpose in the Far East.'[19] Soon after Kolchak moved to Omsk, and in early November was appointed the All-Russian Government's minister for war.

It didn't mean much, because the government had little real power. Internally split (amongst other things, on the extremely hypothetical issue of proportional representation), it had never been able to impose its authority on the parallel Duma government. Nor did it control the Siberian Army, which had started out as a democratic outfit ribboned in Siberian white and green, but since turned revanchist. Its insubordination was on display at a civic banquet honouring Ward, which was gatecrashed by drunken officers who shouted down toasts to English democracy before breaking into a chorus of 'God Save the Tsar'. (The civic dignitaries walked out in protest but befuddled Ward sat on, his interpreter too embarrassed to explain what was happening.)[20]

In London there was disagreement over whether the All-Russian Government was still worth backing. Citing Knox ('sentimental socialists'), the War Office argued that it wasn't, and that Russia's only hope was a military dictator, at least for the time being. Balfour and the Foreign Office took the opposite line: the All Russian Government was moderate, its descent from the elected Constituent Assembly gave it legitimacy, and it would be bolstered by being given *de facto* recognition. The Foreign Office carried its point, and on 14 November the War Cabinet gave its assent. But the decision was never implemented because three nights later the Omsk garrison arrested four out of the government's five-man Directory, and Kolchak declared himself 'Supreme Ruler'.

Was Knox behind the coup? Almost certainly. He had never made a secret of his contempt for the All-Russian Government, and though he absented himself from Omsk for the coup itself, was there for the planning stage beforehand, huddling with right-wing generals and half-humorously telling the Directory that if it did not buckle under he would overthrow it. As one of its members relates, 'General Knox drank tea [and] threatened to gather a band and disperse us . . . "I am becoming a Siberian", he concluded his joke.'[21] Knox's chief of staff and one of his intelligence officers also had meetings with the plotters, and in the immediate run-up Ward helped Kolchak get tactfully out of the way by escorting him to the Urals front. On the evening of the coup itself, 17 November 1918, Ward delivered the Admiral back to Omsk, and the next morning, fearing trouble from the Czechs – in his words 'naturally obsessed with the usual "Liberty, Equality and Fraternity" business' – he posted Maxim guns around government headquarters. Ward also credited himself with saving the lives of the arrested Directory members, by insisting that they be put on a British supply train and taken to the Chinese border. Otherwise they would have been 'dead as mutton . . . quietly bayoneted in the night'.[22]

The All-Russian Government would have fallen anyway. But for Russians with higher hopes for their country than dictatorship it was a heartbreaking moment: the end of any sort of representative government for another seventy years. From Vladivostok, Commissioner Eliot advised the Foreign Office that Kolchak was a bad choice, being said to suffer from nerves. Balfour felt that events were uncomfortably similar to those in Archangel two months earlier – 'Remember General Poole!' The Russian ambassador – triumphant, three days earlier, at the decision on diplomatic recognition – managed to get a meeting with Balfour's deputy Lord Robert Cecil. Wholly wrapped up in getting the League of Nations off the ground, Cecil may not have known that Knox was behind Kolchak's coup. But if he did, his brush-off was shameless: 'We were ready to recognise the Directory. It has been forcibly removed. Who can tell how long the present power will last?'[23]

9

'A feeling of smothering'

I F KNOX WAS the most political of the Intervention generals (and
Graves the least), the best soldier amongst them – later to rise to
field marshal – was the splendidly named Edmund Ironside, the new
commander of Allied forces in the North.

Thirty-eight years old, six foot four and correspondingly broad,
Ironside was the kind of man people love to mythologise. He was a
descendant of Saxon kings, it was said, had been expelled from school
for whipping a teacher, spoke seventeen languages, had disguised
himself as an ox-cart driver during the Boer War. The last of these
stories was true, and it was also true that John Buchan, who met
him in South Africa, used him as the model for Richard Hannay,
straight-up hero of his era-defining thrillers.[1] Behind the stories stood
a less colourful but no less impressive personality: an ambitious and
immensely energetic man, confident bordering on arrogant and
completely immersed in his job, who confided only in his diary
and had in full the soldier's instinctive dislike of Whitehall. ('Must be
some sort of good in him', he wrote after a meeting with Lloyd
George's *éminence grise* Lord Hardinge: 'Suave bearing for dealing
with foreigners perhaps.'[2]) The Tommies' nickname for him was
'Tiny'. The doughboys called him 'Big Bill', and for his evident
professionalism, frequent visits to the front, and the trouble he took
to remember people's names exempted him from their general loathing of the British command.[3]

Ironside arrived in Archangel on the last day of September, after
Poole's too-public connivance in Chaplin's coup attempt. The official removal of Poole, who was in semi-disgrace in London but could
not be seen to be so, was protracted, but Ironside effectively took
command a fortnight later, when Poole departed 'on leave'. He was

immediately confronted by a raft of problems, not least the incompetence of Poole's officers. On the boat over he had worried that they would be second-rate types who had 'got the sack from France', and a first visit to the railway front confirmed it. Of two column commanders one was 'old and stupid', and the second a drunkard, who he put under arrest. ('Damned stinker letting down British prestige like this, especially when commanding French and Americans.')[4] The Archangel staff were lazy and untrained, and the intelligence men, led by 'Russianized' Thornhill, had plainly encouraged Chaplin's putsch. One day who should turn up for lunch in the mess but the 'amusing rascal' Chaplin himself: Thornhill's men, it emerged, had invited him, despite the fact that he was supposed to be confined to the front. Packing Chaplin off again, Ironside

> gave them all a good telling off . . . I told them that as long as I was running things I would have no intriguing, and that they must make no undesirable friends . . . They are a useless crew.[5]

Another problem was bad feeling between the British and the Americans. In Archangel there were squabbles over premises and food aid, the latter because the American Red Cross's aid operation was much bigger than the British one, and relatively unconcerned about where supplies ended up. (Ironside had a furious showdown with a 'most truculent' American Red Cross man after a boatload of flour was seized by 'some local scoundrel' on the disputed Pinega river.[6]) At the fronts, there was ongoing resentment at the Brits' hogging of 'swivel-chair duties' in the rear, as well as at their overall command. A superficially trivial but persistent source of friction was whisky. With Prohibition coming into force at home, American messes were officially dry, but British ones excessively well-supplied. Week after week, Ironside deplored under-the-counter sales and the way American officers hung about 'like so many jackals' cadging drinks. The Americans' unhappiness was exacerbated by the fact that their putative commander in the North, Colonel George Stewart, had the same non-orders as Graves in Siberia, and similarly interpreted them to mean that he should stay as uninvolved as possible. But unlike Graves's, Stewart's soldiers were already in the thick of serious fighting, and took the fact that he barely budged from Archangel extremely badly. To mend matters Ironside asked Stewart to take command of the railway front. He refused, Ironside thereafter putting him down as a 'miserable backboneless individual', 'weak-kneed fool' and 'rabbit'.

Ironside's biggest concern by far, however, was the Russians, specifically the 'Russian Army' being raised by the Chaikovsky government. It had its heroes, for example the haunted-looking young air ace Aleksandr Kazakov, who had escaped north with thirty-seven ex-Imperial Air Force 'planes and crew, and flew from a tented aerodrome at Bereznik. But recruitment numbers were disappointing, as was an embryo Slavo-British Legion. Visiting its training school Ironside reckoned the Russian NCOs excellent but the officers 'lamentable. I simply cannot get them to work hard enough.' When he gave them a lecture on how they should see to their soldiers' welfare and lead by example, there came an indignant question: 'Do you wish us to be valets to our men?'[7] The Russian Army's commander, a mid-ranking former tsarist officer called Boris Durov – 'a sickly little man with a straggle of brown beard' – was unsatisfactory too: too soft to quell a soldiers' strike in Archangel's Nevsky barracks. Hearing that 1,500 recruits had refused to turn out on parade and were instead lounging in their cots listening to agitators from the lumberyards, Ironside went straight to 'old man' Chaikovsky, who he found 'sitting smiling at his desk in a long black frock coat':

> I told [him] that discipline had not been maintained and it must be restored. There could be no such thing as a democratic army . . . I then said that if [Durov and his deputy] did not resign by 12 noon the next day I should take steps to remove them forcibly, and that I was quite sure they didn't want me to do that. With that I left him to make his arrangements.[8]

Durov went and relations with Chaikovsky were patched up, but a note of doubt creeps into Ironside's diary:

> I have been in this country exactly a month . . . I am not in the least frightened, but I cannot see that we are likely to do much good here.

We can keep the fort perhaps during the winter, but if the White Russians in other parts do not manage to do something, we cannot generate a new Russia from this place. Russia is so enormous that it gives one a feeling of smothering.[9]

Things got more complicated with the Armistice. 'The war is really coming to an end at last', he wrote on the evening of 10 November. 'Not our war. We go on. I wonder what effect it is all going to have upon the men here?'[10]

It was a good question, because the news from the fighting lines was mixed. Least problematic was the railway front, which was relatively static and easily resupplied. Most so were the Dvina and Vaga river fronts, where inadequate numbers of inexperienced Americans and worn-out King's Liverpools and Royal Scots were fighting a guerrilla-style war in and around remote villages, without proper supply or communications. A report by river-front commander Brigadier-General Robert Finlayson on the Armistice Day near-disaster at Tulgas was illustrative. The performance of the right-bank column, which had doggedly defended Tulgas for three days despite being heavily outgunned, was 'beyond praise'. But on the left bank thirty Royal Scots had run on coming under attack. According to a local witness, in the first few minutes the lieutenant in command was shot in the throat, upon which all the soldiers 'took to flight, even passing Lt Dalziell as he lay on the ground wounded.' As the enemy approached, the lieutenant raised himself on an elbow and tried to draw his revolver, but two men stepped forward and 'clubbed him on the head with their rifle-butts, killing him outright.' Questioned, the Royal Scots had offered no satisfactory explanation, and Finlayson was worried that the trouble might spread. If one or two men ran away, it was 'easy enough to deal with them', but if thirty out of a small force did so the situation became 'difficult'.[11]

At the end of November winter proper set in, making it easier for Ironside to go and see to things himself. Gone, out in the country-side, the autumn's torrents and wild reds and yellows; in their place stillness, silence and endless black on white. An ascetic semi-Scot who felt most at home with things and people northern, Ironside loved it, the journeys giving him solitude and time to think. His method, quickly perfected, was to travel fast and discreetly, without any escort, in an ordinary country sled. Built of wood and rope, the bottom was filled with hay, for insulation and fodder, and the passengers – two, to keep warm – lay almost at the horizontal, wrapped in blankets with a bearskin tucked over the top. His travelling companions were his orderly, a Russian-Canadian called Piskov, and driver Kostya, 'a most delightful boy' with 'a bright red face', always 'roaring with laughter and singing away to his pony.'[12] The ponies were a joy too; small, hairy and willing, and guided less by rein – their headpieces had no bits – more by voice and flicks of the whip. Trotting along sheltered tracks where the wind did not create snowdrifts, they could cover up to ten miles per hour.

Ironside's first two trips, at the end of November and beginning of December, uncovered niggling problems, but nothing very serious. On a Dvina tributary called the Yemtsa, Anglo-American bickering had delayed defence-building; on the railway there were grumbles about rations, the French wanting red wine and sardines, the twenty-five Italians onions, the Americans coffee instead of tea. Encouraging was an inspection of 'Dyer's Battalion', a new unit recruited from Archangel's prisons and led by a 'tough nut' young Canadian. 'They all looked so keen and eager and in such good health that it did my heart good.' He only wished he had more decent officers for them – the problem the 'morbid temperament' of educated Russians, whose only idea was to 'slink off and enjoy themselves, or to meditate in the extraordinarily pessimistic way they have. That is how so many of them come to commit suicide.'[13]

Grounds for pessimism presented themselves soon after Ironside got back to Archangel, when the soldiers in the Nevsky barracks mutinied again. The background to the protest was the arrival of General Vladimir Marushevsky, the Russian Army's temporary commander-in-chief until another general, Yevgeniy Miller, could arrive from Italy. Marushevsky was no Chaplinesque coupster, but his experiences over the past two years – mass mutiny while in command of Russian troops in France, and three months in a Bolshevik prison – had turned him rigidly conservative. His highest expression of approval for anything was that it was *staraya shkola* – 'old school' – and on the litmus-test issue of epaulettes he would not budge even when his own officers protested that wearing them in public was asking to be beaten up. Ironside found him slightly ridiculous – 'the funniest little man you can imagine' – and was patronising, lecturing him at very first meeting on how Russian officers needed to be more like British ones. He also started a collection of Marushevsky's most pettifogging general orders (which included a schedule for stove-stoking in barracks, and guidance on where to requisition nails for laying linoleum). Not surprisingly, Marushevsky was resentful. He also felt insulted that Ironside was under forty and only a brigadier-general – the appointment an example of how Britain regarded Russia as a 'less cultured country'.[14] It did not help that Marushevsky was only just over five feet tall, and hardly came up to Ironside's shoulder.

In early December Ironside decided that the time had come to put the embryo Russian Army to the test, and went to Marushevsky with a draft order that its founding unit – 1st Company, 1st Archangel Regiment – be issued with weapons and entrained for the front. Marushevsky 'read the order and bowed and said that it must lead to trouble. I told him that all would be ready, and that I expected him to make an effort to get the order carried out.'[15] The day before the send-off, Russian headquarters warned Ironside that the soldiers might attack him as he inspected them, but Ironside pooh-poohed. If the soldiers wanted to mutiny they would have done so already, and taking obvious precautions would be provocative: 'I really cannot stomach the idea of having MGs [machine-guns] round the corner to shoot the people down.' All the same, he went to have a look at some new timber huts the Americans had built opposite the barracks, and was pleased to see that they had solid double walls. Marushevsky came to dinner: 'He says he is ready. Drank a lot of vodka and danced all over the place.'[16]

At ten the next morning, 11 December, came the bad news: all 2,000 men in the Nevsky were refusing orders. Ironside restrained Marushevsky, who was 'rushing about shouting to burn the barracks down', and went to see what was happening. What he found was as much a demonstration as a mutiny. 'The great long white building was full of men, and any number of red flags hanging out, and a desultory fire going on in the direction of our machine-gun school some hundreds of yards away.' Though nobody had been hurt, he ordered the British colonel in charge to bring forward a Lewis gun and aim it at a window. Five short bursts were answered by more rifle-fire, and more flags. Ironside wondered how come the mutineers had so much red cloth at the ready – petticoats? Next he brought forward a Russian mortar team and ordered it to fire. The first shell exploded in a courtyard, the second on the roof, and 'before a third could be tried the door burst open and the men came tearing out with their hands over their heads and shouting that they surrendered':

> As if by magic the red flags fell from the windows and the shooting ceased . . . In a most orderly fashion they fell in without arms by companies, and were then formed in close order on the grass parade ground in front of the barracks. I shouted out for the ringleaders of the mutiny to fall out, and about 13 or 14 men [did so]. When I asked if there were any more, all the 13 shouted out together that there were not, which was repeated by the others. It was really all most weird.[17]

It wasn't so weird in fact, since what Ironside didn't put in his diary, according to a British NCO present, was his threat that if they did not produce the ringleaders, every tenth man in the regiment would be shot.[18] 1st Company was then separated out, harangued and escorted across the river to Bakaritsa, ready for departure to the front as planned: 'such nice round-faced boys, and so hopelessly innocent, that I felt quite sorry for them and their stupidity.'

By 5 p.m., Ironside wrote later that evening,

> the whole thing was over. The ringleaders all shot by a Russian Squad and buried where they were. It all went off so quickly that one hardly had time to think. I am quite sure that the 13 men I shot were really guilty, and they were all oldish men. The example to the recruits was salutory I fancy.

The mortar had killed only one person, a civilian agitator, and the town had apparently hardly noticed that anything was amiss, the trams running throughout. The whole thing had been a strange mixture of 'intense seriousness' and 'comic opera. I hated having to sign the death warrants but my conscience remains quite clear.'[19] In fact it must have pricked him, because writing his memoirs in old age, he pretended that he had commuted the thirteen's sentences, and arranged for them to be sent across the lines to their homes.[20] It would not be the last episode Interventionists preferred to re-remember.

IO

Paris and Shenkursk

WHILE IRONSIDE TRIED to bring order to Archangel, in Paris the Allied leaders were about to reorder the world. Two days after the Nevsky barracks executions, Woodrow Wilson arrived in France for a whistle-stop tour of the Allied capitals prior to the opening of the Peace Conference. His welcome was unprecedented, cheering crowds packing the streets of Brest, all the stations he passed through on the way to Paris, and the capital itself. Riding with Clemenceau in an open landau he looked elated but stunned, half-drowned by the noise and waterfalls of fluttering Stars and Stripes. The crowds were as overwhelming in Rome, and again in London.

But as so often happens, the President was more popular abroad than at home, and had recently lost both Congress and Senate to the Republicans in mid-term elections. Britain's post-war election, held under its new expanded franchise, similarly heralded a swing to the right. It was a personal triumph for Lloyd George, returning him as head of a Liberal-Conservative coalition with an extraordinary majority of 333. But it also filled the Commons with a new intake of right-wing Conservatives – 'Hard-faced men', in Stanley Baldwin's pungent phrase, 'who looked as though they had done well out of the war.' For Lloyd George as for Wilson, the legislature was no longer his to command. The strongest at home of the three was Clemenceau, though he too faced parliamentary elections in a few months' time.

In photographs they contrast nicely, like leads in a movie: Wilson lanky and long-nosed, a nervy greyhound; Lloyd George bouncy and twinkling, an eager terrier; Clemenceau white-haired and shaggy, a cunning old sheepdog. Rounding them up in Paris was already a win for the French premier – Lloyd George had wanted somewhere quiet and neutral – and for the next six months the city would be the capital of the world, the fates of nations decided at meetings, hearings, dinners, dances, bar-room confabulations, fancy-dress parties and outings for tennis to the Trianon or for the races to St Cloud. Everyone who was anyone was there or passed through: Sarah Bernhardt, Marcel Proust, the Wall Street titan Bernard Baruch, Queen Marie of Romania, T. E. Lawrence, the bright young men John Maynard Keynes, Harold Nicolson, Arnold Toynbee and Lewis Namier, Elinor Glyn of the tiger skin, the painters William Orpen and Augustus John. The gathering had a family flavour too. Lloyd George brought along his mistress and teenage daughters, Wilson his new wife and two closest friends.

The leaders' first meeting took place on 12 January 1919, in a tapestry-hung salon in the Quai d'Orsay. The seating had been arranged to give Clemenceau an advantage: the host in front of a grand fireplace, the others facing him, like pupils in front of their teacher. An American aide retaliated by unilaterally opening one of the floor-to-ceiling windows; Lloyd George quipped that it was the room's first breath of fresh air since Louis XIV. The little power-play was indicative. France had suffered by far the most in the war. Nearly 1.5 million of her young men had been killed, and hundreds of her towns and villages ruined. Above all she wanted revenge and security, which to Clemenceau meant reparations, disarmament and surrender of the Rhineland as well as of Alsace-Lorraine. America strode into the Conference as the world's new super-power. Britain and France owed her nearly $8 billion between them, and American food aid was saving swathes of Europe from starvation. To Wilson, it was the New World's chance to bring peace to the Old, meaning national self-determination and a settlement that was not so harsh on Germany that it would push her into revolution or another war. Britain – less battered than France but no fan of self-determination – stood somewhere in between, so that in the months to come Lloyd George often found himself in the role of mediator. Related to the Germany issue was the question of what to do with the remains of the Ottoman and Austro-Hungarian empires. This was not entirely in the victors' gift, since new national armies were forming, and new borders beginning to be fought out on the ground. But the Conference still had to decide which governments to recognise, where to peace-keep and hold plebiscites, and where to establish mandates – the new euphemism for colonies.

Russia policy in particular was influenced by the post-war lifting of censorship. The semi-secrecy of the military expeditions could no longer be maintained, and the press was free to argue that if Russia wanted to turn Bolshevik, that was her business. 'We are sorry for the Russians', ran a leader in Max Beaverbrook's *Daily Express*,

> but they must fight it out amongst themselves. Great Britain is already the policeman of half the world. It will not and cannot be the policeman of all Europe . . . We want to see our sons home again . . . The frozen plains of Eastern Europe are not worth the bones of a single British grenadier.[1]

Douglas Young, former British consul in Archangel, threw away a promising diplomatic career to write an excoriating anti-Intervention article for the left-wing *Herald*, and in the House of Commons, a trio of Liberal MPs – two of them with distinguished war records – started asking awkward questions and became known as the 'Three Musketeers'. On the left, a new 'Hands Off Russia' movement pulled in Sylvia Pankhurst, H. G. Wells and E. M. Forster, and held mass meetings in the Albert Hall.

A similar campaign got underway across the Atlantic. In Wisconsin and Michigan – home states of the Americans in the North – protestors gathered, and newspapers ran anti-war cartoons. In one, a lone figure faces a giant Bolshevik bear; in another, a snowbound pair of soldiers blow on their fingers, one asking the other 'Say, when did we declare war on Russia?' The Intervention was even less popular in Canada, as demonstrated when it was time for the two battalions waiting at Victoria to sail for Vladivostok. Marching through the city to the docks, a group of French-Canadian soldiers came to a halt at a downtown street corner. The colonel in charge ordered them to get moving, but their leader – a Québécois farmer called Onil Boisvert, who had earlier petitioned for demobilisation in time for harvest – refused. The colonel fired his revolver at Boisvert's feet; Boisvert shouted back 'On y vas pas, à Sibérie!' Two other companies – English-speakers from Toronto and Kingston – were then ordered to take off their belts and whip the recalcitrants into motion. As a lieutenant wrote home, 'They did it with a will, and we proceeded, [the protestors] more closely guarded than any group of Germans I ever saw.' The troopship sailed with Boisvert and twelve others handcuffed in the hold.[2]

At the same time, a figure of unmatched energy and eloquence on the other side of the argument joined Lloyd George's Cabinet: Winston Churchill. Forced to resign as First Lord of the Admiralty after the Dardanelles disaster of 1915, Churchill had been brought back into the government as Minister of Munitions, in which role he streamlined arms production and partially mended the government's relations with the army. Promoting him to Secretary of State for War, Lloyd George hoped he would fix a badly designed demobilisation programme, and generally inject his tired Cabinet with some of his own bounce and optimism.

Churchill's own priority was to retrieve his military reputation and with the war proper over, the remaining field for achieving this was Russia. During the December 1918 election campaign, therefore, he had played the anti-Bolshevik card to the hilt. 'Hopping and capering' about 'the ruins of cities and the corpses of their victims' like 'troops of ferocious baboons', he told the voters of Dundee, Lenin and Trotsky had reduced the country to 'an animal form of Barbarism'. He continued in zoological vein in a memorandum ahead of his second Cabinet meeting, on 31 December. Russia, he informed his colleagues, was 'a very large country, a very old country, a very disagreeable country, inhabited by immense numbers of ignorant people.' She was also 'a long way off'. Britain, on the other hand, had just finished an 'important and expensive' war, and now wished to cut taxes and bring her soldiers home. This was understandable, but Russia could not be fobbed off:

The bear is padding on bloody paws across the snows to the Peace Conference. By the time the delegates arrive she will be waiting outside the door . . . 'I bled for you . . . But for my sufferings you would have perished. Are you really going to leave me to stew in my own juice?'[3]★

In the subsequent discussion Churchill expanded his 'honour bound' argument with the airy proposal that if the various Russian factions could not be brought together for talks as the prime minister hoped, the Allies should 'use force to restore the situation and set up a democratic Government.' Bolshevism, he assured Cabinet, was supported by 'a mere fraction' of the Russian public, and would be 'swept away by a General Election held under Allied auspices.' If, on the other hand, nothing was done, revolution would roll across the continent and Britain would 'come away from the Peace Conference rejoicing in a victory which was no victory, and a peace which was no peace.'[4]

Lloyd George was not convinced. To plunge into Russia would be 'a tremendously serious undertaking'. Germany had entered the country with a million men and occupied a large part of it, but had never managed to capture Petrograd. The Allies had far fewer, and they were scattered round the country's fringes. And meanwhile Lenin and Trotsky were building a proper army. More generally, trying to suppress Bolshevism by force might only strengthen it, at home as well as in Russia, and it was better to let it fail of its own accord. All in all, the Russian situation was perilously tangled and unpredictable: 'a jungle, in which no one could say what was within a few yards.'[5] But as was to happen again and again, Lloyd George did not follow through on his well-justified scepticism by insisting that the Intervention be wound up. Instead he prevaricated, refusing to commit large numbers of new troops, but also agreeing that the existing ones stay and be relieved or reinforced where necessary. For waverers like him it was a sensible compromise, but for the committed on either side of the argument, no policy at all.

On Christmas Eve 1918, Private Scheu organised a little party for his hosts in the Dvina village where he was quartered. The day before he

---

★ Churchill liked his animal metaphors. At various points the Bolsheviks were also mangy hyenas, blood-sucking vampires, plague-bearing rats, 'mastermind crocodiles' and tame cobras.

had cut down a small pine tree and hidden it in bushes with the intention of bringing it secretly indoors after dark. A child spilled the beans on his surprise, he wrote that evening:

> however we gather together a few candles, bully beef tins, stew tins, hardtack, cigarettes, a few canteen goods – salt, sugar and tea – wrapped in small packages, and decorate tree. We loaned an accordion, invited the peasants and made merry until the wee small hours. During height of entertainment seven or eight Russians approached us and swore fidelity to the Americans present, and boy how they can swear. We reciprocated likewise and passed the cigarettes, stripped the tree to the children, bid all 'da da', and turned in a tired but happy lot.[6]

Festivities were equally convivial in the genteel Vaga town of Shenkursk. 'Private Tomlin put on his famous cheese dance', wrote medical orderly Anderson of a 'singfest' in the school-turned-hospital, 'and Eddie Kramer sang his cootie song to the tune of *Over There*.'[7] The headmaster brought some of his pupils to perform more songs, and a Russian nurse and her friends danced with the Americans to a balalaika orchestra. The YMCA also laid on a concert, the programme including 'Duet by American soldier violinist and Russian lady pianist' and '*Down in Texas Town* by Russian teacher'. The convent hosted a special Christmas service in its chapel, for which chairs were provided and the icons covered. (Americans crossly noting that at the end 'God Save the King' was sung, but not 'The Star-Spangled Banner'.)

In Archangel, in contrast, the atmosphere was distinctly louche. It is captured in the diary of Zoya Mikhailova, a pretty seventeen-year-old who had moved there from Petrograd with her wealthy parents. Early in the Allied occupation she had been invited to a dance on board the aptly named *Attentive*, and been surprised to find herself one of only six women, three of them 'Night Butterflies'. When its Captain Altham asked her to waltz he held her much too tight, rubbed his legs against hers and kept trying to kiss her on the lips. She should have protested but had been too embarrassed; next time she would show him that he should not treat her as though she were 'a promiscuous girl'.[8] There was more sexual harassment from American ambassador

Francis, to whom her parents had rented out part of their house. She didn't know what to make of his patting, hand-holding and squeezing until her eyes were opened by her governess. 'He keeps disturbing her with dirty proposals. Every night he knocks on her door and once, when she forgot to lock the door, he came into her room and started hugging her, [saying] he wanted French language lessons.'[9] After Francis departed Russia (on a stretcher), Zoya became a general pet, falling innocently in love with every man in uniform she met. It was

> dancing at 5 o'clock tea; dancing in the evening at the English club; dancing at the American Mission . . . I feel as if I were twirling, twirling through life . . . I have already twirled myself beyond my limit, but don't have the strength to stop and don't want to either.[10]

In a photo she is enchanting: leaning back laughing, pearls at her neck, fingers inexpertly flourishing a racy cigarette.

Notably absent from the partying was workaholic Ironside. He disliked the sexual licence (even his soldier-servant had managed to catch venereal disease), but accepted that in a town filled with refugees it was inevitable. He also disliked the many odd characters washing up in Archangel, amongst them a French journalist with a 'nasty artistic look about him' who 'walked about fingering a rosary all day', and the 'terrifying-looking' Latvian mistress of the French intelligence chief, said to have earned the St George's Cross she wore on her 'ample bosom' by poisoning eight German officers at a dinner-party in Riga.[11] A genuinely remarkable visitor was twenty-nine-year-old 'Madame' Mariya Bochkareva. Born into a dirt-poor Siberian peasant family, she had had a grim life – domestic abuse, homelessness – until war broke out and she persuaded the commander of the local garrison to take her on as a soldier. At the front she was twice wounded and won a medal for gallantry, and in 1917 was allowed to form a much-publicised 'Women's Battalion of Death', which fought briefly but bravely in western Ukraine and was guarding the Winter Palace at the time of the Bolshevik coup. With the help of the activist Florence Harriman, she later left the country and went on a publicity tour of America, giving interviews and meeting President Wilson. In London she had an audience with the King, and the War Office asked that she go to Archangel to spur recruitment to the Russian Army. It was an imaginative idea but stillborn, because neither Ironside nor Marushevsky was having any of it. Ironside describes Bochkareva in his diary as 'a great ugly prostitute' with 'legs like an elephant', and Marushevsky publicly ordered her into civvies, because women in uniform were 'a disgraceful stain on the whole population of the Northern Region.'[12] She ended up returning to Siberia, where she was arrested and executed the following year.

Less easy to get rid of was the polar explorer Ernest Shackleton. Before the expeditionary force set out, he had been asked to specify its winter kit, which had proved excellent except for the lethally slippery 'Shackleton boot'. Invited to Russia by General Maynard, he turned out to be promoting a private business venture, involving coal-mining on Spitzbergen, on the side. Having been strict on similar side-dealing by others, Ironside was put in an embarrassing position.

> It does disgust one when one's own show is not clean . . . He comes over here dressed up as a Major . . . I cannot be hard on the man, and yet I cannot let him disgrace the British uniform.[13]

Much more welcome was the reappearance of Ironside's old sled-driver Kostya, who turned up one day at headquarters with his long-bearded peasant father in tow. A permanent job was quickly offered, the father sent away happy with a packet of tobacco, and Kostya washed, reclothed and fed: 'The amount he eats is simply colossal, and he sleeps like a log.'

Two British blunders in the same period had far-reaching consequences. The first was the botching of a new paper currency – the notes, on arrival from the printers in London, turning out to feature the imperial crown and double-headed eagle. Though individually ink-stamped over, they looked a mess and never caught on. The second – a major blot on the British record – was Mudyug, an island prison camp forty miles north of Archangel on the Dvina estuary. It had been set up in the early days by Chaplin and Thornhill, to hold high-risk political arrestees, and by the time Ironside took over contained several hundred people. In his voluminous diary Ironside mentions it only twice, the first time on 25 October 1918. Inspecting Archangel's gaol, he had been angry to find incarcerated many obviously harmless people – children, elderly peasants and a 'crippled schoolmaster reading a book in Hebrew' – and had ordered that they be released. 'The real Bolsheviks' were 'kept down at Moudjoug [sic] Island. I have never been down to see them, but must get Needham [his chief of staff] to go.' Whether Needham actually went is not recorded, but in practice Mudyug was left to rot. According to a Soviet-inflected but plausible survivor memoir, the lieutenant and sergeant in charge, both French, were drunks and thieves, using the prison flour ration to barter with local peasants for extra food for themselves.[14] Sadistic guards dealt out frequent beatings, and unheated, cripplingly small dugout punishment cells equated to a death sentence. As in the town gaol, many inmates should not have been there at all. Socialists had been scooped up alongside genuine Bolsheviks, and in some cases it appeared that the English had confused the word Bolshevik with *bolshak*, local dialect for the eldest son in a fatherless family.

Around New Year, rumours of mistreatment began to reach Archangel. 'Scurvy seems to be beginning amongst the Russian prisoners on Moudjoug Island', Ironside wrote on 6 January: 'I have sent down McDermott [head doctor at the military hospital] to see if something can be done. We cannot have a scandalous camp.' Not allowed to visit, despite repeated applications to gatekeeper Thornhill, was the Northern Government's interior minister, Vladimir Ignatyev. When he finally made it there, accompanied by a doctor and a lawyer, in early spring 1919, he found seventy-eight fresh graves – an enormous number given that the camp only held between two hundred and three hundred people. Emaciated and covered in scurvy ulcers, the survivors resembled 'living corpses, waiting their turn'.[15] Historians estimate that about a thousand prisoners were held at Mudyug during the camp's twelve months of operation, and that of those up to three hundred died. Later, the Soviets turned it into a cartoonishly propagandistic but essentially fact-based museum – toured, like Baku's eternal flame-equipped memorial to the Twenty-Six Commissars, by generations of Russian schoolchildren.

To escape Archangel's gamey whiff and his unease over the Nevsky barracks executions, Ironside took two long midwinter trips to the fronts. Conditions for the troops were now extremely harsh. It was not dark round the clock, as in Murmansk, but the four hours of pearly half-light per day – from ten in the morning to two in the afternoon – hardly counted, and temperatures sat at minus twenty or below. Spotter 'planes could not fly, frozen bogs and rivers no longer gave protection from attack, and the workhorse Vickers machine-guns were liable to pack up without warning, especially if their alcohol-laced coolant had been drained off and replaced by water. (Scheu preferred his newly issued Colt: 'peppy and spits fire when you want it to . . . no caressing, wrapping in warm blankets.') Frostbite was a constant danger, and despite Ironside's nagging about preventative measures, claimed many victims, especially amongst the Russians and French. In a photograph taken for the medical record, hospital orderlies hold up a white sheet, against which an emaciated, shaven-headed teenager obediently displays black fingerless hands, and lopped-off stumps where his feet ought to be. Looking sideways at the camera, his expression is one of bleakest despair.

In human ways too the war was brutal. On the Red side, mutilation of corpses was common, and on the White, killing of prisoners. Writing up his diary while on guard duty, an American private had only to look up to

> meet the eyes of one of the wretched half-animals that were captured
> by a patrol today. There were four. One has already been executed by
> the Russians. We do no executing although God knows they deserve
> no mercy the way they mutilate and torture our men.[16]

Though Allied involvement usually consisted, as here, of turning a blind eye to Russian colleagues' actions, Allied soldiers also sometimes killed prisoners themselves. On one of his early visits to Dyer's Battalion, Ironside heard an 'unsavoury story' about the shooting of a captured Armenian doctor – in the standard formula, 'while attempting to escape'. Ironside gave Dyer a telling-off: if he wanted to make his battalion a success, there could be 'no kind of play of that sort.' But he nonetheless thought Dyer 'a fine type of youngster', deserving of his recent promotion. Thornhill – co-creator of Mudyug and on the scene for the Kem killings – was 'jubilant', he remarked, at the doctor's demise.[17]

For the civilian population, perhaps harshest of the winter's brutalities was the burning of front-line villages. Both sides did it, but rattled, out-of-their-depth Allied troops – ready to see a collaborator in every uncommunicative local – especially so. In early January a false alarm panicked American units into completely destroying the Vaga village of Kitsa, and Scheu describes putting part of disputed Tulgas to the torch:

> We throw a cordon of troops around village to prevent interference, notify natives, and set fire to village at 9 p.m. It ignites rapidly, lighting up surrounding country. Have difficulty with natives; we gave them 3 hours notice to pack and vacate. 'Twas a sad sight.

The next day the cottages were still smoking, 'a big black smudge upon the snow.'[18]

That Ironside could not push his luck was forcibly brought home to him at the end of the year, when a small offensive on the railway, designed to test and motivate the troops, flopped dismally. (To blame, an alcoholic British lieutenant colonel: 'on the verge of DTs' according to a subordinate.) After this 'thoroughly abortive damned show',[19] large-scale winter operations were obviously out, and on 10 January Ironside set off on another inspection of the river front – to Shenkursk, the furthest south and most exposed of his bases. Overnighting at a village on the way, he was surprised when Piskov and Kostya – the latter now picking up English at a great rate – slept across his door. Asking Piskov why, he 'couldn't get much out of him except that there was great unrest round Shenkursk and he thought there was going to be fighting. Most curious.'[20] Intelligence at Shenkursk itself had heard nothing, but that did not mean much, and Ironside told the American colonel in command that if pressure became severe he should withdraw in good time, because there was no relief force to send if the town got cut off. In public, however, Ironside put on a show of confidence, and when the convent's abbess – a 'fine old lady of the upper class' – invited him to tea and prayed him to keep the Bolsheviks away he assured her that he would – making him feel 'a bit of a slippery customer.'[21]

On the same day that Ironside set off back to Archangel the Bolsheviks did indeed attack, their target Ust-Padenga, a straggling village fifteen miles on from Shenkursk up the Vaga. Its northern-most cluster of cottages, 'High Hill', housed 1st Battalion, A Company's headquarters and field hospital; and its southernmost and closest to the enemy, 'Low Hill', a forty-seven-man platoon. In the pitch-black of 6.15 a.m. on 19 January, Bolshevik guns opened up on Low Hill from the forest fringe on the Vaga's oppos-ite bank, and as the sun came up four hours later the platoon found itself surrounded, enemy soldiers having crossed the river in the dark and lain hidden in dips and thickets. The platoon's mile-long retreat to High Hill was a desperate, each-for-himself scramble. Only seven out of the forty-seven made it through unwounded, six were killed within sight of their comrades, and nineteen went missing. Of the missing, two men reappeared in the night, having been hidden by an old woman in her farmhouse, but the rest were never seen again. On High Hill, A Company endured another two days of high-explosive bombardment, until on 22 January the Bolshevik infantry came on again, slowed by newly arrived Canadian gunners. The same afternoon a shrapnel shell hit the field hospital, killing five including the company doctor, and when night fell the whole force began a fighting withdrawal to Shenkursk.

The town, meanwhile, held its breath, the barrage rumbling like distant thunder. In Anderson's description, the columns of smoke from its chimneys seemed to stand on tiptoe, and the green aurora borealis overhead at night to writhe in agony. On 24 January came news that Ust-Padenga had fallen, and orders were given to prepare for evacuation. Soldiers were told to pack only what they could carry, and at the hospital – 'a bedlam of confusion' – Anderson and his colleagues dosed their hundred-odd patients with rum, got them into sleeping-bags – the insufficiently sedated screaming, the shell-shocked struggling – and loaded them onto ambulance sleds. Surplus equip-ment was dumped in the front courtyard, for anyone who wanted it to pick up. By midnight the streets were jammed: soldiers dozing, mounted officers shouting, children wailing, calves skittering at the end of ropes, the convent bell clanging on and on. Gradually, a column formed up and moved off. Russian cavalry took the lead, followed by Canadian guns, fifty-odd ambulance sleds and about one thousand Allied and Russian infantry. Last came several thousand townspeople, their sleds top-heavy with household belongings.

It was a hard march, initially on a lightless track through woods because the enemy had already cut the road along the river. Guns got stuck, sleds tipped, men stumbled in the snow-holes made by horses' hooves. Kit was abandoned, including the slippery Shackleton boots, so that some men marched in their socks. The night's saving graces were that there was no wind and no fighting – either because the Bolsheviks missed the column's departure or because they deliberately let it go. Towards the evening of the following day the straggling procession reached the large village of Shegovary, where the sick and wounded were unloaded into a barn. Only one patient, Anderson was surprised to find, had not survived the journey: the school head – a 'sensitive, lovable sort of person' and a consumptive – who had brought his pupils to the Christmas concert. Next morning, having set fire to Shegovary's principal buildings, the column set off again, and another twenty-four-hour march brought it to a settlement not far from the Vaga's confluence with the Dvina, where orders came to dig in. 'Notify people in village', a private wrote in his diary,

> that they will have to leave. People we are billeted with are crying and in great distress ... They start out in morning, leaving behind cow and several sheep. Give them one of my blankets to help keep baby warm, as it is snowing and very cold. Someone kills sheep for food.[22]

Shenkursk's loss made Ironside angry – with intelligence head Thornhill for not having got wind of the attack, with the 'pig-headed' American colonel at Shenkursk for not having evacuated earlier, and with Poole for having occupied the town in the first place. 'To add to my troubles', he wrote in his diary on 25 January,

> they tried to assassinate me today. I was walking down to the office with Kostia [sic] following me when a man ran out of a side-street and [fired] an automatic pistol. As usual I couldn't get at my own pistol, if I actually had it. I ran on and dodged a bit and really didn't know what to do ... Luckily Kostia kept his head and actually shot the man before he had let off five shots. Really providential as he is only a boy

and only had a revolver . . . I shall stick to him now and take him away
from Russia when I go. A damnable experience.

The Nevsky barracks mutiny; the midnight flit from Shenkursk; and
now an assassination attempt so nearly successful that it tore his clothes
– it was Ironside's third close shave in two months. Even troop-filled,
carefree Archangel was not safe, and there were another three months
of winter to go before the sea ice broke and reinforcements could
arrive.

11

Prinkipo and Siberia

WHILE FIGHTING RAGED in the North, in Paris Lloyd George was winning Clemenceau round to an idea originally floated by Borden: that all parties to the Russian Civil War – the Bolsheviks as well as the various White and national governments – be brought together for peace talks. The venue settled on was Prinkipo, largest of the Princes' Islands, not far from Constantinople in the Sea of Marmara. Drafted by Wilson, a general invitation was issued on 23 January 1919, not via the usual diplomatic channels but publicly, by means of a press release and a shortwave radio announcement transmitted from the top of the Eiffel Tower.

The responses were immediate and decisive. Moscow's reply, also broadcast, was ostensibly 'Yes', but couched in such insulting terms that it might as well have been 'No'. The White governments rejected the idea outright. The new leader of the Northern Government, General Yevgeniy Miller, declared he would not treat with 'robbers and murderers', and was echoed by Chaikovsky, who had stepped down to join émigré representatives in Paris. In Omsk, Kolchak issued an order making it treason even to discuss the possibility of negotiations, and from the Don steppe, the Volunteer Army's General Denikin sent a personal protest to Marshal Foch.

The keenest Interventionists were equally appalled, regarding the offer of talks as tantamount to diplomatic recognition. From Vladivostok, General Knox sent a 'really fuming' telegram – the proposal put 'brave men . . . fighting for civilisation' on a par with 'the blood-stained, Jew-led Bolsheviks'[1] – and in Archangel, American consul DeWitt Poole threatened to resign. Happening to be in Paris, Churchill burst in on Lloyd George while he was shaving, and thundered that if one were going to recognise the regime, 'one might as well legalise sodomy.'² Churchill and Foch both also privately assured White contacts that even if they rejected talks, military aid would keep flowing. The Prinkipo proposal thus died at birth.

In the middle of February the Peace Conference's main proceedings paused, while Wilson returned to Washington to present the League of Nations Covenant to Congress, and Lloyd George to London to deal with a wave of strikes. Briefly but dramatically, Clemenceau too was put out of action, after a lone-wolf French anarchist leapt from behind a *pissoir* and fired at his car. No bullet hit a vital organ, but one lodged in his ribs (and stayed there for the rest of his days). While the Tiger traded quips with his nurses, a second, more discreet approach to the Bolsheviks got underway. At the beginning of the year an idealistic young State Department man in Paris, twenty-eight-year-old, Yale-educated William Bullitt, had suggested that a small mission, with himself as 'general bootblack', should go to Moscow 'to see what the Bolsheviki are about.'³ Before leaving for home Wilson had approved the idea, and in early March Bullitt set out, accompanied by the original Progressive Era muckracker, journalist and campaigner Lincoln Steffens.

In Russia for a week, the pair were given the full works: rooms in a requisitioned mansion, long meetings with Chicherin and Lenin, 'piles' of caviar. Like Raymond Robins before them, they were also made an apparently generous diplomatic offer: in return for an end to the Intervention, the Soviet government would cede all claims to territories held by the Whites at the time of the Armistice. They returned to Paris converted, Steffens declaring to waiting reporters that he had 'been over into the future, and it works.'⁴ During their absence, however, the mood had changed. While on his trip to Washington President Wilson had been bruised by Republican opposition to the League, and made aware of voters' impatience to get peace in Europe done. His priority now was to get the League over the line, even if it meant concessions to France on Russia as well as on Germany. When Bullitt reappeared in Paris excitedly claiming a diplomatic breakthrough, therefore, neither he nor similarly impatient Lloyd George thought taking him seriously worth the price of antagonising the still violently anti-Bolshevik French. Their caution was reinforced by the fact that while courting Bullitt, Lenin had also launched the Communist International, and pulled off a revolution in Hungary (where Bela Kun seized power on 21 March). Adding to their difficulties, on 3 April strained and overworked Wilson had what was probably a small stroke. Though soon back at work, thereafter he was not quite the same man: anxious, unpredictable and absent-minded.

The end result was that Bullitt was thrown over. Wilson cancelled a meeting with him, pleading a headache. Lloyd George asked him for a breakfast briefing, but then denied all knowledge of him in the House of Commons. They were right to be sceptical, since Lenin was indeed only playing for time. They were also under pressure from their legislatures and press. But it was hard on Bullitt, who resigned from the State Department – off to the Riviera, as he told reporters, to 'lie in the sand and watch the world go to hell.'[5]

While the diplomatic dance proceeded in Paris, in Siberia events took a course of their own. By New Year 1919 Vladivostok was full of foreign troops – Japanese, American, Canadian, Czech, British, French, Serb and Italian. Unlike in the North, they were under separate commands. Least effectual was that of newly arrived French general Maurice Janin, appointed the Czech Legion's new C-in-C under an Allied agreement with Masaryk. The Czech regiments themselves had other ideas, and since Kolchak's coup had been dropping out of the war, refusing orders to go into action and withdrawing from the front. The exception was the Legion's Colonel – now General – Gajda, who had accepted command of Kolchak's army in the Urals. As disengaged as the Czechs were Vladivostok's 4,192 Canadians. Barred from anything more than garrison duty by Borden, they killed time exercising their magnificent horses and having sex. Their newsletter, *The Siberian Sapper*, records ice-hockey games and comedy nights, but also an Aquarium nightclub and its hostesses Temp'ramental Betsy, Moora, Husky Babe, Douska, Leena and Meena. A poor quarter, 'Kopek Hill', sprouted brothels, and more than one in four Canadian hospital cases were for venereal disease.

Keenest of the Allied generals in Siberia, as ever, was Knox. With only token troops at his disposal – the invalidish Middlesexes and a newly arrived battalion of Hampshires – he made up for lack of heft with busyness, shuttling back and forth between Omsk and Vladivostok – a distance of 2,700 miles – in a comfortable train nicknamed the Express. Life at mission headquarters is described by one of his aides, Captain Victor 'Teenie' Cazalet, a twenty-one-year-old high society sprig who had been given the posting in part so that he could try to salvage his family's Russian investments. In between legal bulletins – recoverable, maybe, a cargo of tallow languishing in Vladivostok port – his letters home are a feast of period camp. Siberia is 'a terrible place; one can't imagine why anyone lives here.' And he hates it that he's missing the post-war London parties. What did his mother – 'Angel' or 'Beloved' – wear? 'I want to know *all*.' For a Christmas dance, he organises the 'old man who comes up whenever we have a dinner party' to spend five days making sugar baskets: 'I fear it is rather a scandal when sugar costs £*1000* a ton.'[6] On the Intervention, he took his views straight from Knox, violently disagreeing with anyone who questioned its wisdom, or that Kolchak was anything less than 'a really good, honest, determined man.' Though he got to know everyone of importance in Vladivostok, frustratingly for the historian his invariable comment on all and sundry is that they are 'very nice'.

As kind as he was feather-brained, Cazalet took various elderly refugee aristocrats under his wing, amongst them Baroness Buxhoeveden, the former lady-in-waiting disconcerted by Czech outspokenness on a train to Omsk. Given an onward lift to Vladivostok on the Express, she was surprised to find that its carriages were those of a Court train in which she used to travel with the Tsarina. Painted with Union Jacks, they were now filled with the click-clack of typewriters and all things British, down to the dining-car's jars of jam and pickle. Needing 'constant hard work' to 'keep level', she threw herself into copying and translating, feeling pleased as a schoolgirl every time a Major Campbell gave her an approving nod. At each halt the Tommies of the guard kicked a cocoa tin around – an odd compulsion – and each evening the officers changed into their regimentals for dinner and bridge. Buxhoeveden had only the dress she was wearing, but smartened it up with a white collar and cuffs, and sang for her supper with stories of life at court – made more poignant by the presence aboard of Tsarevich Aleksei's pet spaniel, found near the

Romanovs' last house in Yekaterinburg. Angel Mother, Cazalet was sure, would be delighted to have her to stay: 'You will love the Baroness . . . She is quite *one of us.*'

More strenuously engaged in the White cause was Captain Maurice Howgrave-Graham of the Hampshires. Having been in India through the war and thus missed out on 'real soldiering', he was excited to be in Russia, and had spent the first half of the winter barracked in an empty girls' school, getting his men fit and taking Russian lessons from his interpreter, a former colonel in the Imperial Guards. Progress was slow – the grammar 'too ghastly for words' – and the colonel was a bit of a puzzle too: 'We like him, but there is a shifty sort of look in his eyes . . . He has lost his home, his income, his livelihood and everything, but does not seem to worry very much about it.'[7]

Linguistic torture was suspended at end of January, when Howgrave-Graham was ordered to pick twenty Hampshires for a morale-boosting expedition to the Orenburg Cossacks, militarised settler-farmers who controlled the Russo-Kazakh borderlands, and whose capital had just fallen to the Bolsheviks. On the train out the expedition's leader, Knox's chief of staff Lieutenant Colonel John Neilson, gave a briefing. 'We are going to "stick out our chests" and convince the down-hearted, dispirited Cossacks that the English really are taking an interest in them, and at least thinking about giving them armed assistance.' A 'don't-care-a-damn-for-anybody type' with a 'cheery, racy way of talking', Neilson also handed out copies of one of White propaganda's old chestnuts, the 'nationalisation of women' decree. Titillatingly ordering that unmarried women be made state property and allotted partners by committee, it was an obvious fake, but to judge by the number of copies Interventionists brought home with them, widely believed, or at least fantasised over. (Howgrave-Graham copied the whole icky thing out by hand.[8])

The group detrained at Troitsk, a simple, wood-built, one-storey place – 'rather attractive in an indefinable way' – with the usual big frozen river, straight criss-cross streets and clutch of verdigris domes. Setting out again on sleds across the steppe – a treeless, gently rolling plain covered in wave-shaped snowdrifts – felt like putting to sea. Their destination was Verkhnye Uralsk, a garrison town 160 miles to the west, and at the villages on the way they were greeted warmly – eggs, milk, best rooms – and anxiously asked when the British were going to send reinforcements. Howgrave-Graham was touched but embarrassed:

One can't help feeling awfully sorry for these poor people. They clutch at the possibility of help from the Allies as a drowning man clutches at a straw. 'How many men can you send us and how soon?' they ask, and it is rather pathetic that we can promise nothing beyond rifles and ammunition.[9]

At Verkhnye Uralsk there were three days of welcoming ceremonies: bread and salt, 'God Save the King' so many times over that Howgrave-Graham's saluting arm ached, and a punishing series of banquets ('English captain blotto'). Against a backdrop of glittering Ural peaks the Cossacks gave a demonstration cavalry charge, and the Hampshires reciprocated with a drill – not very successful since the parade ground was deep in snow. A welcome interlude, on a still, pearly-pink evening, was a visit to a convent. An elderly nun with the 'gentlest, saintliest face' handed round honey-cakes while a choir sang softly in the next room, and when the English party made their goodbyes, blessed them and presented them with hand-knitted gloves and socks. The visit culminated with Neilson and Howgrave-Graham being awarded Cossack ranks, which involved being kissed by every man in the room and tossed to the ceiling in a chair – 'a giddy operation which was repeated time after time amidst yells.' By the end of it all Howgrave-Graham's heart was won. Physically, he wrote in his diary, the Orenburg Cossacks were an 'extraordinarily fine type . . . straight, fearless [and] manly'. And though they had a reputation for savagery they could also exhibit 'most engaging tenderness', tucking one into one's sled in a 'delightfully motherly way'. Hardy and industrious, not adaptable to new ideas but 'quite solid and sensible', they closely resembled 'our English South-country farmer'.[10]

On 24 February, after more ceremonial back in Troitsk and a meeting with the Orenburg Cossack leader Ataman Aleksandr Dutov ('a bit of a tiger'), the Hampshires set off on a second trip, this time southwards towards the fighting. Arriving in a village in a blizzard, they found the main street littered with abandoned military stores, and all the accommodation taken by refugees. Howgrave-Graham talked to a headmistress stranded with sixty of her pupils. 'She got as far as this three weeks ago, and can't get sledges to take her any further. Many of the children have lost their parents – murdered by Bolsheviks when Orenburg fell.' The British party scraped together fresh sleds for itself – uncomfortable flat ones, meant for baggage – and pushed on in a white-out to the next settlement. There Howgrave-Graham was forced to acknowledge that for all their cavalry-charging and chair-tossing, the Cossacks were not putting up much resistance:

> One sees lots of able-bodied men sitting about and doing nothing in particular, and so far we have come across practically no wounded . . . They seem to think that we are going to march out, and by some miraculous means stem the oncoming tide while they stand by and clap. Much as I like and admire the Cossack, I cannot help seeing that he has much of the Russian about him . . . He gives up, says it's hopeless and waits patiently for the end, drinking if he is male and weeping if he is female . . . If this were a British village, people would be out making defences, sticking up barricades, fortifying their houses and so on, so that at least they could sell their lives dearly.[11]

What the British did on this occasion, however, was join in the rout – part, for the next ten days, of a 'long, crawling procession' of fleeing soldiers and peasants. One night they put up in a smoke-filled Kirghiz mud hut. ('Funny little creatures . . . a kind of Tartar . . . very kindly treated by them.') Another they slept in a byre, cut through by a knife-edge wind. Just in time – on 6 March – they reached a railhead and caught a train back to Omsk. The expedition, Howgrave-Graham admitted to himself, had been nothing but 'a damned nuisance', using transport and consuming food desperately needed by others, and raising false hopes:

> The simple-minded peasant, beholding our arrival, thought that at the eleventh hour the Allies had come to his rescue, and that he was saved. The next thing they saw was their village sacked by the Bolsheviks, and the same heroic allies joining in the general stampede. Of course

it could not possibly be otherwise . . . But it is unfortunate that events
worked out as they did.[12]

It could have been the epitaph for the whole Intervention.

Polar opposite to the British mission's performative activity was the
stance taken by America's General Graves, who despite pressure from
the pro-Intervention State Department steadily refused to visit
Kolchak in Omsk, or to move his troops west to fight. To bolster his
position he asked the War Department for confirmation that he was
correct in treating 'the Bolshevik trouble in Siberia' as 'an internal
trouble, in which I should take no part.' After some bluster from State
he received it, plus a private letter of support from army chief of staff
General March. ('Keep a stiff upper lip; I am going to stand by you
until hell freezes over.')[13]

Graves's stand infuriated Knox, who fulminated to Cazalet that he
and 'that **** Wilson' had 'not the faintest understanding of the situation out here . . . They talk rot about a free Russia and democracy
– you might as well talk about social reform to a cannibal.'[14] The clash
of world-views was underlined at a lunch aboard the USS *Brooklyn*.
Present were the *Brooklyn*'s Admiral Rogers, Cazalet (who was seeing
off Buxhoeveden), the American ambassador to Japan and the engineer John Stevens, builder of the Panama Canal. Cazalet proceeded to
lecture the three distinguished, much older men on how the only
way to deal with Bolsheviks was to put them up against a wall:

> I said that . . . there was only one remedy – 'shooting'. They said – if
> you shoot a Bolshevik you've made ten others, [and that] Bolshevism
> is only what Russia deserves for the awfulness of the old regime . . .
> Such are the American theories![15]

Presumably they humoured Cazalet because they hoped via him to
influence Knox. They may also have known that he was a family
friend of Churchill's and writing him regular letters. If so the tactic
failed, Cazalet coming away more convinced than ever that the
Americans had 'big idealistic views, quite honest', but 'simply [didn't]
understand the Russian character in the least.'[16]

Graves had good reason to keep his distance from Kolchak, because the Supreme Ruler was off to a bad start. Highly strung, and without any previous experience of politics or administration, he found his position overwhelming. In public he looked tense and unhappy, and in private suffered volcanic losses of temper, throwing things and tearing at upholstery with a knife. His insecurity was apparent in his appointments, his chief of staff a parvenu, much-disliked young colonel, and his civilian ministers ineffectual paper-pushers. (Not one, wrote Colonel Ward, would he have trusted to 'manage a whelk-stall.'[17]) Also symptomatic of weakness were Kolchak's atrocities. A month after he took power, the army put down a workers' rising in Omsk's factory quarter with wildly disproportionate ferocity: mass round-ups and floggings, and several hundred extra-judicial executions. The victims included twelve Socialist Revolutionary politicians, members of the party's moderate wing and former delegates to the Constituent Assembly, who were taken from the city gaol at dead of night, sabred to death and left on the river ice. The following month another elected SR, the mayor of a railway town near Krasnoyarsk, was also abducted from prison and killed, his assailants soldiers belonging to the same Cossack officer – now promoted to colonel – who had arrested the All-Russian Government during Kolchak's coup. An eye-witness describes the mayor being marched past his own house, so that his wife and children came running out, and down to the station.

> There, in the presence of a huge crowd and in full view of his family, [he] was hanged. Just before the noose was thrown over his head, [he] called out 'Long Live the Constituent Assembly!' . . . His body was hoisted high on the arm of a water pump, and there it hung for twenty-nine hours, with trains passing under it.[18]

With the introduction of conscription, the army started harassing the countryside too. Typical of the many petitioners Graves received were six peasants who described to him how a recruiting party had arrived in their village, failed to find the men they wanted, and beaten the women with ramrods instead. Sending officers to investigate this and similar cases, Graves concluded that so-called

'Bolsheviks' were usually just ordinary people trying to resist 'unjust treatment by troops'.[19]

The bad blood between him and Knox bubbled over on 2 March, when the Far East's military governor, General Pavel Ivanov-Rinov, arrested four of Vladivostok's leading citizens, including a newspaper editor and the deputy head of the provincial council. Early the next morning the men's wives door-stepped Graves as he arrived for work. Impressively 'quiet and determined', they informed him that if their husbands were executed there would be a rising, and that in that case, they trusted he would not take Ivanov-Rinov's side. Graves, in his account, listened but made no promises. Next to call, 'very excited', was Britain's Commissioner Eliot:

> He asked me if I would use American troops in case of an uprising, and I replied that I would not make any definite statement . . . until I knew the nature of the uprising and the cause. He became more excited and said that the lives of British subjects and British property were involved, and that he must know my attitude.
>
> I finally told Sir Charles, after some more words, that I was well aware that he wanted to know my attitude towards protecting Ivanoff-Rinoff . . . The answer would be that . . . the United States had never been in the habit of protecting murderers, and that I did not intend doing so now, and so far as I was concerned they could bring Ivanoff-Rinoff opposite American Headquarters and hang him from that telegraph pole until he was dead, and not an American soldier would turn his hand.[20]

Knox tried the worldly-wise approach. Not for a moment, he wrote to Graves, did he pretend that Kolchak was 'the Angel Gabriel'. But he had 'energy, patriotism and honesty', and Knox's years in Russia had taught him that such a man was 'a man to keep'. The club-room tone cut no ice, and probably thanks to Graves's stand, the four arrestees were released a few weeks later.

There was one genuine bright spot to the Allies' presence in Siberia that winter: medical aid. Everywhere the Allies operated, they set up military hospitals, which treated Russian as well as Allied soldiers, and some Russian civilians. But the effort was much bigger in Siberia than elsewhere, thanks to the lead taken by the American Red Cross, under missionary doctor Rudolf Teusler.

Pioneering founder of Tokyo's first modern hospital but also ardently pro-Intervention and an antisemite, Teusler was a divisive figure. Amongst those who disliked him was Graves, who felt that he turned the Red Cross into a Kolchak supply effort. On the other hand, he undeniably got things done. His biggest, 250-bed hospital opened in November 1918, in the small west Siberian city of Tyumen. Buxhoeveden spent time there before moving to Omsk, interpreting in exchange for lunch, and was bolstered by its blessed atmosphere of ordered normality. She particularly admired the head matron, Florence Farmer, 'a born organiser – young, active and absolutely indefatigable', who seemed to be everywhere at once, issuing orders right and left and 'always cheerful and ready for any emergency.'[21] Equally indefatigable was its director, Dr Charles Lewis, who in order to penetrate a local prisoner-of-war camp, faked a *propusk* for himself by carving an official-looking stamp from the rubber heel of a shoe. Most pitiable of the people he found inside were 116 Chinese labourers, all suffering from severe frostbite because guards had stolen their boots. Lewis asked the camp management if he could supply wood for their barracks stove, but was refused on the grounds that the European prisoners would resent it. After some persuasion he was allowed to distribute blankets. Not one of these poor men, Lewis recorded – the evil 'Chinese torturers' of White propaganda – 'left the place with any toes.'[22]

Most celebrated of Teusler's initiatives was the Inter-Allied Typhus Train, for its painted wagons better known as the 'Great White Train'. Long endemic to Russia – it was what felled Napoleon's Grande Armée – typhus was not yet well understood. There was no effective vaccine for it, and apart from good nourishment and nursing, no cure. What was known was that it was spread by lice, which flourished in wartime dirt and overcrowding. Realising that it would be impossible to set up de-lousing stations in every town, Teusler conceived and organised a mobile sanitation and treatment facility. Equipped with a bath-house, steam laundry, head-shaving station and clinic, the Great White Train set off from Vladivostok on 2 February

1919, and for the next sixteen months puffed back and forth across White-held Siberia, processing up to 990 people (its record) daily. The project's lavishness raised some resentment, and its design had flaws. (As an American doctor observed, though Russia needed the supplies, she had plenty of well-trained medics of her own, who spoke the language.[23]) Treating over a million people in total, the Great White Train nonetheless undoubtedly did more good – and probably won more hearts and minds – than the rest of the Intervention put together.

12

L'Entente de ma tante

Half a world away from Vladivostok, on the morning after the Armistice the Mediterranean Fleet made its way through the Dardanelles. The weather was perfect – calm and bright, the coastline pale gold, the sea turquoise. As the line of ships steamed at a brisk twenty knots towards the mouth of the strait, the officers aboard divided: classicists to starboard, to contemplate the knobbly headland that once was Troy, the rest to port, where the detritus of the Gallipoli landings – ruined villages, wrecked ships – lined the shore. 'I can't quite express what I felt as I passed again each familiar spot', Captain Herbert Wyld of the destroyer *Nereide* wrote to his wife; 'It seemed so incredible . . . It was a wonderful day, and a day worth waiting for.'[1]

The Interventions in Siberia and the North had grown out of the First World War – extensions, in essence, of wartime supply missions to the tsarist army. But over the winter of 1918/19 the Allies also entered a completely new theatre – the South. Densely populated, long-summered and famous for its fertile soil, it bore no resemblance to Arctic tundra or Siberian *taiga*. On the Black Sea's northern coast, west to east, the great grain port of Odessa, then the shipbuilding centre of Nikolayev (today's Mykolayiv), then the Dnieper-mouth port of Kherson. In Crimea – Riviera-like with its cliffs and coves and Italianate summer palaces – Sebastopol and a string of fashionable seaside resorts. Further east, the busy commercial port of Novorossiysk, and beyond that, in present-day Georgia, Batumi, terminus of the Baku-to-Black Sea oil pipeline. Behind, Ukraine's gently rolling, well-wooded farmland, the coal-mines and ironworks of the Donbass and the prairies of the Kuban, rising to the green foothills of the Caucasus.

Since the Revolution the Ukrainian portion of this vast area – 'South Russia' in the parlance of the time – had seen three changes of government. When Nicholas II abdicated in March 1917 Ukrainians had their first modern-day stab at independence, when moderate socialists led by a professor of history formed a parliamentary or Rada government. Three months after the Bolsheviks took power in Petrograd it was thrown out by a rival Ukrainian Bolshevik government that had declared itself in Kharkov. Then in March 1918, after Lenin's peace-for-territory deal at Brest-Litovsk, the Germans marched in, setting up a puppet administration under a big land-owner called Pavel Skoropadsky.

Styling himself 'Hetman' – an antique Cossack title – Skoropadsky was a figure of fun, mocked by all for his reliance on Berlin and folk-operetta trappings. (Nicely, his surname combined the word for 'quick' – *skoro* – with *padat* – 'to fall'.) His German-backed rule was nonetheless something of a peaceful interlude. In the countryside, grain was seized and sent west, but in the cities crime abated and businesses reopened. Passing through Kiev, the satirist Teffi – Russia's Dorothy Parker – was amazed at how safe and lively the city felt after Moscow. There were posters up for plays and for a performing-dog show; the shops were bursting with food, and the cafés with the capital's upper classes – like her, on their way to Odessa and emigration. What amazed her most – 'like a dream from a life forgotten' – was the sight of a Russian officer, in epaulettes, calmly standing at the door of a bakery eating a piece of cake. In Moscow he would have been in hiding, like a hunted animal.[2] In Crimea, an English nanny similarly found that the staff at German headquarters behaved most courteously when she reported there fortnightly as required, and she opted to bathe from the enemy half of the beach, since unlike the Russians the Germans wore bathing-suits.

Waiting in the wings, when the Germans started to withdraw after the Armistice, were four different armies: the Polish army, under Poland's new leader Józef Piłsudski; the Ukrainian People's Republic army under another 'socialist on horseback', former Rada minister Symon Petlyura; the Ukrainian Soviet army, led by the Ukrainian Bolshevik Vladimir Antonov-Ovseyenko; and General Denikin's Volunteer Army, based in the Kuban. The Don and Kuban Cossack

'Hosts' – another archaic term back in use – also had their own armies, which cooperated uneasily with Denikin. In addition four major warlords, the most colourful of them an anarchist called Nestor Makhno, operated in Ukraine, plus innumerable peasant bands known as Greens.

The result was chaos. In the course of 1919 Kiev changed hands at least a dozen times. ('The inhabitants', wrote the Kiev-born novelist Mikhail Bulgakov, 'reckon that there were eighteen changes of power. Some stay-at-home memoirists counted up to twelve of them; I can tell you that there were precisely fourteen.') Criminality ran riot, and new slang terms were coined for murder: you could be 'put against the wall', 'changed', 'liquidated', 'expended' or 'sent to Dukhonin' – the last commander-in-chief of the Imperial Army, lynched by his own troops the year before. Setting off from Kiev to Odessa, Teffi's train jolted to a halt just outside the station. There were shots, shouting, dancing lanterns, rumours that a hospital train had been attacked:

> Dead. Wounded. How accustomed we had grown to these words. No one felt any particular alarm or distress. No one said 'How awful!' or 'What a tragedy!'
>
> Our way of life had changed, and in accord with this new way of life we just thought 'Remove the dead and bandage the wounded.'
>
> The words were part of our everyday language. And we ourselves could well become 'dead' or 'wounded', perhaps at this next junction, perhaps soon after it.[3]

Most preyed upon, amidst all the violence, were Ukraine's Jews. The first major pogroms of the period took place in December 1918, in and around Lviv, near Ukraine's present-day border with Poland. Having driven Ukrainian forces out of the city, the Polish Army set fire to Jewish-owned buildings, killed and raped. The recorded death toll, probably an undercount, was 132, and doctors reported that sixty twelve-year-old girls were recovering in hospital from soldiers' 'hooliganism'. Setting a pattern for the months to come, the British military representative to the Polish government, one-handed, one-eyed Adrian Carton de Wiart VC, denied the violence. In Lviv trying to broker Polish-Ukrainian peace talks two months later, he made no attempt to investigate, and dismissed pogrom 'rumours' as 'grossly exaggerated'.[4]

Into the gathering maelstrom, at the end of 1918, plunged the French and British armed forces. (America only observed, and ferried food aid and refugees.) The two countries had sketched out a division of responsibilities twelve months earlier. France was to take control of the northern Black Sea coast, from Odessa to Novorossiysk, and Britain the northeastern, from Novorossiysk to Batumi. But they still had a decision to make: which of the anti-Bolshevik forces in Ukraine to support?

The obvious candidates, being by far the largest population group, were the Ukrainians themselves. But Petlyura's Ukrainian People's Republic was both weak – it held Kiev for barely two months after the German withdrawal – and unfriendly. Meeting the Ukrainian leader outside Lviv in February 1919, de Wiart and his French counterpart – both strongly pro-Polish – found him 'very churlish and unforthcoming'. Though he sent representatives for further talks, according to de Wiart they made no concessions and 'had come for the sole purpose of wasting our time . . . Finally I flew into a rage and called them *un tas de cochons*' – a bunch of swine.[5] Petlyura troops then actually machine-gunned the flag-draped Anglo-French train as it set off back to Warsaw, killing two Polish officers on board.

More broadly, the French and British viewed the Ukrainian national movement as a hopeless mess. A British major expressed the general attitude: 'Ukrainians of every national complexion . . . were busily engaged in a series of civil wars which nobody appeared likely to win, as nobody remained long enough on the same side to have a chance of doing so.'[6] *Express* correspondent John Hodgson cared so little who was who that he described Petlyura as Romanian. The sentiment was flippant, and picked up from Russians, who across the political spectrum, then as now, could not accept that Ukrainians were a separate nationality, let alone deserving of their own state. Today, Ukrainians view the Allies' failure to support them as a tragic missed opportunity, but in truth the scoffers were probably right. Split, by the end of 1919, between two paper governments, one allied with the Poles against the Russians and the other the reverse, they did not have the leadership or unity to win power, even with outside military aid. For independence they had to wait another seventy years, until the collapse of the Soviet Union.

Instead, the Allies sought out Denikin. Bald and stout, with a neat white beard and a reserved, slightly awkward manner, he had an unusual background for a tsarist general. His father, born a serf, had been an ordinary soldier, and his Polish mother a seamstress – disadvantages he had overcome on doggedness and talent, in unfashionable regiments of the line. Politically, however, he was conservative, one of the military would-be coupsters who tried to overthrow the Provisional Government in September 1917, and later escaped south to found the Volunteer Army. As with Kolchak, on first meeting outsiders usually liked him, interpreting his quiet style as reliability, and his refusal to talk politics as soldierly honesty. Again as with Kolchak, shortcomings emerged on closer acquaintance.

At the end of November, soon after passing through the Dardanelles, a British delegation arrived at Yekaterinodar (today's Krasnodar), administrative centre of the Kuban and Denikin's headquarters. To head it, the War Office had chosen two passionate anti-Bolsheviks: General Poole – the same man who had connived in the coup against Chaikovsky in Archangel – and Lieutenant Colonel Terence Keyes, an ex-Indian Army political officer who had organised the government's early covert money transfers to the Volunteer Army. The pair were given the same sort of treatment as Neilson and Howgrave-Graham in Verkhnye Uralsk: banquets, parades, Cossack ranks and tsarist honours. ('I got the 3rd class St Vladimir', Keyes boasted to his wife. 'In the old days this made me a noble – an awfully good order, quite equal to the C.B.') A financial incentive seems to have been thrown in too: amongst Poole's papers is a legal document, dated 9 January 1919 and certified by Yekaterinodar's notary public, transferring to him without charge all the shares in a new Caspian oil-drilling company. What they were not given was a proper look at military operations, their sole, spectacularly uncomfortable day-trip to the front seemingly designed, as Keyes shrewdly observed, to 'choke off our curiosity by nearly killing us with cold'.[7]

This soon-to-be well-honed public relations package – flattery and crippling amounts of alcohol, plus a deliberately brief and uninformative glimpse of the actual fighting – did the trick. Denikin's campaign plan was totally unrealistic – as Keyes put it, 'a beautiful paper scheme' requiring eighteen Allied divisions. And Poole saw for himself that the Volunteer Army was disastrously under-resourced, with no repair shops, field hospitals, veterinary units or even winter bedding and clothing. But in the report he delivered on his return to London, he nonetheless strongly recommended that Denikin be given Britain's backing. Admittedly, he wrote, Denikin did not 'stand out as a brilliant soldier or administrator'. But more importantly, he was 'honest and reliable', brimmed with 'determination and patriotism' and enjoyed 'universal confidence and popularity'. His staff were devoted and hard-working, and his generals capable and dashing. Poole even put in a good word for Andrei Shkuro, a notorious rogue commander who roamed the land in a train painted with ravening wolves. ('A good, useful, Cossack . . . full of energy and drive.') If Britain stepped up, the report went on, victory was assured. Red forces, 'mostly unwilling conscripts kept in the ranks by terroristic methods', would melt away, and peasants 'flock to the standard of law and order.' Appended was a long list of the military supplies the Volunteer Army needed, and another of the consumer goods that it would be good if it were able to distribute, the latter including 7,500 tons of tea, 50,000 boxes of pen-nibs, and 3 million pairs of galoshes.[8]

Urged on by Churchill, the War Cabinet gave its authorisation, on the proviso that the new mission should not engage in fighting, and concern itself only with supply. In March the first ships arrived in Novorossiysk, carrying guns, stores and about two thousand officers and soldiers to act as advisors and trainers. The mission's leader, after Churchill replaced an insufficiently gung-ho initial pick, was Lieutenant General Herbert Holman, a 'huge bulk' of a fifty-year-old Indian Army cavalryman, described by juniors as 'very dogmatic' and 'utterly contemptuous of Regulations'.[9] The equally conservative but more cerebral Keyes, who stayed on as political officer, thought him politically reliable but ill-bred: 'sound but a real hairy-heeled creature.'[10] Whereas in Siberia Knox was balanced by a High Commissioner, no diplomatic representative was sent to Denikin, so that London subsequently only had the benefit of Holman's and Keyes's highly partisan views.

Three weeks after Poole and Keyes had their first meeting with Denikin, at the other end of the Black Sea the French occupied Odessa. An initial three divisions of Senegalese were joined, in late January 1919, by three Greek divisions (pawns in a back-room deal between Clemenceau and Greek prime minister, Eleftherios Venizelos), bringing the whole force up to some forty-five thousand. Its commander, General Philippe d'Anselme, reported to Bucharest-based General Henri Berthelot, who had rallied the Romanians to the Allied cause during the war, and hoped to do similarly in Ukraine. A young Russian general, Aleksei Grishin-Almazov, was installed as Odessa's governor.

From their new bases at Odessa and Novorossiysk, the French and British navies fanned out to the smaller ports in between, in support of whichever non-Bolshevik forces present were strongest. The trickiness of their position – and their general out-of-depthness – comes over in the letters Captain Wyld of the *Nereide* wrote to his wife. In mid-December 1918 he was sent to Kherson, eighty miles east of Odessa at the mouth of the Dnieper. On arrival he found it between occupations, four boatloads of Volunteer Army men about to leave as Petlyura's Ukrainians – 'a sort of Bolshevik gang' – moved in. Though his orders were not to take sides, at the request of the provincial governor he took on board all the cash and bonds on deposit in its banks; 'forty large cases, which are locked up in the magazines . . . We [feel] rather rich for the time being.'[11]

After a brief diversion to ferry Nicholas II's sister-in-law – 'most extraordinarily nice' – to Constantinople, Wyld returned to Kherson to find it occupied by the Petlyurists. A Volunteer Army unit – 'appalling specimens some of them' – still held a small town a few miles away on the Dnieper's opposite bank, and the two sides were exchanging desultory gunfire. On the advice of the local harbour-master – his 'interpreter, philosopher, guide and friend' – Wyld tried to act as peacemaker, asking the Petlyurist commander, a Colonel

Kochubei, that he give the Volunteer Army men safe passage to leave. He also put in protests on behalf of mistreated civilians, who included Kherson's imprisoned mayor. 'I had a pleading letter from his wife. I think I got him off; at least, they promised me he would be released.'[12] Another petitioner, the daughter-in-law of a local businessman, described the murder of her husband and father-in-law; a gang of fifteen men had come to the house, demanded 20,000 roubles, and when only 12,000 could be found, took them out to the garden and shot them. When Wyld tackled Kochubei about the incident the colonel first professed ignorance, then dismissed it as 'an everyday occurrence'. Wyld 'insisted it should be investigated and extra police placed. However, I doubt if anything will be done.'[13] Alongside the awful stories came a blizzard of desperation-edged social requests: 'Tea parties every day, and hardly a day passed we didn't have an enormous Russian cake or something sent to us, and they were jolly good too, especially a sort of apple pastry.' Every evening he ate at a different private house, and twice he attended the theatre. The show was *Charley's Aunt*, 'all in Russian of course, but most amusing.'[14]

On 26 January orders came for the *Nereide* to leave. Afraid that if he did so Kherson would descend into wholesale mob violence, Wyld stalled, pointing out to his superiors that departing in a hurry would damage British prestige, and that with an icebreaker manned by German PoWs at his disposal he was in no danger of getting frozen in. To his wife he wrote 'I simply cannot [go]. Lives of citizens here are threatened, and it is only our presence here which prevents, well, goodness knows what. People come to me all day imploring protection and help.'[15] Tension increased the next day, with the news that the powerful Ukrainian warlord Nikifor Hryhoryev had swopped allegiance from Petlyura to the Bolsheviks. Looting broke out and Kochubei and his deputy came to Wyld begging for protection. He put them on his icebreaker, along with some fleeing Volunteer Army officers and a priest: 'All were sworn enemies, and it really was very comical.'[16] For two days he held talks with a 'Revolutionary Committee' that set itself up in the town hall, until on 30 January French troops steamed into harbour, and he could hand over the imbroglio to them. The next morning the

Nereide crunched out to sea, blowing her whistle to clear away sleds and skaters. Two pigs asleep on the ice 'never stirred, though we passed within fifty yards of them.' Throughout Wyld had not noticed – or thought it better not to mention? – that one-third of Kherson's population was Jewish.

Along the coast, wrapped in a stole of midwinter fog, Odessa was dancing away her sorrows. Like Kiev, the city was filled with upper-crust refugees from Moscow. By day they traded away jewellery at commission shops, queued for visas at the Hôtel de Londres or gathered in cold rented rooms to exchange rumours and gossip. By night they tried to forget, packing the casino and will-o'-the-wisp new *cafés-chantants*. 'Stupefied by wine, gambling and cigar-smoke', remembered Teffi, 'bankers and sugar manufacturers would emerge from these clubs and blink their puffy eyelids at the sun. Shadowy figures from the Moldavanka [Odessa's poor quarter] hung about in doorways, sifting the piles of nutshells and sausage skins for scraps.'[17] Asked to come up with a name for the latest night-spot, she suggested *L'Entente de ma tante*.

Amongst the new arrivals was a twenty-six-year-old law student turned officer, Prince Andrei Lobanov-Rostovsky. In France since the Revolution, he had to learn the ropes. Old army friends he bumped into had grown beards and carried false passports, and warned him not to have his photograph taken or let his name be put on any sort of list. Paper money had to be spent as soon as possible: while he waited his turn at the barber's, the price of a shave doubled, and shops gave change in ribbons of uncut rouble notes. A night at the opera – chandeliers, gilt, women in full evening dress – felt like the old days until it was time to go home, which meant hiding away rings and watches, walking in a group, and avoiding the side-streets. A mugging, in new Anglo slang, was a *gobstop*.

Atop the tinderbox sat the French. Too few properly to occupy the region, they felt threatened from within and without: by the hungry, angry poor inside the city, and by warlord Hryhoryev's rag-tag army outside it. The Senegalese, smiling and shivering as they came ashore with their pack-donkeys, did not convince, and there were bitter fallings-out with the Greeks. Four thousand Volunteer Army troops were more of a hindrance than a help, Berthelot complaining to Paris that officers outnumbered men, and that they 'gambled, drank and amused themselves as in the past', with no thought for public opinion.[18] Denikin's representatives, for their part, felt betrayed by French command's dealings with the Petlyurists in Kherson and elsewhere, and insulted by its general high-handedness and arrogance. The first complaint was unjustified: had the Whites themselves condescended to build an anti-Bolshevik coalition, they might have won the Civil War. But on French arrogance they had a point. Illustrative – and typical of the Intervention in general – is a story from Lobanov-Rostovsky. Posted to Sebastopol, he acted as interpreter at a meeting between the French garrison chief and a delegation of local and refugee scholars:

These professors were venerable men, old and learned, all highly cultured and some with an international reputation. The French colonel received them as if they were naughty children requiring advice, and I had the greatest difficulty in softening what he said as I translated. At last I could stand it no longer, and I said to the professors in Russian, 'May I suggest that you do not carry this interview any further?' As some of them spoke French and understood what the trouble was, they agreed immediately and we left.[19]

Things started to fall apart in late February, when Hryhoryev began advancing from the east. On 2 March he attacked Greek-defended Kherson, which fell after a week's fighting. A sizeable portion of the city's civilian population, including women and children, joined in on Hryhoryev's side – 'a striking example', British naval communications sarcastically noted, 'of the popularity of the Allies in South Russia.'[20] Four days later Nikolayev was evacuated, so precipitately that guns, tanks, and according to gloating Denikin the wounded, were left behind.

Berthelot asked to be relieved of his command, and on 20 March the commander-in-chief of French forces in the Near East, General Franchet d'Espèrey ('Desperate Frankie' to Brits) arrived in Odessa to assess the situation. A hard-headed realist, d'Espèrey had warned at the start that the expedition was not big enough, and would be unpopular with the army. Now he declared in public that there was no question of Odessa being abandoned, while privately wiring to Paris for permission to evacuate.* The crisis caught Clemenceau at a politically vulnerable moment. On the defensive because he had failed to persuade the Peace Conference to allot France the Saar coal basin, and with left-wing opposition to the Intervention coming to boiling-point in parliament, he was in no position to pick a fight with the army as well. On 29 March he cabled his assent, and on 2 April d'Anselme received orders to start embarking Allied and Russian civilians.

Out walking that evening, Lobanov-Rostovsky realised that something was up when three French staff cars in a row sped by, all heading for the docks. Next he came upon a line of people camped on the pavement outside a bank. A nod was as good as a wink, and by seven thirty the next morning he was packed and sitting with his baggage in the lobby of the Hôtel de Londres, waiting for its visa office to open. As maids vacuumed around him, the guests read in their morning papers that the French were leaving. In an instant the lobby filled with people:

> Two streams of humanity, going up and down the stairs, met on the landings between the floors, where free-for-all fights took place. Women caught in the crush were shrieking, and from these landings valises came tumbling down on the heads of those below . . . To add to the confusion a huge and menacing crowd of ruffians had assembled in the street, and with shouts of death were trying to force their way into the hotel. The massive doors were hastily bolted, and headquarters' small military guard, with rifles in hand, took up a position behind them.[21]

Chaos reigned throughout the city. French soldiers joined in looting and haphazard shooting; workmen's pickets, armed with rifles,

---

* D'Espèrey was a canny planner. Later, as a Marshal of France, he kept a supply of biscuits inside his screw-top marshal's baton to see him through ceremonial occasions. A former Interventionist, Charles Drage, observed him eating them at Haile Selassie's coronation.

appeared from nowhere; currency traders formed little knots in the squares, urgently gesticulating. Trains stopped running – the Reds were said to have blown up the bridges – and sullen steamship crews had to be physically threatened or paid stupendous sums to set sail. The British commander in the Black Sea, Rear-Admiral Michael Culme-Seymour, deliberately stayed away, explaining to headquarters that there were more than enough admirals on the scene already, and that 'the less the British were officially connected with such a discreditable operation the better.'[22]

After two failed attempts Lobanov-Rostovsky escaped with the help of his brother, who smuggled him aboard a civilian refugee boat scratch-crewed by sailors from an Italian cruiser. Though the weather was calm, it took five days instead of the usual two to reach Constantinople. On arrival

> it was pathetic to see the barges . . . leaving for the quarantine station. Old men and women of good families and wealth, accustomed to luxury and courteous treatment, stumbled down the gangway under the oaths and coarse shouts of French sergeants who treated them like cattle.[23]

After vicissitudes, Lobanov-Rostovsky ended up lodging in a hilltop monastery on one of the Princes' Islands. Sleeping in his coat, and subsisting on tinned rations and goat's milk, he was soothed by the view, the smell of lilacs and the sound of the Easter Week liturgy, floating from the monastery chapel. 'Here life had come to a standstill. *Byzance* was still alive.'

The last act of the French in Ukraine was a naval mutiny. As the evacuation of Odessa commenced, the Red Army broke through Volunteer Army defences at the isthmus joining the Crimean peninsula to the mainland, and started advancing south. Not wanting more Romanov deaths on its conscience, London arranged for HMS *Marlborough* to whisk Nicholas II's mother, the Dowager Empress Marie, plus relatives, away from Yalta. (She sailed with a brace each of grand dukes, English nannies, rolled-up Rembrandts and pet Pekingese, plus a large collection of wigs.)

On 8 April the Reds took the Crimean capital, Simferopol, and on the 16th attacked Sebastopol. A bombardment by the Allied battleships in harbour forced a ceasefire, upon which the crews of two French ships – Admiral Amet's flagship the *Jean Bart*, and the *France* – went on strike. Hosing unpopular officers out of their cabins, they announced that they would no longer fire on the Bolsheviks, nor obey any other orders until a date was fixed for their return home. The next morning, to loud cheers, the Red Flag replaced the French tricolor at the two ships' jack-staffs, and some five hundred French sailors went ashore and joined a pro-Bolshevik demonstration. The marchers were confronted by a unit of French-officered Greeks, who followed warning shots with three rounds of shrapnel. Forty-odd sailors were wounded, and though they returned to the *Bart* and the *France*, the anger was such that the crews of all the other French ships in harbour also tore down their tricolors. Every time a Greek boat passed a French ship there were shouts of 'à bas les Grêques!', to which the Greek flagship replied by hanging a dummy Frenchman at her yard-arm.

The situation stabilised the next day, with the arrival of four British dreadnoughts and Admiral Culme-Seymour. Calling on Amet, Seymour found him 'very much distressed', keen to blame the mutiny on war-weariness rather than radicalism, and resigned to surrendering Sebastopol, which he wanted to hand over intact in exchange for a ceasefire extension. Disagreeing strongly on the last point ('the Bolshevists are not the kind of people with whom arrangements can be made'), Seymour instead ordered that as much as possible of Sebastopol's naval equipment be requisitioned or destroyed. Smaller Russian vessels in harbour were sent to Novorossiysk, and the engines of large, un-crewable battleships disabled using explosive charges. Submarines were towed out to sea and sunk, and a wireless station and eight seaplanes smashed with sledge-hammers. Left alone was the ordnance in the arsenal: blowing it up would have destroyed half the town, and there was not time to remove it safely.[24]

On 23 April the *France* sailed for home, lowering the temperature considerably, and on the 28th the last shore troops embarked. The British cruiser HMS *Calypso* stayed on for a few more days, watching from a prudent distance as the Red Army took over. Except for a seaplane dropping propaganda leaflets, an engineer wrote home, the only excitement was the appearance alongside of a 'boatload of Bolshies' armed with 'hand grenades, pistols and a concertina.' When they began 'serenading', the sailors instantly pelted them 'as hard as they could throw with potatoes . . . Fortunately they did not retaliate with grenades, but pulled as rapidly as possible out of range. They are a nasty lot.'[25]

In Soviet legend, the French mutiny at Sebastopol was a fraternal proto-revolution. Ideology certainly played a part, the mutiny's leaders – engineer officer André Marty on the *Bart* and twenty-one-year-old fitter Charles Tillon on the *France* – both being committed Communists. (Sentenced to hard labour on return home but soon pardoned, they entered parliament and had long political careers. Marty became political commissar for the International Brigades in Spain, earning notoriety for his paranoid enthusiasm for executing his own men, and Tillon led the Second World War's Communist resistance.) What most of the Sebastopol mutineers wanted, however, was not revolution but demobilisation – in which they were not alone, there being similar unrest at the time amongst time-expired British sailors and in British army camps. France's igno-minious exit from Ukraine nonetheless caused an international outcry, with the British accusing the French of losing their nerve, and Russian émigrés crying betrayal. The *débâcle* weakened Clemenceau, and damaged his relations with Washington especially, after d'Espèrey tried to shift the blame onto the American Food Commission, for allegedly failing to deliver promised grain. There was more embarrassment when Odessa's former governor, Grishin-Almazov, was captured by a Bolshevik squadron as he crossed the Black Sea on his way to join Kolchak. He and four others commit-ted suicide rather than be taken prisoner, and a letter that he was carrying from Denikin, highly critical of the French, was gleefully published by the Soviet press.

The whole bruising experience turned the French government off the White cause. Though it did not formally discontinue aid to the Volunteer Army for another six months, policy switched from trying to overthrow Lenin to sealing him off behind buffer states – in the metaphor of the time, establishing a *cordon sanitaire*. What this meant in practice was that while in eastern Ukraine, the Don and the Kuban Britain continued to support Denikin, in western Ukraine France transferred her backing to the Poles. Thus a new contradiction was created in the tangle that was the Intervention, and the loudest initially of the Whites' backers became the first to move her chips elsewhere.

PART III

White Advances, April–September 1919

13

'Our poor little unarmed soldiers'

THE 1919 CAMPAIGNING season was when the Civil War reached its climax. As the spring thaw set in, the two sides looked well matched. The Bolshevik regime had survived two winters, still held Moscow and Petrograd – Russia's largest cities by far – and had grown its forces from a scratch collection of volunteer militias into a full-scale, professionally officered conscript army. Vitally, its hold on the centre of the country also gave it the heart of the railway network, enabling quick movement of troops from front to front. But the Whites too had sizeable if scattered armies, plus the rich world's backing and the greater part of the map: the whole of central and eastern Siberia, the Kuban and Don, parts of Ukraine and the Baltics, and Archangel and Murmansk and their hinterlands. Even with the setbacks at Odessa and Sebastopol, it was not easy to predict who would win.

First of the White leaders to make his move was Kolchak. Starting in early March his three armies, totalling about 130,000 men, advanced out of western Siberia in two directions: westward across the Urals towards the middle Volga, and northwest towards Kotlas, the riverport that had been Poole's objective during his rash dash up the Dvina the previous summer. With hindsight, he would have done better to make a single, concentrated push southwest, towards the Don Cossacks and Denikin. He did not do so either because he was overconfident, believing he could win on his own, or possibly – as a cynical insider thought – because he was swayed by the 'infants' on his staff, who feared that if the Volunteer and Siberian armies combined they would be replaced by more experienced figures.[1] Military historians also criticise Kolchak for impatience. He should have waited until the conscripts mobilised over the winter had been properly trained and equipped, and for

Denikin's own offensive, so that the Red Army could not pick them off one by one.

Nonetheless, the offensive was initially spectacularly successful. The Siberian armies almost immediately captured Ufa, on the western flank of the Urals, and were soon within reach of the Volga. By mid-April some 180,000 square miles of territory had been taken, as well as twenty thousand prisoners and dozens of guns and armoured trains. In the Allied capitals, sceptics started coming round, and manoeuvring began for Kolchak to be given full diplomatic recognition. In London his promoter-in-chief was of course Churchill, who circulated a paper to Cabinet urging recognition on the irrelevant grounds that if Britain took the lead France and America would follow, and the specious ones that recognition would so boost Kolchak's authority that he would be able to join with Allied forces at Archangel. Acting foreign secretary Lord Curzon was half convinced, writing to Balfour in Paris that now if ever was Kolchak's moment, and that recognition would repair the diplomatic damage done by Prinkipo.

On 9 May (two days after the Peace Conference handed the German government the text of the Treaty of Versailles), the issue was discussed by the Allied leaders in Paris. Lloyd George repeated Churchill's lines. Things were looking promising for Kolchak; it was wrong to think of him as reactionary, and if he were to join up with Ironside in the North 'that would be the end of Bolshevism.' As usual, President Wilson took the other side of the argument, expressing scepticism about Kolchak's promises of reform, and concluding that the best policy was to 'clear out of Russia and leave the Russians to fight it out among themselves.' The Japanese government, which had thus far undermined Kolchak by backing the Siberian warlord Semyonov, then threw everyone with the announcement that it intended unilaterally to recognise Kolchak as leader not only of Siberia but of the whole of Russia, the *démarche* intended as a reminder that the Russian Far East was Japan's backyard. Churchill fired off another of his Russia memos to Lloyd George: the Whites 'should be treated with proper consideration, and not simply as a pack of worthless emigrants', because 'in a very little while' the wheel of fortune might put them back in power.[2] At the leaders' next Russia meeting, on 20 May, Wilson was persuaded, and it was agreed to draw up the terms on which a recognition offer would be made.

Knox, meanwhile, was as active as ever, his most striking improvisation the two British ships of the Kama River Flotilla. Created by ex-officers of Russia's Baltic Fleet and based just west of the Urals at Perm, the Flotilla consisted of thirty-eight armed paddle-steamers, whose normal trade was towing rafts of logs. The British contribution was a thirty-four-man detachment, including naval guns, from Vladivostok-based HMS *Kent*. Over the winter the detachment had fought from an armoured train, and when the river ice broke in April it transferred to a tug and a barge, dubbed the *Kent* and the *Suffolk*. Through May and June the little fleet played cat-and-mouse with a Red counterpart up and down the Kama, between Perm and its junction with the Volga. Russian commander Admiral Smirnov – an imperturbable man who let nothing disturb his tea – often rode aboard the *Kent*: the only time that a Russian admiral has flown his flag from a British warship.

As Kolchak's armies advanced, Knox went on a seven-week victory tour in the comfortable Express, now additionally equipped with an observation car. Stopping in towns large and small, he and his staff were treated to the usual dinners, concerts and parades. British prestige was high – 'of course, we are "Lords of Creation"', Cazalet wrote to his mother – but proceedings also had a touch of the absurd, even of mockery. To everyone's great inconvenience, the Express was always met by a guard of honour even at dead of night, and handovers of token soldiers' comforts – socks, cigarettes – were ridiculously over-blown, with bands and speeches. Since Knox failed to visit the actual front – fobbed off with talk of broken bridges – a prisoner-of-war camp was a rare collision with reality. 'You never saw such misery', wrote Cazalet. 'No floors, nor any food. One hut with everyone suffering from Typhus was awful – 4 dead bodies and another dying – ough – a nightmare for ever.'[3] In early May the Express arrived back in Vladivostok, and soon afterwards Cazalet sailed for home, laden with sables, semi-precious stones (Angel Mother was to make an appointment with the family jeweller – 'I am imagining *lovely* things for you'), and wads of Omsk treasury bills, tissue-thin and printed slightly off-centre. (Back in England, his first diary entry is 'Lunched at Knole . . . Very nice.')

The most ambitious of Knox's spring 1919 initiatives was an Anglo-Russian Brigade. He had already set up four small training schools, and now had in mind a much larger scheme: four battalions of 1,000 men each, to be led by British officers and senior NCOs. Assigned to the new Brigade was Howgrave-Graham, who arrived at its Yekaterinburg headquarters (another empty school) in early May, and on the 15th took delivery of his first 600 recruits. Drawn up on the parade ground, they looked

> about as unpromising as any human material could look. Some in old skin coats and fur hats, some in a cotton shirt and nether garments made of odd pieces of material tied together with string, many with-out boots . . . a patient, smelly, long-haired, dirty, ill-fed swarm.[4]

Getting them de-loused and uniformed in the days that followed, he guessed that they were the fag-end of Kolchak's latest mobilisation, off-loaded onto the British because if the Brigade were a success it would show the Russians up. Within his own company one in four recruits failed their medicals, and even those who passed were so emaciated that it made him 'almost cry' to see them stripped. Though they gave their ages as eighteen or nineteen they looked younger – sent to the army, he thought, by parents too poor to feed them.

The Brigade expanded quickly, coming up to 178 British officers and NCOs, 586 Russian NCOs and 1,430 Russian soldiers. Howgrave-Graham was delighted to be promoted to brigade major, and that the Hampshires' CO, a pompous former president of the Oxford Union, left for home. Training, he thought, was going well, his 'little fellows' keen when interested, and extraordinarily adaptable and patient. The major problems were a shortage of interpreters – Russian words of command, it was decided after much debate, would have to be used except where the Russian for something was 'quite hopeless' – and the inefficiency verging on obstructionism of the city authorities, on whom the Brigade relied most vitally for water-carts. The British did not help matters by making fun. When the local fire chief mistook a bonfire at Brigade stables for a conflagration and came dashing, the

British corporal in charge walked forwards, bowing and smiling as if to apologise, then reached out and attached a joke medal, made out of red ribbon and a tin lid, to one of the fire chief's uniform buttons. The fire chief flung it away and turned on his heel.[5]

Real friction with the Russians began mid-June, with an 'astonishing and disgusting' outbreak of 'soldier-beatings'. Kolchak's officers, it had always been clear, resented the Brigade, routinely upbraiding its soldiers for saluting English-fashion when passing on the street. Now the hostility turned violent. In the past forty-eight hours, Howgrave-Graham wrote in his diary on 14 June, seven of his 'poor little Russian soldiers' had been assaulted – punched in the face and their flashes torn off and trampled. 'What exactly [was] at the bottom of it all' he and his colleagues could not make out. Was it a demonstration against the Allies? Or against General Gajda, who was the Brigade's chief patron and had fallen out with Kolchak? Maybe the whole idea of an Anglo-Russian Brigade was unwise. But even so, the attacks were 'a pretty poor kind of gratitude':

> Apart from the insult to England, what makes us boil over more than anything is the disgusting cowardliness [sic] . . . If they had a grievance against us why didn't they have the pluck to try their tricks on the British personnel themselves? Instead they knock our poor little unarmed soldiers about, merely for following the orders they have received.[6]

The recruits were too frightened to identify their attackers, and though Russian headquarters pretended to be 'very much shocked and giving every assistance', in fact nothing was done.

At the same time there was even more discouraging news: Knox had decided that the Brigade could not go into action under British command. Interpreters, it was explained, were too few, and the Russian army could not be relied upon for logistics. Instead Russian officers would gradually take over, starting with platoon leaders and working upwards. Howgrave-Graham and his fellow-Hampshires were extremely disappointed; not leading the Brigade into action themselves 'knocked the bottom out of the show.'

The unspoken reason for Knox's sudden caution was that militarily, the tide was turning the Bolsheviks' way. In the building for twelve months already, the Red Army was a different beast now from the previous summer. It shared many of the White armies' weaknesses: ill-discipline, lack of equipment, mass desertions. But it was bigger, better propagandised, and at Trotsky's insistence had started calling up professional officers in large numbers. Overseen by political commissars, some seventy-five thousand in total joined the Red Army by the time the Civil War ended, including 775 ex-tsarist generals and 1,700 former members of the Imperial General Staff. One of its best assets was Trotsky himself, who having being appointed commissar for military affairs in spring 1918, was blossoming into a war leader of near-genius: shrewd, decisive and boundlessly energetic, dashing from front to front in a much-mythologised armoured train.

In mid-May Trotsky launched his counter-offensive. Three weeks in the Red Army recaptured Ufa, and to the north it turned Gajda's army around, pushing him back to Perm. The Kama River Flotilla, by now ferrying retreating White units, had a narrow escape at Sarapul, a small riverport downstream from Perm and just captured by the Reds. Caught the wrong side of it, the paddle-steamers had to run the gauntlet of gun-batteries positioned in the alleyways running down to the water. Dmitri Fyedotov, the young naval officer who had escorted Admiral Glennon in 1917, was aboard Smirnov's flagship and describes the 'tremendously exciting' noise of machine-gun ballets hammering on its armoured wheelhouse as it braved 'a lane of tall, feathery waterspouts'. But it was strange and upsetting firing at civilian buildings, and at such close quarters, and he didn't cheer with the rest when a lucky shot toppled the town fire station's watchtower.[7] Thanks to the Red gunners' inexperience only one boat, the last in line, was lost, but it was the Flotilla's last hurrah before being disarmed and destroyed just ahead of Perm's abandonment on 30 June.

The reverses came just in time for the Allies to swerve giving Kolchak diplomatic recognition. A week after the 20 May decision the Allied governments had sent him their terms. He had to commit to calling elections as soon as he reached Moscow, and consent to independence for Finland and Poland, and autonomy for the Baltics, the Caucasus and Ukraine. Any border disputes had to be submitted to the League of Nations, and all sovereign foreign debt repaid. After a pregnant pause Kolchak replied, agreeing in principle to every-thing but giving himself wiggle-room on elections: they would be his 'first thought' once the Bolsheviks were 'definitely crushed'. But before negotiations could proceed any further news started coming in of defeats, and the Allied governments simply let the initiative drop. From Vladivostok, Knox continued to urge recognition, but in London even Churchill back-pedalled, telling the House of Commons, quite untruthfully, that he had never encouraged 'extrava-gant hopes' that Kolchak would be 'at the gates of Moscow within a short time.'[8]

In Yekaterinburg, Howgrave-Graham was told to start packing. It brought back uncomfortable memories of the expedition to the Orenburg Cossacks − another undignified skedaddle. The govern-ment would have done better, he gloomily decided, to have either just sent arms to Siberia, or a proper, self-sufficient fighting force. The halfway house had done 'very little good to the Russians and a great deal of harm to ourselves.' The following evening he and a friend got into an altercation with drunken Cossacks at the officers' club, and had to make a swift exit. 'It was just as well. They caught a few Jews after we'd gone and beat them pretty badly.'[9] Soon after came more disheartening news: instead of deploying as a unit, the Anglo-Russian Brigade was to be broken up and used to plug gaps at the front. A 'strong protest' against thus using its 'unfortunate, half-trained brats' as cannon-fodder got nowhere, and on 7 July a Russian colonel appeared at Brigade barracks, expecting to 'take delivery as one does a pound of meat at a shop.'[10] So that some decent ceremo-nial could at least be arranged, Howgrave-Graham made him go away and come back later.

The day after the handover all the British left for Omsk. In his diary Howgrave-Graham is light-hearted − tucked comfortably into the corner of a cattle-wagon, smoking a cadged cigar and contem-plating the 'upside-down-ness' of being the wrong side of the Urals and listening to a drawling major play the violin. In a later version, he is ashamed:

> The day of departure was not altogether pleasant. However much we tried to brazen it out, always there came back the haunting thought,

which refused to be stamped on: What sort of dirty trick was this that we were playing on the simple-minded Siberian peasant? . . . We could only put our tails between our legs and creep quietly away . . . hoping that, though they could not understand, they might at least forget.[11]

A week later, after a day of Cossack-led mob violence against its Jews, Yekaterinburg fell to the Bolsheviks.

14

Dyer's Battalion

A SIMILAR STORY OF White hostility to British-led local forces played out over the winter of 1918/19 in the North. It began shortly after General Maynard's July 1918 seizure of the White Sea town of Kem, when a delegation of Karelians – the Finnic-speaking nationality, fishermen, hunters and farmers, who made up the majority of the local population – approached British headquarters and offered their services in exchange for rations. The offer was accepted and recruits flocked in, quickly numbering over five hundred. Put in charge was Lieutenant Colonel Philip Woods, in pre-war life a textile designer for a family-owned Belfast linen mill. Having 'got their whiskers off to see what was underneath', Woods was delighted with his new charges. Russian acquaintances kept warning him against them – 'crucifixion at their hands' was the least he could expect – but he found them cheerful, alert and humorous as well as superb marksmen. To foster regimental pride he kitted them out with shamrock cap-badges, cut from the green baize of an old billiard table, and when the baize ran out, with metal versions made from old cartridge cases.[1] Recruitment continued, and in August the 'Irish Karelians' were ready for their first expedition – westwards up the Kem river to clear the back-country of Finns, at that point still in alliance with Germany.

On a cloudless blue and green day, three hundred boats gathered along a placid reach outside the town. All were rowed by women, whose bright headscarves were reflected in the ripples, and whose voices carried above the clunk of rowlocks to make 'a cheerful babel of sound'. Getting under way, some broke out flour-sack sails, and others caught the breeze by stepping baby pine trees in their bows. The picturesqueness was deceptive, for as Woods soon discovered, the

Karelians were ruthless fighters. Early on a pair of female rowers ignored rifle fire to ram and overturn a boat carrying Finnish scouts, then drowned the Finns by hitting them over the head with their oars. (A feat for which they were later awarded the Military Cross.) Even more startling was the Karelians' practice of skinning scouts' corpses, then stuffing the skins with leaves and hanging them from trees as warnings. On seeing his first – it looked like a tattered sack hung with streamers – Woods insisted that they desist.

> This was agreed to, but I strongly suspect that the agreement was taken to mean that I should hear no more of barbarities. Certainly I saw none, and the few other exhibits of the taxidermist's art I came upon were old and weather-worn.[2]

Other captured Finns were no luckier. Whenever Woods wanted one for questioning 'the answer was invariably "I arrived too late to save any of them", or "They were all killed in the first attack."' Later he was haunted by the memory of two battle-end massacres. One was at a place called Lousalma, where the beaten Finns were driven onto a sandbank and 'butchered to a man'. The other was at a big lakeside village near the Finnish border, where they took refuge in a meeting hall. The Karelians placed machine-guns at a window and in the doorway, and the gory result reminded Woods of 'a bombed dug-out in France'. Woods was able to purchase the life of one prisoner – 'a nice lad . . . some sort of clerical worker and quite out of his *métier*' – with tobacco, but did not have enough on him to save any more.[3] His powerlessness chimes with a Karelian veteran's account of the expedition, according to which the Karelians themselves initiated and organised it, and the British just tagged along.[4] Either way, militarily it was a resounding success, securing the whole Kem river system and ending the Finnish threat to the Murmansk railway line.

As winter approached Woods turned down General Maynard's suggestion that he move to Brigade headquarters at Kandalaksha, and instead stayed on with what Maynard called his 'most excellent bandits' in Kem. Initially, the atmosphere was peaceful and friendly. Quartered at the railway station, in rooms fitted out with wood panelling and wall-lights fashioned from biscuit tins ('quite a Mayfair effect'), Woods whiled away the long hours of darkness recording the Karelians' woodcraft codes (crossed sticks, smoke signals) and taming a bear-cub called Knobs. He also got War Office permission for a fur-trading scheme to raise money for Karelian wounded and widows, which raised over £600. The local amateur dramatics society, run by the postmaster, put on play-readings in the town theatre, and the abbot of the Solovetsky monastery sent regular gifts of smoked salmon.

The mood changed with the arrival of a thuggish contingent of Russian officers, part of an offshoot of the Northern Government's Russian Army. Openly hostile to the Allies, they accused Woods and his colleagues of encouraging Karelian separatism, and intimidated the locals into shunning them. All but a few townspeople, wrote Woods, became 'afraid to offer us hospitality or to be seen in our company.'[5] While he was away touring outposts the officers tried to disarm his Karelians, and when the theatre, in which he had offices, went up in flames he suspected arson. He was probably right, since Russian suspicion of British motives was acute and went to the top. All the major figures in the Northern Government – from ultra-conservative General Marushevsky to socialist interior minister Ignatyev – fulminate in their memoirs that the Karelian nationality was 'invented by the English', who were 'trying to cut out their first colonial foothold in our North.'[6]

That the Karelians wanted independence was true. In February 1919 a delegation appeared at Woods's door with a petition. Hand-written and signed by fourteen local notables, it declared that for centuries Karelia had been under

Russia Rule and slavery . . . holding her in darkness, preventing any education and sucking all the goods out of us . . . To live with Russia we cannot, and point blank refuse to do so . . . We all desire, from the bottom of our hearts for the British Government to take us under their protection, giving us the right to govern Karelia as we desire. Delegates from all parts of Karelia wish to visit England and to let Britain know the History of Karelia and how the Country is at present.[7]

Passing this touching but awkward document upwards, Woods was immediately ordered to nip the Karelians' hopes in the bud. The idea of a protectorate, Maynard cabled from Murmansk, was 'preposterous'; Karelia's future lay in a restored Russia, 'great, unified and free'. The chargé d'affaires, Lindley, came down from Archangel to reinforce the message. The Karelians were bitterly disappointed, pointing out that the rejection flew in the face of the Peace Conference's solemn declarations about self-determination. Having fantasised that the Colonial Office might be tempted by Karelia's timber and minerals, Woods was angry and upset. Deprived of his command, he accused Maynard of knuckling to Russian prejudice, and told his replacement, a man fresh from the King's African Rifles, that if he intended treating the Karelians like 'ignorant natives' he was 'wanting a little in brains' himself. In the spring the 'Irish Karelians' were broken up and assigned to Russian units, or melted back into their forests.

The one aspect of Russia policy the Peace Conference had agreed on in the early weeks of 1919 was that with Germany beaten, the occupation of Archangel and Murmansk no longer made sense. The Arctic supply route was redundant, and the region had no strategic resources or cities. Spurred on by the Intervention's growing unpopularity, in mid-February the State Department announced that American troops would be withdrawn as soon as the spring thaw allowed. On 4 March the Cabinet similarly decided that British troops would not spend a second winter there, but made no announcement and kept the withdrawal date open.

A tacit reason behind the move was that more and more, since news of the Armistice got through to them, Allied troops in the North were refusing to obey orders. It was not surprising. Though small in scale – Ironside termed it 'platoon fighting' – combat through the second half of the winter was nasty and unrelenting. On the Vaga, soldiers struggled to hold onto the riverside villages where they had dug in after fleeing Shenkursk, their diaries a snowstorm of skirmishes, ambushes, bad food, sleep deprivation and lice. Unusually for the highly mobile Civil War, the railway front congealed into static trench warfare. In cathedral-like pine-forest, the two sides built complex networks of trenches and dugouts, and so much ordnance was flung about that even today, a metal-detector swept over the forest floor beeps every minute. Scuff the cushion of pine-needles, and twisted chunks of shell-casing emerge, sharp-edged and heavy. No-man's-land is easily identifiable by its shorter trees, their parents having been destroyed in the blasts.

Added to the knowledge that the war proper was over, the danger and discomfort sapped morale. In the half-burned Dvina village of Tulgas, still held by the 339th's Company B, Private Scheu became progressively angrier. 'It looks like another Dardanelles to us', he wrote in his diary on 12 February: 'No relief, no reinforcements, no definite advice as to why and wherefore . . . British command – bah.'[8] On 1 March a disastrous patrol resulted in five killed and twelve seriously wounded; headquarters were treating them 'like cattle'. Even in the rear – where perennially buoyant medical orderly Anderson spent his time shooting up weathervanes and entertaining 'cute young barishnas . . . mostly blonde' – homesickness bit. 'The general principals [*sic*] of Russia', another private wrote home,

> are three in number, namely log houses, snow and pine trees . . . I have seen nothing else for about eight months . . . Truly old man I wouldn't wish this country on my worst enemy, or on anyone who knows what it is to live in the land of milk and honey, yes Michigan if you please.[9]

Discontent broke into the open in February and March, in a rash of what were technically mutinies but better termed soldiers' strikes. An early warning was a letter of complaint, dated 9 February, signed by fifty-five Royal Marines at Kandalaksha. If they were not given a withdrawal date at the next day's parade, they would 'down tools' for forty-eight hours:

> If nothing happens then, we will commandeer the first train travelling in the direction of Murmansk . . . We think we have been out here for long enough and what is more have been messed about like a flock of sheep . . . Everyone is fed up with everything in general, and our one aim is *England* and we will have that or trouble.[10]

Appeased by a visit by their CO, the Marines did not carry out their threats and do not seem to have been punished. An enquiry blamed their junior officers, for lacking grip.

The first soldiers to refuse orders outright were a battalion of the Yorkshire Regiment. Cobbled together from remnants of units eviscerated in France, the Yorkshires had already given serious trouble back in October 1918, on embarkation in Dundee. Denied shore-leave before sailing, 150 men had left the ship and stormed the dock gates, telling their colonel, when he pulled out his revolver, that if he did not put it away rifles 'would soon be fetched out to him.'[11] In Murmansk they had been set to building work for several months, before being sent south and marched cross-country to Seletskoye, a small town on the Yemtsa river. There, on 21 February, they dug their heels in, convening a mass meeting that passed resolutions demanding instant demobilisation and an end to censorship of outgoing letters. Though they conducted themselves in an orderly manner, a stretcher-bearer recorded, 'they all positively decline to go up the line or to obey any orders.'[12]

Belatedly informed of the situation five days later, Ironside immediately set off for Seletskoye. On arrival he found that the colonel in charge had managed to resolve matters, arresting the two sergeants who were the ringleaders and persuading the rest to set off for the fighting line. Interviewing the sergeants, Ironside was unforgiving. 'Mealy-looking brutes' of the 'office-clerk stamp', they had been in the Pay Corps through the war, and had never 'heard the whistle of a bullet':

I am afraid I lost my temper with them, and rent them for two cowardly swine . . . If I hadn't had an order in my pocket direct from the King telling me not to carry out the death sentence, I believe I should have had them tried and shot the same day.[13]

After all his strictures to the Russians about the importance of good officer–soldier relations, Ironside couldn't face telling Russian headquarters what had happened. Marushevsky found out anyway and gloated, snarking that the English had mutinied despite travelling soft, 'in sleds, in great comfort'.[14] At their courts-martial the sergeants were given ten years, but Ironside suspended the sentences and sent them back to the line, reckoning it fitter punishment than 'sitting in a warm prison'.

Next to refuse orders, on 1 March, were French colonial troops, who after a month's rest in Archangel refused to entrain back south. Again Ironside took charge in person, going with an armed platoon to the battalion's barracks and ordering that the men fall in. Most obeyed but half a dozen did not. Entering their hut with a sergeant by his side, Ironside found 'a great big brute lying on his elbow and leering at me. I gave him an order in French to get up and come out. He grunted "Non, je refuse."' Ironside told the sergeant to fix his bayonet and load, upon which the soldier 'got up quite quietly and said "Je suis content. Les Alliés vont se tuer."' ('Alright by me. The Allies are only doing themselves in.') Ironside was

> considerably relieved . . . for I had no desire to shoot a Frenchman. Still, their own officers were frightened to go near them, and I thought that if any Britisher had to do the shooting, it had much better be me.[15]

Perhaps because they knew they were going home soon, there was only one comparable incident amongst the Americans, when on 30 March a company refused to load sleds ready for a return to the front. A reminder by Colonel Stewart of the Bolshevik menace – 'If we don't fight we will all be wiped out' – changed their minds, and it was over so quickly that Ironside seems to have been unaware of it. A few days later Churchill sent a message to all British troops, asking them to 'Carry on like Britons fighting for dear life and dearer honour', and promising that only 'a few more months of resolute and faithful service' were required.[16]

At the end of April spring arrived. Roads turned to slush, bogs into tussocky lakes, and the rivers started to move, ice-floes jostling downstream. The villages came to life, people setting to work with wooden ploughs or sitting on doorsteps playing the accordion. Children used long planks to make jump-boards, tossing each other high above dripping cottage eaves, and on Orthodox Easter Day priests led processions to Allied barracks, using bunches of birch-twigs to spray them with holy water.

As soon as the rivers were navigable the Americans started handing over their positions and moving north to Archangel. Among them was Sergeant Douma, who was delighted to see autos and streetcars for the first time in nine months, as well as 'civilised girls' in 'regular dresses and silk stockings.' As soon as he could he was going to 'date up some of them' and 'try to get a little loving.'[17] There were medical inspections, fresh kit and a big remembrance service in the American section of the new Allied cemetery. On 27 June, in beautiful weather, the men of 'Detroit's Own' 339th finally marched down to the water-front and onto their troopships. The streets were full of people, wrote Anderson, 'and from the upper windows along the way the whores of Archangel gave the Yanks a fond and noisy farewell.'[18]

He touched Russian soil for the last time at Murmansk, where his ship was moored next to a British transport going the other way. (The sailors taking the opportunity to throw coal at each other.) The new British contingent was Churchill's doing. The day after Cabinet's 4 March decision not to allow British troops to stay in the North another winter, he had instructed General Staff to begin preparing a new force of between five thousand and six thousand to relieve the existing North Russia Expedition and cover its withdrawal. Since the new troops were to be volunteers, a recruitment drive was necessary. The War Office's line, put about in speeches and a public appeal, was that the existing expeditionary force, exhausted after a long winter and beset by the German-officered Red Army, was hanging on by its fingertips and in dire need of relief. From the *Manchester Guardian* to the *Daily Mail* the press took up the theme, so much so that Ironside – already nettled by what he called 'the W.O.'s paper stunt' – was inundated with worried enquiries from soldiers' relatives. At the same time, recruitment films painted the expedition as a species of wilder-ness adventure. Seaplanes skimmed over lakes, signals men shimmied up trees, and the inter-titles spoke of Primeval Nature, the Pioneer Spirit, and 'the Native, whose customs are so different from our own'. There was almost no mention of the Bolsheviks, and none at all of the Whites. Churchill reinforced the holiday impression in answer to a parliamentary question. 'Judged by Western Front standards', he told

MPs, there was 'really no fighting going on except occasional raids about the magnitude of trench raids.'[19]

Churchill's other propaganda initiative, agreed by Cabinet a few days after the Armistice, was a 'Blue Book' of Bolshevik atrocities. Put together by the Foreign Office and published on 3 April 1919, it comprised accounts taken from recently returned expatriates, and reports by diplomatic and military personnel. Vilified by Cold War-era historians on the left as absurd and hysterical,[20] most of the material is in fact perfectly credible, covering topics such as the mass arrests and executions of summer 1918, requisitioning, price rises, peasant resistance and the breakdown of discipline in schools. (Two of the respondents were teachers.) Among the exceptions, though, are the penny-dreadful stories, lifted straight from White propaganda, contributed by Knox and Poole. Knox claimed to have established that it was a Jewish faction in the Yekaterinburg soviet that had insisted on killing the Romanovs; Poole regurgitated shlocky stuff about Chinese torturers and 'commissariats of free love'.

Exaggerated and contradictory as the recruitment drive was, it worked. Volunteers flocked in, and towards the end of May the first of two battalions of 4,000 men, including no fewer than six VCs, sailed for Archangel in transports injudiciously named the *Tsar* and *Tsarina*. They were greeted with maximum fanfare: greenery-laden triumphal arches, bread and salt in front of the cathedral, an unctuous speech by the mayor. With their arrival and the Americans' departure Archangel became more staid and more British. No more pie-eating contests and 'lunch-and-smokers'; instead, new Boy Scout and Girl Guide troops. Enrolled in Beaver Patrol, Yevgeniya Gherman was taught 'drilling, doing good deeds and suchlike' by 'an English lady dressed in navy blue uniform', and enjoyed a summer jamboree complete with campfire and sausages.[21] Notices went up threatening severe punishment for street-fighting, and a guard was put on the stretch of riverbank in front of the Ghermans' house, to stop soldiers ogling the peasant women who bathed there with their children. A new nickname for the English was *kumony* or 'Come *on*-ers', from their endless exhortations to get a move on. Russians passing through Archangel on their way into emigration found the atmosphere grating. 'They have taken all the best buildings', complained a Petrograder;

'Everywhere, English flags and English speech', not to mention a 'really terrible' band in the public gardens. The actual *Arkhangelski*, he had to concede, seemed to regard all the outsiders in their midst, Russian or foreign, as equally alien. When 'accused of being interested in nothing but the price of cod . . . they would always reply, "Well, did we ask you to come and defend us?"'[22]

The new leader of the Northern Government, General Miller, was a fifty-one-year-old, luxuriantly moustached Baltic German who had commanded an army corps during the war and narrowly escaped lynching during the 1917 mutinies. Though less inflexible than Kolchak and Denikin – for example, amongst his troops *gospodin general* ('Mr General') replaced 'Your Excellency' – he was unequivocally authoritarian, as demonstrated by the summer's political scandal: the trial for sedition of a local trade unionist, M. I. Bechin. A popular moderate who had reined in the Archangel soviet prior to Poole's landing, Bechin's crime was to have organised a rally to mark the second anniversary of the February Revolution. In defiance of protests by the diplomatic corps, he was sentenced to fifteen years hard labour. Ironside liked Miller but patronised him, lecturing him during only their second meeting on Russian officers' 'laziness' and 'lack of method', and on how 'they seemed to be quite incapable of looking after their men.' In Ironside's telling, Miller conceded that many were indeed 'impossible', but begged him to believe 'that they were not all like that before the war.'[23] A later encounter was also characteristic. Some incoming ships having space for extra cargo, Ironside asked Miller for a list of needed supplies, and was astonished to see that it included hundreds of sets of French lingerie:

> I told Miller that I really could not have that, and he calmly said that he thought it was most important. 'You see, our men fight much better if they know that their wives are properly clothed and comfortable.' He was quite unabashed when I [pointed out] that less than 1% of the officers had their wives in Archangel . . . I told Miller that he could order long cloth in bulk and that the women could make their own underclothes – more especially as they had nothing to do.[24]

More seriously, Ironside repeatedly urged Miller to build up his army. In this Miller was partially successful, using conscription to bring troop numbers up to 25,000 – a good number given the region's small population. The problem was incentivising them, and the first half of the year was dominated by mutinies. The first Ironside heard of took place in April at Tulgas, with nine officers killed and three hundred men deserting. Ironside blamed it on Bolshevik propaganda, and as always on Russian officers not being close enough to their men: 'A bad show for the new Army. I'm terribly sorry.'[25] In mid-May there was another mutiny at Pinega, with two officers killed. To blame were unpaid wages and Ironside himself, who had appointed a known 'bad character' as district commander, on the reasoning that there was no use in an 'incompetent saint'. Again Ironside went to the scene in person – a lovely boat-ride up the pretty Pinega river – and found the commander cheerful, having already put down the mutiny and shot four men. The rebellious companies, when Ironside addressed them, looked about as dangerous as 'a lot of sheep', but he nonetheless approved another eleven executions. The rogue commander kept his job, though a Scottish colonel stayed behind to take charge of the cash for soldiers' wages.

Ironside's own instructions from London, in the early summer, were to launch a new offensive down the Dvina, with the aim of joining Kolchak's armies at Kotlas, 300 miles to the southeast. The plan was of course Churchill's, hatched at the same time as the Relief Force. Cabinet blew hot then cold on it as Kolchak advanced and retreated, and finally gave the go-ahead at the end of June, on the promise that troops would not be involved in serious fighting and would be withdrawn in good time for general evacuation in the autumn. Though Ironside backed Churchill by telegram to Cabinet, in private he was sceptical. Kotlas was a long way away, the enemy were improving, and Churchill was 'a man with a wonderfully vivid imagination.'[26] He was also suspicious of the way the War Office was keeping him in the dark about how Kolchak was doing. But before he had to decide whether to clash with his superiors or go along with an operation in which he did not believe, the Kotlas scheme fizzled of its own accord, when water levels in the Dvina dropped so low that movement further upriver became impossible.

What turned Ironside abruptly and completely against the Intervention was not the end of the Kotlas plan, but something emotionally close to home: Dyer's Battalion. Though Dyer himself had died of pneumonia, the battalion had become Ironside's pet project, nucleus of a planned 'Slavo-British Legion'. He had conceived it during his first weeks in Archangel, on discovering that Red prisoners of war were being neglected, and that the civilian gaols were filled with random so-called 'politicals' and homeless boys. Over the winter an initial three platoons were recruited and trained, went to the front and performed well. Numbers grew and in April Ironside brought the unit back to Archangel for expansion, under an ex-rugby international and 'very good officer' called Barrington Wells. An attached 'Boys' Battalion' took in the children, and photos show them washed and uniformed, eating up their supper, playing draughts and learning to box.

As with Siberia's Anglo-Russian Brigade, Russian command saw Dyer's as a rebuke. As Marushevsky put it, 'The main idea of General Ironside was . . . that the Russian soldier is wonderful, but the officers are bad: "I will give them English officers and you will see what great results we can achieve."' Nor did Marushevsky like the way the new battalion blurred class boundaries, making 'captains, majors and even colonels' out of 'shopworkers and clerks in Petrograd factories.'[27] (He exaggerated.) The Russians' better-justified concern was that Ironside was not properly vetting his recruits. '[Miller] tells me', wrote Ironside,

that the best and quietest soldiers are often the worst revolutionaries. I tell him that . . . it is all prisoner material and it is much better to use it than to let it rot . . . I notice that he is not very enthusiastic.[28]

Training and re-equipping in Archangel through the spring and early summer, Dyer's nonetheless seemed to be doing well. Ironside was proud of it, showing it off to visiting bigwigs and dropping by its barracks whenever he needed to cheer himself up. On 1 June it took the lead role in a King's Birthday Parade, during which Miller presented it with magnificently tasselled regimental colours. Though Russian onlookers winced at the three hurrahs for George V, Ironside felt vindicated: 'They all went by with a swing to their Regimental tune, [and] looked as good as any Battalion I have seen.' Towards the end of the month, the battalion was sent for final training to the base at Bereznik, on the confluence of the Dvina and Vaga. Inspecting it there on 25 June, Ironside was cautiously optimistic. Led by foreigners against fellow-Russians, it was too much to expect the men to be 'enthusiastic', but he hoped they would 'do well in any fighting. It's all an experiment [but] already one can see the stamp of the British soldier upon them.' A few days later the battalion moved to a tented camp opposite disputed Tulgas, right on the front line.

For six weeks the river front had been relatively quiet. Ironside had a new mobile headquarters, a large Clydeside-built passenger steamer called the *Retvizan*, from which he took fast motor boats or seaplanes to outlying posts. Normally workaholic, he had time to fly-fish – eerie in the midnight sun – and enjoy the 'simply gorgeous' views. Cheerful Kostya was on board, and whenever the boat dropped anchor the whole crew jumped into the water and swam about like otters. Life, he wrote on 26 June, was 'delightful. Up in the morning to an orange, and then straight off the deck of *Retizvan* into the river and then back to a breakfast with plenty of fresh butter, milk and eggs.'

The idyll was shattered in the small hours of the night of 6/7 July, when a group of eight Dyer's men armed with revolvers approached the building in which their officers were sleeping and fired at them through the windows. One man was killed in his bed, and nine more as they rushed outside. The alarm was raised by twenty-five-year-old Captain David Barr, who though hit in seven places managed to get away and swim to a picket boat. It took three hours to restore order, during which time two hundred-odd soldiers disappeared into the woods. 'The experiment has failed', wrote Ironside in his diary that evening. 'I am bitterly sorry. I cannot remember when I have been so sorry for anything . . . I cannot bear to think of it all.'[29] The next day he presented Barr with a Military Cross ('He is very pleased with it, poor chap. I hope it will pull him through'), and attended the funerals of the others. 'I really felt most upset by it all, more so than by anything I have been through in the whole five years of war.' Barr died a few days later, as did another wounded British officer.

Fifty mutineers were court-martialled, and twelve sentenced to death. (The same number as the mutiny's five British plus seven

Russian victims, following War Office orders not to exceed it.) The executions that followed were a grisly, nerve-wracking affair. To discourage copycats, it was decided that the firing squad would be Russian, and that 1,500 Russian troops, from Dyer's and other units nearby, would be brought to watch. Fearing they might riot, the officer in charge, Major Edward Allfrey, hid British-manned Lewis guns in bell-tents around the execution ground, and issued the firing squad with one machine-gun per condemned man, each loaded with only five rounds. Just before the prisoners were marched on, he recorded in his diary, 'an enormous influx of naval people suddenly came along':

> I felt a little ashamed of them, for all the big parade was quite silent, [and] the arrival of a British contingent of sightseers seemed in awfully bad taste. The execution itself was not a very pleasant sight, as the machine-guns, with their five rounds, only killed about four out of the twelve, and the remainder were left kicking, tied onto big posts. One sergeant had not been touched at all, and I am sure the man behind the gun missed him on purpose. Anyhow the end of it was that the machine-gunners were doubled off the parade, and we all had to go with our revolvers and polish the prisoners off. When the sergeant, who behaved like a man although he is a murderer, realised that he had been missed, he took the bandage off his eyes and shouted out 'Long live the Bolsheviks!' I was glad when somebody fired at him and killed him, for he was uncannily cool and collected.[30]

Together with a big mutiny at Onega a fortnight later, the Dyer's disaster changed Ironside. His breezy confidence vanished, and Marushevsky and Miller found him almost unrecognisable – downcast, stiff and aloof. Ironside could sense the 'I told you so' behind their commiserations: 'Their attitude is that we with our cocksuredness have failed, and they are quite pleased.'[31] On 23 July he told the War Office that he wanted to evacuate Archangel by 1 October at the latest, not leaving even a small mission behind. His problem now, he confided to his diary, was less the Reds, more how to get out without the whole White army turning on him as Dyer's had done.

'Watch your step. You will be walking on eggs loaded with dynamite'

American forces land at Vladivostok, 16 August 1918.

British troops on the Dvina.

Reinforced French wagon, Murmansk, 1919.

'We might . . . have actually dashed to Vologda, but for two
very good reasons – there were not enough of us, and
there were too many bridges.'

Archangel market, October 1918.

Billet on the Archangel to Vologda railway.

'A very fine type of Russian. He stood up and answered Rawly's questions whilst looking him straight in the eye . . . He expressed an open dislike of the old type of Russian officer and that was why he was fighting for the Bolsheviks.'

The Slavo-British Legion.

Soldiers of 'Detroit's Own' 339th, Archangel market.

'Commandeering transport from weeping women – a sad but daily duty.'

'Splendid fellows':
Williamson's Don
Cossack escort.

'Often there was no
road at all . . . it was
the biggest place I
had ever seen.'

A forty-foot plywood
'skimmer', as used by
Agar to sink the *Oleg.*

British and Russian troop trains meet, summer 1919.

One of warlord Semyonov's *broneviki*.

A lieutenant of the American Railway Corps, Manchuria: 'What is left of nine so-called Bolsheviks after Semenoff [*sic*] and souvenir-hunters got through with them.'

'A boat was taking me away from my country'

Civilians apply for evacuation passes, Archangel, August 1919.

The Volunteer Army on board the *Emperor of India*, Novorossiysk, 26 March 1920.

15

One last packet

O N 28 JUNE 1919, in Versailles's glittering Hall of Mirrors, the peace treaty with Germany was signed. As the papers were blotted salutes boomed over the great palace's fountains and parterres, and sent pigeons whirring over the roofs of the capital. Crowds filled the hot summer streets, cheering and weeping. The same evening President Wilson left to take passage to New York, and on landing went straight on to Washington, where he presented his League of Nations Covenant to Congress. Looking tired and pale at the rostrum of the Senate chamber he wound himself up to preacher-man pitch. A 'great duty' lay before the country, wrought not by man but 'by the hand of God . . . It was of this that we dreamed at our birth. America shall in truth show the way.' But Wilson was out of touch. Eight months after the war's end, victory euphoria had given way to worka-day worries about unemployment and inflation, and to a rash of race riots. His high-flown call for an American-led new world order, in the words of an Arizona Democrat, went down 'like cold turnips'.[1]

In Britain too the focus had swung to domestic issues. In Cabinet the main subjects of discussion were strikes, food prices, housing and the Irish Republican Army's worsening assassination campaign. There were also new challenges abroad. In Central Europe and the Near East what Churchill called the 'wars of the pygmies' had broken out: Turks against Greeks; Czechs against Hungarians; Italians against Yugoslavs. And after a four-year hiatus, the Empire was bubbling again: in Egypt, a revolution; in India, Gandhi's non-cooperation campaign. Former Baku consul Ranald MacDonell, now in a new job in Whitehall, could sense Russia's slide down the agenda. His inbox was filled with letters from governesses anxious about former charges, invitations to lectures by 'lady enthusiasts with lantern-slides' and draft treaties written by 'university professors, country parsons and retired colonels'.[2]

But much as Lloyd George and most of his ministers would have liked to put Russia aside, its tangled wars were still going strong. Once Kolchak's victories in the Urals started turning into defeats, hopes shifted to the South and Denikin. Well-supplied now by Britain (452 heavy guns, and over ten thousand tons of ammunition), in late May he started pushing out from his Don base in three directions: west along the Black Sea coast, northwest into eastern and central Ukraine, and northeast towards the Volga. The thrust into Ukraine was led by General Vladimir Mai-Mayevsky, one of the abler White generals despite alcoholism and obesity. (He looked like a circus ringmaster, thought the Brits, or a red-nosed provincial comedian.) He took Kharkov, headquarters of the Ukrainian Red Army, on 25 June, and five days later Yekaterinoslav (Dnipro), a trading hub south of Kiev on the Dnieper.

Though British forces in the South were supposed only to be training and supplying, many did much more. The northeastern push towards the Volga was led by Baron Pyotr Vrangel, a ruthless but efficient cavalryman as tall and gaunt as Mai-Mayevsky was short and round. As well as British arms and equipment, he had at his disposal 47 Squadron of the Royal Air Force, comprising two flights of de Havilland bombers and Sopwith Camel fighters, sixty-seven pilots and 273 crew. Led by the Canadian air ace Raymond Collishaw, it had its own four trains, each including workshops, sickbay, kitchens and bakery as well as flatbeds for the 'planes. Thus self-sufficient, they were able to operate far up the line, pulling into sidings and marking out landing-strips as needed. A visitor to one found its mess bar equipped with a piano, cut-out pictures of women 'in advanced stages of déshabillé', and a 'small shrub in a pot'. Sitting round a table were

> five extremely pretty Russian girls, all very young . . . One was playing a guitar, while another accompanied her . . . 'Of course, they are all married', one of the senior officers informed me gravely. 'Or are soon going to be, at any rate.'[3]

Vrangel's destination, 230 miles away, was Tsaritsyn (the Second World War's Stalingrad and today's Volgograd). A straggling way-station for the Volga timber trade, it had become one of the war's trophy towns, besieged on and off by the Don Cossacks, and its defence led, for part of the previous year, by the uncouth but ambitious young Georgian Iosif Stalin. Having advanced towards it in careful stages, Vrangel began his assault in mid-June, and 47 Squadron came up in time to join in the attack's final week. From 23 June the squadron flew raids daily, and a lucky hit knocked out most of the town soviet. (A day earlier and it might have got Trotsky, on one of his lightning visits to the front.)

On the day that Tsaritsyn fell, 30 June, the squadron had a close shave. Two de Havillands were out reconnoitering enemy cavalry and barges. Flying low, one was hit by machine-gun fire from the ground, and started leaking fuel. Its observer, Lieutenant John Mitchell (in civilian life a Durham police constable), climbed out onto a lower wing and plugged the bullet-holes with his hands. But as his pilot turned for home the second de Havilland was hit too, and crash-landed. Mitchell's 'plane landed beside it, and while the pilot of the crashed machine set it on fire, Mitchell and the other observer held up approaching Red cavalry with Lewis guns. As the flames began to lick Mitchell dashed back to his post on the surviving plane's wing, and the other two climbed into the rear cockpit. Overloaded, it lumbered off the ground just ahead of the horsemen, galloping in pursuit. During the hour-long flight back to base Mitchell stayed in position with his hands pressed to the fuel tank, and was badly burned by the de Havilland's exhaust. 'Had the incident occurred on the Western Front instead of in such an obscure backwater as South Russia', wrote Collishaw, 'I am sure it would have resulted in a pair of VCs.'[4]

47 Squadron helped Vrangel hold Tsaritsyn for the next six months, strafing enemy troop concentrations and bombing trains, depots and a Red river flotilla. Since the enemy lacked 'planes and air defences it was relatively straightforward work, and no lives were lost until 28 August, when an observer was killed by rifle-fire from the ground during an attack on an observation balloon. The riverboats, Collishaw wrote to a friend, were particularly easy targets, since their anti-aircraft guns had a range of only about two hundred feet. 'We go above at 2,500 feet and laugh at them.' His pilots were 'full out lads'

who 'enjoyed the show', and compared to France, Russia was a 'splendid holiday'.[5] The low casualty rate made it easy to keep the squadron's real activities from the British public. Ministers dodged questions in parliament with the assurance that it had orders not to join in combat, and it was renamed and officially merged with a flying school. 'None of this', Collishaw recalled, 'made the slightest difference to any of us nor to the squadron's operations.'[6] How useful were they? In Collishaw's account they terrified and demoralised, and staved off defeat during a three-day crisis in early September, when the Red Army pushed within shelling distance of Tsaritsyn's suburbs. Military historians broadly agree, but veterans were less sure. 'We had no detailed briefings', one told an interviewer, 'but we were told that there were Bolshevik risings in various parts, and flew low over these villages firing guns and what have you.' With what results? 'One could never tell.'[7]

Similarly light-hearted was British and French naval support for Denikin's push west along the Black Sea coast, to retake Odessa and Crimea. Inland, natural selection was thinning out the warlords. Hryhoryev was killed by the anarchist Nestor Makhno, and Odessa's legendary gangster Mishka Yaponchik ('Micky the Little Jap') by Petlyura. But along most of the coast local ceasefires held, so that like their Crimean War predecessors, officers were able to land for picnics and dove-shooting, and even pay social calls on the enemy. At the seaside resort of Feodosiya, Commander Lennon Goldsmith of the destroyer *Montrose* went ashore in a tender, flying a bedsheet as a flag of truce, and had drinks with the local Red commander and his ADC, both of whom turned out to have been regulars in the tsarist army. They would swop sides in a moment, he thought, were they not 'tied hand and foot by Soviets composed of madmen, Jews, murderers and dreamers. The trouble is of course that their families would disappear the moment they crossed into the other camp.' In Odessa – draped with puzzling Futurist posters and under the sway of a vicious local Cheka – he was able to anchor undisturbed a stone's throw from the breakwater. As he wrote to his father, it was 'a funny war'.[8]

In mid-June, helped by Allied naval bombardments and seaplanes, Denikin took the Kerch peninsula and control of the narrow strait into the semi-enclosed Azov Sea. Fearing entrapment, Red forces then withdrew from Crimea, and Denikin was able to reoccupy the peninsula more or less unopposed at the end of June – the same time that Vrangel captured Tsaritsyn. For the rest of the summer British ships cruised up and down the gorgeous Crimean coastline, engaged in what sounds less like war than an extended vacation. The scenery, Goldsmith wrote, was

> a mixture of Lucerne and Sicily . . . one of the most lovely combin-
> ations of mountain, forest, valley and cape you can imagine . . . We
> bathe all day, and ashore no-one wears any clothes at all . . . Even the
> ladies splash about, or lie like lizards on the beach, quite naked . . .
> *Montrose* is open to the public from 4 p.m. to sunset and the popula-
> tion streams on board. The men never had such a time in their lives,
> and live a sort of Arcadian existence, which appears to flow very
> happily without the aid of any words.[9]

A photograph from the more innocent HMS *Ceres* shows girls in straw hats and broiderie anglaise dresses posed around the ship's wheel with three gangly midshipmen, labelled 'The Hon Eric Spanners', 'Sir Tulip Rotagivan' and 'Dr Chattercheese'. In another snap the ship's monkey ('Monk') and dog ('Whiskers') chase each other round the deck. The dreadnought *Ajax* turned into a positive zoo, with a tortoise, goat, dog ('Chunky') and bear-cub ('Trotsky') aboard. A seventeen-year-old 'snotty's' Sunday letters home strike a sad note only once, when Chunky's puppy falls overboard.

In tune with the make-believe atmosphere was a visit to Sebastopol by the Mediterranean Fleet's new commander-in-chief, the mustard-keen Interventionist Admiral John de Robeck. Arriving at the battered naval base, he was impressed by the Whites' efforts at smart turnout – much better than the French, he thought, despite lack of paint. The senior Russian admirals, he reported to London, were querulous and inert, but the junior ones seemed keen, and to under-stand the need for 'quite a new relationship between their officers and their men . . . a point that I took the liberty of impressing on them more than once.' All that de Robeck offered them by way of practical help, however, were cloth anchor-badges and good-conduct stripes, for sailors to 'sew onto whatever clothes they were wearing until they had proper supplies of uniform.' What the Russians thought of the lecture plus badges can only be imagined, but de Robeck was bullish:

> I feel sure that the conversations with these officers have done good, and that the sight of a ship like the *Iron Duke* in their inner habour, as well as the behaviour and appearance of our's ship's company in the town, had a wholesome effect.[10]

★

In the first flush of euphoria after his midsummer victories, Denikin issued what became a notorious general order, known as the 'Moscow Directive'. It laid out a hugely ambitious strategy: his armies would simultaneously advance 750, 400 and 300 miles along three separate routes towards the capital, and take it by the end of the year. 'To Moscow!' became the White South's slogan, repeated on posters and banners, and to the chink of glasses wherever refugees gathered. Criticised by Vrangel at the time and by military historians since, Denikin's reasoning was that he needed to keep up momentum. With the Red Army growing and improving time was not on his side, and only by taking new territory could he acquire new manpower, and the loot that substituted for soldiers' wages. His critics, he complained in his memoirs, were thinking in Great War terms. The conventional approach – advancing slowly and method-ically, consolidating each step behind trenches and blockhouses – was not an option.

Mistaken though it ultimately proved, to begin with his 'To Moscow!' gamble appeared to pay off. In Ukraine, the string of vic-tories resumed. Poltava – site of Peter the Great's historic victory over Sweden's Charles XII in 1709 – was captured on 29 July, Kherson on 18 August and Odessa on 24 August, with the help of HMS *Caradoc*. Kiev was taken on 31 August, while to the northeast the Don Cossacks made a deep raid into Russia proper, capturing the town of Tambov. By September Denikin held a vast expanse of territory: the north Caucasus; the Kuban and southern steppe as far as the Volga; Crimea and the Black Sea coast; Kiev and the rest of present-day eastern and central Ukraine. Encompassing a population of about 35 million, it included the old empire's third and fourth biggest cities, and in square mileage matched France and Britain combined.

With the Whites looking to be on their way to victory, the British government started thinking about its exit strategy. Cabinet exhaustively discussed Russia three times, the chief points at issue how much longer to supply Denikin, and when to pull troops out of newly independent Georgia and Azerbaijan. (Where they had been having a good deal of fun. A typical Baku 'guest night', an officer remembered, consisted of racing commandeered droshkys in the street, followed by the casino, followed by a club where the orchestra would be forced to play 'God Save the Tsar' instead of 'the invariable "Gypsy Princess"'. "We'll be shot if we do" they pleaded. "You'll probably be shot if you don't" we replied . . . What it cost us in Tiflis wine was nobody's business.'[11] Soldiers used 'Yellow-blue vase' for *Ya lyublyu vas* – 'I love you' – and in anecdote at least turned down a caviar ration, complaining that the blackberry jam tasted salty.)

On the Caucasian republics there was a bad-tempered split between acting foreign secretary Curzon, who saw them as vital buffer-states for the Raj, and the Chief of Imperial General Staff, Field Marshal Sir Henry Wilson, a right-winger with a family estate in Longford who wanted the troops for Ireland. (Wilson's views on the Caucasians were taken from his regional envoy, General George Milne, who had made a tour in January and not taken to them. The Georgians, he had privately written, were 'disguised Bolsheviks', the Azeris 'uncivilised' and the Armenians 'what they have always been, a despicable race.' Withdrawal would probably lead to anarchy, but the world would not lose much if they all 'cut each other's throats'.[12])

Wilson won the argument, and British personnel withdrew from Tiflis (today's Tblisi, capital of Georgia) and Baku through the summer. Their feelings ranged from shame to 'good riddance', underlaid by apprehension that the betrayed Whites might turn hostile. Interviewed in old age, a former seaplane pilot, Christopher Bilney, caught the mood. Nineteen years old at the time, he spent the first half of 1919 at Petrovsk (Makhachkala), a small port 175 miles north of Baku. It was not much fun, the town run-down and depressing, and so lawless that despite the presence of a double company of Gurkhas and Punjabis the British could only go out in the evenings armed and in pairs, 'and even then they used to take pot shots at us round street corners.' Whether the Russian troops in the area were part of an army or irregulars was never clear; they were 'just a half-starved, utterly ignorant, dirty rabble' and horrible to prisoners:

> They used to dig a hole and bury them up to their necks, and lop off one ear one morning and one the next, and all that sort of thing. We came across some of these cruelties right under our noses, in the harbour.

Also depressing was constant sabotage of the cargo boats he and his colleagues had converted into seaplane carriers. Left unsupervised, their Russian crews would deliberately cause collisions, or pump all a boat's fuel into a side-tank, so that it listed. Bilney and his fellow-pilots were hardly committed to the cause either:

> If it was a question of coming in low . . . and getting shot up for your pains, we stayed out of trouble. It didn't worry us very much whether we hit the target or not. It wasn't our war after all.

When notice came of withdrawal Bilney was put in charge of flying the seaplanes to a Cossack fishing village with an airfield, where they were to be handed over to the Whites. The team arrived to discover it deserted, all but one of the Russian pilots having flown for 'Bolshy-land'. Bilney and the pilot who had stayed behind, a Captain Igurov, had no language in common, but managed to communicate via an elderly, French-speaking refugee. Together the three re-labelled the seaplanes' instruments, and after a couple of training flights Igurov set off on a bombing raid over Bolshevik-held Astrakhan. Bilney was sad but not surprised when he was killed in a mid-air explosion.

> Afterwards we learned that the observer was carrying the bombs on his lap, pulling out the safety pins with his teeth and throwing them over the side. It didn't work very well . . . Poor chap, I was very sorry.

A farewell banquet with 'local potentates' in the village hall was the usual alcoholic assault course:

I made a jolly long speech while I still could, telling them what jolly good chaps they were . . . When the party broke up at 2 a.m. the four Englishmen were all still on their feet. Such Russians who hadn't gone off with the waitresses were under the table, so we thought we'd kept the Union Jack flying fairly well.

Anecdotes aside, his verdict on his time in Russia was thoroughly negative. The Intervention was

a political nonsense. Waste of time, money, and everything else. I suppose it kept a few of us from cluttering up the unemployment bureaux at home, but that's about all . . . It was an uncomfortable business really. A really nasty, dirty little war.[13]

While withdrawal from the Caucasus proceeded, the Cabinet also came to a decision on Denikin. The issues were problematically related, since Denikin regarded the Caucasian republics as part of Russia One and Indivisible. Relations between his government and the Georgians in particular were stormy ('War was declared at 9 a.m., and cancelled at 11.30', wrote an aide of one shouting-match), and the British mission had to broker a series of truces, eventually drawing a line on the map which Denikin's troops were not supposed to cross. The rows added to London's impatience. Armed with a report by Curzon putting the total cost of the Intervention to date at £94 million, Lloyd George argued that though Denikin should be 'given his chance' he could not be supported indefinitely, and that if he had the Russian public behind him as he claimed he would win anyway. Churchill huffed and puffed, but on 12 August it was formally decided to give Denikin 'one last packet' of military aid, and after that, no more.

16

Honorary Cossacks

MILITARY AND FINANCIAL questions drowned out a more fundamental one: could Denikin actually rule? That he neither could nor deserved to is proved by the great stain on the White movement and the Intervention in general – the Whites' 1919 massacres of Jews, and Britain's connivance in them.

In Russia as throughout Europe, antisemitism has a long history, dating back at least to medieval times. But whereas, by the start of the twentieth century, the rest of the continent had long torn down its ghettos, in Russia a whole panoply of anti-Jewish laws was still in place. Jews could not take any kind of government job, nor own land, nor live outside the 'Pale of Settlement' – roughly, today's Lithuania, Belarus, eastern and central Poland, Moldova and most of Ukraine. A quota system meant that few could go to university. The rules were not always enforced: there were local anomalies, and the richest floated above them, building magnificent mansions in Moscow and Petersburg. But they still had enough bite to ensure a steady income in bribes for officialdom, and to constrict Jews to a set menu of professions. Within the Pale, according to censuses, over 70 per cent of barbers, barrel-makers, glaziers, coachmen, tailors, dentists and doctors were Jewish, but very few railway workers or farmers.

Less explicit but deadlier was the tsarist habit of scapegoating Jews at times of crisis. When Alexander II was assassinated by a (multi-ethnic) anarchist group in 1881, gangs of thugs were allowed to run riot in Jewish neighbourhoods. The same happened during the mass pro-democracy demonstrations of 1905, the violence deadlier this time and whipped up by a state-sponsored religio-nationalist movement called 'the Black Hundreds'. When war with Germany broke out in 1914 there were hopes worldwide that high rates of Jewish volunteering might nudge the regime towards emancipation. In fact the reverse happened: again, Jews were scapegoated, this time as German spies and sympathisers. Russian newspapers ran outlandish scare stories (Jews were using prostitutes to spread venereal disease), and almost incredibly, official lists of the fallen only gave Jewish soldiers' initials, so as to disguise the fact that young men called Abram, Chaim or David were dying for their country. When the Germans broke through the Carpathians in spring 1915 the Imperial Army started randomly hanging and taking hostage Jews living in the conflict zone, then expelled them en masse. Together with Roma, Muslim Tatars and ethnic Germans (descendants of settlers invited to Russia by Catherine the Great), about a quarter of a million people were made homeless and forced to moved east.

The abuses caused a storm in America, but not in Britain, where the government did not want to annoy Petrograd, and establishment 'West End' Jewry itself felt vulnerable to accusations that it was pro-German. Twice, the British emancipation campaigner Lucien Wolf passed detailed dossiers on what we would now call human rights violations to the Foreign Office, and twice they were handed back to him with the comment that 'a very large number' of Russian Jews were war-profiteering, or in German pay. Revealing is a note from foreign minister Robert Cecil to the British ambassador in Petrograd, asking for help in answering parliamentary questions. Pogrom reports, Cecil opined, were

> doubtless untrue or very greatly exaggerated, and if we could be assured that such occurrences as have taken place were due to some local or temporary cause, which is not likely to recur, that would probably very largely meet the case.[1]

Like Balfour's November 1917 declaration of support for a Jewish homeland in Palestine, a speech by Lloyd George promising 'one emancipated land from the Urals to the Atlantic' was aimed at the Jewish-American audience, and when Wolf asked for specifics he got no reply.

With the Russian Revolution and the start of the Civil War a new canard was born: Jew equals Bolshevik. For the Whites it filled the gap where a political programme should have been. The Allies were able to pressure Kolchak, as 'Supreme Ruler', into transparently insincere promises of elections and civil rights (drafted, fingers crossed behind his back, by General Knox). But Denikin continued to insist that he was a mere simple soldier, and that political decisions should await victory. In place of clear commitments on vital topics such as land reform, therefore, the White government in the South had only the slogan 'Save Mother Russia' – which since Mother Russia meant the White armies, translated simply as 'support us'. In this ideas vacuum the trope that the Jews made the Revolution met a need. It explained tsarism's bewildering collapse in one easy phrase, and excused adherents from confronting the real reasons for the old system's unpopularity. (In his memoirs, the best that Denikin could come up with was that the nation had been 'struck by madness'.[2]) An obvious, observable truth – that though many leading Bolsheviks were indeed Jews, not all Jews were Bolsheviks – was bounced aside by a culture-tapping, blame-shifting conspiracy theory.

Antisemitism was fanned by White propaganda. The first director of Denikin's propaganda unit, a figure from the moderate centre-right, employed Jewish writers and designers, and recommended that Denikin make public declarations in favour of representative government, autonomy for the non-Russian nationalities, and labour and land reform. Six weeks into his job he was dismissed and replaced by a notorious antisemite, who sacked all Jewish staff and started producing unabashed hate speech. 'As soon as the Volunteer Army entered a city', wrote the Red Cross organiser and later pogrom historian Elias Heifetz,

> one could find everywhere on the walls, next to the official communications, proclamations against the Jews, which were almost all alike in form and content – 'Underlings of the Red Guard!', 'To All!' – and called on the people to make pogroms.[3]

White publications always referred to the Jewish-heritage Bolshevik leaders by their birth-names – Bronstein-Trotsky, Rosenfeld-Kamenev and so on – and posters showed them with caricatured Jewish features. In one a giant, naked Trotsky, a Star of David around his neck, climbs gorilla-like over the Kremlin battlements. In another he flourishes a butcher's knife over a bound woman wearing a traditional Russian head-dress, in front of an altar to the Communist International. Thousands of new copies of the *Protocols of the Elders of Zion* – a turn-of-the-century fake purporting to show that Jews were plotting to take over the world – were printed, and widely distributed within the army. With every repetition the assertion that Jews were the real enemy became more embedded, less interrogated; turning, for those who needed to believe it, into a self-evident truth.

Of the scope and detail of the 1919 pogroms themselves we know an unusual amount, thanks to the systematic data-gathering undertaken by Jewish organisations working on the ground at the time. Two men in particular – the activist and aid organiser Nahum Gergel and the journalist and philologist Nokhem Shtif – were instrumental, founding a Kiev-based 'Editorial Committee to Collect and Publish Material about the Pogroms in Ukraine'. With agents throughout the region, it photographed, took statements from survivors and witnesses, distributed questionnaires, collected press clippings and official notices, and exhumed, counted and when possible identified bodies. The materials were smuggled out of the country in 1921, and written up in Berlin and New York.

The story they tell is horrible. The 1881 and 1905 pogroms involved more beating and looting than outright killing. The 1919 ones were on a different scale, not seen since the Cossack rebellions of the seventeenth century. Patterns of violence varied. In some places attacks were initiated by soldiers, and townspeople and peasants from nearby villages joined in; in others it was the other way around. Sometimes Christian households sheltered or tried to intercede on behalf of their Jewish neighbours; sometimes they turned on them, having been friends for years. 'Quiet' pogroms – raids, kidnappings, beatings – alternated with wholesale massacres, when every person in every house was dragged out onto the street and killed. Today's leading historian of the subject can confidently name about twenty thousand individuals killed in 770 incidents, but estimates the total death toll at up to ten times larger.[4]

Not only the Whites were responsible; the attacks came from all sides. As already mentioned, the first army to commit large-scale violence was the Polish one, in Lviv in December 1918. Petlyura's troops gave the lie to the Ukrainian People's Republic's claim to ethnic inclusivity by doing the same: at Ovruch in January 1919; in Kiev in early February as it fell to the Red Army; and worst of all in Proskuriv (Khmelnytsky), on 14–16 February, after a failed Bolshevik rising. (Here an estimated seventeen hundred were killed.) In March Petlyura passed through Zhytomyr the morning after a massacre, pausing to congratulate his men on their victory over 'Muscovite robbers and Jews'. The killing recommenced as soon as he left. Next up was the warlord Hryhoryev, whose men went on the rampage in the Odessa region after the French abandoned the city in April, killing over 3,400 people, in fifty-two attacks, over eighteen days. The grim list went on through May: the warlord Makhno at Yekaterinoslav; another lesser warlord at Uman; the Red Army at Odessa, Lubny and Cherkassy; Petlyura again at Rovno (Rivnye).[5]

When Denikin began advancing through Ukraine in June, Jews hoped for a return to normality. That he had Allied backing was reassuring, as was the fact that in its early days, during the winter of 1917/18, the Volunteer Army had included Jewish officers and been supported by Jewish-owned businesses. When it first entered Ukrainian towns, therefore, it was welcomed, and fighting-age men hurried to sign up. Their hopes were quickly dashed, Denikin's Cossack units in particular taking up the violence where the Poles, Ukrainians and Bolsheviks had left off. 'No other group before the Volunteers', wrote Shtif, operated so 'systematically and thoroughly'.[6] One form the violence took was mass executions, officially of 'Bolsheviks' but in fact largely of Jews. There were mass hangings in Kharkov after its capture in mid-June, and over the next three weeks sixty-five people were killed at Balashov (near Tambov, in Russia), 130 at Kremenchuk, 129 at Cherkassy and twenty at Smyela, all Ukrainian towns on or near the Dnieper. According to the *Express*'s (approving) Hodgson, Vrangel 'tried, sentenced and executed' a 'Red commissar' in 'ten minutes' on capturing Tsaritsyn, and 'next morning, no less than six other bodies were wafting in the breeze.' He was told that they were Jews who had been offering big bribes to railway officials for the use of trucks in which they could get their goods away . . . At the time every wheel was needed for the transport of the Army and its food, so Vrangel strung up the whole gang, plus the station master.[7]

Typical of the pogroms proper was what happened at Rossava, a *shtetl* town in between Cherkassy and Smyela. Like the whole region, it had already changed hands several times – from the Germans to Petlyura to the Reds and back to Petlyura – when a Denikin regiment, General Shkuro's notorious 'Wolves', arrived at the railway station on 13 August. A standard sequence of events – in pogrom historian Irina Astashkevich's term, 'the traditional script'– followed.[8] First the town elders came to the station and presented the regiment's commander with supplicatory gifts of money, bread and salt. Then the soldiers divided into groups and systematically looted the Jewish quarter, emptying shops and going from home to home demanding money and jewellery. The bulkier loot was piled into carts and taken back to the train. In the evening some local Christians joined in the robbery, following in the Cossacks' footsteps. The next day the 'carnival of violence' began, with the streets turned into 'public performance areas' where Jews were humiliated, tortured and killed. An elderly couple were stripped naked and chased through the town by whooping soldiers; parents were killed in front of their children and vice versa. On the third day Jews who had hidden in nearby woods and along a riverbank were hunted down and shot or bayoneted. Nobody was allowed to help the injured or collect the dead, so they lay where they were, 'preserving the macabre scene for greater effect.'

What Astashkevich describes as the pogrom's 'focal point' were gang rapes. They began on the first evening and carried on throughout, becoming more ritualised and public as the violence progressed. On day three Shkuro's officers summoned all the town's inhabitants to its central square, where a family called Kozlov was picked out. Soldiers shot the father on the spot and 'picked up' the mother 'by sabres', after which their daughter, Roza, was dragged inside a shed, raped, then thrown out into the crowd again. Other victims included a seventy-year-old woman, a mother who had just given birth, and a twelve-year-old girl, the daughter of the local distiller. (Here as else-where, women's noses, breasts or arms were sometimes lopped off after rape, which could mean that they bled to death.) On the same day peasants started coming with carts from nearby villages and loot-ing Jewish houses of their furniture. On the fourth day the Wolves retired to their train, but continued to raid the town until 27 August, when the surviving thousand or so inhabitants fled on foot to another *shtetl* nearby.

The largest of the White pogroms was committed the following month at Fastov (Fastiv), a medium-sized market town not far from Kiev. It had a Jewish population of about seven thousand, or 40 per cent of the total, with six synagogues and two Jewish schools. It also hosted between three thousand and five thousand mostly Jewish refu-gees from the warlord-scourged villages round about. Like Rossava it had already suffered months of on-off violence when on 6 September a Volunteer Army train rolled in, carrying Denikin's Second Terek Cossack Brigade. As in Rossava, the arrival of regular, uniformed troops was initially greeted with relief. 'So many children, women and old folk came out onto the street', wrote a witness, 'what joy on their faces. Everybody thought their saviours had arrived.' There was genu-ine surprise when at ten that evening a commotion broke out; the Cossacks had started plundering Jewish homes. For the next several days Jewish families hid each night outdoors or in cellars or attics, and watched during the quieter daytimes as their possessions – sewing-machines, mirrors, pictures – were auctioned off in the street. Officers as well as soldiers participated, and the Brigade's colonel summoned the town's rabbi and demanded a large 'contribution' in gold coins.

For a fortnight the violence continued at a relatively low level, until on 21 September the Cossack Brigade abruptly left and another train carrying 700 Red Army troops arrived. For twenty-four hours the Reds desultorily patrolled the main streets, until on the afternoon of the 22nd artillery boomed, and Denikin's army was back. This time there was no restraint. 'Groups of Cossacks openly went around the town', wrote a journalist who interviewed witnesses soon after-wards, 'stopping Jews on the street. Sometimes they would simply ask "Are you a Jew?" and shoot them in the forehead. But much more often they would first search them, even strip them naked, and then shoot them.' Over two hundred women and girls were violated: 'In the presence of mothers, fathers and dozens of strangers the victim was pushed to the ground and raped, even right on the street, by 15 to 20 men each . . . The cries went on for hours.'

In the evening the soldiers started setting fire to Jewish shops and homes, using gunpowder and kerosene, so that by dawn all the buildings around the market square and most of those along the main streets were smouldering wrecks. In some instances residents were forced to fire their homes themselves, then driven inside them. (One burned-out house held twelve corpses.) On the pogrom's third day the local priest appealed to the brigade commander to stop. The commander's response was to order survivors to the synagogue, strip them of all but their underclothes and demand a final ransom. Incomers found about a hundred dead bodies lying in the town's two main squares, and pigs and dogs gnawing on more in a ravine behind a prayer house. The total number of dead was put at about eighteen hundred, with another thousand dying of injuries, exposure, hunger and typhus over the next few weeks. Include the injured who were evacuated to Kiev by Jewish aid organisations and died there, and the Fastov death toll rises to perhaps eight thousand.[9]

The Russian-American anarchist Emma Goldman – already utterly disillusioned by the Revolution and thus no Soviet propagandist – saw the aftermath the following summer, as a member of a fraternal delegation that toured the area after its recapture by the Red Army. The once-prosperous town was two-thirds empty, with only a few small food stalls operating in the ruined market square:

There were more women about than men, and I was struck by the strange expression in their eyes. They did not look you full in the face; they stared past you with a dumb, hunted, animal expression. We told the women that we had heard many terrible pogroms had taken place in Fastov, and we wished to get data on the subject to be sent to America to enlighten the people there on the condition of the Ukrainian Jews. As news of our presence spread many women and children surrounded us, all much excited and each trying to tell her story . . . The greater part of the city had been destroyed or burned; many of the older Jews were trapped in the synagogue and there murdered, while others had been driven to the public square where they were slaughtered. Not a woman, young or old, that had not been outraged, most of them in the very sight of their father, husband or brothers. The young girls, some of them mere children, had suffered repeated violation at the hands of the Denikin soldiers. I understood the dreadful look in the eyes of the women of Fastov.[10]

In the evening a procession of people came to the delegation's railway carriage, with letters for relatives in America. 'Some of the messages bore no addresses, the simple folk thinking the name sufficient . . . It was touching to see [their] deep faith that their relatives . . . would save them.'

Travelling on, the delegations's train was stormed at every stop:

Everywhere masses of desperate people, shouting and struggling to gain a foothold . . . Now and then an agonized cry would ring through the night and the already moving train would come to a halt: someone had been thrown to his death under the wheels.[11]

On arrival in Kiev Goldman interviewed the director of the Jewish hospital, one of the best in the country and the community's pride. Each time the city changed hands, patients had been forced out of their beds to make room for 'the favourites of this or that regime':

The officers of the Denikin army were most brutal. They drove the Jewish patients out into the street, subjected them to indignities and abuse, and would have killed them had it not been for the intercession of the hospital staff . . . It was only the fact that the majority of staff were Gentiles that saved the hospital and its inmates. But the shock resulted in numerous deaths and many patients were left with shattered nerves.

The doctor also related to me the stories of some of the patients, most of them victims of the Fastov pogroms. Among them were children between the ages of six and eight, gaunt and sickly looking, terror stamped on their faces. They had lost all their kin, in some cases the whole family having been killed before their eyes . . . The doctor pointed out a group of young girls aged between fourteen and eighteen, the worst victims of the Denikin pogrom. All of them had been repeatedly outraged and were in a mutilated state when they came to the hospital; it would take years to restore them to health.[12]

Which of the warring groups killed most is not clear, and the subject of defensive blame-shifting by the nations involved. The most recent scholarship puts the total direct and indirect death toll at somewhere between 100,000 and 200,000, with Petlyura's and Hryhoryev's armies the worst. During their period of ascendancy, from July to December 1919, the White armies directly killed somewhere between 8,000 and 16,000 people, in 213 documented incidents, and many more died in their aftermath.[13] What witnesses stressed about Denikin's pogroms was how methodical they were. This was partly because the Volunteer Army, based as it was on old tsarist units, was more disciplined than the Ukrainian National Army or the Red Army, but also because killing and humiliating Jews, in the White mind, had become the same thing as fighting the enemy. Nor was White violence against Jews only a product of frustrated, chaotic defeat. Though Denikin's defence, at the time and in his memoirs, was that regrettably his soldiers sometimes got out of control, in fact violence against Jews increased, in Heifetz's words, 'as the power of the [White] government grew firmer. The victorious regime of Denikin advanced over the dead bodies of the Jews.'[14] It is this, as well as the similarity of White and Nazi propaganda and the awful size of the overall death toll, that prompts historians to regard the pogroms of 1919 and 1920 as a rehearsal for the Holocaust.

How, embarking on this rape and killing spree, did the Whites present it to the Allies? Shtif gave a bitter answer: 'One method could always be counted on: convince the "friends" that all Jews were Bolsheviks . . . The "friends" believed them, or pretended to.'[15]

The French having departed Ukraine, and the Americans not having got involved there in the first place, the 'friends' meant the British. Judging by Interventionists' letters and diaries, not much pretending was needed. Though often startled at the virulence of Russian antisemitism, they were also routinely antisemitic themselves. Major Hudleston Williamson, whose letters to his mother display commendable concern for refugees and ill-treated Russian soldiers, also explained to her that the Revolution was the work of 'omnipotent international Jews who depend on war and discord to provide a fruitful field for their financial enterprises.' In England, everyone needed to '*work work work*' to make the public realise what Bolshevism meant. Churchill understood, and wanted 'to do the thing properly', but opposition was '*very strong*' and 'of course being backed by the brains and money of the Jews.'[16] When Captain Goldsmith sailed into the pretty little Crimean port of Alushta, he was greeted by three separate deputations – Russian, Jewish and Crimean Tatar – all inviting him to services of thanksgiving. 'It was a pleasure to meet the honest Russians and Tatars', he wrote to his father, 'but I confess my gorge rose at the Jews. A Russian Jew is quite the most loathsome type of humanity as a rule, and they are the curse of Russia at this moment.'[17] Elsewhere he wrote of how Russians – 'hard-bitten, blue-eyed, open-faced horsemen', child-like in their 'animal plunges into vice' – were being bamboozled and preyed upon by 'cunning little rats . . . Jews mostly'.[18] Despite – or perhaps because of – his surname, Goldsmith was unusually antisemitic. But many others expressed disgust at Jewish traders and money-lenders – always 'waxing fat' on the war – and took violence against Jews for granted. The first thing a Captain Evelyn Barker wrote in his scrapbook on landing at Odessa was: 'Heard that four Jews had been hung . . . for preaching against mobilisation.' Next to the entry he stuck in the programme for a 'Great Spectacle-Gala in Honour of England' at the opera house, but made no further comment on the hangings.[19]

Though they noticed the 'awful lot' of Jews in places like Odessa, the British managed not to notice that their White allies were murder-ing them. Official communications from the field are discreet to the point of silence. For example, the sole reference to White violence against civilians in the 1919 Navy Record (a compendium of com-munications between senior naval personnel in the Black Sea) is a 29 June telegram to the Admiralty from de Robeck's predecessor as C-in-C, Admiral Somerset Gough-Calthorpe. He explains that he does not want to send a ship to Sebastopol because if, 'as has already happened elsewhere', the incoming Volunteer Army undertakes 'reprisals against suspects and others of the population' his position will be 'extremely difficult'.[20] Private papers keep equally mum. Amongst dozens, the only time the word 'pogrom' crops up is in a jokey anecdote. Two officers were riding home from a snipe-shooting expedition when gunfire sounded in a village ahead. 'We assumed', wrote one, that

> it was either a local Red rising or a pogrom, but we soon met a peasant who said it was only in honour of tomorrow's *praznik* or holiday for the Blessing of the Waters. This we decided was far more dangerous than any number of Reds, so we turned back.[21]

Typical comments on Shkuro, one of the bloodiest White generals, are that he is a 'scallywag' or 'a bit of a brigand'.

It is true that the worst violence happened off-stage, in small towns away from the bases where British personnel spent most of their time. But this was not always so, and there was more than enough opportunity to find out what was happening from Jewish relief organisations, or from survivors who had fled to the cities. Typical of the way the British preferred to turn a blind eye was embedded journalist Hodgson, who tied himself in knots criticising the Volunteer Army's obsessive antisemitism ('a fierce and unreasoning hatred'), while simultaneously denying that it had committed any pogroms. He dismissed a Jewish committee's protest to British command at Constantinople as an 'effusion', and on a tour of newly captured towns claimed not to have found 'a sign or whisper of outrage'. On the contrary, he possessed 'the strongest evidence' that Denikin's orders against pogroms were being 'conscientiously observed', and 'every effort' being made, 'with great success, to prevent unnecessary bloodshed.' As for past pogroms, they were 'grossly exaggerated', and had mostly been 'fanned into existence by the nervous panicking of the Jews themselves.'[22]

Equally dishonest was the Military Mission itself. Its head, General Holman, was notoriously antisemitic even by the standards of the time – according to an expatriate clergyman, 'obsessed by the idea of wiping out the Jews everywhere, and can talk of little else.'[23] Holman's predecessor told Reuters, in an interview in July, that reports of 'various forms of outrage' were 'utterly false' and 'prompted by German and Bolshevist propaganda', and repeated the assertion at a meeting with MPs a fortnight later (with Churchill present).[24] The generals' prejudices were shared by political officer Keyes, who waved away an Anglo-Jewish complainant with the observation that Jews had brought violence on themselves by not denouncing the Bolsheviks sufficiently loudly, and later regaled officer cadets with the hoary, gory propaganda story of Rosa the beautiful Jewish torturess.[25] Another antisemite was the Foreign Office's commissioner to Georgia, the scholar and linguist Oliver Wardrop. In a telegram to Curzon he advised that 'nearly all the present misery of the world' was due to 'Jewish intrigues', and that a new governor of Daghestan would have 'no more trouble' if he handed all Jews in the province to the Volunteer Army for 'appropriate treatment'. He rounded off with an Old Testament quote about Jerusalem being 'a torch of fire among sheaves'. This was a bit fervid even for Keyes, who scribbled on his copy that London's reaction would be 'Look to the strapping up of thy portmanteaux, O Wardrop', but added, 'He is quite right about Jerusalem though!' (Today a statue of Wardrop and his sister, also a translator, stands in Tblisi's Wardrop Square.)[26]

The Jew-equals-Bolshevik assumption was almost as embedded in London as in White Russia. Not only the hard-right *Morning Post* but the respectable *Times* regularly characterised the Bolsheviks as 'adventurers of German-Jewish blood', and *The Times*'s veteran Russia correspondent, Robert Wilton, wrote books blaming the Revolution and murder of the Tsar on 'Lenin's pack of Jews' and 'the hate-laden produce of the Pale'.[27] Anglo-Jewish protest was not as loud as it could have been, taking second place, for Zionists, to the push for a homeland in Palestine, and for assimilationists, to a campaign to get Jewish rights enshrined in the new Polish constitution. For both groups, opposition to the Intervention also risked more accusations of pro-Bolshevism, the net result being that the Ukrainian, as opposed to the Polish, pogroms were only covered in detail by the Yiddish-language 'East End' Jewish press. What protests there were, the government brushed off. On 29 May the MP Josiah Wedgwood – one of the anti-Intervention 'Three Musketeers' – listed recent White atrocities during questions to the Minister for

War. Churchill did not address the charges, riposting that thanks to British arms, Denikin was freeing Russia from 'what my hon. and gallant friend Colonel Wedgwood would no doubt call the blessings of Bolshevik rule.'[28] That Churchill was already well aware of the pogroms, and himself equated Jew with Bolshevik, is indicated by a telegram he sent soon afterwards to Britain's military representative in the Baltics. Anti-Bolshevik 'excesses' would 'alienate sympathies British nation and render continuance of support most difficult', and he should therefore 'tactfully but strongly' advise the White leadership against 'Jew pogroms' when Petrograd was liberated, these being likely 'in view of prominent part taken by Jews in Red Terror and regime.'[29] Following the first round of killings at Fastov he sent two telegrams to Denikin asking him to rein in 'excesses', and instructed Holman to reinforce the message, because 'the Jews' were 'very powerful in England' and it would make his own task easier if it could be demonstrated that Denikin was 'protecting them as his army advanced.'[30] On 22 September – the same day that the Fastov pogrom was getting underway – Churchill made a detailed presentation to Cabinet, urging continued military support for Denikin. He made no mention, of course, of massacres or mass rapes, and the only hint that his protégé might not be quite the democrat of War Office press releases was the observation that Denikin needed political guidance, so as not to 'fall into the hands of reactionaries'.[31]

The rest of the Cabinet did not ask questions. When Sir Alfred Mond – a millionaire industrialist and the minister of works – sent Lloyd George a letter detailing Volunteer Army pogroms on 7 October, the prime minister forwarded it to Churchill with a slightly facetious covering note:

I wish you would make some enquiries about this treatment of the Jews by your friends. Now that we are subsidising the Volunteer Army and providing them with weapons we certainly have a right to protest against outrages of this character . . . Apart from the iniquity of the proceedings and one's natural repugnance to be associated with it, it provides material for a most disagreeable debate in the House of Commons.

Churchill replied to Lloyd George three days later, admitting that Denikin's armies had committed some 'particularly fearful massacres', but explaining that they were unavoidable given 'very bitter feeling' against Jews, as 'the main instigators of the ruin of the Empire' and lead players in Bolshevik atrocities. Stopping military aid to Denikin, he argued, would deprive Britain of the leverage to 'exercise a modifying influence', and of the chance to steer 'National Russia', now 'on the eve of its restoration', towards 'mercy and democracy'.[32] Denikin, he assured the prime minister, had given 'solemn assurances' that he was doing everything possible to prevent further violence, and his *bona fides* on the matter were endorsed by General Holman – all of which Lloyd George seems to have taken at face value. (Tellingly, in his memoirs Churchill quotes a third, October, note that he sent Denikin, but does not mention the Mond letter that prompted it.[33])

Applications to the Foreign Office met the same fate. Having earlier kept clear of the Russian quagmire, in September the well-connected Zionist campaigner Chaim Weizmann submitted a detailed pogrom report, and asked permission to lead a Jewish delegation to Denikin. 'I do not at all like the proposal', minuted senior mandarin Sir Eyre Crowe, 'I am most reluctant to take up the question of Jews in Russia.' The application was refused.[34] So was a similar application by Lucien Wolf, who was fobbed off with assurances that Denikin was doing 'all in his power to restrain his troops', and that 'any excesses' were 'expressly against his orders'. Deputy foreign secretary Robert Cecil told a Yiddish-language journalist that pogroms were the 'terrible results of earlier misdoings', there being 'scarcely a revolutionary movement in any part of Europe which has not at the back of it a Jew' – albeit that they had been driven to it by tsarist injustice.[35]

For the British government, in short, Denikin's massacres and mass rapes were a side issue, only of serious concern in so far as they caused political embarrassment. The admonitory telegrams were gestures, not taken seriously and not expected to be. At no stage did the government tell Denikin that unless the pogroms ceased it would withdraw military aid, nor did it even consider doing so. On the contrary, right up to his final defeat new loans and deliveries continued to flow. Hardly present in the debate of the day, or in historians' since, the pogroms answer the question 'Was the Intervention worth it?' at a stroke. The answer is No. Even at the distance of a century, with 1919's killings long overshadowed by the Holocaust, the fact that Britain knowingly funded, supplied, trained and sent men to fight alongside the armies that committed them is shocking and shameful.

17

The stubborn German eagle

BY SPRING 1919 the Allies had forces present in the North, the South, Siberia and the Caspian. The fifth piece of the puzzle – and the only place where the Intervention can be said to have succeeded – was the Baltic. Like Ukraine, the region was in turmoil. During the 1917 revolutions, rival national and Bolshevik governments had declared themselves in Reval (today's Tallinn, capital of Estonia), and Riga (capital of Latvia), before the German army occupied the whole area under the Treaty of Brest-Litovsk. It was still in occupation when the Armistice was declared in November 1918, and fearing Red risings and with no troops of their own to spare, the Allies agreed with Berlin that it would stay on for the time being. The German soldiers themselves, however, wanted only to go home, and kept sullenly to their barracks as local militias skirmished around them. By the end of the year a national Estonian government held Reval, and a Red Latvian one Riga, the Latvian national government having fled to the seaside resort of Libau (Liepāja) on the other side of the Courland peninsula.

Intervention proper opened in early 1919, with the arrival of two new commanders. The first, at the head of an Anglo-French cruiser squadron, was a pepperpot of a British admiral, Walter Cowan. Five foot six and nicknamed 'The Little Man', he loathed women and loved action, carrying a dog-eared copy of one of Nelson's up-and-at-'em battle-orders in his breast pocket. On land he spent all the time he could hunting, and when docked at Copenhagen, it was said, always went to pay his respects to the fox in the city zoo. The second, dourer, figure was General Rüdiger von der Goltz, a bullet-headed Prussian who had helped Finland's new leader, General Carl Mannerheim, put down the Finnish Reds. Like most senior German officers he despised the new German republic, and dreamt of using the Baltic as a base from which to restore the Reich. Regular troops being unenthusiastic, he turned instead to irregulars. His first formation was the Landeswehr, a six-thousand-strong militia raised by the region's German-speaking landowners, the 'Baltic barons', and his second the Freikorps, bands of demobbed soldiers who like him felt that Germany was no longer their country, and for whom fighting had become an end in itself. The first Baltic Freikorps was the Stahlende Division or 'Iron Division' – quickly nicknamed the Stehlende Division, from *stehlen*, 'to steal' – and more formed after the desperate Latvian national government offered volunteers land and citizenship. (German newspapers ran advertisements for farms 'in the beautiful *Baltenland'*.) Most, though, signed up simply for the violence. A rootless seventeen-year-old, the future writer Ernst von Salomon, joined a unit commanded by a 'big dark angular' lieutenant with a tooth that protruded over his lower lip like the tusk of a boar. Brilliantly honest on the experience of battle – hand-to-hand combat takes him outside time and space; gunnery is a form of orgasmic release – Salomon's repeated theme is his and his comrades' nihilism.

> What we wanted we did not know . . . To force a way through the prisoning walls of the world, to march over burning fields, to stamp over ruins and scattered ashes? . . . I do not know, but that was what we did. And the search for reasons why was lost in the tumult of continuous fighting.[1]

When Britain's diplomatic representative to the Baltic governments, a Harrow-and-Oxford civil servant and Irish Guardsman called Stephen Tallents, arrived in May, he found Goltz very much in charge. In Libau he had ousted the leader of the Latvian government, a US-educated former agronomist called Kārlis Ulmanis, and replaced him with his own puppet, a Lutheran pastor. Two Latvian ministers had been arrested and the others were sheltering at the British Legation and on a British-manned steamer in the harbour. Goltz was also on the point of recapturing Riga, and after he did so on 23 May let no Allied representative into the city for two weeks. First to get entry was a French colonel, who confirmed rumours that in revenge for atrocities committed by the Bolsheviks on departure, the Landeswehr was executing dozens daily in the yard of the central prison. With the help of an American who had been granted a pass, Tallents got in a few days later, and went straight to the Ritterhaus – the Baltic barons' old assembly building – for a meeting with Landeswehr commander Major Fletcher (Prussian despite his name). His protest at the executions fell on deaf ears. 'Formal and wooden', Fletcher

> told us that he had 4,000 prisoners to deal with. Of these 200 had already been shot. He was executing a fixed number of 33 men and seven women every morning, and no court on earth could avoid the necessity of several hundred further executions. He described some of the horrible crimes they had committed, and on my referring to the execution of a girl of seventeen, said that the worst crimes had been committed by women. We could get from him . . . nothing but minor concessions, such as that he would personally review the cases of condemned boys and girls in their teens.[2]

Forty miles northeast, the Landeswehr was fighting the Estonian army for the town of Wenden (Cēsis). Tallents's formal order to Fletcher that it should cease – delivered in 'the heaviest military style that I could assume' – was also ignored, as were Berlin's repeated orders to Goltz to round up his Freikorps and return to Germany. It was an extraordinary situation: despite having defeated Germany six months previously, the Allies found themselves powerless against a renegade German army partly of their own making. When Tallents asked London for more security his superiors evidently found the situation incredible too, querying whether 'lethal weapons' were really needed.[3] (The French foreign ministry was even less *au courant*, issuing a mission member with yen in the belief that Latvia was an island off Japan.)

Things started moving the Allies' way on 22 June, when the Landeswehr lost Wenden to an Estonian counter-attack, and news came that the German government was about to sign the Treaty of Versailles. A few days later Tallents attended the formal demolition of a Baltic-German monument – a bronze eagle perched on a granite column – that stood in front of Libau's Kurhaus. The ceremony lasted a while, the column proving to be 'of very solid construction. For two hours sweating men hacked at it, while the populace and we stood by with increasing weariness and impatience.' At last a rope was tied to the eagle's legs, and it crashed to the ground to cat-calls and whistles. 'Then a band played God Save the King four times and the Marseillaise twice' and everyone could go home.[4]

On the night of 2/3 July, the Estonians' continuing advance allowed Tallents to pressure Goltz into signing a truce. The negotiations took place in an empty schoolhouse in a front-line village, in a room lit by candles stuck in bottles. One by one, Tallents called in representatives of all the fighting forces in the area – German, Baltic German, Estonian and White Russian – and at three-thirty in the morning, after hours of side-meetings and re-draftings, an agreement was signed. German troops would withdraw from Riga to Mitau (Jelgava), thirty miles southwest across the Daugava river, and the capital would be handed over to Ulmanis's Latvian government. Proclamations were posted later the same morning, and for four days Tallents acted as interim governor, installing himself in the same ornate Ritterhaus where he had had the fruitless interview with Fletcher a few weeks before. The night of the 4th/5th – the deadline for the Germans' departure – was tense, broken by rifle shots and the sound of soldiers singing 'Die Wacht am Rhein' as they marched to the station. But next morning they were gone, and on 7 July lovely Riga – shabby and empty but not much damaged – was handed over to the Latvians with all requisite fanfares, speeches and little girls in white frills presenting roses. On the same day Tallents got a telegram telling him that his wife had given birth to a son. Ulmanis suggested that to mark the occasion the baby should be given a Latvian middle name. From a list, Tallents chose Wiswaldis, meaning 'ruling over all'. 'My elder boy thus acquired . . . an outlandish Christian name and . . . a pretty christening present of a knife, fork and two spoons from the Latvian government.'[5]

A pause followed, the Freikorps keeping to their camps, but still refusing to return to Germany. (To Salomon, drinking and slapping at mosquitoes in a wet wood next to a railway line, his homeland felt like 'an empty space on the map – a country with no real existence.'[6]) Goltz stayed too, declaring that he would not desert his men. At a meeting with Tallents and other Allied representatives halfway between Riga and Mitau he refused to shake hands, spoke only through a deputy and muttered inaudibly when asked if he accepted Versailles. An Allied success, during this stalemate, was the handover of the blood-soaked Landeswehr to British command, as specified under the schoolhouse truce. Chosen to head it was Tallents's twenty-seven-year-old aide, Lieutenant Colonel Harold Alexander, a much decorated fellow-Irish Guardsman who had been with him at the Somme. He turned out to be an inspired choice. The high-spirited third son of an Anglo-Irish earl, he had the same sort of ethnic tension-infused, Big House, boggy-acres background as the Landeswehr's own Baltic barons, and got on with them famously. He also fell in love with the region in general, toying with the idea of buying an estate – 'a couple of thousand pounds would get a place of several thousand acres and a nice house'[7] – and kitting himself out in Russian-style thigh-boots and an astrakhan hat. Reorganised and retrained, at the end of August the Landeswehr moved east to face the Red Army, and thanks largely to Alexander's charisma, stayed there for the rest of the conflict.

With the Landeswehr neutralised, the situation around Riga was sufficiently stable for Tallents to return briefly to London, to lobby for more supplies for the Latvian army. But while he pushed the Balts' cause in Whitehall, in the Gulf of Finland Admiral Cowan was helping prepare the ground for an advance on Petrograd by the Balts' inveterate enemies, the White Russians. The previous year, under the protection of German occupation, a small White Russian force had gathered at Pskov, an ancient town just east of the Estonian border. Dubbed the Northwestern Army, it was led by General Nikolai Yudenich, formerly commander of tsarist forces in eastern Turkey. A tiny man with a round head and long, propeller-like moustaches, he made his headquarters at Helsingfors, in a large seaside hotel. Cowan's squadron was based along the coast at Biorko Sound, a large and scenic bay in which the Imperial Fleet had held its reviews.

The War Office's representative in the Baltic, tasked with persuading the various anti-Bolshevik forces to cooperate, was General

Hubert Gough. Another Anglo-Irish hunting man, he had commanded the Fifth Army in France, and been scapegoated for its collapse in the face of the Ludendorff offensive in spring 1918. The Baltic appointment was recompense. True to Intervention form, he had been given the vaguest of instructions. At the Foreign Office, Curzon stressed the importance of non-interference, while at the War Office, Churchill paced excitedly up and down in front of a wall map, explaining that with Kolchak, Denikin, Ironside and Yudenich all converging, Lenin was about to fall. In Gough's words,

> he seemed to overlook the scale of the map, [and] when I remarked that the forces were too widely separated to afford each other any mutual support . . . assured me that Bolshevik morale was so low that the resolute advance of any armies, however small, would cause their organisation to disintegrate.[8]

The presence of German troops, Gough claims, was not mentioned at either meeting. He and Tallents rather warily worked out a division of labour: Tallents would deal with the Baltic governments and Goltz from Riga; Gough with Yudenich and Mannerheim in Helsingfors.

Yudenich having only about six thousand men, it was obvious that to take Petrograd he would need the help of the Finns, whose southern border was only twenty miles north of the city, and whose army was by far the biggest in the region. Since, like Denikin, Yudenich was officially subordinate to Supreme Ruler Kolchak, formal negotiations had to go via Omsk. Using Gough as an intermediary, on 8 July Mannerheim outlined his conditions: recognition of Finnish independence, self-determination for Karelia, and the secession to Finland of Pechenga, the barren Arctic inlet where the *Cochrane's* marines had fought the year before. Kolchak's more realistic advisors pleaded with him to accept, arguing that the Bolsheviks should be beaten first and the empire rebuilt after. But Kolchak was immoveable. Mannerheim's conditions, he declared, were 'fantastic . . . one would suppose that Finland had conquered Russia.'[9] That left the Estonians, about whom the Whites were even more emphatic. Estonia, Yudenich spluttered, was 'a piece of Russian soil, a Russian *guberniya*', and the Estonian government – led by a conservative half-Russian former newspaper editor called Konstantin Päts — 'a gang of criminals' with whom he could have 'no conversation'.[10]

Exasperated by weeks of shuttle diplomacy, and by the Whites' endless internal intrigues and complaints about slow-to-arrive British aid, on 10 August Gough gave them an ultimatum. Summoning Yudenich's civilian representatives and other White notables to Reval, he charged his Russian-speaking chief of staff, Colonel Marsh, with bringing matters to a head. Speaking in what a White source describes as 'a particularly rude and insolent manner',[11] Marsh told the meeting that too much time had been wasted talking and squabbling. They must here and now form a government, and sign an agreement with the Estonians. It was now twenty past six. If they did not do so by seven, that would be the end of Allied aid. Handing over a list of ministers and the agreement's text, he then tapped his pocket-watch and left the room.

This brisk approach caused an uproar. Yudenich did form a 'Northwestern Government', but protested furiously at the notion of Estonian independence, as did White representatives in the West. (Estonia had 'no class sufficiently intelligent to govern the country', the Russian ambassador to London snorted, and as for the opinions of Western so-called Russia experts, 'all the dustbins of the world' did not suffice.[12]) Unrestrained by Balfour or Curzon, who were away in Paris, Churchill recalled Gough and gave him a carpeting. Gough put his own side of the story to army chief Field Marshal Wilson, telling him that Yudenich was 'a waste of time and money'.[13] Wilson, for whom the Intervention was a distraction from Ireland and Egypt, lost no time in passing on Gough's views to Lloyd George, so that when Churchill delivered another of his aggrieved Russia memoranda to Cabinet, the prime minister's reply was unusually sharp. Again and again, Churchill had promised that in Russia 'great opportunities' were 'dangling at our fingertips', but again and again, they had come to nothing. In Siberia, Kolchak was in retreat, and in the Baltics Yudenich — a 'notorious reactionary' — had managed to recruit only a few thousand men out of a local population of several million. Their failures were not Britain's fault; she had already spent over £100 million on Russia and sent 'excellent' troops. Churchill should drop his Russia obsession, and focus, as asked, on cutting costs. 'Russia does not want to be liberated . . . Let us therefore attend to our own business and leave Russia to look after hers.'[14]

While all around wrangled, Admiral Cowan quietly launched a plan of his own – one of the most daring in British naval history. It had its genesis in a revolutionary advance in boat design – the planing hull. Commonplace today – RIBs, speed-boats and racing dinghies all have them – planing hulls are shaped like a shallow V, and when moving fast enough, lift off the water, giving extra speed. Prototypes were patented in the 1870s, but for practical purposes had to await the invention of the combustion engine. Designed and built by John Thornycroft at his yards on the Thames, the first working planing boats debuted at the 1908 Olympics. When war broke out it was realised that they had military potential; Thornycroft was asked to come up with a design, and in August 1916 delivered an initial twelve examples. A training base was set up on Osea Island, at the mouth of Essex's Blackwater, and the 'skimmers' – officially Coastal Motor Boats or CMBs – went to work, harrying German inshore craft and laying smokescreens during April 1918's Zeebrugge Raid.

Their deployment to the Baltic was shrouded in secrecy. In February 1919, twenty-nine-year-old Lieutenant Gus Agar, a Zeebrugge veteran and trainer at Osea, was told to report to the Admiralty and ask for naval intelligence. Directed to distant offices on the top floor, he was confronted by Mansfield Cumming, eccentric head of the newish and bumblingly amateur Secret Intelligence Service. Cumming needed someone to take two CMBs to Finland – 'I won't ask you take it on, for I know you will' – and use them to run couriers to Petrograd, where a British agent was working undercover. (As Agar found out later, this was the musician Paul Dukes, formerly assistant to the chief conductor of the Mariinsky Opera.) Back at Osea, Agar picked out two lieutenants, a midshipman and two skilled motor mechanics – all under twenty-one, since Cumming had told him to choose men with no dependants. Posing as motor-boat salesmen (for which purpose Agar bought a brown Moss Bros suit), they sailed to Helsingfors in a Swedish coaster. Two 40-foot CMBs followed on a small freighter, painted white so as to look like pleasure-craft. A final lunch with Cumming was pure Buchan. A speed addict who had lost his leg and his only son in a car crash four years earlier, Cumming drove Agar to his club in his Rolls Royce, roaring through the arch of Horse Guards Parade.

> During luncheon Russia was not mentioned. We talked about sailing boats. Nor was there afterwards any awkward or dramatic goodbye. He just gave me a pat on the back and said 'Well my boy, good luck to you' – and was gone.[15]

After consultations with the Helsingfors consulate, for his base Agar chose a shuttered sailing club at a place called Terijoki, a quiet resort village in pinewoods just west of the Russo-Finnish border. (Along with half of Finnish Karelia, Terijoki went to the Soviet Union at the end of the Second World War, and is now Zelenogorsk.) Their presence could not be secret, since its summerhouses were inhabited and a Finnish garrison was based nearby. But it could be discreet, since a high stone breakwater hid the little harbour from the sea. One of Cowan's destroyers towed the CMBs from the Finnish port where they had been unloaded to Biorko. There they were painted grey, and in defiance of Cumming's instructions, equipped with torpedoes, hidden under tarpaulin covers.

Agar now had to plan a route for Cumming's couriers into Petrograd. The city was and is guarded from the sea by the island naval base of Kronstadt, itself connected to the southern and northern shores of the Gulf of Finland by a line of sea-forts. The main shipping channel into the city lay to the south, and was closely watched and heavily mined. To the north, however, passage between the forts was blocked only by a submerged breakwater. Agar realised that since his CMBs drew less than three feet, so long as they were not caught by the forts' searchlights they could skim over the breakwater without difficulty. This would allow his first courier – an absurdly noticeable six-foot-four Olympic footballer called Pyotr Sokolov – to be dropped directly into Petrograd's outer suburbs, on one of the islands at the mouth of the river Neva. It had to be done soon though, because it was already late May, and in a few weeks' time it would be light or semi-light round the clock. The commander of the Finnish garrison, a Colonel Sarin, came up with a local fisherman cum smuggler to act as pilot – a 'weird-looking ruffian, but he knew the coast.'

Agar made his first trip on the moonless night of 13 June, after Sarin told him that the troops manning Krasnaya Gorka, a large land fort on the other side of the Gulf, had just risen against the Reds. Trusting that the rising was keeping the enemy busy, and wearing leather jackets and caps so as to look from a distance like Bolshevik despatchers, Agar, Sokolov, motor mechanic Hugh Beeley and the pilot set out in a single CMB at 10.30 p.m. Covering the twelve miles to the forts in about half an hour, they flew safely over a defensive minefield, then slowed to pass quietly between the forts themselves. 'The strain was terrific' but no searchlights flashed, and once out of range Agar opened up the throttle again, reducing speed only when city lights gleamed ahead. Creeping up to the low black outline of one of the Neva islands, he came to reed-banks and moored barges. A pram dinghy was lowered, and Sokolov rowed himself to shore. He was to hide the dinghy, take his message to agent Dukes, and be back at the same spot in forty-eight hours' time. With only two hours of darkness left, Agar turned for home. Crossing the forts, 'again that awful feeling of tenseness. One felt one's collar too small for one's throat, and had difficulty in swallowing. At last we were through and found ourselves leaving them behind.'[16]

On the return journey he detoured south, towards Krasnaya Gorka. Since its guns pointed inland it was vulnerable from the sea, and sure enough, there in the distance were the Red Fleet's two battleships, the *Andrei Pervozvanny* and the *Petropavlovsk*, anchored ready to bombard. In Agar's telling, he was there and then struck by an idea. With a torpedo in his locker, and complete surprise on his side, why not attack? He had ordered that the torpedo be primed and was picking up speed when there was a clatter, and the CMB settled back into the water. The engine had failed. After half an hour during which the group expected at any moment to be spotted by a nearby lighthouse or by one of the battleships' screen of destroyers, Beeley got it going again, and they were able to limp 'like a lame dog' back to Terijoki.

The next day Agar got a lift with a neighbouring villa-owner along forest tracks to Biorko. He was not able to see Cowan, who was at sea, but picked up his second CMB, which had been undergoing repairs. Motoring back along the coast, the roll of big guns – the Red bombardment of Krasnaya Gorka had begun. Later the same evening, he and his crew set off again to Petrograd to pick up Sokolov, the trip passing without incident. The next morning the bombardment of Krasnaya Gorka resumed. Invited by Sarin to his observation point in the bell-tower of a nearby church, Agar watched the distant puffs of smoke through a telescope. Sarin and Sokolov were both desperate for Cowan's squadron to take action, arguing that if only Krasnaya Gorka were helped to hold out, Kronstadt's sailors would rise against the Bolsheviks too. Agar explained that with only lightly armoured cruisers at his disposal, Cowan could not go up against battleships, but privately 'thought immediately of our two CMBs and the torpedoes we carried. Surely they could provide, like a couple of hornets, the very sting to drive those Red bombarding ships away?' In the course of the day he sent two cipher telegrams by radio to Cumming, explaining the need for immediate action, and that even if the CMBs were lost there was enough time to send out replacements before the next courier run was due. Cumming's replies were unequivocal: 'Take no offensive without direct instructions from SNO [Senior Naval Officer] Baltic', and 'Boats should not be used for any other but intelligence work.'[17]

Trusting that Cowan would back him up, Agar went ahead anyway, timing the CMBs' departure so as to arrive at Krasnaya Gorka at early dawn, when there would be just enough light to see, but not enough, with luck, to be seen. But half an hour in the mission had to be aborted, when one of the boats hit a floating object – probably a dud mine – and snapped its propeller-shaft. Agar spent the next day back in the bell-tower, inwardly debating whether to try again with only one boat and one torpedo. What was happening at Krasnaya Gorka was not clear either, the bombardment pausing as the two battleships were replaced by a heavy cruiser, the *Oleg*. He decided to take the plunge, and that evening – 17 June – set off in his remaining CMB, together with Beeley and Lieutenant John Hampsheir. Bouncing into a strong headwind and choppy sea, their first challenge was to pass unseen between the destroyers guarding the *Oleg*. They slowed, and the anchored ships were about two hundred yards away when the CMB jerked and shuddered. 'I thought we had hit something and stopped. Hampsheir appeared from below the hatch with an agonized look on his face. "The charge has fired, sir."' The charge propelled a hydraulic ram, which normally shot the torpedo tail-first over the stern. In this case, by good luck, stops had been in place to prevent it from launching. For the next quarter of an hour, in darkness and wet and with the boat wildly rolling, Hampsheir struggled to fit a new cartridge:

> All through this time of intolerable suspense my eyes were on the destroyers on either side of us . . . We might at any moment be seen, as it was then just before one o'clock in the morning and the first streaks of early dawn were due to appear. Beeley remained wonderfully calm. There was nothing to be said . . . At last Hampsheir popped up from the hatch. 'It's all right sir, we have reloaded.' With a sigh of relief, I slipped in the clutch . . . put on full speed and headed straight for the *Oleg*.[18]

At 500 yards he fired, a moment after the *Oleg* loosed her own first salvo.

> We looked back . . . and saw a large flash abreast the cruiser's foremost funnel, followed almost immediately by a huge column of black smoke . . . We tried to give three cheers but could scarcely hear ourselves for the din of the engines.

For a few minutes they were still within range, but the shells fell wide, poor light and the CMB's speed making it a hard target. Wanting the Reds to think that he had come from Biorko, Agar kept on west until out of sight, before turning north for Terijoki. At ten to one, freezing and soaked to the skin, they arrived back at the yacht club, to cocoa and wild congratulations – the explosion had been audible across the bay. Agar sent signals to Cumming and Cowan – 'Have attacked *Oleg* and have hit her' – and before he went to sleep wrote a long, elated letter to his fiancée and a short, sober note in his diary: 'Hope all the decent sailors were taken off by the destroyers . . . What a life!'[19]

Later in the day it was Agar's awkward job to placate Sarin, who had been assured that the CMBs were only doing reconnaissance work, and was furious at the deceit. Worried that the Bolsheviks would now bomb Terijoki from their airbase on the other side of the Gulf, he insisted that Agar move his CMBs to Biorko. As the team motored into the great bay the next day, one CMB towing the other, they found the whole squadron manned to greet them, sailors cheering and klaxons sounding on ship after ship as they passed down the line. The next day Agar took a Finnish seaplane to assess the damage to the *Oleg*.

> The machine descended to two thousand feet, and how shall I express my feelings when, in the exact position where I had attacked her, we could see quite clearly the hulk of the cruiser lying on her side like a large dead whale.[20]

But over Krasnaya Gorka Red Flags were flying; the fort had surrendered and the sinking had come too late. On the return journey the plane broke down and Agar did not get back to Biorko until after midnight. Cowan, who received him in his pyjamas, was undismayed at the news: Krasnaya Gorka would probably not have held out for long anyway, and now the Reds knew that if they 'showed their noses outside Kronstadt', he had 'a sting' waiting for them. He was also recommending Agar for a VC.

There was now a pause, while the CMBs were refitted and midsummer's twenty-four-hour daylight passed. Installed in a large wooden summer-house equipped with housekeeper, tennis court and a French boxer dog called Dinah, Agar and his officers paid calls on their neighbours. Each household was missing at least one member – wives waiting for husbands, parents for children, children for parents – and they seemed to live off sugarless tea and hope, 'one and all . . . imbued with the firm belief that the British Navy had arrived to succour them.'[21] Cowan, meanwhile, was developing an audacious new plan – a raid on Kronstadt itself. While aeroplanes distracted the fort's guns from the air, a flotilla of CMBs would dash into the harbour, fire at the two battleships lying there and speed off again, just as Agar had done with the *Oleg*. Required would be more 'skimmers' – the larger, 55-foot type that carried two torpedoes – the 'planes and a new landing-strip at Biorko. Agar was doubtful. The entrance to the harbour was only fifty yards wide, and inside it manoeuvring would be extremely difficult, since CMBs had large turning circles and no reverse gear. There was also the trickiness of the torpedoes: they had no aiming mechanism, and if launched when the boat was going too slowly went into a 'death dive', which in a shallow harbour meant hitting the bottom and blowing up the boat itself. Discussing the plan with Cowan during the admiral's daily walk, however, Agar found him bullish: striding along 'as fast as his short legs could carry him', never was a man 'more confident and full of enthusiasm'.[22] The date was set for the dark of the moon round the middle of August.

While the aeroplanes and new CMBs made their way out from England (the 'planes on a converted cruiser, the CMBs under tow), Agar's team resumed its courier duties. These were harder now that the enemy was on the alert. One boat was spotted and fired on at the forts, and a new drop-off point had to be established after the first was discovered. What was supposed to be Dukes's final pick-up ended in near-catastrophe when a new dinghy turned out to be missing its bung, and sank as Dukes and the courier rowed out to the waiting CMB. (They swam back to shore, and later escaped overland.) The Kronstadt raid itself took place on the night of 17/18 August. After only one rehearsal, and with engines barely resuscitated after soakings on the tow out, nine CMBs set out from Biorko at dusk. The weather was good – calm and overcast – and at midnight, gathered off a small point to the west of the forts, they were ready for their attack. The plan was for a first CMB to hit the guardship at the harbour entrance, the *Gavriil*, then for the rest to dash inside in two waves of three, the first group, skippered by the most experienced officers, exiting before the second entered. Their targets were the battleships *Andrei Pervozvanny* and *Petropavlovsk*, a submarine depot ship, the *Pamyat Azova*, and the harbour's dry dock, without which the damaged ships would be harder to repair. Agar was to lead the CMBs to the harbour mouth and then wait outside, blocking the exit from another smaller basin next door. At the same time twelve biplanes – a mixture of models – would attack from the air, knocking out or at least distracting the guns on the harbour walls.

Knowing that there was no chance of nine boats passing the forts unobserved, the little flotilla sped between them at full throttle.

Machine-guns rattled but they got through unharmed, and arrived at the harbour entrance just as the 'planes made their first bombing run. As Kronstadt's sailors scrambled to their stations, the first of the CMBs dashed through the harbour mouth – providentially, not blocked by a boom – and straight ahead for the *Pamyat*, which was tied up to a central pier. It released its torpedo, and the *Pamyat* burst into flames. Outside the harbour, the CMB whose job it was to knock out the guardship *Gavriil* missed, and the *Gavriil* was able to blast it to pieces. While its crew floated in the water, the remaining two first-wave CMBs made their runs on the *Pervozvanny* and the *Petropavlovsk*, moored in the harbour's left-hand corner. With great skill – the manoeuvre involved switching off one engine, turning sharp left, then switching it on again, all under fire – they both hit their targets, and as smoke erupted from the stricken ships, roared out again into the bay.

Here the raid should have halted. All the targets save for the dry dock had been successfully hit. One CMB had been destroyed, its crew dead or wounded, and the skipper of the CMB that targeted the *Petropavlovsk* had been shot in the head. The air attack was almost exhausted – only two 'planes still dived at the harbour guns – and the forts' defenders were now blazing with everything they had. Two of the three second-wave CMBs – one had dropped out earlier with engine failure – nonetheless made their runs as planned, and met with disaster. The first immediately sputtered to a halt, its carburettor damaged by bullets or shrapnel. The second carried on into the harbour mouth, where it collided at full speed with the last of the first-wave boats coming out. Spotlit by searchlights, the two craft wallowed helplessly while the surviving crew of the most damaged of them climbed into the other. Amazingly, they then managed to push clear, exit the harbour, and fire their torpedoes at the waiting *Gavriil*. They missed, the *Gavriil* opened up, and the CMB sank. Back at Biorko, the bill came to two men dead or dying, and seventeen missing presumed dead. It turned out later that nine of the missing had been pulled from the water by the *Gavriil*, bringing the number of lives lost down to ten.[23] (The rescued men were returned to Britain in a prisoner swop seven months later.) Despite the losses it was a stunning action: a handful of small plywood motor boats had sunk or disabled three of the Red Fleet's heaviest warships, inside its own fortress harbour.

When the First Lord of the Admiralty announced the triumph in Cabinet, his colleagues were disappointingly unexcited. Russia was a distraction, and with angry demobilisation demonstrations ongoing, that Britain was involved there at all was not something to shout about. But for the Navy – relatively inactive during the war proper and feeling like the junior service – the raid was a fillip. Another two VCs on top of Agar's were awarded, plus four DSOs and Conspicuous Gallantry Medals for all the ratings involved. The raid also made a significant difference militarily. Cowan's squadron continued to patrol and to lay mines, and the RAF to bomb Kronstadt, where the *Pervozvanny* was raised and moved to dry dock. But there was only one more ship-to-ship action during the Baltic campaign – on 31 August 1919, when a Red submarine sank a British destroyer – and Yudenich and the Estonians were thereafter safe from the sea. Agar went on to a long naval career, retiring to grow strawberries after Japanese divebombers sank his ship in 1942. Of his two original 'skimmers', one was written off when he and Beeley hit a breakwater on a final courier trip. The other, in which he sunk the *Oleg*, is on display at Portsmouth's naval museum, her long lean lines as sharky as ever.

18

Ironside's bed

IN LATE JULY 1919, a Socialist Revolutionary doctor and former
secretary to the Provisional Government, Boris Sokolov, took ship
to Archangel. After a year abroad, he was taking up the post of medical officer to the North's Russian Army. On board he got talking to a
British major returning from leave. The conversation was discouraging. Soon, the major said, the British would have been there for
a year:

> We wanted to help your fight against the Bolsheviks. But what do we
> see? Russians don't want to fight. At the front, it's us holding all the
> key positions. The Russians just organise rebellions, and we have to
> suppress them.

In short, the expedition was an expensive waste of time, as well as
very unpopular with British workers. Sokolov asked if the Russian
Army would be able to stand alone. 'Of course not', said the major.
'The day we leave the Bolsheviks will come. You can bet on it.' In that
case, what were two hundred-odd Russian officers, mostly released
from German prisoner-of-war camps, doing on board? Why ship
them to Archangel just to get killed? The major shrugged: 'We
thought it was pointless. But the Russian command insisted, so we
dressed them up and brought them over. It's none of our business
what happens to them.'[1]

As Sokolov had discovered, the Dyer's mutiny plus the end of the plan
to join with Kolchak's armies at Kotlas meant that Ironside was now
wholly focused on how to evacuate his forces before winter, without
collapsing Miller's army in the process. His plan was for the newly

arrived, VC-garlanded Relief Force to make quick thrusts down the rivers and the railway, hand over to the Russians, then withdraw and take ship in late September or early October. By putting the Reds on the back foot, the offensive would avoid a repeat of the chaotic French exit from Odessa, and give Miller breathing space before he had to take over the region's defence alone.

The War Office approved the plan, and sent out one of its biggest hitters, General Henry Lord Rawlinson, to oversee it. Former commander of the Fourth Army in France, Rawlinson was not thrilled at the appointment. As he wrote in his diary,

> North Russia is a nasty job, but . . . the Government is in a hole, and I consider it my duty to go and try to help them out of it. [Field Marshal] Wilson thanked me profusely for going, saying it was a very sporting thing to do.[2]

Going aboard Rawlinson's ship when it docked on 11 August, Ironside found him lively and cheerful, with a 'twinkle in his eye' and a 'jumpy sort of way of talking'. Thereafter, instead of resenting being supplanted, Ironside cannily made the most of his proximity to the great man, learning from him – 'Rawly' was acutely observant, listened more than he talked and 'never bothered himself for a minute about trifles' – and appreciating the cover he gave in London. (The award of a knighthood, organised by Churchill, helped: 'I was really so astonished that I could hardly believe it . . . My little ADC is almost overcome.') Rawlinson, for his part, was pleased with Ironside's arrangements and let him get on with them while he himself toured the fronts. (And got in a little painting: 'Rawly was like a child', wrote his slightly baffled deputy, 'seeing the wonderful colours of the forest.')[3]

By the time Rawlinson arrived, rumours that the British were leaving had already been circulating for a few weeks, to White Russian anger and despair. At the Bereznik aerodrome the air ace Kozakov, not long ago awarded a DSO, skipped a farewell dinner for departing British colleagues, got into his Sopwith Snipe, circled to 1,000 feet then dived vertically into the ground, crashing right next to a hangar. Ironside regarded the suicide as desertion, but conceded that 'most of the other pilots seem to think that he did something very fine indeed.' (Today there is a stone memorial to Kozakov outside Bereznik's cottage museum. Below a photo-engraving of his narrow, expressionless face the inscription reads, 'Shot down 17 German aeroplanes. Glory to a Hero of Russia!' The clue that he was White is a tasselled sabre.) The day after his death, Miller tightened the emotional thumbscrews with a parade to mark the first anniversary of the Allied landing. Obliged to take part, Ironside squirmed: 'Here we are going to sneak off very shortly, and these wretched people wish to celebrate . . . I really felt like nothing on earth.'[4] Miller also made a last-minute stab at democratic legitimacy, by bringing what Sokolov sarcastically called 'two and a half SRs' into his government, and by allowing a convention of town councils – promptly dissolved again when it demanded amnesty for non-Bolshevik political prisoners.

Rawlinson's first action on disembarkation was to go to Miller and make it as clear as possible that the evacuation really was happening. 'I think Miller had been hoping against hope', wrote Ironside, 'that it might be possible to retain us here. Rawly put it very clearly . . . so that there could not be a shadow of a doubt.'[5] The following day Ironside went to Miller again, and strongly advised that he move his government and army to Murmansk, since it was easier to defend than Archangel and ice-free in winter, allowing evacuation by sea if necessary. The other, unspoken reason Ironside wanted Russian troops gone was because he feared that they might mutiny wholesale as his withdrawal began, and that his own men would have to fight their way back to Archangel. Rawlinson agreed, writing to Wilson that though some complained that Britain was 'deserting her friends', personally he would be thankful to 'get away without opening fire on them.'[6]

Their fears were shared by Miller's younger and more junior commanders at the fronts, who knew that they would end up being left behind if the army collapsed. At a general meeting called by Miller they unanimously voted that safe evacuation from Archangel was impossible without the British, and that the army should regroup at Murmansk as suggested. Some of Miller's headquarters staff agreed, but his unpopular and newly arrived chief of staff did not, and bolstered his argument by misrepresenting Kolchak as having ordered that the North be defended at all costs. Determined to talk to Miller alone, the junior commanders bearded him in his quarters later that evening. Miller, according to an observer, 'tried to calm them with his cordial tone', but made no concessions beyond promising that measures would be taken to improve soldiers' morale.[7]

The next day the meeting reconvened, but remained deadlocked. First comically bureaucratic Marushevsky completely lost his head, proposing not only that the Army should stay in Archangel, but that it should make the British stay too. Miller asked him how this was to be done. 'General Marushevsky replied that we could resort to force, at which Miller could only spread his hands.' It was then decided to make a formal appeal to the British government, and at midday the group went to Rawlinson and requested that he convey it to London. Rawlinson was gracious but firm: he would of course pass it on, but it would not help. Even if the Russian Army captured 'not only Vologda and Vyatka but also Moscow and Petrograd', he would still have to obey orders and evacuate. Ironside joined the meeting and was much blunter, asking each regimental commander in turn if he could honestly vouch for the steadiness of his men. When they all replied in the negative he told Miller and Marushevsky that they were fantasising – Who was going to take over logistics? Had they trained up the necessary officers? – and called staying in Archangel 'pure folly'.[8]

Civilian petitions flooded in too. Gluing one into his diary – schoolroom English, painstakingly neat handwriting – Ironside noted Rawly's 'lofty way' of brushing them aside. Not having got to know the locals, for him it was easy, but Ironside himself had lived through 'a most trying winter with them', and could not but feel 'a certain amount of sympathy'. A week later he stuck in another, from a group of country parishes: 'Poor devils . . . We really did promise them that we were going to help them. What they cannot understand is that they have done so little to help themselves.'[9] Convinced as ever that trying to hang on in Archangel would be a death sentence for Russian officers up the rivers and railway, he had another go at Miller on 19 August. 'Poor old man, he is simply buried in stupid little routine matters, which should be done by his *chef du cabinet*. He is always ready to smile and talk.'

His insistence was counterproductive, and at the end of August Miller issued a statement that the Northern Province need not fear, because although the British were leaving, he and the Russian Army would remain. Dishonestly, he cited Kolchak, who had in fact explicitly given him permission to withdraw to Murmansk if necessary, or even to leave the North altogether and join Yudenich or Denikin.[10] A grandstanding speech to his officers – 'I will be the last to leave the *oblast*' – went down like a lead balloon. As a Russian colonel present put it, they 'had heard the same pretty words in the past, and no longer believed them.' British headquarters responded by posting notices, printed on orange paper, urging civilians to leave and giving dates and times of sailings. Miller countered with green ones telling them that the front was stable and there was no need to panic. The townspeople, the colonel wrote,

> ran from one announcement to the other, and begged passing soldiers to tell them which colour they should believe. Green being the colour of hope, many put their trust in it, and left their already-purchased steamship tickets in their pockets.[11]

★

Meanwhile Ironside activated his pre-evacuation offensive. Designed more to disrupt than to take territory, it was notably violent and indiscriminate, and in the imperial context would have been called a pacification campaign. Major Allfrey, the man who had been put in charge of the Dyer's executions, led raids into no-man's-land around Seltso, on the upper Dvina. 'All the fighting during the morning', he wrote on 10 August, 'was most awfully amusing, for we took them so completely by surprise that Heaton, who commands D Company, ran through three villages quite easily, and killed or captured quite a number of Bolos.' A messenger arrived with news that the enemy were landing men downriver, and to avoid getting cut off, his company and Heaton's moved on to a fourth settlement, a cluster of time-silvered log cabins by the name of Lipovyets:

> Immediately they saw our bayonets, the whole lot simply dashed off as hard as they could, and we ran close behind them into the village, shouting and firing at them . . . The Bolos were simply terrified, and went helter-skelter into any house they could. The cracking of single

rifle-shots went on for about a quarter of an hour while my men were digging the Bolos out of all sorts of extraordinary places, such as up chimneys and underneath mattresses.[12]

British casualties were one dead and nine wounded.

Lipovyets being reckoned unsafe for the night, in the evening the two companies set off again, together with their stretcher-cases and some four hundred prisoners. Allfrey had 'collared' some carts, and, when they could go no further, the drivers, all women, were told to unharness the ponies, get on them and stay close. After five hours' scrambling through boggy woods choked with fallen pines, the column reached a river, the bridge across it posts and planks. A pause to rest; the front of the line began to cross; and just as it reached the other side, a fusillade from the opposite bank. The result, wrote Allfrey, was 'horrible to watch ... Several of the men on the plank were shot down and drowned, [as were] the Russian women drivers, who had got on splendidly until then.' The 'Bolo prisoners dumped down all our wounded and stampeded, followed by quite a lot of our own men, who were still half asleep.' When the shooting ended he was 'left with half the column lying down behind the trees, and we could not find the rest of the men anywhere.'[13] At nine in the morning he and the other survivors reached a British-held village, where a colonel gave him 'the most glorious breakfast' he had ever had. Twenty-five officers and men had been killed in the ambush, and sixty were wounded or missing. Though buglers were posted and an observation balloon sent aloft to guide stragglers home, Allfrey was not hopeful, assuming that they would be picked up by 'rather desperate' groups from the villages they had just raided. In fact, by the end of the following day all but three had returned – 'not a bad after-battle muster at all'.[14]★

★ The ambush's society casualty was Lord Settrington, twenty-year-old heir of the Duke of Richmond. An Australian volunteer, twenty-two-year-old Corporal Arthur Sullivan, carried him and three others from the bridge, but he died of his wounds. Sullivan was awarded a VC, and in 1937 came to London as a member of the Australian delegation to George VI's coronation. Strolling along Birdcage Walk he tripped, hit his head and died. A plaque on the railings next to the Guards' Chapel marks the spot.

For the next four weeks, Allfrey helped manage the withdrawal downriver. Like Ironside, he worried less about the Reds, more about the possibility that nearby White units might turn hostile, rushing barges or setting fire to landing-stages. It wasn't an overblown fear. Organising the Russian Army's medical services on the railway front, Sokolov was shocked at officers' 'instinctive' loathing of their British counterparts. 'When they talked about them it was always with sarcasm or ridicule, and often they took advantage of the English not understanding the language to use the filthiest swearwords, right to their faces.' Tackling a group on the subject he got a tirade: the English had taken charge, they were arrogant, they weren't saving Russia but killing her, 'and so on and so forth'.[15] Well aware of the resentment, Allied personnel constantly suspected plots, which sometimes translated into vigilantism. As recorded by Allfrey on 30 August:

A few nights ago a Russian officer was dining with the French Foreign Legion, who are also here . . . [He] got drunk and let slip a remark about an organised mutiny which was about to take place amongst his Russian soldiers. Unfortunately for him, the French Foreign Legion is made of a very hard and lawless material, and they carried him out and put his feet in the fire until he betrayed the names of the affected Russians. The officer, who was quite badly burned, had to be killed, and the Frenchmen then went off to the Russian Battalion, where they arrested the mutineers and shot them on the spot. There are things of this description happening frequently here, but they do not come to light unless one happens to be on the spot.

There were friendly encounters too, but they had a pathetic undertow. Allfrey was billeted not far from a monastery (as nobody bothered to find out, the sixteenth-century Antoniyevo-Siyisky, delightfully positioned on a lake.) Its white-bearded abbot, Father Porfiriy, had long been hospitable to passing British officers, showing them round his gardens and playing a pedal harmonium. Allfrey and colleagues were invited to lunch – mushrooms followed by 'excellent' cakes with raspberries and cream – and shown the monastery's treasures: jewel-studded crucifixes, manuscript Bibles, and a collection of pearl-framed eighteenth-century miniatures.[16] Allfrey invited Porfiriy to a return meal the next day, during which the abbot presented him with an icon and singlehandedly polished off his last bottle of gin. A few days later he appeared again, this time bearing an 'old Roman buckle'. Given no warning, Allfrey was only able to rustle up bully beef, for which the old man sang 'a very long grace, during which we all sat in silence feeling very hungry':

> When he had finished he asked if we ever did that sort of thing in England. I determined not to be outdone . . . so gave the Padre the tip in English to sing 'Three blind mice'. We kept it up for about a minute. Old Father Purfere [sic] was quite taken in, and sat through the performance very seriously. We all kept a straight face and were heartily congratulated on our harmony.[17]

Militarily, the pre-evacuation campaign was notable for a technological innovation – a new sort of gas bomb called the 'M Device'. Developed by the government laboratories at Porton, and containing a deadly new derivative of arsenic, it had come just too late for the war against Germany. Churchill was initially reluctant to reveal the weapon's existence, but changed his mind: though not as worthy of its potential as the Western Front, Russia would be a useful testing-ground.

Receiving his first consignment of the sinister canisters back in March, Ironside had been dubious: 'I must ask what I am to do with this stuff, which is something quite new and terrifying. As there is no wind, the only thing I can do with it is drop it from aeroplanes.'[18] Trials by a team of specialist gas officers proved him right, and to adapt the canisters for air-dropping, a tinplate sleeve was devised which landed them nose-down, setting off the thermal reaction that turned the arsenic powder into a cloud of poisonous green smoke. Shown a rough prototype, Ironside thought it 'extremely clever', and ordered 2,000 sets. A plane's observer, he reckoned, would be able to throw over a hundred or so bombs in thirty minutes, though a rack that released several at a time would be even better. He would use them 'as a *bonne bouche* as I go away.'[19]

The first bombings took place on 27 August, when three 'planes dropped 119 canisters on Yemtsa, the sleepy village – church, wooden cottages, few thin fields, ring of pines – that was also the Red Army's front-line headquarters on the railway. Ironside was frustrated at not being able to inspect the results: 'I should have liked to have made a big [ground] raid at the same moment, in order to get actual specimens.'[20] He also thought that with each strike spread over twenty minutes, most people would have had time to run away. Yemtsa was nonetheless bombed again the next day and the one after, together with Plesetskaya, the next settlement down the line. 'We have no evidence as to what effect these things are having', Ironside wrote on 2 September, but 'I am certain that they can't be nice.'

'Good smokes' continued almost daily until at least 11 September, when part of the gas unit moved to Murmansk, to support General Maynard's parallel pre-withdrawal push. A final eighty M Devices were dropped – by two seaplanes, on a village near Lake Onega – on 22 September, by which time 2,718 had been used in all. Evidence as to their effectiveness remained patchy. Though prisoners described people staggering and collapsing in the evil green smoke, incoming Russian Army troops found surprisingly few corpses. But the bombs certainly incapacitated, causing violent symptoms – bleeding from ears, nose and mouth, vomiting, giddiness – for up to forty-eight hours, and crippling lassitude after. A member of the British gas team whose respirator failed during a test was still in hospital four months later, and a pilot who crash-landed and got the powder in his wounds lost the use of his arms. What the long-term health damage was to Russian civilians, we do not know.[21]

The final withdrawal took place mid-month, preceded by what sounds like a massacre on the river front. Over the past three days, Ironside wrote on 8 September, enemy casualties were reckoned at 163 killed and 200 wounded, to his own one killed and ten wounded. 'One little lot of the 45th Fusiliers' – probably its notoriously fierce Australians – had 'bayoneted 17 men like sheep . . . it really shows what good troops can do.'[22] Apart from some sniping from the banks, the transport barges made their way north unopposed. On board the *Retvizan*, an unlucky officer was killed by a rifle round that pinged through his cabin, but the only major loss was the gunboat *Glow-Worm*, lost together with twenty-seven crew when a nearby ammunition-carrier caught fire and exploded. Beneath sky-filling skeins of migrating geese, the last barges passed Bereznik on the 16th.

In Archangel new billboards announced the Allies' departure and again urged civilians to leave. Fewer than expected – only about six thousand – did so, the majority not townspeople but refugees from elsewhere. A major cause of bitterness was the removal and destruction of equipment and supplies. The War Office initially wanted everything to go, so as not to risk it falling into Bolshevik hands. At Ironside's insistence a substantial amount, including all surplus food and six tanks that Rawlinson had brought with him, was in fact handed over to the Russian Army. But a great deal more – ammunition, vehicles, aeroplanes, and a CMB and two gunboats after they got trapped in shallows – was burned or dumped in the Dvina. Sokolov was aghast to see nearly all medical facilities packed up and removed; his corps was left with only one field hospital and no de-lousing stations, *banyas* or canteens. Over forty-seven thousand unused M Devices – 'Miller made a plea for them', wrote Ironside, 'but I said no' – were towed downriver and sunk in the semi-enclosed White Sea, where they have presumably been poisoning marine life ever since.[23]

The final countdown was tense, Ironside noting that the town was 'weirdly quiet', with no 'smiling faces . . . Nobody says good morning as they used to.'[24] Not wanting to 'get done in at the last moment', he ordered an extra guard for his quarters at night. On 22 September he hosted a small farewell supper for Miller. 'We drank his health and I handed over to him all my cooking things. Poor devil; I wonder how much I should require to insure his life.' On the same day the first troopships sailed, and he was relieved that the local pilots did not deliberately ground the ships so as to block the channel. From the 25th, all troops were 'in marching order, ready to embark at a moment's notice. I do not think that the Russians can realise how quickly the last 6,000 will get away.' Miller came to him, and 'again said rather sadly that he didn't see what all the hurry was about.' A Russian colonel who Ironside knew well and had decorated was less restrained:

He entered my office and saluted me. He then threw his D.S.O, on the table between us. For two minutes he told me what he thought of the Allies and their behaviour. He then saluted again and marched out of the room. I sat in silence looking at the discarded Order which he had so gallantly won.[25]

On the 26th the last troops were embarked, from different points so as not to make it obvious that none were left in barracks. Ironside waited out the day in his empty office, playing patience. Departure day, 27 September, dawned still and clear; the town silent because Miller had ordered a curfew.

At noon exactly Miller came down in a motor car with his ADC and stayed a few minutes. He had tears in his eyes as he took me by the hand for the last time and I can hardly blame him. Not a sign of man, woman or child in the streets.

At half past the convoy weighed anchor and set off downriver; past houses and boatyards and out into the braided estuary. The last Ironside saw of Archangel was the golden domes of its cathedral, catching the sun. He remembered how he had admired them on arrival, exactly a year previously. Now 'there didn't seem to be quite the same life in them. One felt older somehow or other.'[26]

A couple of weeks earlier he had made an uncharacteristically introspective diary entry. The whole North Russia expedition, he confessed to himself, had been a failure, and it would have been better 'never to have started the show at all.' As it was, Britain had 'incurred the everlasting enmity of both sides – the Whites for deserting them, and the Reds for opposing them.' What would his emotions be once he was home? 'Shall I feel disgusted with myself, or shall I say "Thank goodness that is over?"'[27] Given a peerage at the end of a long and spectacularly successful military career, he nonetheless chose as his title Lord Ironside of Archangel, after the small far-northern port of which he had briefly been virtual governor. The region didn't forget him either. In the village of Ust-Vaga – rusting cars, derelict school-house, birdsong and muscled, hurts-your-eyes blue river – a farmer shows off his collection of Intervention-era shell casings, ferreted out of the woods and lined up in height order on shelves in his shed. His prize exhibit is out the back – a hinged iron bedstead, rescued from the abandoned house next door. Ironside stayed there, he says, while visiting the Vaga front in the winter of 1918/19, and left the bed behind. It looks a bit short for a man of six foot four, and Ironside makes no mention of folding beds in his diary. But who knows? It could be true.

PART IV

White Retreats, September 1919–March 1920

19

'We liked the Balts'

COMING UP TO a year after the victory over Germany, and two after the Russian Revolution, the Whites' chances still looked good. As Churchill never tired of showing visitors to his office, though Kolchak had been pushed back across the Urals he still held three-quarters of the map, all the way to the Pacific, and Denikin a vast swathe of Ukraine and the South, from Odessa to the Volga. Distracted by new troubles at home and abroad, the Allies were beginning to wind down their involvement. They had gone from the North, trimmed their ambitions in Siberia, and given Denikin notice that aid had an end-date. But they still had tens of thousands of troops in Russia, and no set date for withdrawal. Policy was still essentially 'wait and see'.

Of the White generals, apparently closest to victory was Yudenich, poised less than a hundred miles west of Petrograd. Chaotically governed and with its economy in tatters, the city was ripe for picking. The Russo-French novelist Victor Serge, who worked in its Comintern bureau at the time, describes it as dead-alive. In the hotel the Comintern had commandeered for its offices, the 'one-eyed gaze' of a machine-gun behind the reception desk had not yet dispelled the ghosts of old guests – 'She, shapely in furs . . . he, slender, light dancing off his monocle.' In the smokeless factory district only the occasional drive-shaft still turned, with a sound 'like an out of breath heart', and workers were dismantling machinery to make cigarette lighters and rabbit cages. In the bread queues the talk was of soaring prices and the likelihood that the city would fall: 'If the English come, you'll see. Everybody who raised his hand for the Communists even once will be hanged.'[1]

To take it, Yudenich now had a, by Civil War standards, quite large and well-equipped army: 17,800 infantry, 700 cavalry, fifty-seven guns and four armoured trains. Rations, clothing and trucks came courtesy of America, which though officially present in the Baltic only for diplomatic and humanitarian purposes, in practice supplied him via the American Relief Association. (The ARA's head, the mining millionaire and future president Herbert Hoover, lied on the subject in his memoirs, claiming that no food aid went to White troops except when they plundered stores during their retreat. Actually he arranged for shiploads of flour and beans to be delivered to Northwestern Army depots at Vyborg and Narva.[2]) Britain's most eye-catching contribution was a tank unit. Six machines – christened *First Aid*, *Deliverance*, *Brown Bear*, *White Soldier* and *Captain Cromie* – and forty-four officers and soldiers landed at Reval in August and September 1919, and training commenced of Russian crews. Like Cowan's squadron, the unit was a political embarrassment at home, and its leader, Major Ernest Hope Carson, was instructed to use only volunteers for active operations, and to make sure that they were not subject to 'undue strain' – in other words, to avoid casualties.[3]

All through the summer, Gough had pushed Yudenich to take advantage of Petrograd's weakness and begin his advance. When he finally did so, in the first week of October, the operation was immediately thrown into disarray by one of White Russia's rich cast of exotically uniformed military chancers, Pavel Bermondt-Avalov. Black of moustache and flashing of eye, he styled himself a Georgian prince, but the gossip was of syphilis and of pimping for generals on the Austrian front. For Tallents he was

> a figure of mystery . . . We lightheartedly accepted alternative legends that he had been conductor of a Russian orchestra, or bandmaster of a Caucasian regiment. Nothing in his manner or appearance gave the lie to either of these stories.[4]

His rise was due to Goltz, who instead of leading his Freikorps back to Germany as ordered by Berlin, handed them over to the rogue Russian. The rebranded force spent September rampaging through the Courland peninsula, and on 7 October it attacked Riga, on the excuse that the Latvians had broken their promise to give German volunteers citizenship.

Tallents realised an attack was underway when two aeroplanes flew over the parade ground where he was inspecting Latvian troops, parading in new British uniforms. That night he was woken by the sound of tramping feet and singing – students, marching out of the city to meet the Freikorps. By the end of the afternoon they were streaming back again, and Ulmanis and his ministers came with a request. They were leaving, but would be grateful if Tallents stayed, since his presence might check German atrocities. He reassured them and gave them a case of port 'to revive their drooping spirits . . . Thus fortified, they motored off into the country, while [Major-General Alfred] Burt and I settled down in the Ritterhaus to await events.' Fully expecting Riga to fall overnight, the two men went to bed armed and dressed, but the next morning the Germans had still not crossed the Daugava, and Ulmanis reappeared for 'a somewhat gloomy breakfast'. All that day the streets were whipped with rifle- and light artillery-fire from across the river, and when Tallents went for a walk in the evening he saw several burning buildings and a young man lying dead on the pavement. A Latvian acquaintance he bumped into had just passed another body, 'a little schoolboy with his school books by his side.'[5]

Outside the city, the Freikorps went on a killing spree. Salomon describes it almost with relish: cottages are torched and their inhabitants flung into the flames, an old man found hiding under a cart is beaten to death with a sledge-hammer, a cow shot in her byre, a 'little bristly dog' pulped with a revolver butt. Shelling of the city centre continued until 15 October, when three British cruisers and a French destroyer arrived in harbour. Bermondt was given an ultimatum – withdraw or we fire – but defied it, protesting that he felt nothing but friendship for the Allies, and was only putting down Bolshevism. At noon the ships duly opened up on his positions, allowing the Latvians to cross the Daugava in force and start driving the Freikorps back towards Mitau.

Bermondt's audacity was a serious blow to Yudenich. As well as undermining his authority, it meant that the Estonian army, with which he had been in uneasy alliance, left for Riga to help the Latvians. Yudenich regarded this as desertion, and his furious reaction scotched any chance of renewed cooperation. Like Kolchak's springtime offensive in Siberia and Denikin's summer one in the South, his march on Petrograd was nonetheless initially strikingly successful. With the help of Cowan's ships, which bombarded Krasnaya Gorka, and Hope Carson's tanks, which were hard to manouevre – too heavy for many bridges – but effective when they could be got into position, it took him only a week to reach Gatchina, outermost of the old capital's satellite palace towns. Four days later he reached Tsarskoye Selo – 'Royal Village' – twelve miles from Petrograd itself. Standing on top of a hill, the American sports-turned-war-correspondent Arthur Ruhl could see the dome of St Isaac's, the gilt spire of the Admiralty, and a train pulling out of the Nikolai station, plume of steam trailing. It felt as if 'one could slip a couple of sand-wiches in one's pocket', tramp across the fields, and be there by evening.[6]

Inside the city, the Bolsheviks prepared for last-ditch street-fighting. Barricades of logs and paving stones were thrown up across the main streets, gun emplacements dug at street corners and, to encourage waverers, lists posted of the latest 'spies, criminals, black-mailers, bandits and deserters' executed by the Cheka.[7] There was corresponding excitement at Churchill's War Office. He and Field Marshal Wilson spent the evening of 20 October deciding which British general would join the entry into Petrograd, and even drafted his instructions – which reveal their thorough knowledge of the likely nature of White rule. Yudenich was to be warned against military dictatorship and encouraged to 'clothe his action[s] with as great an appearance of constitutional support as possible'; public trials were preferred to 'indiscriminate or wholesale executions'; and, above all, 'anything in the nature of a Jewish pogrom would do immense harm to the Russian cause.'[8] In Washington President Wilson, just off his near death-bed after a major stroke, signed a letter authorising the US Grain Corporation to send Petrograd 29,000 tons of flour.

It was not to be, because Yudenich's army was faltering. Kept permanently in the fighting line by a lack of reserves, the infantry lost heart. The overworked tanks started breaking down, and without them soldiers refused to go forward. Good junior officers and NCOs, Hope Carson thought, could have rallied them – but Yudenich didn't have enough of those either. Worse, as Hope Carson admitted to a journalist, some of the breakdowns were sabotage carried out by his own Russian crewmen. Woken one morning with the news that the Reds were close and the tanks would not start, he had raced to the field where they were parked. The engine of one, he discovered, had been smashed with a sledge-hammer. Another had been robbed of its magneto, and the carburettor of a third had been stuffed with cotton wadding. 'And mind you, this Russian tank unit was supposed to be all ex-officers and picked men.'[9] White command seemed to sink into fatalism. In Tsarskoye Selo Ruhl interviewed Yudenich's deputy, a former Olympic showjumper called Aleksandr Rodzianko. Ruhl had expected a dashing, daredevil figure, but found the general 'slow-moving' and 'lustreless . . . with the air of surveying, with good-natured, somewhat weary irony, a hopeless job.'[10]

Rodzianko had good reason, because Petrograd was now better defended. Making a dramatic entrance on his famous train, Trotsky had reshuffled the Red 7th Army's command, and brought in 20,000 fresh troops from Moscow. (Why Yudenich failed to cut the Moscow–Petrograd railway line is a mystery; one theory is that the commander ordered to do so wanted instead to be first to ride up the Nevsky.) On 21 October the bolstered 7th Army made its counter-attack, and two days later it drove Yudenich off the Pulkovo Heights, a low ridge just north of Tsarskoye Selo which was also the closest Hitler got to the city twenty-two years later. On 3 November, after defending Gatchina for ten days, the whole Northwestern Army fled in disorder for Estonia. The campaign had lasted only four weeks.

Its coda was the miserable fate of the army's rank and file. While Yudenich repaired to the Riviera, allegedly taking remaining army funds with him, his soldiers were disarmed and interned by the Estonians, who were already in ceasefire talks with Moscow. They were imprisoned in the border town of Narva, in two ancient forts and a disused textile mill. Inspecting a couple of months later, Tallents saw 'ghosts of skeletons'. American Red Cross man Loy Henderson, leader of a team that arrived in February 1920, was more specific:

Lying on the floor in disorderly rows were several hundred men clothed in remnants of old uniforms . . . Through the long hair that covered their heads and faces we could see their eyes, frequently bright with fever, peering at us, some angrily, some pleadingly, some without any emotions at all.

Portions of the hair and beards of many . . . were of a bluish-grey colour, and on closer examination I found that the colour [was] due to closely packed columns of lice. Captain Robinson paused and pointed at the bluish-grey column that was moving slowly across the floor towards a patient who was either asleep or unconscious. The column was leaving the beard and hair of a man who I saw was dead.[11]

Washing, shaving, fumigating, feeding, the Red Cross and local auxiliaries subsequently saved uncounted lives by preventing typhus's spread to the general population. Henderson caught typhus but survived; two of his American colleagues died.

Though Yudenich had been defeated, and fighting between the Estonians and the Red Army was coming to an end, the Latvian government still had a winter of warfare ahead, first with Bermondt's Freikorps, then with the partly Latvian Red 15th Army, which held the ethnically mixed province of Lettgallen, on Latvia's present-day borders with Russia and Belarus.

From 15 October, when Cowan's ships first bombarded Bermondt's positions outside Riga, driving out the Germans took five weeks. The navy continued to take a hand, but on land the only Allied contributions were two wireless operators and an anti-aircraft gun. (The Ritterhaus caught a stray piece of shrapnel, which 'entered . . . the bathroom one morning and destroyed the pyjamas of two members of the Mission staff who were shaving.')[12] The Freikorps abandoned the southern bank of the Daugava in mid-November, when an east wind froze the river and Latvian patrols started coming across, and were driven out of Mitau on 21 November, setting fire to the Mitau Palace – a baroque monster built by Empress Anna for a favourite – as they went. Over the next few weeks a new inter-Allied mission under a French general brokered a ceasefire, and as autumn turned to winter the brutal, brutalised Freikorps finally returned to Germany.

Cowan's squadron also left at the end of the year, partly to avoid getting iced in, partly for fear of mutiny. In October and November,

British sailors bound for the Baltic had protested or deserted ship in Edinburgh and in Copenhagen, and in December only a quarter of the crew of Cowan's flagship, the *Delhi*, obeyed the bugle when told that instead of spending Christmas in Reval, as expected, they were to lift anchor for bleak Biorko. It took several hours to restore order – in an officer's description, a 'jumbled kaleidoscope' of 'interviews with senior ratings, deputations going here and there [and] false alarms of worse things.'[13] Cowan was something of a martinet, but the discontent was also Whitehall's fault for refusing to recognise that a Baltic posting amounted to war service. (A total of 128 naval and RAF personnel were killed during the campaign, mostly by mines.)

Having driven out the Germans, the Latvian army turned its attention to Lettgallen and the Red 15th Army. Helped by Alexander's Landeswehr, in January 1920 it drove the Reds a hundred miles east. Despite bitter cold, to judge by his letters Alexander enjoyed every minute of it. His most fearsome adversaries, he told his family, were the Flintenweiber, or Bolshevik Latvian riflewomen – 'four of whom we shot the other day – brutes!'[14] It was all a splendid opportunity 'for people who are fond of Adventure!', and there were comic doodles of matchstick men and horses sliding on ice. When he gave up his command in March 1920 it was with regret. The Landeswehr were 'such nice fellows', who he had grown as fond of as his own regiment. England was going to feel tame: 'a garden, so small, compact and beautifully cultivated.'[15]

Nineteen-twenty was the year of peace-making. In February the Estonians signed a treaty with the Bolshevik government at the university town of Dorpat (today's Tartu). In June the Lithuanians did the same, though they continued to fight the Poles for Vilnius. (They lost, and for their capital, had to make do with the town of Kaunas.) The Latvians followed suit in August, and the Finns in October.

Tallents spent the year attending conferences and inaugurations, involving Balts, Russians and Poles in various permutations. Travelling back and forth across the region, he enjoyed the wide-skied, unassertive landscape – windmills, reed-thatched barns, 'dun stubbles, pale grasses and grey willows' – and the picturesqueness of the people. When summer came, children made flower wreaths for their cows and sold wild strawberries at the roadside, and stopping at a cottage to ask for water, he was invited into a brick-floored room with rabbits hopping about, and given a handful of blackcurrants from a bush by the door. He also took advantage of the fact that the Baltic barons were selling up, snaffling a Wedgewood dinner service and a print of Bligh being set adrift from the *Bounty*. English prints, he was told, had once been the fashion, 'but the next generation had despised them and passed them on to their local vicarages.'[16]

His trickiest diplomatic challenge was settling the status of Walk, an ethnically mixed border town claimed by both Latvia and Estonia. After four months of deadlocked talks he lost patience and unilaterally drew a zig-zag line through the town centre. 'I was determined not to wait and argue . . . So as soon as I had unrolled my map on the table, I walked quickly to the door without making any farewells, entered my car, and drove straight off.'[17] Cartoons in the local press depicted him as a baby-chopping Solomon, but the storm blew over, and unusually for an Interventionist, he closes his memoir on a confident note. It was 'clearly desirable' that the Baltic 'gateways to Russia should be in good working order . . . Meanwhile we liked [the Balts], and we admired their courage and desire for freedom. Their friends were our friends and their enemies our enemies.'[18] He was right to be a little proud. Unlike British-sponsored Georgia and Azerbaijan, the three Baltic states kept their independence until 1940, when the Red Army invaded again under Stalin's pact with Hitler. For the next half-century they languished under Soviet rule, but in 1991 played a leading role in the collapse of the Union. Today they are robustly democratic, twice as wealthy per head as Russia, and members of NATO and the EU. Tallents's off-the-cuff, get-it-done border through the middle of Walk – today's Valga-Valka, municipal slogan 'One Town, Two Countries' – is still there.

20

To Moscow!

S LEEPLESS IN A railway carriage one autumn night, a young
medic with Denikin's army in the Caucasus, Mikhail Bulgakov,
wrote what was to be his first published work, a jeremiad against
international indifference to Russia's fate. He had been leafing
through some English journals, admiring their 'marvellous photographs', when suddenly 'it all made sense'. In the West, the war had
ended. Now the great powers were licking their wounds, but soon
they would recover. 'And what about us?' Russia would fall behind,
so far that who knew when she would be able to catch up – 'or
whether we'll ever catch up at all.' First, 'we must fight . . . fight for
our own capitals.' The English would remember how 'we covered
fields with bloody dew in our battle with Germany', and 'lend us
some more overcoats and boots so we can reach Moscow.' Only then
would Russia start getting back on her feet; only then would she
regain her rights and be 'welcome in the halls of Versailles. Who
will see those bright days? Us? No chance! Perhaps our children,
perhaps our grandchildren.'[1]

As the future novelist intuited, October 1919 was when the Whites
in the South as well as in the Baltics reached their high tide. Having
entered Odessa and Kiev in the last week of August, in mid-September
Denikin started his three-pronged advance towards the capital itself.
Kursk – east of the present-day Russian–Ukrainian border, and on the
main road to Moscow – fell to General Mai-Mayevsky on 20 September,
amidst mass desertions from Reds to Whites. Ten days later Voronezh,
also on a major road, was captured by Shkuro's Wolves, then occupied
by the Don Cossacks. Oryol – only just over 200 miles from Moscow
– was taken on 14 October.

Accompanying the advance, as liaison officer to the 1st Corps of the

Volunteer Army, was Captain John Kennedy. The twenty-six-year-old son of a Galloway manse, he was a sober, methodical, reading young man (and destined, in 1940, to become Churchill's director of military operations). His intelligence, plus the fact that his job meant that he spent most of his time with Russians, made him an unusually insightful observer. Checking in with British headquarters on landing, he was not impressed. 'Disobliging and of a somewhat low type', its personnel were hard-drinking, 'obviously inefficient, and the last people to be representing us here' – 'the scum', he thought, of the old Salonika Forces.[2] Having received his appointment he went straight on to Kharkov, where he met the Russian inspector of artillery to whom he would be attached, General Belayev – 'a little dark bearded man, very amiable and eager to help.'[3] Friendly and (apart from the usual antisemitism, which Kennedy shared in diluted form) sensible, Belayev subsequently became a close friend.

Though Denikin's 'To Moscow!' advance was just beginning, for three weeks Kennedy was prevented from seeing any action by non-stop hospitality. The Volunteer Army laid on the usual cavalry charge, toasts and tossings in the air, and local and refugee grandees a whirl of dinners and dances. His interpreter, a Prince Dmitri Golitsyn, took him and another British officer to supper with his father – 'we rather gathered that they were somewhat hard up . . . didn't eat much' – and to a nearby estate, where the manager showed them round the vandalised main house and served pancakes stuffed with cream cheese. Back in town there were trotting races, a concert, and an 'exquisitely pretty' ballet by a Madame Sadoff and her pupils:

> When encored Madame S. said 'I will dance again – for the English' . . . Afterwards we had supper, and were given a table out on the balcony with the Princess G. and her cousin, Countess K., and were shewn the greatest attention – quite a banquet. We finally got away about 2.30am, went for a run in the car with the ladies, and then dropped them at their house and got home quite ready for bed.[4]

Quite an evening for a country vicar's son.

At the end of September he travelled with Belayev to newly liberated Kursk – much sadder and emptier – where he was besieged by would-be interpreters. He ended up taking on a 'nervous, spectacled youth of twenty', whose father, a history professor, was one of thirty prominent citizens who the Reds had arrested during their occupation and taken with them when they left. The boy's health and language skills were poor – his luggage consisted 'chiefly of medicine bottles and dictionaries' – but pity won out, and Kennedy subsequently got by mostly in French. The most striking event of his stay was a mass funeral for about one hundred people executed by the Cheka. It was held outdoors, in front of the cathedral, and translating the bishop's sermon – on forgiveness – Belayev explained that the clergy were hedging their bets, too afraid of the Bolsheviks' return openly to condemn them.

On 9 October the two men finally set out by car for the front itself, 100 miles away up the Moscow *chaussée*. It was a monotonous journey, across flat wheat-growing country, and slow because the Bolsheviks had destroyed the bridges, which peasant details were replacing with timber causeways. (Their skill was remarkable; there was no need for a corps of engineers.) Billeted in farmhouses, Kennedy came into close contact with ordinary Russians for the first time. At first they struck him as heartwarmingly pleased to be liberated:

An old peasant came in, bowed deeply, and told us how welcome the Volunteer Army was, and how badly they had been treated by the Bolsh. Great curiosity about the English officer!

Our room was swept out, after a peasant woman had sprayed the floor with water by taking mouthfuls from a jug, and blowing and spitting it forth in all directions. The geraniums in the windows were dusted, and fresh straw laid down for beds. The walls were of timber, the interstices stuffed with grass. In a corner were the ikons, and the walls were pasted with sweetmeat wrappings, with a modern postcard or two in frames. A table was brought, and presently we had a sumptuous repast of cold goose, pies, potatoes, bread, honey and tea.[5]

Over the next few days, as the army splashed from village to village in rainy weather, he learned that actually, for the rural population Reds and Whites were as bad as each other. At halts, he made a practice of talking to the curious groups – 'shaggy, bearded, long coats' – who gathered round. The Bolsheviks, they complained, had taken their livestock and grain, and now the Volunteer Army was doing the same. Kennedy could see it for himself: long lines of country carts, carrying poultry and sheep with their legs tied, and he had never eaten so much goose in his life. The only bread on sale, meanwhile, was 'awful looking stuff', and the locals were obviously 'in the last stages of misery and poverty.'[6] In his end-of-expedition report he stressed the need for land reform. Peasants' 'first questions . . . were always with respect to Denikin's Agrarian Policy.' In other words, would they have to give fields they had occupied during the Revolution back to their owners? Since Denikin was ducking the land issue, Kennedy had no answer for them, and no more did his Russian colleagues.[7] The Bolsheviks, in contrast, told the peasants what they wanted to hear and put up posters everywhere; he took down two, bright and well-designed, from a schoolroom wall.

Entering the town of Oryol with the army on 14 October, Kennedy also saw for himself that Whites as well as Reds mistreated civilians and prisoners – and made no secret of it. Walking with Belayev to the cathedral for the usual thanksgiving service, he saw a man being dragged out of his house – a Communist, Belayev told him, who would 'probably be shot'. And on their way back they came upon a 'freshly killed man lying on the pavement' – again, 'a Jew or a Communist, I suppose.' At the evening's victory banquet, shouting over the noise of a band, a young colonel boasted that he had shot all the Red officers he had taken prisoner, and would shortly *fusiller* a divisional commander and his staff too. In line with Intervention practice, Kennedy was careful not to find out more, claiming in his report to have had 'no opportunity of verifying this'. The next day, waiting for a train back to Kursk, he saw some of the victims on the other side: fifteen 'miserably pale and ill looking' men and women in prison clothes. They were some of the Bolsheviks' arrestees, found imprisoned in a Cheka torture-house. The rest had been executed – amongst them his interpreter's history professor father.[8]

Coinciding with Yudenich's advance on Petrograd, the capture of Oryol made it possible to believe that the Whites were on their way to victory. In the Kremlin, the Politburo held emergency meetings.

In London, Churchill gloated. Ever since Cabinet's vote two months earlier to send Denikin 'one last packet' of aid but no more, he had been pushing for the decision's reversal. It was 'a cheap thing', he had written in a memo of 15 September, 'to mock at Denikin's efforts, and to indulge to the full the easy wisdom of pessimism and indifference.'[9] But Denikin was fighting Britain's war, as she would realise too late if the Bolsheviks were allowed to win. More notes followed on the 20th and the 22nd, the latter accompanied by a proposal that Denikin be granted a new £14-million loan. Sensitive to the accusation that Churchill was out of control – for headline-writers, the Intervention had become 'Mr Churchill's Private War' – Lloyd George let rip in an exasperated blast of a reply. Churchill's latest letter, he wrote, 'distressed' him. Again and again, he had asked Churchill to turn his mind to cutting the War Office's 'enormous expenditure', but again and again, Churchill's answer had related to Russia:

> I invited you to Paris to help me to reduce our commitments in the East. You then produce a lengthy and carefully prepared memorandum on Russia. I entreated you on Friday to let Russia be for at least 48 hours, and to devote your weekend to preparing for the Finance Committee . . . Your reply is to send me a four-page letter on Russia, and a closely printed memorandum of several pages – all on Russia. I am frankly in despair.

Churchill, the prime minister went on, might be eager to spend the hundreds of millions it would take to reconquer the country and prop up a new regime, but would not find 'another responsible person in the whole land' who agreed with him. Even Clemenceau and Foch, who used to 'talk a good deal about Anti-Bolshevism', were now clear that they would do no more. 'I wonder', he concluded, 'if it is any use making one last effort to induce you to throw off this obsession which, if you will forgive me for saying so, is upsetting your balance.'[10] Churchill did not give him the last word, replying from the leathery recesses of the Turf Club that Lloyd George was being 'very unkind and I think unjust', and that whether he himself got rid of his 'obsession' or Lloyd George got rid of him, the prime minister could 'not get rid of Russia'.[11] When Oryol fell three weeks later, the self-pity turned into triumphalism. War Office press releases predicted imminent victory for the 'National Russians', and a new memo to Cabinet was a six-page 'I told you so'. Over lunch with Field Marshal Wilson, Churchill confided that his ambition was to 'go out as a sort of Ambassador', and 'help Denikin to mould the new Russian Constitution.'[12]

But in reality, Denikin had reached the end of his punch. His armies were outnumbered, his overstretched supply lines were failing, and more broadly the military aid arriving at the Black Sea ports was being fed into a dysfunctional machine. Russian mismanagement and corruption had always been a problem, and after an August tour of the front Holman exploded in a letter to Denikin. Though 200,000 complete sets of clothing and equipment had been issued to the southern armies, he wrote, he had seen not a single soldier properly kitted out. Instead many were 'barefooted and in rags, fighting on cold nights without greatcoat, blanket or waterproof sheets.' Equally deplorable was the state of the military hospitals, where sick and wounded lay filthy and untended on the floor, despite the fact that 'a rich store of British medical equipment' sat waiting in Novorossiysk.[13] What was happening – as Holman did not allow correspondent Hodgson to report – was that equipment was being sold on the side. 'About the middle of 1919', Hodgson wrote later,

> the British sent out a complete 200-bed equipment for a hospital at Yekaterinodar. Not a single bed ever reached its destination. Beds, blankets, sheets, mattresses and pillows disappeared as if by magic. They found their way into the houses of staff officers and members of the government.

Fifteen hundred nurses' uniforms also vanished. During his whole time in Russia he never saw a nurse in one, but did see 'girls who were emphatically *not* nurses, walking the street of Novorossiysk wearing regulation British hospital skirts and stockings.'[14] The most notorious example of White carelessness – or perhaps of sabotage – was the loss of ten British tanks, which sat for weeks on a Novorossiysk jetty, until one stormy night they broke free of their lashings and rolled into the sea. Holman eventually extracted an order from

Denikin that British staff should remain in charge of supplies until they reached the front. But it made little difference: as he admitted in his final report, 'the incompetence and corruption of the administrative services and departments could not be overcome by any scheme.'[15] The root cause was the collapse of the economy. As Belayev pointed out to Kennedy, army pay was not nearly enough to live on. At the real as opposed to official exchange-rate, a Russian captain earned the same per month as Kennedy did per day. 'Speculation' was inevitable. When the Corp's second-in-command was caught selling a goods wagon's worth of leather on the side, what was his CO to do? 'Must he hang his own chief of staff?'[16]

By far the ghastliest symptom of Denikin's weakness was his continued reliance on pogroms to let the steam out of rank-and-file discontent. Standing outside Kursk's cathedral watching the mass funeral, Belayev had told Kennedy that the Jewish family in whose house he was staying were 'in great fear of being attacked and murdered' – because, Belayev explained, Jews identified 'largely with the Bolshevik movement', and held most of its top jobs.[17] The family were right to be frightened, because a new wave of antisemitic violence was about to break. In Kiev, taken by the Don Cossacks at the end of August, it was already dangerous for anyone of Jewish appearance to go out on the street. Random attacks turned into an outright pogrom on 16 October, when as described by the secretary to the Belgian consulate, 'organised bands of soldiers and officers from the Volunteer Army arrived by car, on horseback and on foot with the deliberate intention of attacking and looting defenseless Jewish homes.'[18] They systematically raided the stucco mansion blocks of the city centre, leaving the suburbs to lower ranks, and Podil, the commercial district down by the river, to an allied warlord. The Central Committee for the Relief of Pogrom Victims, an umbrella group co-founded by Nahum Gergel, collected over three hundred witness statements. One man was killed by soldiers who burst into his apartment shouting 'All Yids must die'. Another was shot dead from the street as he stepped out onto his balcony. Two Red Cross staff, a clerk and an accountant, were held hostage then murdered. At least five survivors of the previous month's pogrom at Fastov were killed in their hospital beds, after soldiers burst in demanding to know which patients had come from there. Many testimonies hint at rape. 'As long as I live', wrote the Belgian of the sounds coming from a neighbouring apartment, 'I will not forget the screams . . . [They] continued for about an hour and then ceased. The lone voice of a woman, resembling the bark of a dog, could then be heard.' In another flat that he was taken to he saw a whole family, 'father, mother, and a little girl', lying 'in a pool of blood, their bodies terribly mutilated, their hands torn off, separated from the body by sabre blows.'[19] As in Ukraine at the time of writing – again under unfathomably bloody occupation – people were not able to get their relatives to cemeteries for burial, and instead dug graves for them in flowerbeds and courtyards. Final estimates of the death toll ranged from four hundred to six hundred.[20]

As usual, the White authorities denied any responsibility. The same day that the Kiev pogrom began, a local paper published an interview with the military district's governor, General Vladimir Dragomirov. Fresh from a diplomatic mission to London and Paris, he knew the form. Asked about the recent atrocities at Fastov, he intoned that the whole Jewish nation could not be held responsible for Bolshevik crimes, and promised courts-martial for the perpetrators. He also cited a telegram from Denikin, ordering him to take 'proper measures' against 'excesses'.[21] What he actually did, however, was allow the rapes and killings to run for five days. Government newspapers fanned the flames with fabricated scare stories, and accused Jews of bringing the violence on themselves. 'Will the Jews learn something from these nights of terror?' asked one; would they 'beat their breasts, cover their heads with ashes and repent before all the world' for having taken 'such active part in the Bolshevik madness?' Or would they carry on 'denying well-known facts, and thus still more inflame anti-Jewish feeling?'[22] There were no courts-martial or punishments, and Dragomirov stayed in his job.

The British reaction was as token as ever too – another finger-wagging War Office telegram, sent on 25 October. A remark Denikin had let drop in a meeting with Jewish delegates from Constantinople a few months earlier showed that he knew not to take it seriously. Having detailed recent White pogroms, the delegates asked Denikin to make a strong public statement against them. Kolchak, they reminded him, had already done so. 'As for Kolchak', Denikin replied, 'that's different. There, there are Americans.' British protests, it was implied, were for show, and could safely be ignored.[23] Deserving of honourable mention is Lionel Gundry-White, a twenty-five-year-old major with the Mission's offshoot in Odessa. Sent to attend a signing ceremony (for a short-lived alliance between the Volunteer Army and the formerly Polish-ruled western Ukrainians) in the town of Vinnitsya, he threw off the Russian staff captain acting as his inter-preter-cum-minder, and made his own enquiries as to why the town was full of destitute Jews. We know of his initiative thanks to the Volunteer Army's letters of complaint to Gundry-White's CO and to Mission headquarters. 'Tactlessly' and with an 'undue degree of persistency and nervousness', Gundry-White had used his 'superficial French' to ask questions 'of a political character'. His conclusions were 'extremely careless', unsurprisingly so since he was 'obviously a Jew himself by origin' and thus unable to take a 'sufficiently object-ive point of view'. It was 'extremely desirable' that he be recalled. But Gundry-White was the exception that proved a rule. All the other British in Odessa, Mission HQ was assured, correctly understood matters and did everything possible to strengthen Anglo-Russian ties.[24]

On the last day of the Kiev pogrom – 20 October – Denikin lost Oryol again, having held it for only a week. Four days later Voronezh fell to the Bolsheviks' new 'Horse Army', mostly made up of Bolshevik Cossacks. From then on the Red Army – still badly equipped and trained, but now much bigger than the White ones, steadily pushed Denikin's forces back south.

Witness to Denikin's advance and retreat was keen-as-mustard Major Hudleston Williamson. A convinced Interventionist, his early letters home breathe enthusiasm. The campaign, he wrote to his mother after an August tour of the front, was like something out of 'the days of Marlborough'. The Cossacks were 'splendid fellows', and riding over the thyme-covered steppe – 'blue and gold and pink, wonderfully sweet-smelling for mile after mile' – was 'tremendous', with 'always a glorious bathe in the Don in the evening.' His concerns were for the Russian soldiers – only 60 per cent of them had boots, and you could see their knees and elbows through their uniforms – and the military hospitals, which had '*no* anaesthetics, *no* anti-tetanus, *no* sheets, *no* blankets, *no* ambulance carts, millions of flies.' His mother should collect supplies – sheets, bandages, lint, soup-squares, sugar and flour – and send them at once: 'Parcels and packing cases – no matter how small or large, and do rouse public sympathy for us here.'[25]

A fourth letter, of mid-September, is undimmed. He has been flying about with the RAF (looking, as he does not say, for misplaced M Devices), and Denikin is 'doing wonderfully'. Her parcels have started to arrive and he has more orders for her: two 'good *large* pictures of our King and Queen', to hang in British-run hospitals, and 1,000 Christmas puddings, so as to give all the patients 'Christmas dinner à l'Anglais. Can you start a fund for that? . . . Some firm like Harrods would do it but I should think it would come to about £250.'[26] With the loss of Oryol and Voronezh, notes of doubt start to creep in. The military amateurishness that had been charming in high summer, during an advance, was less so in rain and snow, on retreat. Visiting a Russian observation point, he had discovered thirty officers and soldiers eating round campfires, the smoke obvious to the enemy only a few hundred yards away. The commander told him that 'if the O.P. was located, well it was just too bad. Nothing very desperate would happen, and they would just have to find another one somewhere.' Williamson asked him why he was wasting ammunition 'dropping shells here and there but nowhere near any worthwhile target that I could see.' With disconcerting candour the commander replied that if he stopped firing his infantry would abandon their positions. After a while a captain dressed in a covert coat and tweed cap galloped up, with the news that a hundred Red cavalry 'were somewhere behind us.' He galloped off again, nothing more was seen of him or of any Red cavalry, and 'the operation being concluded, we all rode back to Divisional Hqrs for tea and vodka.'[27]

Harder to frame as amusing, though like all British Interventionists Williamson did his best to ignore them, were White atrocities. Unmentioned in letters home was a massacre of prisoners that he and a colleague chanced across. As recounted in a later memoir, they happened to stop for the night at a just-captured village into which a Don Cossack unit had just rounded some three hundred prisoners.

The prisoners were terrified, pleading that they had been forcibly conscripted and their families taken hostage. The following morning they were nonetheless 'taken out of the town and all shot with machine-guns . . . It was a sickening experience, but . . . as our opinion was never asked, it was wisest to try not to see what happened.'[28]

With few illusions to lose was Prince Andrei Lobanov-Rostovsky, last seen sleeping on a monastery floor in the Princes' Islands, having fled Odessa. In August he had returned to Russia to join Denikin, now headquartered in the Azov Sea port of Taganrog. Shortages and a brief alarm at warlord Makhno's approach aside, the town felt like 'a little capital, or a parody of one', with the military missions filling the role of embassies, and the Volunteer officers' regiments that of the old Imperial Guards. With Denikin's star still rising, a pseudo-court gathered around him, and busied itself with seating plans and etiquette. Assigned to intelligence, Lobanov-Rostovsky found his colleagues paranoid – the fact that he had briefly held a British commission was a cause of suspicion – and comically ignorant. Processing files on suspect persons, he came upon one on himself, and discovered that people who he had thought friends were informing on him. ('Dutifully I wrote on these papers "Case settled. File under letter L."') On another occasion, Denikin personally instructed him to look into an intercepted letter. An entirely innocent invitation to tea from one young woman to another, it had been written on YMCA notepaper. The intelligence men had mistaken the YMCA's triangular logo for a Masonic sign, 'and the Masons, in the eyes of the average Russian officer, were the paid servants of International Zionism.'[29]

Though the dinners and receptions went on, after Oryol was lost the mood changed. Every few weeks Lobanov-Rostovsky interpreted at a regular joint meeting on Allied aid. Under the surface formalities it had always been scratchy, the Allied representatives complaining of inefficiency and delay, and the Russian ones, *sotto voce*, that they were being dumped with outdated, sub-standard equipment. Once Denikin went into retreat, Allied impatience became much more marked. It was Lobanov-Rostovsky's 'painful task' to brief the meeting on the latest news from the front. 'Standing in front of a large map with flags and pins, I repeated over and over that the retreat was due to a shortening of our lines in preparation for a new offensive, which of course no one believed.' The Poles, who 'hoped to be able to get Kiev', were 'jubilant; their smiles broader and broader as the news became worse . . . The French shook their heads and said "Mon Dieu!" The British remained charming, but somewhat more reserved and mysterious.'[30]

By early November it was obvious that Denikin had no hope of taking Moscow, this season at least. To the east Vrangel still held Tsaritsyn, with the RAF's help. And to the west, the Volunteer Army still occupied Kiev. But the march on the capital had gone into reverse. In Kursk, Kennedy underwent the standard Interventionist awkwardness of saying goodbye to Russian friends. He had spent three pleasant weeks there with the Belayevs, learning Russian in the mornings and riding in the afternoons. The lowlight was a public hanging in the town square, the highlight a village wedding: starlit sled-ride, rings and crowns and a blushing bride who signed her name with a cross, sugared *kasha* and guest beds made up on the floor with sweet-smelling straw. On 5 November a telegram arrived ordering him to report to headquarters. His feelings, he confided to his diary, were mixed. It was flattering to be asked to join the Mission staff, but he was 'really *very* sorry' to leave the Belayevs, who had shown him 'the greatest hospitality and kindness', and made him feel 'quite one of the family'.[31] On the three-day, stop-start train journey back to Taganrog he was hosted by a friendly Colonel Sakhnovsky. Chatting, Sakhnovsky showed Kennedy some official stamps he had picked up in a commissar's abandoned office, and used them to print five-pointed Communist stars in Kennedy's notebook. In return Kennedy showed the colonel some English banknotes, and when he admired the picture of the Houses of Parliament on a £1 note, gave it to him as a souvenir. Sakhnovsky insisted on paying him 400 roubles for it, but before they parted Kennedy hid the money in one of the colonel's files, with a cheery note saying that the exchange rate had once been ten roubles to the pound, and that 'when this rate obtained once more with the returning prosperity of Russia', he would claim his ten roubles back. Sakhnovsky's name and address are written in big, careful capital letters on the notebook's last page. Kursk fell to the Boksheviks a week later.

21

'Russia is a quicksand'

Denikin went into reverse so quickly in part because Trotsky was able to transfer troops from the east, where Kolchak was already in steady retreat. The largest Allied forces in Siberia were still the Czech Legion, with about seventy thousand troops, and the Japanese, with thirty thousand – well down on the year before, although Tokyo was also still supporting Semyonov and an equally bloodstained warlord called Kalmykov, based north of Vladivostok at Khabarovsk. The third largest force in Siberia, with only 7,000 men, was America's, under General Graves. Tasked, under an Inter-Allied Railway Agreement of the spring, with protecting sections of the Trans-Siberian east of Lake Baikal, in practice it helped Kolchak. But posted to remote railway towns, the Americans also witnessed White cruelties that were easy to ignore in Omsk or Vladivostok.

Graves's anti-Intervention instincts were confirmed by an eight-week late summer trip to Omsk and back. Ever since arriving in Russia he had resisted visiting Kolchak, arguing that to do so would make it look as though the United States were giving him official recognition. Back in Washington, however, the pro-Intervention State Department won out, and in early July Graves was ordered to make the trip in company with the equally pro-Intervention ambassador to Japan, Roland Morris. Unlike Knox on his Express, on the outward journey they did their best to canvas a broad range of opinion. In the towns they stopped at on the way they met civic representatives as well as the military, and during refuelling halts, sent their interpreters to talk to refugees, with instructions to focus on likelier-to-be-outspoken women. At Verkhnye-Udinsk (on the still-active camel-caravan route from China, and today's Ulan-Ude), Colonel Charles Morrow of the US 27th Infantry described the extravagant brutalities being inflicted on the region by Semyonov, and on the other side of Lake Baikal, at Krasnoyarsk, they heard almost as lurid stories about General Sergei Rozanov, Kolchak's appointee as regional governor. By the time they got to Omsk, in the third week of July, even Morris had to admit that they had not found 'a single individual who spoke a good word for the Kolchak regime.'[1]

On arrival Graves asked permission to go on another 180 miles to Petropavlovsk (just into today's Kazakhstan) to see for himself a much-advertised new mobilisation. Kolchak's staff tried to dissuade him with talk of train-jams, and when he persisted, suggested that he go north to Ishim, from where he could easily get to Petropavlovsk by car. It soon became obvious that they intended a wild goose chase. On the first day, Graves's train puffed out of Omsk on time, but then sat in an isolated siding for twenty-four hours. On the second, the train was stopped by Kolchak officers, who told the American corporal in charge of the guard that it was needed for military purposes, and that Graves and his party would have to disembark. 'This corporal', Graves gleefully recounts,

> decided that he could handle the situation without reporting to me. [He] ordered his guard to load their rifles, and notified those Russia officers that 'if they started anything there would be more dead Russian officers in that town than they had ever seen.' This resulted in us moving on toward Ishim.[2]

At Ishim itself 'the ubiquitous English officer appeared', and told Graves not to go any further because he would certainly be captured, 'spoiling all we have accomplished over here'. Graves then went in search of the Russian in charge, who first pretended to be having a nap, and when Graves insisted on an interview became 'exceedingly unfriendly':

> I asked him for an escort, and told him that I was directed to do so by [Kolchak's C-in-C] General Diterikhs. He replied that he had no soldiers he could trust as an escort for me. I then asked him if I could have the motor cars General Diterikhs told me I could have, and he replied that he could not let me have any cars. I then asked him if there

were any cars in the town [that] we could hire to take us to Petropavlovsk. He replied 'Yes, but you will not get them.' In the meantime, [he] had sent for a glass of tea, and sat there and drank it in our presence without asking us to join him, so we arose, said 'Goodbye' and left.[3]

Put on his mettle, in the early evening Graves set off in his own staff car, accompanied only by driver, interpreter, two officers and a soldier. After covering sixty-three miles on what Omsk had promised was a highway but was actually a faint track, they parked for the night in an oatfield, plagued by mosquitoes. The next morning they reached the river Ishim and a village, where they handed out Hershey bars to the children, and were just able to fit the car – a seven-seater Cadillac – onto a hand-operated cable-raft. Thirty miles on they arrived at Petropavlovsk, where there was no sign of what Omsk had promised were 100,000 new troops, nor of any train-jam. The Russian general in charge had not been notified of any American visit, but in Graves's words,

threw his arms around me and was very hospitable. I asked him where his troops were and he said that he had none. I asked him how they expected to start an offensive in two weeks if they had no troops there. He said that if an offensive was contemplated I knew more about it than he did.[4]

Back in Omsk, Graves asked General Diterikhs for an explanation. Diterikhs replied that the Petropavlovsk commander didn't know what he was talking about, and that Graves had gone to the wrong place. Graves wired Washington that the new mobilisation had obviously utterly failed.

Graves's general revulsion at the whole White scene was intensified on the journey back to Vladivostok, during which he heard an eye-witness description of a recent Semyonov atrocity from three lieutenants of the American Railway Service Corps. On 18 August they had been at Adrianovka – a tiny stop east of Semyonov's headquarters at Chita – when a trainload of about four hundred prisoners pulled in. It being common knowledge at the station that the prisoners were to be executed, they decided to keep an eye on the train, and find out what they could. The next morning Semyonov and Kolchak officers – the latter identifiable by their British uniforms – went aboard, plus a machine-gun and a work detail carrying long-handled shovels. When the train moved off one of the Railway Corps men, John McDonald, jogged after it, and caught up with it only about a mile away, idling at a curve. Before he could get near a sentry ordered him to turn back: 'I pretended not to understand Russian, but he put a [round] into his rifle to assist . . . I understood.' He walked back to the station, and a while later the train returned, empty.

The next morning, in heavy rain, all three lieutenants walked down the line, passing on the way a woman carrying what was obviously looted clothing. At the curve they found heaped bullet casings and three newly dug mass graves, one so perfunctory that the limbs of the dead protruded. Further on were three older graves, which had been dug up by stray dogs. Some of the bodies, McDonald recounted, 'had the feet cut off, one had no head, one had the genitals cut off. Of course, dogs might have done it, but it didn't look like the work of dogs.' Two days later the Americans went again to the execution ground, and were shown more mass graves by small boys who were working through them for valuables. The same night, Semyonov and his Japanese advisors arrived at Adrianovka and held a 'big banquet', with women, music and 'plenty of booze'.[5] Telling were the contrasting reactions when the lieutenants reported their findings to Allied personnel at Chita. An American intelligence officer went to the site himself, and sent a report on it to Washington. But in discussion with Ambassador Morris, a British Captain Raynor was 'indignant that the Americans had the gall to suggest that the ataman would execute men without a fair trial.'[6] The Adrianovka atrocity was only one of dozens – executions, rapes, abductions and beatings – witnessed or heard of by the Railway Corps over the summer.

When Graves arrived back in Vladivostok in early September, the city was simmering. The source of tension was the presence of General Gajda, who had been dismissed by Kolchak in July, decamped east and joined forces with a group of centre-left Siberian politicians led by the former chair of Tomsk's regional assembly, Ivan Yakushev.

Proposing that the failing, brutal Kolchak regime be replaced with an assembly of municipal and rural councils, they approached the Allies for support. The transfer of power, they promised, would be bloodless, and they would establish friendly relations with Denikin. Graves and Ambassador Morris – fully cured of Interventionism by his Omsk trip – were strongly sympathetic. More cautiously so were Knox's deputy, Brigadier-General Blair (in charge of the Mission while Knox was in Omsk), and Eliot's replacement as high commissioner, William O'Reilly, a career diplomat without previous Russia experience. O'Reilly wired to London that political as well as military solutions were needed, that the 'Kolchak or Bolshevism' argument was a 'bogey', and that the Yakushev group deserved a hearing.[7]

Matters came to a head when Kolchak's new appointee as military governor, the same Rozanov who had been terrorising Krasnoyarsk, responded to coup rumours by filling Vladivostok with the Japanese-backed warlord Kalmykov's irregulars. On 26 September all the Allied military mission heads – including, oddly, the Japanese one – lodged a joint demand that they be removed within three days. The denouement exposed the divide between the more open-minded Allied camp in Vladivostok, and the strongly pro-Kolchak one 3,000 miles away in Omsk. On hearing that Blair had put his name to the ultimatum, Knox ordered him to rescind it, and took away his command. He also targeted O'Reilly, wiring to Churchill that the new commissioner had fallen for 'local tittle-tattle'.[8] Churchill duly pressured Curzon to give O'Reilly the push:

> His ignorance of the Russian situation, his want of conviction as to policy, his fatuous verbosity – are really the limit. Why should he be allowed to choke the wires with . . . unending abuse and detraction of Kolchak? All this stuff circulating about the Cabinet does harm. People who are not closely informed on the Russian situation fasten on this or that phrase . . . Forgive this fury. We are so near to immense events.[9]

Curzon acceded, and soon-to-be-justified O'Reilly was posted to Bolivia. (Whether he thought this better or worse than Siberia, history does not relate.)

Similarly typical – on the American side this time – of the way pro-Interventionists tried to suppress anti-White views was the treatment of an American aid organiser, Dr Frank Rosenblatt. An émigré from western Ukraine, with a PhD in economics from Columbia and several years in US government service, Rosenblatt represented the Joint Jewish Distribution Committee or 'Joint', a New York-based aid organisation set up by the banker Sigmund Warburg at the start of the war. Arriving in Vladivostok in spring 1919, he found fewer Jewish refugees than expected, but was swamped with complaints about White antisemitism. Passing them on to the Joint, however, proved difficult. When he wrote his first report Graves was away, so instead he went to the Red Cross's Dr Teusler, and asked if he might use his cablegram machine. To his amazement Teusler flatly refused, telling him that any pogroms would be 'fully deserved', and that if he really wanted to serve his people he should persuade them to cease Bolshevik activity and profiteering. Rosenblatt later discovered that Teusler would not employ any Jews, not even Americans, and had instructed Red Cross headquarters that when recruiting Russian-speakers they should 'always watch out for Jewish blood, and if found DON'T enrol.'[10]

When rumours reached Vladivostok of the White's pre-evacuation pogrom at Yekaterinburg in July, Rosenblatt wrote a second report, this time turning to Graves for help. Graves cabled it as requested, and also made his own enquiries of Kolchak's staff, who made 'no direct admission, but . . . hinted that something had occurred at Yekaterinburg that would give the Jews something to think about.'[11] On its passage through the State Department, the report was noticed by pro-Intervention Lansing, who asked the American consul-general in Omsk, Ernest Harris, for more information. Harris replied with outright lies: Rosenblatt's claims were 'absolutely false'. There had not been 'a single pogrom, or any Jew discriminated against, since Kolchak came to power', and rumours to the contrary were put about by Jewish draft dodgers. Harris also wired Rosenblatt with a threat: his 'false and irresponsible reports' would 'embitter the Omsk government against the Jews.'[12] Lansing did not pass Rosenblatt's report on to the Joint, and instructed Graves to send no more cables on Rosenblatt's behalf, nor any that had 'not been checked for accuracy'

– in other words, been passed by Harris. If Harris meant to criticise Rosenblatt's estimate of the Yekaterinburg death toll, Graves drily noted, he 'could probably justify his statement, as no one was in a position to give the exact number.' But 'if Mr Harris meant to say that there were no Jews killed, he was woefully misinformed.'[13]

The British attitude to Rosenblatt was satirised by Knox's aide Gerhardie in his novelised memoir *Futility*. At a Vladivostok supper-party, a Jewish dentist describes asking an Allied diplomat – unnamed but resembling Eliot – to protect Jews from Kolchak's soldiers:

> The diplomat was . . . a wonderful linguist, a marvellous specimen of humanity. There he sat before me, maintaining a most distressing silence in twenty-eight foreign languages. 'I beg of you to intercede', I said, 'to prevent their being massacred. I entreat you, sir, to protest.'
>
> 'My dear Mr Eisenstein,' he said at last, 'how can I protest – before they are killed? . . . I have been a diplomatist now for thirty-six years, and never once in my career, sir, have I said anything that – well, could be misconstrued – to mean something. And I am certainly not going to revise my methods now.'[14]

Gerhardie's Knox character chips in with 'You Jews . . . are all damned Bolsheviks.'

Graves's refusal to join in the prevalent culture of antisemitism – in particular, his refusal to dismiss Jewish interpreters – helped turn him into a hate figure of the Vladivostok right. In August and September the mutual dislike spilled into physical clashes between American and Russian soldiers. There were endless stand-offs over trains; an American captain and corporal were abducted and beaten by Kalmykov's men; and an American was shot dead by a Russian officer in Vladivostok railway station, after the Russian told him he was a 'bloody Bolshevik' and he waved a fist in response. 'To make the scene more effective', wrote Graves bitterly,

> some Japanese officers, who were at the station and saw the murder, congratulated the Russian by shaking hands with him over the American's body. The Russian went at once to the fake civil court . . . was tried, and in one hour acquitted. This Russian was a part of

Kolchak's fighting forces to whom the United States was turning over arms and ammunition.[15]

From then on Graves refused to hand shipments of American rifles to Rozanov, but insisted on sending them under American guard direct to Omsk.

The Civil War, meanwhile, was reaching its climax. In western Siberia, a White counter-offensive briefly forced the Red Army back over the river Tobol. The mood in Omsk swung from despair to euphoria, but the Reds regrouped, and in the middle of October resumed their push east. On the 24th they captured Tobolsk, 300 miles from Omsk and Siberia's oldest city. And on the 31st, after a three-day battle, they took Petropavlovsk, the town that Kolchak's staff officers had tried so hard to stop Graves getting to in the summer.

It was the turning-point. In the past twelve days, the Whites had been defeated outside Petrograd and driven back from Moscow, and now they were about to lose Omsk too. Between 6 and 8 November, the Allied representatives in the city packed up and departed. For Lloyd George, it was perfect timing. On the evening of the 8th, as Knox sped east for the last time in his Express, he stood up in the Guildhall to make his annual speech at the Lord Mayor's Banquet. The subject — which he had not spoken about in public since the spring — was Russia. He had made his preparations carefully, keeping his own thoughts to himself but letting others air theirs thoroughly before he made his move. Cabinet, now back to its peacetime size of twenty-two, had discussed the question twice, and there had been a fiery debate in the House of Commons. Liberal MP Cecil l'Estrange Malone, one of the anti-Intervention 'Three Musketeers', described his recent visit to Moscow, complete with ride on Trotsky's train.* Colonel John Ward,

---

* Malone was a remarkable character. A much-decorated naval aviation pioneer, he had commanded a seaplane-carrier at Gallipoli, and was elected to parliament in the post-war 'khaki' election. His Moscow trip turned him into a passionate Communist, and at a rally in the Albert Hall the following year he called for revolution at home: 'What are a few Churchills or a few Curzons on lampposts, compared to the massacre of thousands?' When the police raided his flat they found a ticket for a left luggage locker, and in the locker, booklets on bomb-making and bank-raiding. He was prosecuted for sedition and sentenced to six months in gaol.

back from Siberia with his Middlesexes, riposted by recounting how with his own eyes he had seen victims of the Cheka brought up from under the ice of the Kama river – many, he added, obviously ordinary working people. Churchill weighed in with his famous metaphor for the Germans' despatch of Lenin to Petrograd in 1917. They had put him on his sealed train 'in the same way that you might send a phial . . . of typhoid or cholera to be poured into the water supply of a great city.' (Leaving the chamber after the debate, Balfour complimented him on 'the exaggerated way you tell the truth.')[16]

Having allowed the intractability of the Russia question to sink in, and without telling even his foreign secretary what he intended, Lloyd George launched his Guildhall bombshell. 'I would feel much happier', he told his audience, 'if I knew that the Russian tangle were in the course of being cleared up.' Only a few weeks ago the news had been 'distinctly promising'. But now it pointed to 'a more prolonged and sanguinary struggle.' Yudenich's 'daring raid' on Petrograd had 'not come off', Denikin's 'brilliant advance' on Moscow had been 'temporarily checked', and reports from Omsk were 'certainly not reassuring'. He was not predicting Bolshevik victory: he had 'seen the Russian skies look just as black before' and it was 'a land of surprises'. But what he dreaded was 'an interminable series of swaying contests', with all the 'cruelties, the reprisals and counter-reprisals which are inseparable from such warfare.' He also predicted, though it would not make him popular, that Bolshevism 'could not be suppressed by the sword.' Back in January, the Powers had tried to bring the two sides to the negotiating table with the Prinkipo proposal. It had been premature, but he hoped that soon a renewed attempt would have better success. Finally he came to the nitty gritty. He did not regret a penny of the £100 million of military aid already sent. If the Russian people wanted freedom, 'we can always say that we have given them the chance.' But Britain could not, 'of course', keep up such an expensive effort indefinitely. To close, he invoked Napoleon's doomed Grande Armée: 'Russia is a quicksand. Victories are usually won in Russia, but you sink in victories; great armies and great empires in the past have been overwhelmed . . . Russia is a dangerous land.'[17]

The speech caused a furore. *The Times* hinted at conspiracy: like Prinkipo, the change of policy was the work of 'prominent Jewish financiers in New York, whose interest in Trotsky is of old standing.'[18] From the War Office, Churchill launched another barrage of notes – arguing for renewed pressure on Finland to attack Petrograd, for more pleas to Washington and Tokyo that they help Kolchak, for a new arms shipment to Murmansk, and for more aid for 'poor Denikin'. In Paris, Clemenceau told colleagues that Lloyd George was 'a deserter in the face of the enemy' – hypocritical since he himself had sent no more troops to Russia since the Odessa *débâcle*. From Washington alone there was not much reaction, the whole business of government having been semi-suspended since 2 October, when President Wilson suffered a massive stroke. (Brought on by a punishing speaking tour to drum up support for his League of Nations, it paralysed his left side, and for the remainder of his presidency his wife and doctor kept visitors away and made decisions in his name.) With the large majority of his Cabinet behind him, Lloyd George sat out the storm. There would be no precipitate withdrawals; the missions to Siberia and the South would stay for the time being. But in sum the Whites were failing, Britain could not support them for ever, and they should start thinking about making peace.

22

'The falls of Niagara'

SIX DAYS AFTER Lloyd George's Guildhall speech, Kolchak abandoned Omsk, triggering the longest and grimmest of the Civil
War's great retreats. The last few days were frantic, as the government
imploded (Diterikhs resigned) and people scrambled for any sort of
transport east. Czech Legionary Becvar had the heart-rending task of
turning away the streams of desperate people who came begging
for 'just a corner' on a Legion train. Some resorted to trickery, one
man turning up 'accompanied by an attractive young girl, begging
us to save his daughter, and incidentally himself, from the fury of
the Bolsheviks.' She turned out to be a local prostitute, hired for the
occasion. Though under strict orders not to let on any non-Czechs,
Becvar cracked when a Russian colonel, 'well over fifty' and looking
'utterly worn out', asked for places for his (genuine) wife and
daughter.

> His voice trembled. It was most painful to listen to . . . I could see
> from letters he had brought that he had many friends in the Legion,
> and had often cooperated with our troops during the Siberian
> campaign. Suddenly I felt that I could not refuse anyone again.[1]

Space was made for them.

Kolchak and his entourage left Omsk on 13 November 1919, in a
convoy of seven trains: six for his mistress, ministers and staff, an
armoured *bronevik*, and a special goods train, twenty-nine trucks long,
to transport up to £65 million of bullion – the remainder of the
tsarist gold reserve. Amongst the troops left in the rearguard was
Lieutenant Fyedotov, back from the Kama River Flotilla and in charge
of a battalion of marines. That evening, having arranged his patrols,

he went to bed fully dressed, 'rather surmising' that the regiments still in Omsk would 'join the Red Army as soon as things got too hot for us go keep an eye on them.'[2] At dawn he was shaken awake by an adjutant, who told him there was nobody left at headquarters, and that their instructions were to keep order in the streets, and retreat when the enemy drew near. About noon Red patrols appeared on the far bank of the Irtysh, amongst the chimneys of the factory district, and Fyedotov and the adjutant gathered the marines and rode at their head out of town, the men's hobnailed British boots making an incongruously cheerful clinking sound on the frozen road. That evening, having supper in a village, Fyedotov noticed that his Naval Guard insignia – a cross-shaped medallion engraved with Nicholas II's monogram – had come loose from his jacket. The loss upset him more than the sight of a dog chewing a roadside corpse had done earlier in the day. The adjutant taxed him with 'joining the ranks of the superstitious':

> I told him I felt that I should never again wear the Naval Guard uniform, never again be a real officer of a real regiment of which one could be proud. We were now a mere rabble, pretending to be soldiers. [He] did his best to cheer me. Our armies would rally, we should defeat the Reds, and Moscow would yet see our flags. I did not argue.[3]

Meanwhile the Red Army had entered Omsk unopposed, capturing dozens of artillery pieces, thousands of machine-guns, over forty locomotives and hundreds of goods wagons, many of them loaded with supplies.

Three days after Kolchak fled Omsk, in Vladivostok Gajda and Yakushev made a bid for power, declaring a Siberian National Directorate. As shops put up their shutters and the everyday sound of stray rifle shots quickened into a steady rat-a-tat, the Allied missions met and decided to stay neutral. The deputy commander of Japanese troops, General Oi Shigemoto, also set up checkpoints all over the city, forestalling any pro-Gajda popular rising. It was the green light for Rozanov, who with the help of 500 cadets from a British-run officer training school quickly pinned down Gajda's supporters on the three-mile tongue of land – wharfs, sidings, sheds – enclosing the commercial harbour. The centre of the battle was the railway station, an 1890s fantasia – Muscovite monastery cum Loire château – situated at the peninsula's landward end.

Headquartered directly opposite the station's main entrance, the British had a ringside seat. From his office window Gerhardie watched as 'a fearless cadet in British khaki' took up a position on a bridge over the tracks, 'and rattled off his machine-gun. Then he lay still. Several bodies were already lying on the square, some dead, others wriggling.'[4] At six in the evening, as drizzle turned into snow, Gajda captured the station's main building, and the green and white Siberian flag rose over its mansard roof. Rozanov's response was to put machine-guns at the windows of his offices, which occupied the same premises as the Mission, and train them on the station opposite. The firefight went on all night (when not lying flat on the floor, the British brought in both sides' wounded) until at five in the morning the cadets went in with grenades, dislodging Gajda's men room by room. Three hours later a final batch of prisoners were brought across the square to Russian headquarters – 'for trial', the British were told. Shortly afterwards eighteen were marched back inside the station, made to descend its grand central staircase, and executed by machine-gun at the bottom.

'I was able to get all over the scene of the fighting immediately afterwards', an appalled young Royal Engineer wrote home:

The dead were lying thickly along the road, wharves and railway lines – about 500 bodies – and the ghastliness of the whole thing is indescribable. The interior of the station was the worst and this actually ran with blood. The remainder of the prisoners were marched to a distant part of the harbour and shot with machine-guns. Thus ended the revolution of November 17th–18th, the result of which will only be to create a thirst for vengeance ... What struck me most was that both Govm't troops and insurgents were wearing British clothing and boots, and firing British ammunition out of American rifles and Canadian machine-guns. There you have in a nutshell the result of Allied 'help' in Russia.[5]

Gerhardie walked over the grisly scene too. In *Futility* he describes it with Waugh-esque flippancy: the snow-covered bodies lay in 'horrid postures'; Rozanov's soldiers were bayoneting the wounded 'amid unspeakable yells'. Since he had not seen active service during the war, in reality it was his first experience of mass killing, and in letters home he did not attempt the pose. 'The horror of the sight of a dead body', he wrote to his parents,

> is that it brings home to you, stronger than perhaps anything else . . . the *temporary* nature of a human being. What was once a human being is now an object – like a stone, or a stick . . . This was done by the people whom we are helping, and honestly, with the best intention in the world it is difficult to see any difference in the methods of the Bolsheviks and the reactionaries.[6]

Gajda was captured during the fighting, but after a beating, allowed to sail for Shanghai. To Graves's embarrassment, five of his most prominent supporters managed to make their way to American head-quarters and there begged for asylum. Graves's dilemma – breach neutrality, or send them to their deaths? – was solved by a resourceful Colonel Bugbee, who without asking for orders quietly took them out of town at nightfall, and let them 'escape'. Gajda's collaborator Yakushev was less fortunate, washing up dead on the shore a few days later.

On departing Omsk a week before its fall, Knox had asked for volunteers to stay behind for as long as possible and report on developments. Thirteen – four officers, four NCOs and five soldiers – raised their hands, and another two officers, who had been with Kolchak units, joined at the last minute. Led by Major Leonard Vining, a steady, middle-aged Indian Army man who played the bagpipes, the group included two notable figures. The first was Brian Horrocks, a twenty-four-year-old infantry captain not long out of a German PoW camp, and in time to come one of Montgomery's corps commanders in the Western Desert. The second was Francis McCullagh, forty-five-year-old son of an Omagh publican, and a well-known war correspondent and author. A lively writer with an eye for the absurd, he had covered the Russo-Japanese, Libyan and Balkan wars, and commanded a company at Gallipoli. He was also the only Mission member liked by Gerhardie, who found that his 'dry, shrivelled-up exterior concealed a good deal of subtle humour.'[7] The rest of the group included another Irishman – a musical-hall pianist called Joseph Rooney – two Canadians and an American. Also attached to it – fatally, as things turned out – were about two dozen civilians; a mixture of elderly Russians promised rescue by Knox, and stray British citizens (or people claiming to be such) taken pity on by Vining.

Delayed by blockages at the station – Vining and a sergeant spent a night shunting wagons out of the way by hand – they left Omsk twenty-four hours later than planned, on the same day that the Red Army entered the west-bank half of the city. They joined a mass movement of humanity eastward along the Trans-Siberian and its parallel road, the old penal transportation system's dreaded *trakt*. The journey had the repetitive, closed-loop quality of a nightmare. Attached to a Polish train, the group's two carriages travelled at not much more than walking pace, passing and repassing a stream of soldiers on foot and on horseback. 'I used to drop off to sleep at dusk', wrote McCullagh, 'watching the busbies of the Cossacks bobbing endlessly past the window.' Each time he woke in the night they were 'still passing, and for a fraction of a second . . . I was uncertain whether the dream was not the reality and this incredible, infinite procession the dream.' Though the soldiers still had their weapons and kept more or less to their units, the retreat felt unstoppable, like being 'manacled in a rudderless boat shooting down towards the falls of Niagara.'[8]

The group's overriding task was keeping their locomotive going. Wood for fuel was relatively plentiful, but most water-towers had frozen, and when one did still function there were near-fights with soldiers from other trains. Sometimes they were able to fill the boiler at a village well – adding a bucket-chain to several already radiating from it – but mostly they had to 'snow', which was hard work in heavy clothing, and frustrating because so little water was produced that in a few hours the engine began to flag again. They also had to mount a round-the-clock guard to prevent their locomotive from being stolen by other crews, and to stop its driver, who they suspected of Bolshevism, from deliberately letting its pipes freeze. There were more tense scenes at stations, where echelon commanders crowded into stationmasters' offices, shouting for priority and fingering their revolvers. 'Failing somehow to inspire terror', the small British group was usually left last in line. (There were wry smiles at a telegram from Vladivostok headquarters, instructing that if the situation warranted it, they should 'not hesitate to take complete control.')[9] Enviously, McCullagh watched unattached officers 'train-jumping' – walking to the front of the queue during halts, and grabbing a place in the foremost train. He and the others would have done the same, he thought, had not Knox lumbered them with his Russian 'aged people of good family', who while complaining of British betrayal hogged all the bunks, used up all the water and demanded the services of a private as cook.

On 30 November, having covered only 550 miles in eighteen days, they arrived at Novo-Nikolayevsk (Novosibirsk). After a five-day halt they got going again, but even more slowly than before. Both the up and down lines were now jammed nose to tail, and often they passed stacks of frozen corpses – typhus victims, left behind by Russian Red Cross trains, whose staff 'made a practice of stripping [the dead] stark naked, and then piling them in the open, like logs of wood, alongside the track.'[10] (Only children's corpses, McCullagh noted, were treated with respect – wrapped in shrouds and garlanded with pine boughs.) On 16 December, at a stop called simply Bolotnaya ('Marshy'), their already much-repaired locomotive gave up the ghost. Horrocks, who had picked up some Russian in his PoW camp, was sent to beg a replacement from the stationmaster, but to no avail. Instead the civilians and the baggage were transferred to another train, and the rest of the group travelled on by sled.

For the next five days and ninety miles they experienced the *trakt*: days sitting immobile in temperatures of twenty degrees below zero, bumping along a narrow, high-sided snow road; nights sleeping on the floor in a peasant cottage, packed tight with possibly typhus-bearing strangers. Falling off your sled, as everybody did at least once, was potentially fatal, because the half-asleep driver usually carried on oblivious, and the drivers behind hit out with their whips if you tried to climb aboard. It happened to McCullagh, who was floundering and beginning to panic when a gun battery picked him up and took him on to the next village. Pre-war, he could see, the area had been prosperous – Siberia's famous dairy country, not *taiga*. But now the farmhouses were filled with 'endless relays of armed men, who ate up all the food, used up all the fuel, took away all the fodder, sleighs, horses and cattle, and frequently compelled all the men and boys to accompany them.' In the towns where the army halted, it left behind 'thousands of these unfortunate peasants – their horses lost, their sleighs smashed, themselves without money or food or any means of getting back to their homes.'[11]

On Christmas Eve the group came together again at another wayside stop, and celebrated with tinned soup and rice. Vining played the bagpipes and there was a singalong to a banjo. The next morning the civilians were attached to a Red Cross echelon and again went on ahead. After another long wait for a train willing to take them, Vining, McCullagh, Horrocks and the rest crawled onwards with more halts than ever. By New Year's Eve they had travelled only another 150 miles, to the station of Achinsk – an awful sight because an ammunition train had just exploded there, and corpses and wreckage still strewed the line. The nightmare came to an end on 6 January 1920. Eight weeks but less than eight hundred miles on from Omsk, they had almost reached Krasnoyarsk. As they waited for the usual train-jam to move – a delay they put down to it being Orthodox Christmas Eve – a mounted courier rode past, and the stationary engines all blew their whistles. The banjo-player was launching into 'Take Me Back to Dear Old Blighty' when someone remarked, 'A Russian officer has just thrown his sword over the bank.' Six miles ahead, Krasnoyarsk had been taken over by Bolshevik-affiliated Socialist Revolutionaries. Exhausted and utterly demoralised, Kolchak's soldiers continued to trudge in, giving up their weapons 'with the peaceful unconcern of railway travellers surrendering their tickets to the ticket-collector at the end of their journey . . . Soon a huge pile of rifles, swords and revolvers arose in the snow outside our carriage.'[12]

Unsure what happened next, the group sat tight:

There was no shooting – nothing. So, working on the principle 'when in doubt, feed', we decided to have supper. Then into our carriage came a soldier with a huge red cockade in his fur cap. He was followed shortly afterwards by a couple of officers, one of whom said he was the Red battalion commander. We were now their prisoners, but discovering that we were British, they beamed with delight and asked us whether they might join us for supper.[13]

Otherwise ignored by the authorities, after a few days the group moved out of the train and into Krasnoyarsk. Situated on another of Siberia's giant rivers – the Yenisei – the city was reasonably orderly but typhus-ridden and desperately overcrowded. Hundreds of emaciated horses wandered about, chewing fences and nosing pockets, and at the railway station, the whole of a large wall was covered with handwritten notes begging for news of lost relatives.[14] When the Red 5th Army moved in, McCullagh noticed how many soldiers wore British uniform – sign of the past weeks' mass desertions. About one in four were fully kitted out in 'the khaki of King George', and the rest always had 'some little token to remind one of home' – a 'British Warm' perhaps, or a regulation water-bottle.[15]

The Mission group were not taken into custody, but allowed to move freely about the city. White currency having been declared illegal, to raise money for food and accommodation they sold spare clothing and blankets at a street market, and found odd jobs. Several gave English lessons, and Sergeant Rooney played the piano in a café. The two Russian-speakers, McCullagh and Horrocks, did the rounds of the commissariats, trying to obtain ration-cards and registration papers. This was their first encounter with actual Bolsheviks, the most communicative of them the 'commandant', a man 'of some education' – according to rumour a former pharmacist – with 'the thin face of a fanatic'. With evident sincerity, he delivered an impassioned lecture on how revolution was about to sweep England too. 'Captain Horrocks and I . . . looked at each other with amazement, for we realised that we were dealing with a state of things of which we had no previous conception.'[16] They eventually got their papers with the help of a former Mission interpreter, now working in the commandant's office.

There were thoughts of escape. The only possible route was south, over the Mongolian border. An Anglo-French group, on retreat with the Orenburg Cossacks, took a similar one at the time, successfully crossing today's Kazakhstan into China.[17] Horrocks in particular, having already spent years in German captivity, was eager to make the attempt. But Vining discouraged him: they were in already Red-held territory, and it was too cold and too far. Privately, McCullagh also thought that the young English officers would give the game away through naïvety; already, they were far too chatty with chance-met Russians, refusing to take seriously his warnings that they could be informers. As things worked out, the only person who got away was McCullagh himself, by the simple expedient of swopping his uniform for civvies and re-registering himself as a journalist. With the help of an old cuttings file that proved his anti-imperialist credentials (he had exposed an Italian massacre in Libya, and supported Russia's short-lived democratic revolution of 1905), he ingratiated himself with the commissar in charge of propaganda. Either unaware that McCullagh had been with the Mission, or more likely, hoping for favourable press, on 1 February the commissar gave him a pass for a train that was leaving immediately for Yekaterinburg. Without time to bid farewell to Vining and the others, McCullagh just caught it, and spent the next several fascinating if nerve-wracking months in Red Russia before making his way home.

The rest were detained until October 1920, when they were released under a government-negotiated prisoner exchange. Though they saw the insides of two grim monastery gaols in Moscow, they were treated relatively well – certainly much better than their White counterparts. Some time in the spring Fyedotov, who had had an infinitely worse journey from Omsk, been stripped of all his belongings on capture, and locked up with murderers and thieves, coincided with them at a station:

> These clean, well-dressed men strolling up and down the sunlit plat-
> form smoking their pipes, talking calmly to each other and completely
> ignoring the sentries and the commissars, were to me like a vision
> from another world. I longed to join them, but forced myself to turn
> away.[18]

It is nice to know that he got out of Russia two years later, and ended up a senior executive of the Cunard–White Star shipping line.

And what of Admiral Kolchak – so ill-judging, so rigid, so far from the sea? For the first three weeks or so of his journey east he continued to go through the motions of Supreme Rulership – issuing decrees, reshuffling his generals, appointing a new prime minister. It was a pantomime, but he might have got away safely had it not been for his bad relations with the Czech Legion. Always regarded as uppity, since dropping out of the war the Czechs had been loathed by the Kolchak regime, and loathed it in return. They nonetheless still controlled the Trans-Siberian west of Irkutsk, and under inter-Allied agreements were formally responsible for Kolchak's safe passage. Their first priority, however, was getting away themselves, and as conditions deteriorated Kolchak's convoy became increasingly burdensome. In December the Legion's acting commander switched it to the slower of the Trans-Siberian's two lines, so infuriating Kolchak's latest army chief that he challenged the Czech to a duel. Remaining trust evaporated when the Czechs intercepted a hysterical wire from Kolchak to Semyonov, authorising him to blow up the Baikal tunnels so as to force the Legion to stand and fight.

Kolchak's fate was sealed on 27 December, when halfway between Krasnoyarsk and Irkutsk his convoy came to a halt at the small town of Nizhne-Udinsk, which had just been taken over by a revolutionary militia. From then on he was held semi-prisoner, hemmed in by Legion trains while the Czechs negotiated with the militia leaders. When he tried to contact General Janin, still notionally the Legion's C-in-C, the Frenchman was elusive. 'The Czechs outwardly agreed to summon this or that person to the telephone', a Kolchak officer wrote in his diary, 'but it [always] turned out that either communications were cut, or the person wanted had not come to the instrument.'[19] The soldiers of Kolchak's personal guard started packing their haversacks, and his band walked off into town playing the 'Marseillaise'.

Up ahead, a White regiment and a Bolshevik-affiliated local revolutionary group fought for Irkutsk. Janin, the new British commissioner and America's Consul Harris watched the battle from their trains, and after White troops swopped sides, hosted ceasefire talks before departing together with the defeated Kolchak general. The general's last act was to hand over thirty-one political prisoners – the usual rag-bag of hard left, soft left, and vaguely suspicious-looking – to a Semyonov henchman, who had been sent to Irkutsk to see if there was any chance of appropriating Kolchak's gold. The Semyonov men then drove the prisoners into the hold of a Baikal steamer, and in a drunken spree that night clubbed them all to death.

The morning after the bloodbath Kolchak announced that he was stepping down. Governorship of the Far East was transferred to Semyonov, and Supreme Rulership to Denikin. Two days later, on 8 January, the Czechs moved Kolchak and the remainder of his entourage into two second-class carriages flying Allied flags, and sent him under guard to Irkutsk. By the time he arrived six days later, the Allied representatives were long gone, and at midnight the Czechs handed him over to the revolutionaries, in exchange for a formal receipt. Together with his mistress and prime minister, he was then marched over the frozen Angara to prison.

It still wasn't quite the end. Over the next three weeks a five-man panel interrogated Kolchak nine times, courteously and ostensibly in preparation for trial in Moscow. The sessions turned into a sort of leave-taking, Kolchak recalling his whole life and career unprompted and with remarkable frankness. He only became evasive during the last, harsher, session, pretending ignorance of the mass executions with which he had put down the workers' rising in Omsk after his coup. (A lawyer on the panel had been involved, and survived only because he was in the prison's typhus ward at the time: Kolchak's men had not dared enter it to abduct him.) Challenged on Rozanov's punitive village-burnings, he simply said that they were usual practice in war. The final scene was precipitated by the march on Irkutsk of a thousand-strong White force that had escaped the Krasnoyarsk encirclement. When it reached the Angara the nervous Irkutsk authorities decided that Kolchak made them a target, and that their best course was to get rid of him. (It seems without asking Moscow first.) On the night of 7 January 1920 the Supreme Ruler duly walked the same road as hundreds of his own prisoners before him: the high bank of the Angara; the dazzle of headlights; shots; a kick down a worn-smooth snow-slide to a bloodstained ice-hole. A week later the

Legion came to an agreement with the Red 5th Army, under which its trains were able to proceed unmolested. An unsolved mystery is what happened to the trainful of imperial gold. Probably the Czechs handed it over to the Red Army in exchange for safe passage, but the story persists that they took it home and founded Czechoslovakia's National Bank with it.

For the Allies Kolchak's end was a hideous embarrassment, and recriminations flew. Chief scapegoat was Janin. Commander of the Legion and thus responsible for Kolchak's safety, why had he not waited in Irkutsk for Kolchak to catch him up? And why had he let the Legion hand him over to revolutionaries? In a pother of telegrams, Janin came up with excuses military and legal, but divulged his real feelings in a message to Paris: 'Many men have been shot who have done less harm to Siberia and to Russia than the Admiral.'[20] He was never given another high-profile command, but there was no official enquiry into his actions.

Knox — the man who spotted Kolchak in Tokyo and helped him take power — was bitter. 'He came to see me', Graves remembered of their last meeting, 'and said that he had completely failed; that he had done nothing for Russia, his own country or himself.'[21] Even ever-flippant Gerhardie was sufficiently upset to march into Knox's office and go 'on and on' at him about the Intervention's pointlessness as the general sat typing his final report. Knox jumped to his feet, 'by the look of it to kick me out of his room', but got caught up in his typewriter, allowing Gerhardie to make a 'Pierrot-like' escape. An undated note amongst Gerhardie's papers reads: 'I think that the only good Siberia has done to me, is that it has taught me to foxtrot.'[22]

At the end of December, Graves got orders to withdraw his troops to Vladivostok ready for departure. Before leaving their sections of the Trans-Siberian they had a final clash with Semyonov, after the 27th Infantry's Colonel Morrow forced one of Semyonov's *bronevik* commanders, a General Bogomolyets, to release Verkhnye-Udinsk's stationmaster from arrest. Bogomolyets retaliated by steaming to another small station sixty miles away, and machine-gunning the sleeping-wagons of a thirty-eight-man American detachment stationed there. Forewarned by a sergeant's Russian girlfriend, the Americans were unhurt, and counter-attacked. Their senior officer, a twenty-one-year-old lieutenant, stuck his automatic into a *bronevik* porthole and silenced a machine-gun, while at the same time a group de-coupled one of its two locomotives. With suicidal bravery Sergeant Carl Robbins – 'a tall boy from Tennessee' – climbed on top of the second and threw a grenade into its cab. He was killed but so were five of Bogomolyets's men, and after another American unit came up, Bogomolyets and fifty-four others surrendered. When their train was searched it yielded 177 stolen pocketbooks and wallets, and question-ing established that over the past ten days they had robbed and murdered at least forty civilian men, and gang-raped and murdered three or perhaps four women. They did not get what they deserved, because when Morrow left Verkhnye-Udinsk two weeks later he let them go.[23]

By the time the 27th Infantry arrived back in Vladivostok the city had a new government. Rozanov had fled, and been replaced by a 'council' government made up of elected local officials. Graves liked the look of it, but was off – on April Fool's Day, to the sound of a Japanese band, sent to the quayside by General Oi, derisively playing 'Hard Times Come Again No More'. Almost as soon as the Americans dipped below the horizon, Oi ousted the 'council', and after a few chaotic days the Rising Sun fluttered over all the town halls in the Russian Pacific. (And continued to do so until summer 1922, when the Japanese withdrew and left the region to the Soviets.)

Uniquely among Allied generals, Graves wholeheartedly slated the Intervention in his memoirs. It was a 'fiasco' and a 'fundamental error', and America should never have got involved. Though in command of US troops in Siberia, he himself had had no idea what the government was trying to achieve there.[24] Viewing developments from London, Curzon summed things up in one and a half words. When the paperwork winding up Knox's mission crossed his desk, he saw that his permanent secretary, suave Hardinge, had added a comment: 'So ends a not very creditable enterprise.' Curzon crossed out 'not very', and substituted 'highly dis'.[25]

23

The Heartland

W HEN CAPTAIN GEORGE Lever of the Royal Engineers – a loungy, slangy, fag-in-hand type of regular officer – landed in Novorossiysk, his first job was to find accommodation for a group of Russian nurses, who had arrived on the same ship and been temporarily lodged at the YMCA. It was difficult, first because Novorossiysk was already bursting at the seams, second because the nurses refused – with 'tears and bewailings and talk of suicide' – to leave Allied shelter, believing that if they did so they would be forced into prostitution. Landlords' leers forced Lever to the same conclusion, but told that it was the rooms he had found or nothing, the women 'dwindled away to offices, hospitals, dance-halls, cabarets etc.' The fate of some at least 'hardly bore thinking about'.[1]

In charge of supplying Denikin with radio communications, Lever quickly became acquainted with all the usual Intervention difficulties: bad interpreters ('I never said all that!'), misuse of equipment (delicate radio sets left in a damp truck), misdirection ('striking off at a tangent re the weather, how we liked Russia, were we married, etc. etc.'), and antisemitism. A warning in his induction interview that when dealing with the Whites the vital things were 'patience and *the avoidance of Jewish acquaintances*' turned out to be so to the point that a fellow-officer, when discovered to be Jewish, had to be sent home.[2] British personnel were not much better: most officers had signed up for the pay, and judging by appearances most of the men were on the run from the law.

How badly the war was going he began to appreciate on a late-December 1919 train journey to Mission headquarters at Taganrog. Kharkov and Kiev had both just fallen to the Reds, and thousands of people were fleeing south, packing station buildings so tight that they blurred the outlines of walls and benches, like a swarm of locusts. Stretching his legs at a stop, Lever noticed a group looking at something on the ground. It was a dead man, curled up into a ball.

> Death was due to exposure through riding on the outside step of the train, from which he had apparently just rolled off. The lookers-on were very phlegmatic . . . One rolled the corpse over with his toe . . . The body was still there as we started on our way again.[3]

He arrived in Taganrog in time for Christmas Day, which headquarters celebrated with roast turkey and 'dancing, musical chairs, hunt the slipper etc' with its female telegraphists and typists, all local hires. As British records do not note, that same evening Denikin's troops committed another pogrom, in Tetiyev, a half-Jewish town eighty miles southwest of Kiev. They had already plundered it during their September advance, and now did the same again in retreat, murdering between fifteen and thirty people, and setting fire to market stalls, shops and houses.[4]

Also in Taganrog, since leaving Kursk in early November, was Captain Kennedy. He had had an uneventful few weeks, working office hours and spending his spare time ice-yachting and listening to Denikin's superb court orchestra. The wretchedness of the general population made him uncomfortable: 'One feels rather rotten walking about here in warm clothes.' But it did not stop him trawling the commission shops for bargain-price furs, sold by departing refugees to raise cash: 'A fox lining for an opera cloak is offered for 5,000 roubles, which I should think is good value. A squirrel stole, which rather takes my fancy, is 4,000.'[5]

On Christmas Eve he was shaken out of his torpor by the reappearance of his friends the Belayevs. Just come from the front, they described scenes of confusion and panic, and warned that at the Volunteer Army's present rate of retreat Rostov-on-Don – the junction between Taganrog and Novorossiysk – would fall in ten days' time. Front-line officers had lost all trust in high command, who were busy evacuating their own families while refusing to contemplate general withdrawal. On Christmas Day Kennedy went to church, walked and thought, then rejoined Belayev and offered to write up his assessment in English and present it to Holman's deputy, a 'rather fussy old boy' called General Cotton. (Holman was at the front.) Though it risked getting him into trouble with Vrangel (broken-down Mai-Mayevsky's replacement as commander-in-chief) Belayev agreed, and Kennedy sat up until 3 a.m. putting together a seven-page report. Later the same morning he went over it again with Belayev, typed up a corrected version and took it to Cotton.

Except for its assertion that the Red Army was doing well because it employed German officers – an oft-repeated canard born of reluctance to accept that former tsarist ones were choosing the other side – the report's analysis was brutally accurate. The Volunteer Army was greatly outnumbered, and thanks to bad pay and rations, fatally prone to pillaging and desertion. The railways were 'choked and disorganised', and supply services had 'completely broken down'. The enemy would probably reach Novorossiysk in about six weeks. Defence lines round the port should be established immediately, and all available ships summoned ready to evacuate the White armies to Romania or Crimea. Reading the report through Cotton was 'absolutely flabbergasted', and when he had recovered the power of speech told Kennedy that Belayev obviously 'had the wind up'. Kennedy retorted that this was what the Russians always said, when 'asked to look past their noses. In fact one or two rather biting remarks passed!'[6] Cotton, he could see, would not take responsibility, and evacuation orders would have to await Holman's return.

Over the next few days, incoming British officers reinforced Belayev's warnings. 'The whole army', Kennedy wrote in his diary on 29 December, 'is running hard and not fighting at all. Wrangel [sic] is hanging people all over the place.' A sergeant fresh from just-abandoned Belgorod (close to the present-day Russian–Ukrainian border), described how for three nights running he had watched

men and women accused of being pro-Bolsheviks hanged in the town square. They were not given a drop, but were simply strung up, and drunken Cossacks hewed their arms and legs off with their swords, while the wretched people were still alive.[7]

Vrangel himself passed through Taganrog in his train on the night of 30/31 December. Kennedy went to the station to take a look at him, and was impressed by his height, commanding manner, 'thin, rather pale face and eagle eye'. The general shook hands and exchanged a few words, but when Kennedy tried to photograph him 'stalked away . . . glaring about him as if seeking whom he might devour.'

In the small hours of 1 January 1920 Denikin left, giving the Mission only a few hours' warning. Kennedy and about half the Mission staff got away early the same morning, and reached Rostov three hours later without incident. Lever was with a later group, who after waiting all morning at the station, were told to leave everything they could not carry, and board a train in a distant siding. The hurry was unnecessary, because it turned out to have 'no ruddy engine!!!! Somebody has walked off with it and left us sans puffer. Situation . . . is parlous to say the least.' It took four hours to find another, during which the 'rather electric atmosphere' was 'enlivened by spasmodic bursts of rifle fire . . . Russkies scrapping amongst themselves most likely.' Lever went to see what had become of the abandoned baggage, and found 'every bally thing' ransacked. The train finally left at 11 p.m., only to stop again 'about a mile out, what time a Russian officer went to "interview" the driver with a revolver. Don't know what happened to the driver but the train gets a move on.' Sitting in an icy goods wagon, pitch-black except for the odd glowing cigarette, he pondered his lost laundry, gloves, boots and primus stove, all 'probably by now sculling about some Russky kitchen'.[8]

Also lost at Taganrog, more seriously, were twenty of 47 Squadron's Sopwith Camels. There for refitting, they could not be flown out, and were instead torched on the airfield. The RAF train carrying squadron leader Collishaw, which had been operating around Kharkov, arrived after the line east to Rostov had been cut, so instead headed west towards White-held Crimea. Expanded to ninety trucks and three engines so as to carry two thousand civilian refugees, it travelled agonisingly slowly, hampered by torn-up rails and the need to 'snow' whenever the engines ran out of water. (The women aboard joined in the work, carrying snow in their outspread skirts.) When typhus broke out in the refugee wagons, Collishaw ordered that the dead be dumped. 'Distrait mothers', he wrote, hid their children's bodies, doubtless accelerating the spread of the disease, though it was hard to blame them.[9] There was need for hurry because they were being pursued by an enemy *bronevik* armed with a nine-inch gun. By ripping up rails behind, Collishaw's team managed to keep it out of firing range, but disaster struck at a country station, when anonymous 'Reds' sent an unmanned locomotive careering down a slope into the RAF train's rear. In his published memoir Collishaw wrote that luckily nobody was hurt, since the smashed wagons contained only stores. But in a private letter he admitted that 'hundreds' were killed or injured, and that 'with heavy hearts, we had to abandon all the Russian people in our train who had come to us for succour, and so steamed out of that hell hole just in time.'[10] Minus refugees, the train reached Crimea on 4 January.

Taganrog abandoned, Denikin moved to Yekaterinodar, the other side of the Don and only sixty miles from Novorossiysk. A young town – streets so straight and steppe so flat that one could always see the horizon on both sides – it felt to staff officer Lobanov-Rostovsky less like a capital, more like a trap. Hourly expecting mutiny, he and his colleagues slept with their boots on, and on patrol, took care to walk behind their men with rifles at the ready, and to never turn their backs on them. In the way of war zones, cafés were open though ordinary food shops were shut, and he and a friend tried to lift their spirits by stuffing themselves with pastries, 'feeling dismal all the while'.[11] The offering at the town theatre was no cheerier: fatalism-saturated *Uncle Vanya*, with Chekhov's widow Madame Knipper in the lead. During the climactic scene, when Vanya shoots and misses, a woman in the audience went into hysterics and was carried out screaming.

Major Williamson – the man who had asked his mother to send Christmas puddings – was still with the Don Cossacks in Novocherkassk. On 6 January he wrote to her again. As she probably knew, things were 'pretty bitter here', with eight months' work undone and the Don Army in full retreat. Thankfully he had persuaded 'sullen' railway men at the station to send off British personnel and 'a quantity of Russian ladies and children' – just in time, since the enemy were now only thirty versts away. He and a couple of others had stayed behind but were keeping their horses saddled. He refused, though, to accept defeat.

> Personally, I *won't* believe that we shall lose until it is *lost* . . . By Jove, if only we can stop them now and push them back again . . . I should be so happy if poor old Novocherkassk could be saved.

It was the fault of Kolchak and Yudenich for giving up, of 'German intrigues', and of the British people, who could have prevented the disaster, but were 'allowing it to happen':

> allowing the Jews and criminals of whom the whole Red organisation is composed to murder, loot and torture; allowing women and children to be driven from their homes in a Russian winter, to plod along miles of open Steppe; allowing sick and wounded to die side by side of typhus or hunger on the railway platforms of every station . . . allowing her ally to be slowly strangled to death.

'So sorry to bore you with all this', he closed,

> I expect everyone thinks I have lost my sense of proportion by being so long away. Perhaps I have, but Russia is a very big country . . . and though we are a very small country, yet we have a very large responsibility to humanity, if nothing else.[12]

For the final couple of nights he and his colleagues moved into the town's once smart central hotel, now with an upturned pot plant in the lobby and a Cossack captain, said to be a deserter, hanging from a tree outside. ('I hate that part of the business.') On Orthodox Christmas Eve they foraged for supper in the hotel kitchen, and woke next morning to find half the townspeople looting and starting fires, while the other half went to church as normal. ('That maddening Russian nonchalance.') The railway line having been cut, when evening fell they joined a retreating cavalry column, riding out of the town into the cold serenity of the moonlit steppe. At midnight they reached the Don river, crossing the ice on a path marked by small fires, and after resting at a village, left the column and struck out for a still White-held railway town twenty miles on. Leading their exhausted horses, they reached it just in time to catch a Mission train. From it Williamson wrote once more: 'As far as I am concerned *it is all finished!!!* . . . pretty heartbreaking from every point of view.' In time, the Allies would 'start again and work up a new Volunteer Army', but for now all they could do was see to the safe evacuation of refugees: 'I shall probably send some to you!! Poor Mother, cheer up!'[13]

He arrived in Yekaterinodar to find the regathered Mission furious with Holman, who had tried to shift the blame for Taganrog with a circular accusing his officers of panicking. Lever spoke for all: the 'babyish' letter was 'a considered insult', and Holman should have 'stayed occasionally at the Base and made some attempt at running his show', instead of 'sculling about in an aeroplane . . . doing spectacular stunts in the way of bomb-dropping. Most of us have never had a glimpse of the man.'[14] Holman's new deputy and Williamson's new boss, Lieutenant Colonel Frederick Lister, hinted at an affair: Holman had been 'bombing Bolos' with a 'good-looking and very young pilot', who he declared 'the finest fellow in the world' and with whom he had exchanged uniform buttons.[15]

There was also dreadful news from Rostov, which had fallen on 8 January. A week before leaving Novocherkassk, Williamson had sent one of his captains – a twenty-four-year-old, three times wounded in France, Rugbeian called William Frecheville – to Yekaterinodar to fetch money and stores. Passing through Rostov, Frecheville had run into Holman, who ordered him and three others to go and supervise defence-digging at a village ten miles away. Almost as soon as they got there the village was attacked and the group became separated. Two of the four had since reappeared, but Frecheville and another were still missing, and the rumour was that they had been captured and tortured, then slashed to death in Rostov's main square.

As Frecheville's poor father – a professor of engineering at Imperial College – discovered by advertising for information, this was substantially true, the details emerging two years later when Frecheville's interpreter, a Lieutenant Kozma, escaped Russia and gave a statement. Dashing back to Rostov in a pony-trap, he and Frecheville had seen a group of cavalry approaching, and assumed they were Denikin's.

In fact they were from a Bolshevik regiment, and the pair were taken captive and stripped of their money and clothes. As they were being whipped half-naked along the road more horsemen appeared, and suggested killing the prisoners at once. One drew his sword and said 'I will begin.' Kozma translated for Frecheville, 'who merely replied to the effect that nothing could prevent him. The man then cut three times at Frecheville's head, and at the third blow he fell.' Kozma was saved by the arrival of a Bolshevik officer, who reprimanded the soldiers and ordered that Kozma be given back his clothes. Kozma subsequently worked as the regiment's clerk for six months, before deserting and making his way to Poland. According to Williamson, the Volunteer Army made a retaliatory raid into Rostov and captured a commissar wearing Frecheville's tunic. 'I was told he was beaten to death with steel ramrods, a not abnormal fate for prisoners in this civil war.'[16]

By this time even Churchill privately accepted that Denikin was finished. On New Year's Eve he wrote to Field Marshal Wilson that the South seemed to be 'a complete smash-up', and that the best that could be hoped for now was 'guerrilla resistance in the mountains'.[17] On 11 January he sent a 'Personal and Secret' telegram to Holman, telling him to advise Denikin to appeal for British mediation in peace talks with the Bolsheviks. Lloyd George 'would go a long way to try to save as much as possible from the wreck', and if Denikin acted quickly, while he still had bargaining power, he might be able to establish a refuge of some sort for the Volunteer Army, and autonomy for the Cossacks. (Negotiations, Churchill blithely opined, would take 'a fortnight or three weeks'.)[18]

But this relative realism was only for Holman and intimates. In public and with political colleagues, Churchill mounted a rearguard action to prolong the Intervention. Its first prong was a scare campaign. In a lurid anti-Bolshevik speech to a rally in Sunderland, in a War Office press release predicting 'combustion' in the Middle East, and notoriously, in a piece of race-theory claptrap for the *Sunday Herald*, he asserted that revolution was being plotted world-wide, by 'International' and 'Terrorist' Jews. Rightly condemned by the *Jewish Chronicle* for adopting 'the hoary tactics of hooligan anti-Semites', in his *Herald* article Churchill also denied Denikin's pogroms, claiming that in White-held territory 'protection was always accorded to the Jewish population', and that White officers 'made strenuous efforts to prevent reprisals and to punish those guilty of them.' Foreshadowing, ironically, a late-Soviet propaganda trope, he blamed what pogroms there were on Ukrainian 'hordes'.[19] At a birthday lunch for Lloyd George during Allied talks in Paris, he added a tantrum to the mix. 'A most amusing meal', the prime minister's secretary and lover Frances Stevenson wrote in her diary. Having not got his way on Russia at a Cabinet meeting that morning, 'Winston arrived simply *raving*.' Churchill went to sympathetic Wilson with one of his by now routine resignation threats, and at five they went together to Lloyd George's hotel to tackle him again. But the prime minister was inured: he had spent the afternoon playing golf and was fast asleep.

The second prong was the Mackinder mission. For several months, Churchill and Wilson had been urging the Foreign Office to send a 'really high-class' man as high commissioner and political advisor to Denikin, in the same way that Eliot had been sent to Kolchak. After some hesitation the Foreign Office approved the idea, and alighted on the unlikely figure of Halford Mackinder. A fifty-eight-year-old academic geographer turned Conservative MP, Mackinder was an interesting man – one of the founders of the London School of Economics and inventor of what we today call geopolitics – the school of thought that geography, more than governance or ideology, determines the political world order. His association with Russia, however, was a purely theoretical one: the notion – reiterated in a new book published in time for the Peace Conference – that Russia and Central Asia (the 'Heartland') naturally dominate Eurasia and Africa ('the World Island'), and hence the world.

His chance to visit the Heartland in person came in October 1919, when Curzon offered him the commissionership and an accompanying knighthood, plus the assurance that he would 'probably enter Moscow beside General Denikin'.[20] Mackinder accepted the following day but was in no hurry actually to depart, spending weeks gathering a large staff. Chivvied by Curzon, he finally left London on 4 December, and stopping in Paris, Warsaw, Bucharest, Sofia and

Constantinople on the way, did not reach Novorossiysk until 1 January – the same day Denikin fled Taganrog.

For the next six days Mackinder refused to leave ship (the Dowager Empress's *Marlborough*), complaining that the accommodation arranged for him ashore was inadequate, and that neither Denikin nor Holman was there to greet him. Feather-smoothing fell to political officer Keyes. Though talk of bandits and derailments made Mackinder 'rather nervous', Keyes persuaded him to meet Denikin at a small railway station halfway between Rostov and Yekaterinodar. Denikin himself they found preternaturally serene, happy to give them a five-hour meeting with only brief interruptions for incoming messages. In a 'very pleasant' atmosphere, the man from the LSE told the tsarist general that his advance on Moscow had been 'a great adventure'. But now it was time for him to ally with the Georgians and Poles, and set up a 'modern' government, even if not 'fully democratic in the Western sense'. Britain could not donate any more arms or money, but would lend its 'economic methods and organising brain'. Denikin made the usual replies. His armies were 'mere militias' that disintegrated if they stood still; 'All-Russia, great and indivisible' would rise again; constitutional arrangements would be decided once victory was won.[21] It was a ritual exchange, but there was progress on immediate issues. Having been advised by Keyes that unless Volunteer Army officers knew that their families were safe they would desert, Mackinder gave what became known as the 'Mackinder guarantee': a formal promise on behalf of His Majesty's Government that officers' wives and children would be evacuated on all available ships, naval and commercial. (The rank and file, it was assumed, would be able to merge back into the general population.) In return, Denikin undertook to recognise the Caucasian republics, and to accept international mediation of the Russian–Polish border.

Unmentioned by either side, so far as the records show, were White pogroms. Four days before, the Volunteer Army had celebrated Orthodox Christmas by ravaging the *shtetl* of Krivoye Ozero, halfway between Kiev and Odessa. 'On Christmas night', a witness reported, 'to the sound of church bells, wild killing began.' Soldiers broke down doors, wielded swords, bayonets, axes and knives, and dragged girls to the building they used as a brothel. Others danced, played cards, and drank toasts to victory over the 'Communist-Yids', all 'in the very centre of town, on streets that were streaming with blood.' A local schoolteacher who came in with the Red Army shortly afterwards saw corpses 'lying around the streets like garbage', and helped survivors transport over four hundred to a mass grave in the cemetery.[22] On appointing Mackinder commissioner, Curzon had promised the Jewish Board of Deputies that he would make a 'thorough investigation' of pogrom allegations, and do 'all possible' for victims.[23] In addition, the Jewish-rights campaigner Lucien Wolf had offered to put Mackinder in touch with the Kiev-based aid organisations collecting witness statements and data.[24] But in his five hours with Denikin, Mackinder seems not to have brought up the subject at all.

With the usual halts and alarms, it took Mackinder three days to cover the 200 miles back to Novorossiysk, and on 13 January he went aboard the *Marlborough* and sailed away, as he put it 'to run home for a few days.' The plan had been that he would stay in Russia for at least six months. Not counting his malingering on arrival, he had stuck it out for slightly over a week. The charitable interpretation is that he wanted to make sure his evacuation promise was fulfilled. The more obvious one is that he was frightened, his Heartland proving less tractable in the flesh than on paper. The recommendations he presented to Cabinet on his return – trade deals, export credits, a new syndicate of 'Merchant Adventurers' – were utterly divorced from reality. And his analysis – that the Red Army was directed by 'subterranean German agencies, probably through Jewish channels' – parroted White delusions, presumably via Keyes.[25] Cabinet's reaction was uniformly negative; his commissionership was wound up and he never returned to Russia. His Heartland theory, however, flourishes there, its promise of geographically predetermined world domination catnip to Putin's Kremlin.[26]

24

Tak!

WHILE WILLIAMSON AND his colleagues shuttled between the plain-Jane railway towns of the Don steppe, a Mission offshoot spent the winter in louche, once-luxurious Odessa. After Kiev's fall in mid-December 1919, the city grew increasingly tense. Trains in and out stopped running, sailings to Constantinople multiplied, and power cuts halted the trams and doused the street lights. In mismatching typefaces, one-page government newspapers ran assurances that reinforcements were on the way, alongside decrees threatening 'on the spot' capital punishment for 'assemblages', and small ads for second-hand jewellery, Persian rugs and furs. Carrying water home each day from a standpipe, the writer Konstantin Paustowsky read the litter on the pavements. Here a reminder of peaceful times – a hair-ribbon, an empty packet of Egyptian cigarettes. But there a spent cartridge, drops of blood, torn-up documents or a ransacked purse. The logs he bought to heat the empty doctor's surgery where he lodged were acacia, from the city's famous old street trees, now being felled for firewood.

General British out-of-depthness is nowhere better illustrated than by the reports the chief of British intelligence, Captain J. W. C. Lancaster, received from his local informers. They read like notes for an absurdist play. The Bulgarian consul is trading cloth and nails and has 'a very unsavoury Dossier'; the White officers starting fights with British ones in cafés are Bolshevik provocateurs in disguise; a raid on Fanconi's restaurant has netted 200 'Jewish Profiteers'; the ex-mistress of the tsar's ex-chef, now a murderer for the Cheka, has been arrested at the Londonskaya Hotel; a turncoat postmaster is 'an incorrigible drunkard'; at the Popoff tobacco factory, a Committee has been formed. A supposed list of the twenty-one members of the Odessa

Cheka specifies that seven out of eleven named individuals are 'the Jew' so-and-so, and the remaining ten 'All Jews, names unknown'. The code-word Lancaster used to transmit this mass of nonsense to headquarters was SVANGALI [*sic*], later changed to MARZIPAN.

With defeat looming, Odessa's White leaders turned on each other, and drew Lancaster into their intrigues. The rivals were the province's military governor, General Nikolai Shilling, and his deputy, Colonel Aleksandr Stessel. Lancaster already disliked Shilling, for his inanition and for 'the enormous amount of thieving and peculation . . . almost openly going on' at his headquarters. (As he put it in his final report, its 'entire business . . . was the sale and shipment of Government and private stores.')[1] His pro-Stessel informers stoked his distrust with a variety of allegations, the most plausible that on abandoning Kiev Shilling had left behind British-supplied arms in favour of wagon-loads of exportable barley and sugar, the least that he was linked to the Bolsheviks via his alleged 'regular mistress', the popular singer Isa Kremer. (A habituée, naturally, of 'strong Hebrew circles'.) The Stessel faction also targeted Shilling's head of counter-intelligence, a twenty-eight-year-old former zoology student called Kirpichnikov, who had clashed with Stessel over appointments and arrests. Lancaster had been working closely with Kirpichnikov, who he describes as a 'very pleasant personality' with 'an intimate knowledge of the under-world'. But by Lancaster's own admission, an after-dark meeting with one of Stessel's associates was enough to convince him that Kirpichnikov was actually a closet Bolshevik – the 'master spirit', in fact, behind all Odessan dissent. At a second meeting, Lancaster goes on, 'it was decided that [Kirpichnikov] should be assassinated':

> They asked from me cordite and explosives with which to dynamite the road leading to Kirpitchnikoff's headquarters, as it was their intention to blow him up. I protested against this method of execution as being far too open to accident, and told them that I considered shooting was much the safest method, by either holding his car up and shooting him, or turning a machine-gun on him on his way to the office.

Lancaster also promised the plotters that if 'any of them got into trouble', he would provide passports and do his 'utmost to get them

away'.[2] A few days later – on the evening of 30 January 1920 –
Kirpichnikov was driving home from a reception at Shilling's residence when his car was stopped by four armed men. They demanded
his passport, and as he put his hand into his pocket, shot him five
times in the chest. According to Lancaster, a radio transmitter was
subsequently discovered on the roof of his house, together with two
'trusted operators, who were both hung.' What was really going on?
Who knows, but it would be in line with Odessa tradition if it had
mostly to do with the profits from the port. What is clear is that
Lancaster – an accessory to murder – had not a clue either.[3]

Two days after the assassination, news arrived that the Red Army
had captured Nikolayev, seventy-five miles to Odessa's northeast.
Four days later, by which time the rumble of artillery could be heard
in the distance, mass civilian evacuation began. At the docks, the
crews of the *Ceres*, *Cardiff* and *Ajax* erected barriers, checked papers
and patrolled, together with teenage cadets from the local military
academy. 'To buck the inhabitants up a bit', the *Ajax*'s band led five
companies on a march through the city centre. On the afternoon
of 6 February, with the enemy still fifteen miles off, Shilling threw in
the towel, sailing with his staff and their families to Sebastopol. The
British insisted that he take in tow three refugee-filled lighters, the
junior officer who 'blew aboard' to deliver the message finding him
'quite pleasant, but helpless and ready to do what he was told.'[4]

As news of Shilling's departure got out, the soldiers manning
Odessa's defences left their positions and straggled into the city. The
same evening the Red Army began its final advance along the coast
road, slowed by the destroyer *Sportive*, whose guns flashed through
the night from across the bay. At ten thirty the following morning
Bolshevik supporters inside the city seized a signals station and set up
a machine-gun under the filigree plane trees of the Nikolayevsky
Promenade. As fighting spread, the streets down to the harbour filled
with lorries and carts, and the quaysides with mostly middle-class
civilians, sitting grim-faced on their baggage in incongruously smart
coats and shoes. Inshore, an icebreaker and a tug worked back and
forth freeing trapped vessels, and further out, ships rafted up, coaling
or transferring refugees. A Greek destroyer, the British were half-
amused to see, turned refugees away but hoisted aboard several luxury

cars. *Ceres* and *Ajax* took the boy cadets, who had been among the last defenders of the coast road. A second lieutenant noted with approval that they were 'smiling and cheerful' and showed 'not the slightest sign of nerves'. One 'little fellow' had been shot through the knee, but was 'cocky as anything when the PMO told him he wouldn't have to have his leg cut off.'[5] Not so the civilians, who stampeded on seeing the cadets going. Paustowsky, who had decided that rather than join the mob he would stay and take his chances, watched from above the harbour, and describes a maelstrom of gaping mouths, wild eyes and outstretched arms, with marines' rifle-butts 'crashing down overhead'. Whenever someone managed to grab hold of a gangplank or ship's rail others clung onto them, until the weight grew too much and the whole cluster fell into the water.

By midday, in the lieutenant's words, things looked 'rather black', with enemy machine-guns 'practically on top of us' and still no sign of the Mission staff. Just as the marines were about to make a foray to the rescue they appeared, revolvers in hand, and at 1 p.m. the *Ceres* cut her ropes, a farewell spatter of bullets from the shore wounding a sailor in the arm. Out in the bay she transferred her last load of refugees to transports, and anchored – 'everyone looking a little jaded' – with the rest of the squadron for the night. 'Quite an interesting week. Rather tragic, but several very amusing incidents.'[6]

Next it was Novorossiysk's turn. 'If the other towns and cities to the north had been disasters', wrote Williamson, 'Novorossiysk was the worst of the lot, as the wreckage of a whole nation funnelled down . . . to the only remaining [White-held] seaport in the area.' During January and February the immediate threat was not the Red Army, which had not yet taken Yekaterinodar, but independent guerrilla bands known as Greens, made up mostly of local peasants. Controlling the coastal villages, they ambushed trains and even raided Novorossiysk gaol. Occupying a cement factory in the outskirts, the port's Mission offices were vulnerable, and a defensive 'Heath Robinson Line' was hastily put together in the hills behind. At the end of January a British patrol was fired on and slightly wounded ('semi-Blighties'), and HMS *Benbow* retaliated by bombarding a suspect fishing village – turning it into what Lever called 'a large hole'.[7]

Deadlier than any Green, of course, was typhus. Lobanov-Rostovsky visited the military hospital to take a sick friend some money:

When I asked at the office which room Captain So-and-So was occupying the clerk laughed. 'We have 500 beds and 5,000 patients. They come in and out so rapidly we have no time to keep a record. You'll have to look for him yourself.' Every bit of space in the hospital was occupied. The corridors and the spaces between beds were crowded with the sick, some lying on straw, some directly on the floor. Many had lice swarming over them. I stepped cautiously over the prostrate figures and finally found my colleague. Across from his bed a man was shouting in delirium. Next to him a man had died, and the body had not yet been removed. A few nurses were going about in a daze, with an expression on their faces that made one fear for their sanity. They could do nothing as there were no medicines available. My friend was very touched at seeing me, but said 'Please don't stay here' . . . Coming out of the building, I noticed a truck at the back entrance being loaded with white bundles. As I came nearer I saw they were corpses wrapped in white sheets. 'Can't you give the dead a decent burial?' I asked one of the men loading the truck. 'No time and no coffins', he snapped, and the truck drove away.[8]

The other mass killer was cold, worst during Novorossiysk's notorious blizzards, which could bowl men down the street and blow over horses and carts. Sorting radio equipment at the railway station, habitually light-hearted Lever felt impotent rage at the appalling state of the refugee trains, which paused next to his depot before being shunted off to sidings. Living conditions aboard them – frozen excrement, the dead mixed up with the living – were beyond comprehension, and every time one drew up he had to make 'a strong effort of will . . . to return to prosaic official duties.'[9] Russian kindnesses – rarer since Lloyd George's Guildhall speech – were discomforting: the little party thrown by Russian colleagues at the Mission to celebrate Orthodox Christmas; the colonel who pushed a ring onto his finger on being issued with some radio equipment; a passing stranger who, on seeing that his nose was frostbitten, wordlessly picked up a handful of snow and rubbed it pink again.

In Yekaterinodar the White leadership was imploding. A new, deckchairs-on-the-Titanic government was appointed and Vrangel resigned, publicly accusing Denikin of incompetence. Denikin replaced him with Shkuro (who had just been awarded the Order of Bath: 'Fancy that debauched little bandit commanding an Army!'[10]). On 20 February Rostov was retaken in a last-throw counter-attack, but fell again three days later, upon which the Allied representatives in Yekaterinodar met to discuss evacuation. As Lister put it 'they all wanted to bolt', the Poles complaining that when they asked Russian headquarters for trains they were told, '*Debrouillez-vous*'– 'Sort yourselves out'.[11] That there would be a rising in the town was taken as a given, but with luck it had been delayed by '400 arrests and 200 executions'.[12] Determined to remain to the last was Holman, to whom Lister had to 'speak out very straight' to get permission to recall outlying officers. 'His usual reply if you mention unpleasant facts is "Let's take an aeroplane and a tank and bomb the blighters", or something to that effect.'[13] Keyes too begged Holman to move the Mission to Novorossiysk, arguing that it would be 'a poor return to Winston', who had backed the Mission 'magnificently', to get cut off and necessitate a rescue. When the Mission did finally leave, on 7 March, it was mid-blizzard and in undisinfected wagons. Holman stayed behind, and speaking Hindustani for security, continued to put in long calls with grand plans for a general counter-attack. He rejoined his staff on the 11th, riding a motorised trolley-car.

The man responsible for carrying out the 'Mackinder guarantee' was Keyes. Still convalescent after a bout of Spanish 'flu, he was harassed on the one side by Denikin, who wanted the guarantee extended to non-military men, and on the other by Curzon, warning him not to over-promise. Individual requests rained down too: one from a Reverend Cragg, on behalf of 380 'boys of good family' from a Novocherkassk boarding-school; another from the British Museum, hoping that in return for a berth, a Madame Terletzky might donate her collection of coins. Too late, the Foreign Office made a query about pogroms. Keyes stonewalled: in territory still under White control Jews were few in number and 'not being ill-treated'; elsewhere, 'direct evidence' was no longer available.[14] In the second week of March he suffered a nervous breakdown, apparent in the increasingly odd letters – 'obscure factors'; Germans 'lying perdu' – he wrote to his wife. He nonetheless kept begging London for more evacuation ships, and by 9 March had succeeded in getting away 5,300 officers' families and 2,800 wounded – decent numbers, though the process was marred by widespread fraud and bribery.[15]

On the 15th Yekaterinodar fell, and Lister wrote in his diary that the threat from the Greens was getting 'really serious'. Soldiers were deserting to them in droves, and they could take Novorossiysk 'any day they liked'. Though the trains had stopped running, between 100,000 and 150,000 civilians were reported to be heading for the city on foot and in carts: 'Heaven knows what can be done with them. There will be famine in no time.'[16] Others besides Keyes were cracking. On the Russian side, Lobanov-Rostovsky knew for sure that everything was up when his normally calm and courteous CO went into hysterics at a coding mistake, and with twitching face seized an inkstand and flung it at his head. On the night of 17/18 March the colonel in charge of British intelligence shot himself dead in his bed, apparently in general despair. Initially thought to be the work of the Greens, the suicide was made the excuse for an intended-to-impress full dress military funeral, attended by Denikin and lent pipes and drums by newly arrived Royal Scots Fusiliers. On the same day as the funeral, 20 March, Lister came down with typhus and was stretchered, delirious, onto a hospital ship. When he came round twelve days later, Williamson was in the next bed. 'My head was burning', Williamson wrote,

> my joints shaking, and I felt rotten in body and rotten in heart. It was all over – one long list of failures, which became more complex and more irremediable the more I looked at it . . . Failure in ideals, failure in plan, failure in execution. What would history say of the failure of the British Mission to South Russia?[17]

★

During their delirium the final act had played out. On 20 March the Mission was ordered to start packing, and to make out rosters for round-the-clock manning of the Heath Robinson Line. Denikin moved his train to the dockside and refused visitors. 'The huge map of the front', wrote Lobanov-Rostovsky, still hung on the wall, showing an impressive number of divisions occupying the line. That some of these divisions were reduced to thirty or one hundred men seemed not to be taken into consideration. 'Well, what news?' I asked a young officer on one of my visits. 'Nothing', he replied. 'So and So has been decorated, and So and So promoted. He is younger than I' . . . I looked out of the window. There were the dark gloomy hills where the Reds were relentlessly driving the Whites down to the sea. To the right were the foothills along the coast highway where the Greens were cutting off our retreat. I marvelled at human nature. Children playing soldiers whilst the house was on fire.[18]

On the 25th, having spent the previous days 'dashing about like a cat on hot bricks . . . hourly expecting interruption from local brother Bolshy', Lever got orders to destroy his papers and dismantle his radio station. By eight forty-five the following morning everything was packed into lorries, and he climbed into the last of them for the drive to the docks:

> At one spot a drunken Cossack officer, brandishing a couple of re-volvers, stood in the middle of the road hurling curses at somebody – us? – and occasionally firing. To my driver's query I said 'keep going', and really wondered what was likely to happen. As we closed with the berserk Cossack I rose in my place, and as I reached full height brought my hand to a pukka salute and beamed at the Russky. To my eternal relief he pouched his right revolver and gave me a pukka Russian salute [in return]. We were well past before I really breathed normally again![19]

Compared to Odessa, military embarkation was orderly. Barges and destroyers laid alongside the quays, and transferred White troops to the big ships out in the bay – battleships HMS *Benbow* and *Emperor of India*, cruis-ers HMS *Calypso* and USS *Galveston*, and France's six-funnelled *Waldeck-Rousseau*. To Allied relief, the Russian soldiers were passive. As described in a letter to Lister by Holman's replacement, General Jocelyn Percy,

> They came into the town in mobs, and all flocked to the Eastern Quay. It was quite impossible to keep them out of our enclosure, and

it was equally impossible to persuade them to guard the heights around the town, or even picket the enclosure we had made . . . In spite of this they just stood quietly and patiently outside the wire on the quay and waited their turn to be put on board a ship . . . We got off several thousand and those that were left behind never made any fuss, but just took things as a matter of course. All they seemed to want was to get somewhere near the ships, and they had the greatest possible faith that the British would take them off if it was possible to do so.[20]

Civilian embarkation, in contrast, was chaotic. With tickets and without, whole communities packed the waterfront: a school's pupils and staff; a hospital's patients and medics; shopkeepers with their goods piled onto barrows; whole Cossack villages with their sheep and cattle; Kalmyks in little tented carts. As in Odessa, part of the crowd panicked, breaching a cordon and swarming onto moored boats. A paddle-steamer cast off and capsized, tipping hundreds into the sea. ('It was *bloody* awful', a witness told an interviewer long after; 'It really was. I think it was the worst thing I've ever seen in my life.'[21]) 'Last day' accounts often gain a great deal in the telling, but there are stories of Cossacks trying to swim out to the ships on their horses, and of a father shooting dead his wife and children before turning his revolver on himself.

By early afternoon the only British troops left on land were the Scots Fusiliers, who held the dock perimeter. Having 'raised Cain' to get his radio gear aboard, Lever was able to watch from the deck of a destroyer: 'Guns, guns and again guns, line upon line of them, stretching along the distant bays of the dock sidings. Wagons, clothing, cars etc etc . . . Tons and tons of valuable material, left for brother Bolshy.'[22] Across the harbour, dabs of white marked where field-pieces and vehicles were being pushed into the water; nearby, a tank squashed flat a row of aeroplanes, before trundling into the sea with its own mighty splash. Late in the afternoon three large fires broke out in the town – one at the ordnance sheds, two at oil stores, Lever thought – and black smoke billowed against the grey sky. As dusk fell, the Red guns in the hills behind started firing shrapnel, booms and crackles echoing. Playing their searchlights, the ships out in the bay replied, first the *Emperor*, 'stately and methodical', followed by the cruisers and destroyers, 'barking like a lot of terriers'. Speechless in the overwhelming noise – 'hell with the lid off' – everyone on deck was grinning, pleased to be 'kicking' if only with 'the parting kick of a runaway'. At 11 p.m. the squadron lifted anchor and set off for White-held Crimea. Twenty-two thousand White soldiers and officers were left behind, some to be captured, others to flee south along the coast towards Georgia. (About nine thousand were later taken off at Sochi and Batumi.)

Out at sea, there was time to think. Watching the coastline merge with the night from the deck of a small cargo boat, Lobanov-Rostovsky remembered how two and a half years earlier, he had expected that about now, life would be returning to normal.

> Instead, a boat was taking me away from my country. Around me people were excitedly talking of returning in two or three months. I did not believe them. I felt that it would not be for fifteen or twenty years – possibly never. I had saved my life, but it was dreadful to feel at twenty-eight that one was a living dead man.[23]

Lever, in a photograph, looks as jaunty as ever, leaning against a sail-bag with his cap pushed back, cigarette dangling and legs crossed at the ankle. But in his diary he wrote of 'anger and self-condemnation', and of Madame Dronova, a nurse at the military hospital who had refused evacuation. Saying goodbye, he had asked her what would happen if 'the Bolsh' found out she had worked for the British. The answer was *Tak!* – 'So!' – and a finger across the throat. Among Lever's papers there is a three-quarter-length photograph of a woman in nurse's uniform. Tall, probably in her mid-thirties, she has a strong, handsome face and gazes levelly at the camera, irony in her almost-smile and a wisp of fringe escaping from her nurse's wimple.

PART V

The End, 1920

25

'Do we not trade with cannibals?'

To ALL INTENTS and purposes it was the end. Kolchak was dead; Denikin, Miller and Yudenich had fled, and White-held territory was down to the half-island of Crimea. Chastened and in some cases deeply unhappy, the Intervention's soldiers were coming home, and its politicians making themselves scarce. While Novorossiysk was being evacuated Churchill was vacationing on the French Atlantic coast, in a lodge borrowed from the Duke of Westminster. The weather, he wrote to Clementine, was 'delicious', and the dark green of pines and gold of gorse perfect for his painting. To Lloyd George a couple of days later: 'I have been having a *complete* holiday and trying to forget about all the disagreeable things that are going on.'[1]

Another sniffer of the wind was officer-cum-journalist Francis McCullagh, now in Moscow and lodging in a new guesthouse for foreigners, a dishevelled mansion still hung with its old owner's Poussins and Corots. Most of his fellow-residents, he was surprised to find, were not foreign Communists but businessmen, on the hunt for government contracts. He did not like them – they 'looked and talked like pickpockets' – but could not help admiring their 'will-power, diplomatic skill and absolute unscrupulousness. They were "out" for "big money", for concessions which would make them multi-millionaires.'[2] They did not make millions, but were right that Allied policy was shifting. When Lenin made peace with Germany at Brest-Litovsk, trade with Bolshevik-held Russia had been banned, and the blockade – in today's terminology, sanctions – had stayed in place after the Armistice. It made little difference to the Russian economy – devasted anyway by war and revolution – but Bolshevik propaganda blamed it for hunger, as did the 'Hands Off Russia' movement. (Former US consul DeWitt Poole, now back in

Washington, resorted to double-speak when receiving a deputation of 'humanitarian women'. No blockade existed, but it was the government's policy 'to refuse export licences for shipments to Russian territory under Bolshevik control.'[3]) Bowing to public pressure, it was lifted in January 1920.

The next stage was an actual trade agreement. At the opening of parliament on 10 February 1920, Lloyd George floated the idea in public for the first time. Bolshevism's 'rapine and plunder', he began, 'revolted the consciences of mankind'. But it was now clear to 'every unprejudiced observer' that it could not be crushed by force of arms. The danger from Bolshevism, he went on, was not in Russia but here at home, where unemployment and food prices were on the rise. Before the war, Russia had supplied a quarter of the world's wheat exports and four-fifths of its flax. Resuming trade would bring prices down and get the mill towns going again. That Russia had not emerged as a democracy was regrettable, but 'When people are hungry, you cannot refuse to buy corn in Egypt because there is a Pharaoh on the throne.' Helped by the fact that Clemenceau had just been ousted by the French electorate, at a meeting of the Supreme Allied Council in Paris on the 24th Lloyd George was able to bring the European leaders with him, and they jointly declared that trade with Russia would now be encouraged 'to the utmost degree'.[4] The outlier was America. Rudderless since Woodrow Wilson's stroke, for twelve months the country had been in the grip of an anarchist 'Red Scare', involving parcel-bombings, an assassination attempt against the attorney general, and harsh police round-ups and raids. (The violence peaked in September 1920, when a horse-drawn cart filled with nitro-glycerine exploded outside the Wall Street offices of JP Morgan, killing thirty-eight – the US's worst domestic terrorist attack until Oklahoma City, seventy-five years later.) Fiercely anti-Bolshevik Lansing no longer led the State Department, but his replacement shared his views, making a statement – broadly, that the Soviet government was bent on subversion and could not be done business with – that defined Washington's position for the next decade.

Even at home, where Lloyd George had the business-minded House of Commons with him, getting trade talks off the ground required all his political wizardry. At the suggestion of a left-leaning civil servant, the preliminary approaches were indirect, not from the Foreign Office to the Kremlin, but from the Ministry of Food to notionally independent producers' cooperatives. As well as preserving deniability this had the advantage of bypassing Curzon, who disagreed with the prime minister's change of policy and whose pomposity irritated. Secrecy ended on 31 May, with the sensational arrival in London of Moscow's official representative, Leonid Krasin, an urbane and dapper figure who until 1917 had combined a revolutionary career with running the Russian branch of Siemens. Outside Downing Street flash-bulbs popped, and Lloyd George met him at the door and ushered him upstairs to meet the Cabinet. Only Curzon had to be nudged – 'Be a gentleman!' – to shake his hand.

Through the summer negotiations proceeded in fits and starts, hampered by a press outcry over the Bolsheviks' treatment of British prisoners of war, by a Labour Party mission's discovery that Soviet Russia was suppressing trades unions, and by the Caspian Red Fleet's ambush of the British garrison at Enzeli.[5] The biggest stumbling-block by far was a new war between Russia and Poland. Under its own austere revolutionary Józef Piłsudski, the Polish army had been edging east for a while, and in April 1920 it launched an offensive on Kiev. Taken by surprise, the Allies debated how to respond. Squarely behind Poland was France, in line with her policy of *cordon sanitaire*. The American government restricted itself to making loans, but allowed citizens to join the Polish Army as volunteers – most famously the twenty-one American pilots of the Kościuszko Squadron. Least keen was Britain, where dockers refused to load munitions bound for Danzig, and Lloyd George told a friend that the Poles had 'gone rather mad', and would 'get their heads punched'.[6]

He was right. With the help of what ended up being substantial Allied aid – sixty aircraft, 100,000 rifles, $56 million in loans – the Polish army occupied Kiev on 7 May. But in part because the offensive prompted a new wave of former tsarist officers to join the Red Army, it was only able to hold it for a few weeks. On 13 June the 'Horse Army' counter-attacked, and by early August it had pushed the Poles all the way back to Warsaw. (To British 'I told you so's, as a friend wrote to Kennedy, 'The Russkis seem to be making that idiotic Polish kingdom rather small, don't they? Can the Red Army really

fight, do you think, or is it simply that their opponents can't?')
Mid-month the conflict turned again with the Poles' 'Miracle on the
Vistula', and in September the two sides started peace talks, without
Allied (or Ukrainian) participation. In October a new border was
agreed along the river Bug – coincidentally, where Curzon had
proposed one the previous December.

The Polish–Soviet war had a matchless chronicler in a twenty-six-
year-old Odessan journalist – Isaac Babel, embedded with a Red cavalry
regiment under a non-Jewish name. In his short stories and even better
in his raw diary, he evokes an oddly bucolic campaign, of dusty roads and
drying clover, insect bites, green apples, and above all of horses – snort-
ing in the drawing-room of a ransacked manor house ('well, we've got
to keep the rain off them'), or in a barn, mouthing wisps of hay from
under his head. One of his jobs was interrogating prisoners, including a
shot-down pilot from the Kościuszko Squadron. The encounter was
one of mutual fascination and misunderstanding. The American's
appearance – 'neck like a pillar, dazzling white teeth' – and general
Western-ness – 'cafés, civilisation, power' – hypnotised Babel: 'I watch
him, can't take my eyes off him.' The pilot – Merian Cooper, later to
script and produce *King Kong* – angled for good treatment by pretending
an enthusiastic interest in Communism, and in a misguided reversal of
Babel's own camouflage tactics, by giving his surname as Mosher. 'Sad
and delicious impression', wrote Babel, who did not detect the ruse.[7]

The irony was very bitter, because although the war was hideously
violent all round – 'Massacre of prisoners', reads one curt diary entry
– those who suffered most, as ever, were Jews.[8] In the village of
Komarow, halfway between Lviv and Lublin, Babel interviewed
survivors of a Polish pogrom:

Indescribable terror and despair. They tell me all about it. Privately,
indoors – they're afraid the Poles may come back . . . In people's
homes – a naked, barely breathing prophet of an old man, an old
woman butchered, a child with fingers chopped off . . . stench of
blood, everything turned upside down, chaos, a mother sitting over
her sabred son, an old woman lying twisted like a pretzel . . . An
agonized Jew showing it all to me, a tall Jew takes over from him . . .
Fifteen people killed.

In an article he wrote about the pogroms for a Red Army newspaper, Babel attacked the infatuated Entente 'governesses' for swooning over the Poles as if they were 'knights of European civilisation'. But in his diary he admitted that his own syphilis-riddled troops were just as bad:

> The hatred is the same, the Cossacks just the same, the cruelty the same; it's nonsense to think that one army is different from another . . . The girls and women, all of them, can scarcely walk. In the evening – a talkative Jew with a little beard, used to keep a shop, daughter threw herself out of a second-storey window to escape a Cossack, broke her arms, one of many.[9]

To boost survivors' morale – and perhaps his own – he had 'my usual system': a consciously untrue set speech:

> I say . . . miraculous things are happening in Russia – express trains, free food for children, theatres, the International. They listen with delight and disbelief. I think – you'll have your diamond-studded sky . . . and feel sorry for them.[10]

★

The trade talks came closest to collapse in August 1920, as the Poles and the Bolsheviks grappled outside Warsaw. For the British government it was a moment of general crisis, with miners, railway men and postal workers striking or threatening to strike, and Irish terror and counter-terror escalating. Both issues inflamed the right, including Churchill and Field Marshal Wilson. They differed on Ireland, Churchill supporting the paramilitary 'Black and Tans', whereas Wilson thought sending in untrained 'scallywags' a mistake. But they were united in regarding all post-war protest, from Cork to Calcutta, as connected – a 'worldwide conspiracy', as Churchill told a City lunch club, 'to deprive us of our place in the world and to rob us of the fruits of victory.'[11] Churchill loved phrase-making, but Wilson seems genuinely to have feared a revolution, repeatedly sounding the alarm in Cabinet, and drawing up emergency plans to deploy troops around London. In private he even suspected Lloyd George, wondering again and again in his diary if the prime minister might not be a secret 'Bolshevist' and 'traitor'.[12]

Two events raised the tension further, the first Soviet defiance on Poland. On 4 August, Lloyd George called Krasin and newly arrived senior Politburo member Lev Kamenev to Downing Street and gave them an ultimatum: unless the Red Army halted its advance on Warsaw, the Royal Navy would sail for Polish ports in three days' time. Sensing irresolution, Moscow called his bluff. The advance continued, the deadline passed and the Navy did not sail. A fortnight later, Cabinet was informed that just as Wilson feared, the Soviet delegation was combining talks with subversion. As revealed by naval intelligence, on 12 August Kamenev had wired to the commissar for foreign affairs that he intended to 'drive in still further the wedge between England and France', and on the 13th he had asked permission to buy enough arms for 50,000 men, to be distributed amongst British workers. Where the money was to come from came to light on the 20th, in a personal telegram from Kamenev to Lenin. In accordance with his instructions from the Central Committee, Kamenev had smuggled a parcel of precious stones into Britain, sold some of them for £40,000, and transferred the money to the trades unionist *Daily Herald*. He hoped that the rest would raise another £60,000.

It was not a very alarming conspiracy. The smuggling showed how strapped Moscow was for cash; no arms had yet been bought, and the *Herald*'s circulation was small. But conspiracy it was, and Churchill made the most of it, urging Lloyd George to publish the intercepts and expel Kamenev and Krasin. Wilson, for whom the prime minister's hesitation was sinister ('my oft-recurring suspicions of LG's loyalty crowd in on me tonight'), rounded up the heads of the intelligence services, Navy and Air Force, and tried to strong-arm Churchill into threatening resignation.

> I told Winston it was the chance of his life to come out as an Englishman . . . I think I have got him pretty well fixed. I warned him that we Soldiers might have to take action if he did not.[13]

Churchill was too wily for him, and agreeing that it was all very serious, left for another of his well-timed holidays in France. Lloyd George was not to be stampeded either. From his own holiday in the Swiss Alps he parried the wires pinging in from London, and stayed away, as planned, until 9 September. A Cabinet debate on his return resulted in a compromise: Kamenev would go, but the talks could continue under Krasin. Officially of his own volition, Kamenev left the following day.

At the same time, the Civil War's end-game played out in Crimea. After Novorossiysk fell, leadership of what remained of the White armies passed from Denikin to Vrangel. British handling of him was characteristically indecisive. When he took power the government sent him a formal note demanding that he abandon a lost cause and seek peace terms. But when he ignored it the Mission, now transferred to Sebastopol, stayed on regardless, training machine-gunners and helping with radio communications. Collishaw's relocated 47 Squadron flew bombing missions, and de Robeck's Black Sea squadron continued to ferry stragglers, and to bombard Red positions on the Kerch Strait.

For the most part, however, the Mission did little more than observe, and like the year before, the Intervention's Crimean summer had almost a holiday air. To convalescing Lister, new Mission head Percy wrote that Vrangel knew in his heart that it was a hopeless fight, but would not give up. 'They don't listen to advice as you well know, and prefer to do things their own way . . . No one takes any notice of me!' The weather and scenery, however, were lovely, so life was pleasant except that 'one is rather bored'.[14] Kennedy, who had seen his friends the Belayevs safely away at Novorossiysk, was stationed in the peninsula's north, and spent his free time shooting teal and riding over the steppe, now busy with bustards and bright with wild tulips. At seaside Feodosiya there were football matches and balalaika evenings, and a subaltern reciprocated formal calls from 'elderly ladies in rusty black, speaking English or exquisite French, [who] over the tea-cups introduced their grand-daughters.'[15] Everyone toured the Crimean War battlefields, and everyone loved Sebastopol's extraordinarily lifelike 360-degree Panorama of the Malakoff Redoubt.

Lever was stationed at Sebastopol, organising radio sets from its Hotel Grand. Though he had the usual fun – picnics, sailing trips – he also caught the town's underlying desperation. From his office balcony, he wrote to his brother, he could see the entrance to the public gardens. There one could hire a rowing boat or listen to an outdoor orchestra, but also buy sex, the sellers not 'flagrant flaunting' professional prostitutes, but respectable women who clearly hated the trade and had been driven to it out of desperation. Though it was 'so easy to dilate one's nostrils', his brother should not condemn:

> Better starve, you say? Withdraw that opinion! . . . Conceive it if you can! . . . Long years of stark, inexorable desolation, utterly complete . . . no apparent goal worth the striving; their accepted canons of virtue, their fetishes, their codes, collapsed all around them like a jerry-built house in a hurricane . . . We English cannot conceive it; [we would have] to go down into the damnable depths of ourselves, and stay there, before realisation came.

Lever also admired the women's resilience – 'badly battered perhaps, but still hoping' – and thought they would return to normal life as soon as circumstances permitted, the sex trade 'thrown away like a dirty ill-fitting coat'.[16]

What Lever only hinted at in his letters were the 'forceful methods' Vrangel was using to keep order. The most notorious of Vrangel's generals was Yakov Slashchyov, formerly Shkuro's deputy and a psychopathic cocaine addict who rode about with a caged crow attached to his saddle. He inspired Bulgakov's jet-black farce *Flight*, in which a 'sick from head to foot' White commander orders hangings at accelerating frequency, to the whirl of a manic waltz. A mass execution at Dzhankoi, the town where Slashchyov was headquartered, was witnessed by a British signals sergeant living in a train at the station. He woke one morning to the sight of two hundred soldiers lying dead on the platform, all shot in the back of the head. When he returned from work that evening more corpses hung 'from every lamppost along the platform . . . including two nurses in their uniforms.'[17]

The sergeant told the story decades later, to an interviewer. Lever similarly recorded an atrocity he was unwittingly involved with only in old age, in a handwritten addition to his diary. One day, without giving it much thought, he had approved a Russian cadet's request for a prisoner detail. At breakfast in the mess the next morning a colleague warned him that he might be in trouble. '"Why?" said I. "What did

I do wrong?"' It transpired that the cadet had made the prisoners dig a trench, then lined them up and described to them how Reds had tortured and killed his grandfather. 'On finishing his tale he drew his revolver and shot the lot – tumbling them into the trench and filling it in. I sweated, but was assured that he'd done it before, and no action would be taken. WOW!!'

In the second week of June, against British advice, Vrangel launched an offensive out of Crimea into 'mainland' Ukraine. The talks with Krasin having just begun, Lloyd George was furious, and told Churchill to wind up the Mission immediately. Fearing that his younger, more impressionable officers might want to stay, Percy gathered them at Sebastopol on the pretence of a training conference, and on 29 June they sailed away. According to Lever, two officers did indeed throw in their commissions, and out at sea, he wondered if he were a cad for not doing the same. Though Vrangel's offensive was initially successful – he took Aleksandrovsk (Zaporizhiye), and Mariupol – he survived the summer only because the Red Army was diverted by the Poles. As soon as the war with Poland ended the Red Army launched a counter-offensive, and on 7 November breached White defences at Crimea's Perekop isthmus. It was the Civil War's last battle, and Vrangel evacuated from Sebastopol a week later, on 14 November. In orderly fashion, about forty thousand people left in total, the civilians sailing for Constantinople, the bulk of soldiers for a camp on the Greek island of Lemnos, just the other side of the Dardanelles. Later Vrangel claimed that the perfidious Allies played no part. It wasn't true: French and American ships took off Russian troops, and though the Admiralty ordered de Robeck 'not repeat not' to breach neutrality by taking part, four British captains – of the destroyers *Seraph*, *Shamrock*, *Tumult* and *Torch* – boarded wounded and medics, and were subsequently reprimanded by a court of enquiry.

The same week, Lloyd George forced closure on the trade talks. On 17 November he announced to Cabinet that a deal was on the table. The two sides would exchange permanent trade missions, cease all hostile propaganda, and free all remaining detainees and prisoners of war. (An earlier demand that Moscow recognise Russia's pre-1917 debts had been dropped.) If signed, he said again, the deal would bring down prices and unemployment, and might even help stabilise

Russia herself, commerce having a 'sobering influence'. As for moral objections to doing business with the Bolsheviks, 'do we not trade with cannibals in the Solomon Islands?'[18] Glowering through the presentation, Churchill handed a note to his friend Lord Birkenhead, threatening to resign if the agreement were approved. At a second meeting the following day it was put to the vote and passed easily, the only dissenters Churchill, Curzon and colonial secretary Lord Milner, who wanted to see Soviet proselytising in India actually cease first. Churchill did not resign, Krasin was sent a draft text a few days later, and after some more to and fro on wording, the Anglo-Soviet Trade Agreement was finally signed on 16 March 1921.

Long-anticipated and overshadowed by events elsewhere, the news created little stir. But it was momentous. Drag her feet on full diplomatic recognition as she might (it was witheld for another three years), Britain had effectively accepted as Russia's legitimate rulers men who three years previously had been obscure exiled revolutionary pamphleteers. It was an astonishing reversal: a triumph for Lenin, and a rebuke to all those who had assumed that he could easily be swept away. The date was momentous for another reason too. A few hours after the signing ceremony, the Red Army attacked the Kronstadt naval base. Six days earlier the Kronstadt sailors – heroes of the Revolution – had thrown out their Party overseers and submitted a list of demands including free elections, a free press and independent trades unions. Without any negotiations, Trotsky now sent waves of infantry across the sea ice to storm Kronstadt's walls. For all but the truest believers, the attack and subsequent executions ended lingering hopes that as it bedded in, the regime would moderate. Just as the Intervention was put to rest, the Bolsheviks definitively proved themselves every bit as ruthless as the tsars.

26

Aftermath

S HORTLY AFTER FLEEING Novorossiysk on the *Emperor of India,*
Denikin issued a list of British naval officers on whom he wished
to bestow decorations. Those on it, wrote one, 'strutted about proudly
for a few days, until someone made the mistake of mentioning the
matter to Sir John [de Robeck].' The admiral's

> eyes flashed and his voice thundered. 'Russian decorations? No sir, I
> do *not* approve! When my officers return to England, they will be
> asked "What did you get out of Russia?" And my officers, sir, will be
> able to answer "Nothing!"'[1]

After the Intervention failed, it was easiest to let its memory fade,
or elide with that of the Great War. No official military histories were
published, nor campaign medals issued, and on the stone crosses that
sprouted in English towns and villages, place-names with a scent of
forest and ice-floe ran seamlessly with the sad, familiar ones from
France and Flanders. The politicians distanced themselves. Lloyd
George tried to shift the blame onto Churchill, joking in a memoir
that his minister's 'ducal blood' had revolted at the Romanov murders,
and to the polymath C. P. Snow that 'the trouble with Winston' was
that he would '*insist on getting out his maps.* In 1914 he got out his maps
of the Dardanelles, and think where that landed us.' And after the
Armistice, 'before I could look round, he'd got out maps of Russia
and we were making fools of ourselves in the Civil War.'[2] On the
other side of the Atlantic, former Secretary of State Lansing brought
his memoirs to a halt at the end of 1917, thus including his initial
advice to sit tight and wait, but omitting his subsequent passionate
advocacy for Intervention. President Wilson's biographers did his

distancing for him, stressing his reluctance to send troops, and blaming his eventual acquiescence on his failing health. Loudly unrepentant, uniquely, was Churchill. The Intervention damaged his career, cementing his post-Dardanelles reputation as an irresponsible adventurer, souring his relations with the trades unions, and contributing to the loss of his seat in the general election of 1922. But to the end of his life he vociferously defended it, arguing that the Bolsheviks could have been overthrown easily if only the political will had been there, and that the Whites had been a good cause. Kolchak, he wrote in a war memoir, 'tried hard to be liberal and progressive', and to Denikin's 'excesses' he gave three sentences, all in reference to his own token telegrams.[3]

What should we think about the Intervention now? The Cold War criticism, developed by American foreign-policy luminary George Kennan and others, was that it sowed the seeds of Soviet anti-Westernism, and made the system more repressive. The second charge is disingenuous, since the Bolsheviks used political violence from the start. Stalinism was not a departure from Leninism, but the same philosophy taken to extremes. There is some truth to the first, in that the Intervention played into a long-standing Russian narrative of encirclement by hostile foreign powers. But it is hard to see, had the Allies stood back, that relations would have been much better. A one-party state explicitly dedicated to worldwide revolution, the Soviet Union was never going to be a normal diplomatic partner.

Much more plausible is the charge that by radicalising the politics and damaging the self-confidence of the democracies, the Intervention contributed to Europe's fragmentation between the wars. The link was most obvious in Germany, where returning Freikorps members took part in March 1920's Kapp Putsch before drifting into the early Nazi militias. (Amongst them the future Auschwitz commandant Rudolf Höss.) More broadly White ideology, in particular the conviction that Jews masterminded the Revolution, fed into Nazism via émigré organisations in Munich and Berlin. The Intervention also destabilised in Czechoslovakia, where the Legion was key to the new state's army and foundation story, but clashed with its democratic political establishment. Most disruptive was Gajda, who headed a fascist party from 1927 and ended up being shot as a collaborator at the close of the Second World War. (Gustav Becvar, in happy contrast, moved to England and bought a Sussex dairy farm, where his descendants still live today.)

In America, the Intervention's failure fed into interwar isolationism, the slogan 'America First' – originally Wilson's – helping the Republican Warren Harding to a landslide victory in the presidential election of November 1920. Britain kept her taste for adventure: with new mandates in Africa and the Middle East, the Empire was in fact bigger than ever. But like the Boer War before and the loss of Ireland after, the Russian humiliation marked a diminution; more and more, she had to bring America with her, and be careful not to bite off more than she could chew. Domestically, it contributed to a general sense of disenchantment, as post-war hopes faded in the face of economic depression. Though far less viciously than in Germany, it also gave antisemitism a boost, the mixed-race anarchist replacing the Hun as default bogeyman in popular culture. (And in parts of the establishment. It is a remarkable factoid that the winner of the 1922 Coronation Cup was a horse called Pogrom, owned by Waldorf Astor. Its dam was Lemberg – the Austrian name for Lviv.) The Intervention was not to blame for appeasement; the Depression and the Great War were far more important. But that Churchill was so strongly identified with it made it easier to question his judgement on Hitler later on.

Of the White leaders, only Denikin had a peaceful afterlife, living quietly in France before moving to America. General Miller also settled in France, until in 1937 NKVD agents posing as German military intelligence lured him to a safehouse, drugged him, put him in a packing case and loaded it onto a Soviet freighter waiting at Le Havre. He was executed in Moscow two years later. Vrangel died suddenly at his home in Brussels, either of a heart attack or, as his family believed, poisoned by his butler's NKVD agent brother. Lesser figures came to more or less deserved bad ends. Shkuro and the Don Cossack leader Pyotr Krasnov both led émigré units for the Wehrmacht during the Second World War, were taken prisoner by British forces at its end, and handed over to Moscow and hung. The Siberian warlord

Semyonov met the same fate after being captured by the Red Army in Manchuria.

And what of the Interventionists themselves? There was a marked difference between British and American remembering. The British accounts are uneasy, with guilt and a sense of failure lurking beneath surface jollity. They also benefit greatly from hindsight. For example in Williamson's memoir, not published until the 1970s, the antisemitism and blind enthusiasm for the Whites of his letters of the time are edited out, and praise for Jewish doctors edited in. (Plus, for commercial reasons, an invented love affair.) American accounts are much less tortured. Some are in the context-free wilderness adventure vein, but most straightforwardly denounce the Intervention as a misbegotten waste of money and lives. Interviewed in later life, veterans compared it to Vietnam.

Some Russo-Allied personal relationships endured. Unofficially, marriages between Interventionists and local women were strongly discouraged, COs generally regarding prospective brides as passport-hunters and bad wife material. (They were 'all pretty *wild* girls. They knew they had to make it somewhere . . . And they were *very, very* attractive.'[4]) There were plenty nonetheless. Colonel Stokes, Dunsterville's political officer in Baku, acquired a Russian wife, and also brought home three 'Mission Boys', for whose passage and new clothes he requested £62 in expenses. The Trans-Caspian Committee's Reginald Teague-Jones married an Armenian girl who he met on a refugee steamer. The relationship did not survive life in a small Barons Court flat, but they renewed contact in old age, dying within weeks of each other in the same south coast nursing home. Several Interventionists brought home personal servants. Philip Woods of the 'Irish Karelians' tried to get a 'very intelligent Karelian youth' settled with his parents in Belfast. He was too wild for them – within days, the cook and maids gave notice – but did well with stronger-nerved Russian friends in London, getting a job at a dentist's and earning a police commendation for catching a bolting horse. Ironside's cheerful Kostya – Konstantin Osipov – came away with him and continued to work as his driver, before serving in the Tank Regiment during the Second World War. Distinctly iffy today but gushingly reported at the time, is the story of America's representative to Denikin, Admiral

Newton McCully, and the seven 'orphans', aged from twelve down to three, he took home with him from Crimea. He made a habit of visiting children's homes – he had earlier tried to adopt in London and Murmansk – and the 'orphans' were not actually parentless; in the case of at least one of the girls, her father wanted payment to give her up.[5]

In total, perhaps two million people left the old tsarist empire in the four years after the Revolution. Britain and America were stingy with visas, but sizeable émigré colonies developed in Constantinople, Shanghai, Paris and Berlin. For those who stayed behind, past association with the Allies could be fatal. After the final evacuations in the South, the incoming Bolsheviks executed thousands in Odessa and Sebastopol, and Archangel province was made the site of the early Gulag. Its very first camp occupied the Solovetsky Islands monastery, whose abbot had sent presents of smoked salmon to Woods at Kem. For the old middle classes in general, survival meant adopting protective camouflage. Back in Russia as advisor to a Labour delegation in 1925, former Baku consul Ranald MacDonell got into conversation with a ragged, bearded man at a railway station:

> I hailed him with the accepted 'Good morning, Comrade'. He totally ignored my fraternal greeting, and pointing to our wagon, asked 'What is all this special train about?' It was evident from his speech that he was not born a peasant. I explained to him that the train carried the British Trades Union Delegation.
>
> 'My God, the British again!' he exclaimed. 'What the devil do they want now?'
>
> I told him this was a delegation of British workers. 'God save us' he said, crossing himself, 'more proletariat'.
>
> I asked him what he was; he replied that he had been on a carpentry job that day. 'But', I enquired, 'what were you before?'
>
> 'You should know', he replied, 'that in Russia today you must not ask even your father what he was yesterday,' and with a chuckle he slouched away.[6]

How are the Civil War and Intervention seen in Russia today? With the collapse of the Soviet Union, the motheaten trope of heroic Red Army versus villainous White Guard and Entente unravelled.

Archives opened, scholarship flourished and cartoonish memorial sites such as Mudyug were left to crumble. The wheel started turning again from the early 2000s, with the rise of Putin. Censorship returned, media and academia were muzzled, and a new story enforced, of unbroken Russian greatness under strong leaders. In: medieval Rus and the Great Patriotic War. Out: Gorbachev, the Gulag and the 1917 Revolution, the centenary of which went almost unmarked. In this pick-'n'-mix, might-is-right narrative, White heroes and Soviet ones are interchangeable, imperial eagle perching next to hammer and sickle. In 2005 Denikin 'came home', his remains moved from New Jersey to a Moscow monastery, and in 2008 a lavish and highly romanticised Kolchak biopic, *Admiral*, broke box-office records.

With Putin's full-scale invasion of Ukraine, history is in some ways repeating itself. Again, the West is sending weapons and money; again, it has imposed economic sanctions; again middle-class Russians are fleeing into exile. Most of all, Russia is again in the grip of a millennial ideology: its leaders denying that Ukraine exists and threatening nuclear Armageddon, its population, save for a brave few, cheering them on or burying their heads in the sand. After the Civil War, trade with the West quickly resumed. But politically and culturally, Russia remained hostile and isolated for the next seventy years. Her current levels of violence and lunacy feel too febrile to last for long. They could be the Putin regime's death-throes, or they could be a prelude to escalation – perhaps another invasion, perhaps even a nuclear strike. Easiest to imagine perhaps only because familiar is something in between – the fighting dying down and resumption of the Cold War, unfriendly but relatively stable. In truth, we don't know. The Kremlin is a black box, and as pointed out in this book's introduction, the Intervention a reminder of how often we get Russia badly wrong.

Unknowability is at the heart of Gerhardie's *Futility*. In it he clumsily woos a girl called Nina, one of a bewitching trio of sisters who have washed up in Vladivostok along with a train of feckless relatives. Nina was a real person: Gerhardie kept a photograph of her lying on a lawn with a dog. But in the book, she and he stand for their respective countries: she mercurial, elusive, selfish; he self-important, busy, naïve. The reader can see that she is thoroughly unsuitable, and that the affair is doomed. But the Gerhardie character does not realise it until the very end, when he discovers that Nina and her sisters have given his name to their pointlessly chirping pet canary. He sails home a sadder and a wiser man.

Acknowledgements

MANY PEOPLE HELPED to create this book. First, thanks to my agent Natasha Fairweather for her encouragement, friendship and shrewd editorial eye. The same to Matthew Marland and the rest of the superb team at Rogers, Coleridge & White. At John Murray, commissioning editor Joe Zigmond gave detailed and immensely useful commentary on the book's first draft, and Caroline Westmore expertly ushered it through final edits and production.

Second, thanks to all those who made my research trips a success. In Archangel, Professor Vladislav Goldin of the Northern Arctic Federal University (NARFU) was extremely generous with his time and knowledge, giving me a fascinating tour of his city as well as invaluable advice on sources and the historiography. So were Dr Tatyana Troshina, also of NARFU, and Dr Yelizavyeta Khatanzeiskaya, now of Moscow's Higher School of Economics. The battlefield archaeologist Aleksei Sukhanovsky hosted me at his base on the railway front, describing amongst other things his rediscovery of the lost remains of Australian VC Sam Pearse. On the once British-run prison island of Mudyug, Marina Titova showed me a memorial to her great-great-uncle, executed after a breakout attempt. All this was organised by ever-enthusiastic, soon to be Dr Yekaterina Yemelyanova. Equally good company, in Murmansk, was Lyudmila Ivanova, who as well as setting up interviews organised a memorable outing to Pechenga, scene of the Intervention's first fighting and now one of Russia's remotest garrisons. A painful note: I made these trips in 2019, before Russia's new invasion of Ukraine. Today I would not go. All the above are happy to have their names cited here; others prefer to remain anonymous.

In Ukraine, Professor Volodymyr Poltorak and Dr Taras Vintskovsky, both of Odesa National University, shared their thoughts on the

French occupation of their lovely and now again front-line city. The historian and journalist Yevgeniy Demenok and the musicologist Professor Yuriy Semenov were a pleasure to meet, as was Professor Viktor Savchenko of the Odesa State University of Internal Affairs, who as well as talking history took me swimming in the Black Sea. In Baku, Ilkin Huseynli was a matchless guide, and enabled revealing interviews with Professor Jabi Bahramov and Dr Ilgar Niftaliyev of the Baku Academy of Sciences. Tahir Gözel put me up in his stunning Fairmont hotel, and Famil Mustafa, director of the Tusi-Bohm Planetarium, showed me round the battlefields outside the city.

At home, I was privileged to be given access to several privately held Intervention diaries. Christopher and Rossana Howgrave-Graham and Charles and Katrina Ironside were extremely kind hosts, plying me with refreshments as I worked through their forebears' papers. Han Dunsterville and Sir Richard Onslow generously passed on precious transcripts. Lord and Lady Ironside have since donated the important Ironside diary, covering the whole of the Field Marshal's long career, to the Liddell Hart Centre for Military Archives at King's College London. For sharing their research and/or giving detailed advice on sources, special thanks to Lieutenant Colonel Colin Bulleid of the Royal Hampshire Regiment Trust, Professors Todd Endelman and Jeffrey Veidlinger of the University of Michigan, Thomas McCall, Tamara Polyakova of the University of Wisconsin-Madison, and Professor David Rechter of Oxford. In the archives, particularly helpful were Katrina DiMuro of KCL's Liddell Hart Centre, Dr Lucy Gwynn of Eton College Library, John Wells of Cambridge University Library, and Stuart Wheeler and Katie Thompson of Bovington's Tank Museum. Ekaterina Aleynikova filleted the Russian-language memoirs, and contributed her own shrewd insights into the writers' motivations and personalities.

Other busy people who gave tips, made introductions or responded to out-of-the-blue emails are Edward Amory, Lucy Ash, Dr Justin Basquille, Anthony and Sarah Becvar, Camilla Beresford, Professor Kate Brown, Professor Andy Bruno, Rohan Collier, Peter Collins, Kevan Darby, Vladislav Davidzon, Salamander Davoudi, Robert Denis, Frank Donald, John and Jane Dunsterville, Louise Fergusson and Sara Lady Fergusson, Jonathan Ford, Archie Fraser, Professor

Krista Goff, Dr Altay Goyushov, Professor Jamil Hasanli, Nikolai Holmov, Dr Tanya Howgrave-Graham, Professor Véronique Jobert, Orysia Lutsevych, Dr Nigar Maxwell, Lieutenant Colonel Stephen May, Giles Milton, Anna Morgan, Catriona Oliphant, Dan Orteu, James Peill, Marina Pesenti, Dr Jane Plotke, Victor Sebestyen, Dr Lyuba Vinogradova, Dr Tatiana Voronina, Tom de Waal, Damien Wright and Yuliya Zaika.

Last but not least, love and gratitude as always to my husband Charles and our sons Ed and Bertie. This book is dedicated to my father Alex, lender together with my stepmother Sian of the perfect writer's cottage up a hill, and a never-failing source of support and ideas.

Picture Credits

Notes

Abbreviations

BHL–UM: Bentley Historical Library, University of Michigan
BL: British Library, London
BL–UL: Brotherton Library, University of Leeds
CUL: Cambridge University Library
ECL: Eton College Library
IWM: Imperial War Museum, London
LHCMA–KCL: Liddell Hart Centre for Military Archives, King's
             College London
NA: National Archives, Kew

Introduction

1. Gerhardie, *Futility*, p. 90.
2. Edmund Ironside diary, 28 November 1918, LHCMA–KCL; Gerhardie, *Futility*, p. 131.
3. Peter Crawford, quoted in Dobson and Miller, p. 49.
4. Hudleston Williamson, in Harris (ed.), p. 15.
5. George Green, interview, recorded 1986, IWM.
6. Williamson, in Harris (ed.), pp. 72, 86.
7. Edward Trombley diary, BHL–UM.
8. R. H. Earnshaw, interview, recorded 1970, IWM.
9. Robert Watson, interview, recorded 1997, IWM.
10. Cudahy, p. 77.
11. Lendon FitzPayne, interview, recorded 1983, IWM.
12. Phelps Hodges, p. 75.
13. Williamson, in Harris (ed.), pp. 27, 33.

14. Ibid., pp. 82–3.
15. Marushevsky, pp. 30–1.
16. Hodgson, p. 85.

Chapter 1: *Unerhört!*

1. Fedotoff White, p. 40.
2. Woodrow Wilson's speech to Congress of 2 April 1918, quoted in Foglesong, p. 51.
3. Lansing, p. 332.
4. See Rappaport, pp. 66–9.
5. Fedotoff White, pp. 145–6.
6. Ibid., p. 165.
7. Lansing, pp. 337–8.
8. de Robien, 19 November 1917, p. 147.
9. Noskov, p. 56.
10. Lansing, pp. 339–40.
11. Ullman, vol. 1, p. 31.

Chapter 2: 'A lot of impossible folks'

1. Bruce Lockhart, p. 275.
2. Jacques Sadoul to Albert Thomas, 7 May 1918, quoted in Sadoul, p. 342.
3. Brogan, p. 202.
4. Bruce Lockhart, p. 226.
5. Ibid., p. 240.
6. Sadoul, p. 376.
7. Churchill, *Thoughts and Adventures*, p. 172.
8. Woodrow Wilson's speech to Congress of 8 January 1918, quoted in Foglesong, p. 65.
9. Charles Drage diary, 30 April 1918, IWM.
10. Ibid., 5 May 1918.
11. Ibid., 11 May 1918.

Chapter 3: Brother Czecho

1. Becvar, p. 74.
2. Ibid., p. 82.
3. Ibid., p. 91.
4. Maurice Howgrave-Graham diary, 10 December 1918, private collection.
5. Ernest Harris to George Emerson, quoted in Graves, p. 50.
6. Buxhoeveden, Chapter 13.
7. Sakharow, pp. 53, 151.
8. Foglesong, p. 163.
9. Kennan, p. 394.
10. Ibid., p. 397.

Chapter 4: Aide Memoire

1. Maynard, pp. 10–14.
2. Ibid., p. 17.
3. A. G. Burn diary, 19 June 1918, IWM.
4. Maynard, p. 39.
5. Bruce Lockhart, p. 286.
6. Maynard, pp. 41–2.
7. Ibid., p. 44.
8. Ibid., p. 51.
9. Philip Woods memoir, in Baron (ed.), p. 157.
10. Charles Maynard to DeWitt Poole, 1 September 1918, quoted in Rothstein, p. 80.
11. Rothstein, pp. 79, 81.
12. Kennan, pp. 371–2.
13. Bruce Lockhart, p. 289.
14. Francis, p. 304.
15. de Robien, 1 July 1918, p. 277.
16. Bruce Lockhart, p. 300.
17. Ibid., p. 255.
18. For the whole 'Aide Memoire', see Kennan, pp. 482–5.
19. Silverlight, p. 44.
20. Poole, p. 172.

Chapter 5: 'We are not here to conquer'

1. Fraser, p. 242.
2. Bruce Lockhart, p. 310.
3. Ibid., p. 316.
4. Ibid., p. 320.
5. Hill, pp. 228–9.
6. Ibid., p. 240. See also George Hill's 26 November 1918 report to General Poole, Poole papers, IWM.
7. Bruce Lockhart, p. 329.
8. Ibid., p. 339.
9. See Ullman, vol. 1, pp. 296–300.

Chapter 6: Charley Chaplin's coup

1. Godfrey J. Anderson memoir, p. 3, BHL-UM.
2. Ibid., pp. 4–6.
3. Francis, pp. 270, 273.
4. de Robien, 6 September 1918, p. 289.
5. US Office of Naval Intelligence report of 21 October 1918, 'Attempted Revolution at Archangel, September 5–12, 1918', in Strakhovsky, pp. 266–73.
6. Strakhovsky, p. 57.
7. Ullman, vol. 1, pp. 241–2.
8. Clarence G. Scheu diary, 8 September 1918, BHL-UM.
9. Ibid., 16 September 1918.
10. Ibid., 21 September 1918.
11. Edwin Arkins diary, 21 September 1918, BHL-UM.
12. Scheu diary, 25 September 1918, BHL-UM.
13. Arkins diary, 4 October 1918, BHL-UM.
14. Anderson memoir, p. 28, BHL-UM.
15. Ibid, pp. 29–30.
16. Henry Katz, 'Short Summary of Activities of Medical Personnel with First Battalion 339th Infantry', Katz papers, BHL-UM.
17. See Novikova, p. 165.
18. Hilton Young to his brother, letter of 24 June 1918, Hilton Young papers, CUL.

19. Young, pp. 255–6.
20. Ibid., p. 259.
21. Ibid., pp. 262–5.
22. Ibid., p. 275.
23. Ibid., p. 281.
24. Ibid., p. 287.
25. Scheu diary, 10, 11, 13 and 14 October 1918, BHL-UM.
26. Ibid., 27 October 1918.
27. Ibid., 5 November 1918.
28. Robert Lansing telegram to David Francis, 26 September 1918, 'Papers Relating to the Foreign Relations of the United States, 1918, Russia, Volume II', Office of the Historian, Foreign Service Institute, US Department of State.

Chapter 7: The Hush-hush Brigade

1. Lionel Dunsterville diary, 6 January 1918, www.gwpda.org/Dunsterville/Dunsterville_1918.html
2. Ibid., 18 February 1918.
3. MacDonell, p. 215.
4. Ibid., p. 222.
5. Ibid., pp. 228, 234.
6. Claude Stokes memoir, 'Pages from Life', pp. 4–5, IWM.
7. Dunsterville diary, 27 August 1918.
8. Dunsterville, *The Adventures of Dunsterforce*, p. 273.
9. Dunsterville diary, 1 September 1918.
10. Stokes memoir, pp. 6–7, IWM.
11. Dunsterville diary, 1 September 1918.
12. MacDonell, p. 263.
13. John Weightman Warden diary, 14 September 1918, Public Archives of Canada.
14. Dunsterville, *The Adventures of Dunsterforce*, p. 309.
15. See Kazemzadeh, pp. 143–4.
16. MacDonell, p. 273.
17. Ibid., pp. 274–5.
18. Erich von Ludendorff, *Ludendorff's Own Story*, vol. 2, London, 2018, p. 258.
19. Dunsterville diary, 28 September 1918.
20. Teague-Jones, p. 120.

Chapter 8: 'Eggs loaded with dynamite'

1. Maurice Jenks memoir, 'Service Memories and Thoughts', 13 November 1918, p. 19, IWM.
2. Young, p. 297.
3. Becvar, p. 198.
4. Clarence G. Scheu diary, 11 November 1918, BHL-UM.
5. Ibid., 12 November 1918.
6. Ibid., 13 November 1918.
7. Ibid., 6 January 1919.
8. Ibid., 11 January 1919.
9. Philips Price, p. 345.
10. Nabokoff, p. 274.
11. Lloyd George speech of 16 April 1919, quoted in Ullman, vol. 2, p. 155.
12. Silverlight, p. 100.
13. Graves, p. 4.
14. Ibid., p. 55.
15. Ward, pp. 12–13.
16. Ullman, vol. 1, p. 132.
17. Maurice Howgrave-Graham diary, 7 December 1918, private collection.
18. Gerhardie, *Futility*, p. 93.
19. Ullman, vol. 1, p. 272.
20. Dotsenko, pp. 53–4.
21. Vasiliy Boldyrev, quoted in Dotsenko, p. 52.
22. Ward, pp. 35, 40.
23. Nabokoff, p. 277.

Chapter 9: 'A feeling of smothering'

1. See Richard Usborne, *Clubland Heroes*, London, 1974, p. 87.
2. Edmund Ironside diary, 1 March 1920, LHCMA-KCL.
3. See for example Costello, pp. 58–9.
4. Ironside diary, 4 October 1918, LHCMA-KCL.
5. Ibid., 7 November 1918.
6. Ibid., 8 November 1918.
7. Ibid., 7 November 1918.
8. Ibid., 29 October 1918.

9. Ibid., 31 October 1918.

10. Ibid., 10 November 1918.

11. Report by Brigadier-General Robert Gordon-Finlayson on actions on the river front, 11–14 November 1918, pasted into Ironside's diary, 16 November 1918. Finlayson misspells the lieutenant's name: he was John Morrison Dalziel.

12. Ironside diary, 7 December 1918, LHCMA-KCL.

13. Ibid.

14. Marushevsky, p. 45.

15. Ironside diary, 8 December 1918, LHCMA-KCL.

16. Ibid., 10 December 1918.

17. Ibid., 11 December 1918. Marushevsky's version of events, in his memoir *God na Severye* ('A Year in the North'), is that he himself gave the orders re the Lewis gun and mortar, and that Ironside did not arrive until after the ringleaders had given themselves up. The French ambassador, Noulens, agrees more closely with Ironside. An American account in Moore et al.'s *The History of the American Expedition Fighting the Bolsheviki* is completely invented.

18. Ironside and Bamford, p. 117. The witness was Company Sergeant Major Frederick Neesham.

19. Ironside diary, 11 December 1918, LHCMA-KCL.

20. Ironside, *Archangel 1918–1919*, p. 70.

Chapter 10: Paris and Shenkursk

1. 3 January 1919, quoted in Gilbert, p. 231.

2. See Isitt, 'Canada's Siberian Expedition', (University of Victoria), http://www.siberianexpedition.ca/index.html%3Flang=english.html

3. Quoted in Gilbert, pp. 227–8.

4. Ibid., p. 229.

5. Ibid.

6. Clarence G. Scheu diary, 24 December 1918, BHL-UM.

7. Godfrey J. Anderson memoir, p. 39, BHL-UM.

8. Zoya Mikhailova diary, 18 August 1918, private collection.

9. Ibid., 13 October 1918.

10. Ibid., 18 August and 24 December 1918.

11. Edmund Ironside diary, 14 November 1918, LHCMA-KCL.

12. Ibid., 21 December 1918. For more on Bochkareva, and on women in the tsarist army in general, see Melissa Stockdale, "'My Death for the

Motherland is Happiness": Women, Patriotism, and Soldiering in Russia's Great War, 1914–1917', https://historycooperative.org/journal/my-death-for-the-motherland-is-happiness-women-patriotism-and-soldiering-in-russias-great-war-1914-1917/

13. Ironside diary, 23 February 1919, LHCMA-KCL.
14. Pavel Rasskazov, 'Notes of a Prisoner', in Goldin (ed.), *Interventsiya na Russkom Severye, 1918–1920.*
15. Vladimir Ignatyev memoir, in Goldin (ed.), *Bely Sever*, vol. 1, pp. 152–3.
16. Edward Trombley diary, 5 December 1918, BHL-UM.
17. Ironside diary, 21 October 1918, LHCMA-KCL.
18. Scheu diary, 1 and 2 February 1919; see also Cudahy, pp. 162–3.
19. Ironside diary, 30 December 1918, LHCMA-KCL.
20. Ibid., 16 January 1919.
21. Ibid., 17 January 1919.
22. Edwin Arkins diary, 26 January 1919, BHL-UM.

Chapter 11: Prinkipo and Siberia

1. Alfred Knox to War Office, 29 January 1919, quoted in Ullman, vol. 2, p. 115.
2. Gilbert, p. 235.
3. Silverlight, pp. 156–7.
4. Brogan, p. 234.
5. Poole, p. 262.
6. Victor Cazalet letter to his mother, 23 December 1918, ECL.
7. Maurice Howgrave-Graham diary, 1 December 1918, private collection.
8. Ibid., 23 January 1919.
9. Ibid., 31 January 1919.
10. Ibid., 5, 6 and 13 February 1919.
11. Ibid., 25 February 1919.
12. Ibid., 6 March 1919.
13. Graves, p. 160.
14. Cazalet diary, 11 February 1919, ECL.
15. Ibid., 19 February 1919.
16. Cazalet letter to his family, 19 February 1919, ECL.
17. Ward, p. 60.

18. Dotsenko, p. 77.
19. Graves, p. 163.
20. Ibid., pp. 170–1.
21. Buxhoeveden, Chapter 12.
22. Robert Speer, *"Lu Taifu": Charles Lewis MD, a Pioneer Surgeon in China,* New York, 1930s, p. 114.
23. See Irwin, p. 95.

Chapter 12: *L'Entente de ma tante*

1. Herbert Wyld letter to his wife, 14 November 1918, IWM.
2. Teffi, p. 80.
3. Ibid., p. 106.
4. de Wiart, p. 99.
5. Ibid., p. 100.
6. Hudleston Williamson, lecture for the BBC, 1965, IWM.
7. Terence Keyes letter to his wife, 9 January 1919, BL.
8. 'Report on Visit of British Military Mission to the Volunteer Army Under General Denikin in South Russia, November–December 1918', General Staff, War Office, Poole papers, LHCMA-KCL.
9. George Lever diary, 9 February 1920, LHCMA-KCL; Charles de Wolff memoir, p. 45, IWM.
10. Keyes letter to his wife, 8 February 1919, BL.
11. Wyld letter to his wife, 17 December 1918, IWM.
12. Ibid., 21 January 1919.
13. Wyld, 'Daily report', 23 January 1919, IWM.
14. Wyld letter to his wife, 2 February 1919, IWM.
15. Ibid., 26 January 1919, IWM.
16. Ibid., 2 February 1919, IWM.
17. Teffi, p. 110.
18. Munholland, p. 48.
19. Lobanov-Rostovsky, p. 320.
20. Culme-Seymour to Gough-Calthorpe, 1 April 1919, quoted in Halpern (ed.), p. 26.
21. Lobanov-Rostovsky, p. 333.
22. Culme-Seymour to Gough-Calthorpe, 8 April 1919, quoted in Halpern (ed.), p. 32.
23. Lobanov-Rostovsky, p. 339.

24. Culme-Seymour to Gough-Calthorpe, 1 May 1919, quoted in Halpern (ed.), pp. 42–9.
25. Percy Shrubsole, letter to a friend, 25 May 1919, IWM.

Chapter 13: 'Our poor little unarmed soldiers'

1. A. P. von Budberg, quoted in Smele, *The 'Russian' Civil Wars*, p. 112.
2. Gilbert, p. 291.
3. Victor Cazalet diary, 31 March 1919, ECL.
4. Maurice Howgrave-Graham diary, 16 May 1919, private collection.
5. Maurice Howgrave-Graham, 'The Siberian Soldier Factory', pp. 284–5, private collection.
6. Howgrave-Graham diary, 11–14 June 1919, private collection.
7. Fedotoff White, p. 230.
8. Gilbert, pp. 296–7.
9. Howgrave-Graham diary, 28 June 1919, private collection.
10. Ibid., 7 July 1919.
11. Howgrave-Graham, 'The Siberian Soldier Factory', p. 296, private collection.

Chapter 14: Dyer's Battalion

1. Woods memoir, in Baron (ed.), pp. 163, 165.
2. Ibid., p.183.
3. Ibid., pp. 177, 183, 186.
4. Fedor Lesonen, quoted in Polyakova.
5. Woods memoir, in Baron (ed.), p. 194.
6. Marushevsky, p. 224; Vladimir Ignatyev memoir, in Goldin (ed.), *Bely Sever*, vol. 1, p. 155.
7. Woods memoir, in Baron (ed.), pp. 264–5.
8. Clarence G. Scheu diary, 12 February 1919, BHL-UM.
9. Kenneth A. Skelleger letter to his brother, 10 April 1919, BHL-UM.
10. Bentinck, pp. 56–7; see also Kinvig, pp. 175–6.
11. F. Hirst diary, 16 October 1918, IWM.
12. Riley Rudd diary, 22 February 1919, IWM.
13. Edmund Ironside diary, 27 February 1919, LHCMA-KCL.
14. Marushevsky, p. 142.

15. Ironside diary, 2 March 1919, LHCMA-KCL.
16. War Office to Ironside, 4 April 1919. Given in War Office 'Blue Book', *The Evacuation of North Russia, 1919*, Appendix F.
17. Frank Douma diary, 8 June 1919, BHL-UM.
18. Godfrey J. Anderson memoir, p. 81, BHL-UM.
19. Silverlight, p. 172.
20. See, for example, Silverlight, p. 191 and Ullman, vol. 2, p. 141.
21. Fraser, p. 253.
22. Boris Sokolov memoir, in Goldin (ed.), *Bely Sever*, vol. 2, pp. 321–2, 350.
23. Ironside diary, 19 February 1919, LHCMA-KCL.
24. Ibid., 6 June 1919.
25. Ibid., 25 April 1919.
26. Ibid., 3 April 1919.
27. Marushevsky, p. 31.
28. Ironside diary, 11 March 1919, LHCMA-KCL.
29. Ibid., 7 July 1919.
30. Edward Allfrey diary, 17 July 1919, IWM.
31. Ironside diary, 7 July 1919, LHCMA-KCL.

Chapter 15: One last packet

1. Berg, p. 607.
2. MacDonell, p. 303.
3. Hudleston Williamson, in Harris (ed.), p. 155.
4. Collishaw, p. 187.
5. Collishaw letter, 1 November 1919, quoted in Loftus, pp. 15, 19.
6. Collishaw, p. 198.
7. Leslie Kemp, interview, BL-UL.
8. M. L. Goldsmith letters to his father, 1 and 20 June 1919, LHCMA-KCL.
9. Ibid., 29 June 1919, LHCMA-KCL.
10. John de Robeck report to the Admiralty, 19 October 1919, quoted in Halpern (ed.), pp. 117–18.
11. Maurice Jenks memoir, 'Service Memories and Thoughts', 13 November 1918, p. 20, IWM.
12. George Milne letter to Henry Wilson, 22 January 1919, in Jeffreys (ed.), *The Military Correspondence of Field Marshal Sir Henry Wilson, 1918–1922*, pp. 77–9.
13. Christopher Bilney, interview, recorded 1972, IWM.

Chapter 16: Honorary Cossacks

1. Levene, pp. 62–3.
2. Denikine, p. 227.
3. Heifetz, p. 110.
4. Jeffrey Veidlinger, presentation given at the Center for Jewish History, New York, 16 May 2016, www.yivo.org/A-Forgotten-Genocide
5. See Veidlinger; McGeever.
6. Shtif, p. 45.
7. Hodgson, pp. 140–1.
8. Astashkevich, pp. 34–5, 42.
9. Veidlinger, pp. 259–68.
10. Goldman, pp. 130–1.
11. Ibid., pp. 131, 133.
12. Ibid., pp. 136–7.
13. Veidlinger, p. 248.
14. Heifetz, p. 122.
15. Shtif, p. 83.
16. Williamson letter to his mother, 12 August 1919, IWM.
17. Goldsmith letter to his father, 29 June 1919, LHCMA-KCL.
18. Ibid., 1 June 1919.
19. Evelyn Barker papers, BL-UL.
20. Gough-Calthorpe to the Admiralty, 29 June 1919, quoted in Halpern (ed.), p. 95.
21. Frederick Lister diary, 18 January 1920, Lister papers, LHCMA-KCL.
22. Hodgson, pp. 63–9.
23. Kinvig, p. 233.
24. Kadish, p. 17.
25. Leonard Cohen letter to Terence Keyes, 20 June (year not given, but probably 1920), and Keyes speech to Quetta Staff College, Hyderabad, 1921, Keyes papers, BL.
26. Oliver Wardrop telegram to George Curzon, 12 October 1919, Keyes papers, BL.
27. Kadish, pp. 22, 24, 26.
28. Gilbert, p. 293.
29. Churchill telegram to Hubert Gough, 6 June 1919, quoted in Gilbert, p. 293.
30. Churchill telegram to Herbert Holman, 18 September 1919, quoted in Kadish, p. 16.

31. Churchill, *The Aftermath*, p. 251.
32. Gilbert, p. 342.
33. Churchill, *The Aftermath*, p. 255.
34. Ullman, vol. 2, p. 219.
35. Kadish, pp. 13–14.

Chapter 17: The stubborn German eagle

1. Salomon, p. 65.
2. Tallents, p. 312.
3. Ibid., p. 313.
4. Ibid., p. 322.
5. Ibid., pp. 340–1.
6. Salomon, p. 99.
7. Harold Alexander letter to Jane de Koughnet, 15 March 1920, quoted in Nicolson, p. 64.
8. Gough, p. 191.
9. David Footman, 'Civil War in the Baltic Area: The Northwestern Army', p. 10.
10. Silverlight, p. 317.
11. Denikin, p. 318.
12. Nabokoff, pp. 299, 301.
13. Gilbert, p. 322.
14. Lloyd George to Churchill, Curzon and Balfour, 30 August 1919, quoted in Gilbert, pp. 324–5.
15. Agar, p. 39. Agar's memoir is hazy on dates; where necessary I have relied on Harry Ferguson's *Operation Kronstadt*, which is drawn from his diary.
16. Agar, p. 71.
17. Ferguson, pp. 159–60.
18. Agar, pp. 86–7.
19. Ferguson, p. 168.
20. Agar, p. 92.
21. Ibid., p. 124.
22. Ibid., p. 153.
23. There is confusion about how many lives were lost in the Kronstadt raid. Geoffrey Bennett's *Freeing the Baltic* gives it as fifteen, and the Commonwealth War Graves Commission as eight.

Chapter 18: Ironside's bed

1. Boris Sokolov memoir, in Goldin (ed.), *Bely Sever*, vol. 2, p. 320.
2. Henry Rawlinson diary, 31 July 1919, quoted in Gilbert, p. 315.
3. Edmund Ironside diary, 1 and 16 August 1919, LHCMA-KCL.
4. Ibid., 2 August 1919.
5. Ibid., 11 August 1919.
6. Henry Rawlinson letter to Henry Wilson, 27 August 1919, quoted in Jeffreys, *Field Marshal Sir Henry Wilson*, p. 232.
7. Dobrovolsky, p. 48.
8. Ibid., pp. 48–9.
9. Ironside diary, 12 and 19 August 1919, LHCMA-KCL.
10. Dobrovolsky, p. 52.
11. Zelenov, pp. 28–9.
12. Edward Allfrey diary, 10 August 1919, IWM.
13. Ibid., 11 August 1919.
14. Ibid., 13 August 1919.
15. Sokolov memoir, in Goldin (ed.), *Bely Sever*, vol. 2, p. 326.
16. Allfrey diary, 29 August 1919, IWM. See also the diary of Lieutenant John Bowen of the *Moth*, 8 September 1919, IWM.
17. Allfrey diary, 5 September 1919, IWM.
18. Ironside diary, 31 March 1919, LHCMA-KCL.
19. Ibid., 3 August 1919.
20. Ibid., 27 August 1919.
21. For more on the M Devices, see Milton, pp. 251–5, and Jones.
22. Ironside diary, 8 September 1919, LHCMA-KCL.
23. Ibid., 17 September 1919.
24. Ibid., 23 September 1919.
25. Ironside, *Archangel 1918–1919*, pp. 176–7.
26. Ironside diary, 27 September 1919, LHCMA-KCL.
27. Ibid., 10 September 1919.

Chapter 19: 'We liked the Balts'

1. Serge, pp. 39, 58–9.
2. See Foglesong, pp. 264–5.
3. Ullman, vol. 2, pp. 283–4.

4. Tallents, p. 362.

5. Ibid., pp. 336–7.

6. Ruhl, p. 109.

7. Serge, p. 189.

8. Gilbert, pp. 350–1.

9. Walter Duranty, *I Write as I Please*, London, 1935, p. 21.

10. Ruhl, p. 110.

11. George Baer (ed.), *A Question of Trust: The Origins of US–Soviet Diplomatic Relations – The Memoirs of Loy W. Henderson*, Stanford, 1986, quoted in 'How Loy Henderson Earned Estonia's Cross of Liberty', p. 3, https://ee.usembassy.gov/wp-content/uploads/sites/207/How-Loy-Henderson-Earned-Estonia.pdf

12. Tallents, p. 368.

13. Bennett, p. 202.

14. Harold Alexander letter to his family, 25 January 1920, quoted in Egremont, p. 159.

15. Harold Alexander letter to his uncle, 22 February 1920, quoted in Nicolson, p. 64.

16. Tallents, p. 286.

17. Ibid., p. 376.

18. Ibid., p. 404.

Chapter 20: To Moscow!

1. Mikhail Bulgakov, 'Future Prospects', 13 November 1919, in Boris Dralyuk (ed.), *1917: Stories and Poems from the Russian Revolution* (trans. Martha Kelly), London, 2016, pp. 209–12.

2. John Kennedy diary, 7 and 8 September 1919, LHCMA-KCL.

3. Ibid., 11 September 1919.

4. Ibid., 21 September 1919.

5. Ibid., 10 October 1919.

6. Ibid., 11 October 1919.

7. John Kennedy, 'Notes on a Visit to the Volunteer Army Front', *c.* 17 October 1919, LHCMA-KCL.

8. Kennedy diary, 14 and 15 October 1919, LHCMA-KCL.

9. Quoted in Churchill, *The Aftermath*, p. 258.

10. Gilbert, pp. 331–3.

11. Ibid., pp. 333–5.

12. Henry Wilson diary, 16 October 1919, quoted in Gilbert, p. 348.

13. Herbert Holman note to Anton Denikin, 3 September 1919, quoted in Ullman, vol. 2, p. 214.

14. Hodgson, pp. 180–1.

15. Ullman, vol. 2, p. 214.

16. Kennedy diary, 1 and 6 November 1919, LHCMA-KCL.

17. Ibid., 7 October 1919.

18. Charles Jacobovitz, quoted in Veidlinger, p. 271.

19. Ibid., p. 272.

20. Ibid., p. 274.

21. Heifetz, p. 119.

22. Vasiliy Shulgin, 'Torture of Fear', *Kievlyanin*, 19 October 1919, quoted in Heifetz, pp. 113–14. In his atmospheric but unreliable memoir *Story of a Life*, Konstantin Paustowsky describes how the Kiev nights were rent with the sound of screaming, but states that there was no actual pogrom. This is false.

23. Albert Carasso, secretary of the Comité de secours aux Juifs de Russie, letter to John de Robeck, 17 November 1919, Keyes papers, BL. The meeting took place on 8 August 1919.

24. VA Odessa chief of staff General Chernyavin to QMG Taganrog, 30 November 1919, and Captain Sokolov report to British liaison, Odessa, 11 November 1919, J. W. C. Lancaster papers, IWM.

25. Hudleston Williamson, in Harris (ed.), p. 123, and letters to his mother, 2 June, 22 July, 12 August 1919, IWM.

26. Williamson letter to his mother, 12 September 1919, IWM.

27. Williamson, 'Note on Operations While Visiting 1st Don Corps, 21 Oct–6 Nov 1919', IWM.

28. Williamson, in Harris (ed.), p. 184.

29. Lobanov-Rostovsky, p. 352.

30. Ibid., pp. 360–1.

31. Kennedy diary, 5 and 7 November 1919, LHCMA-KCL.

Chapter 21: 'Russia is a quicksand'

1. Graves, p. 216.

2. Ibid., p. 229.

3. Ibid., p. 231.

4. Ibid., p. 233.

5. Ibid., p. 241; John McDonald, quoted in Bisher, pp. 184–5. Graves's account was drawn from memory, McDonald's from evidence he gave to a Senate committee. They differ on minor details.

6. Bisher, p. 185.

7. William O'Reilly to Curzon, 15 October 1919, quoted in Ullman, vol. 2, p. 242.

8. Ullman, vol. 2, p. 239.

9. Churchill to Curzon, 10 October 1919, quoted in Gilbert, p. 344.

10. Beizer, p. 43.

11. Graves, p. 266.

12. Beizer, p. 45.

13. Graves, p. 267.

14. Gerhardie, *Futility*, pp. 159–60.

15. Graves, p. 271.

16. Gilbert, p. 356.

17. Hodgson, pp. 191–5.

18. *The Times*, 10 November 1919, quoted in Silverlight, p. 338. For more on *The Times*'s antisemitism, see Kadish, pp. 22–32.

Chapter 22: 'The falls of Niagara'

1. Becvar, pp. 220–1.

2. Fedotoff White, p. 260.

3. Ibid., p. 263.

4. Gerhardie, *Futility*, p. 135.

5. Thomas Ivens letter to his uncle, 23 November 1919, IWM.

6. Davies, p. 80.

7. Gerhardie, *Memoirs of a Polyglot*, p. 161.

8. McCullagh, pp. 22, 28.

9. Horrocks, p. 45.

10. McCullagh, p. 15.

11. Ibid., p. 17.

12. Ibid., p. 22.

13. Horrocks, p. 46.

14. Ilyin, p. 177.

15. McCullagh, pp. 68–9.

16. Ibid., p. 46.

17. See Phelps Hodges.

18. Fedotoff White, p. 343.
19. Fleming, p. 188.
20. Ibid., p. 224.
21. Graves, p. 337.
22. Gerhardie, *Memoirs of a Polyglot*, p. 177; Davies, p. 88.
23. Bisher, pp. 221–2.
24. Graves, pp. 353–4.
25. Silverlight, p. 352.

Chapter 23: The Heartland

1. George Lever diary, early December 1919, p. 32, LHCMA-KCL.
2. Ibid., 16 and 17 December 1919.
3. Ibid., 13 December 1919.
4. See Veidlinger, pp. 276–7.
5. John Kennedy diary, 30 November 1919, LHCMA-KCL.
6. Kennedy, report to Cotton and diary, 26 December 1919, LHCMA-KCL.
7. Maurice Howgrave-Graham diary, 29 December 1919, private collection.
8. Lever diary, 1 January 1920, LHCMA-KCL.
9. Collishaw, p. 209.
10. Collishaw letter to Imogen Aten, 23 September 1961, quoted in Loftus, pp. 25–6.
11. Lobanov-Rostovsky, p. 366. For more on Yekaterinodar at the time, see Bechhofer, pp. 141–60.
12. Hudleston Williamson letter to his mother, 6 January 1920, IWM.
13. Ibid., 13 January 1920.
14. Lever diary, mid-January 1920, pp. 70–1, LHCMA-KCL.
15. Frederick Lister, note he added to a letter he received from Jocelyn Percy, 9 May 1920, Lister papers, LHCMA-KCL.
16. Williamson, in Harris (ed.), pp. 250–1. Kozma's statement is cited in Andrew Bailey, 'The Fallen of Ewhurst and Ellen's Green, Surrey: William Frecheville', private collection. For an account by a Rostov resident who knew Kozma, see Bechhofer, p. 133.
17. Gilbert, p. 364.
18. Ibid., pp. 368–9.
19. Churchill, 'Zionism versus Bolshevism', *Illustrated Sunday Herald*, 8 February 1920.

20. Kearns, p. 202.
21. Halford Mackinder, 'Report on Situation in South Russia', 21 January 1920, p. 4 and Appendix B, NA.
22. Veidlinger, p. 309.
23. Kearns, p. 204.
24. Lucien Wolf letter to the Under-Secretary of State, 5 November 1919, Keyes papers, BL.
25. Mackinder, 'Report on Situation in South Russia', 21 January 1920, p. 6, NA.
26. See Charles Clover, 'The Unlikely Origins of Russia's Manifest Destiny', *Foreign Policy*, 27 July 2016.

Chapter 24: *Tak!*

1. 'A Report by JWC Lancaster on the Evacuation of Odessa, 7th Feb, 1920', J. W. C. Lancaster papers, IWM.
2. 'Report by Captain JWC Lancaster on the assassination of Colonel Kirpitchnikoff', undated, J. W. C. Lancaster papers, IWM.
3. The intelligence officer George Hill appropriated the Kirpichnikov episode in his memoirs, painting it as a dashing stroke and taking Lancaster's role for himself.
4. J. Bostock letter to his mother, 13 February 1920, IWM.
5. Caspar Swinley letter to his mother, 14 February 1920, BL-UL.
6. Bostock letter to his mother, 13 February 1920, IWM.
7. George Lever diary, 31 January 1920, LHCMA-KCL.
8. Lobanov-Rostovsky, p. 370.
9. Lever diary, 31 January 1920, LHCMA-KCL.
10. Frederick Lister diary, 13 February 1920, Lister papers, LHCMA-KCL.
11. Ibid., 24 February 1920.
12. Ibid., 25 February 1920.
13. Ibid., 2 March 1920.
14. Keyes telegram to the F.O., 4 March 1920, Keyes papers, BL.
15. See Bechhofer, p. 202.
16. Lister diary, 15 and 18 March 1920, Lister papers, LHCMA-KCL.
17. Hudleston Williamson, in Harris (ed.), pp. 282–3.
18. Lobanov-Rostovsky, pp. 372–3.
19. Lever diary, 25 March 1920, LHCMA-KCL.

20. Jocelyn Percy letter to Frederick Lister, 9 May 1920, Lister papers, LHCMA-KCL.
21. Maurice Jenks interview, recorded 1979, IWM.
22. Lever diary, 26 March 1920, LHCMA-KCL.
23. Lobanov-Rostovksy, pp. 373–4. Happy to say, after a couple of starveling years in Constantinople and Paris, he had a long and successful academic career at the universities of California and Michigan, loved by generations of lucky undergraduates for what his obituary called his 'matchless ability to enliven his lectures with personal reminiscences'.

Chapter 25: 'Do we not trade with cannibals?'

1. Churchill letter to Lloyd George, 31 March 1920, quoted in Gilbert, p. 388.
2. McCullagh, pp. 227, 229.
3. Poole, pp. 296–7.
4. Gilbert, p. 380.
5. For more on the Labour mission, see the enterprising Charles Buxton's *In a Russian Village*, London, 1922. And for a Russian minder's point of view, Gleb Albert, '"I Have No Qualms About Having Shown Soviet Russia Just Like It Is"', *International Newsletter of Communist Studies*, nos 31–2, 2018–19, pp. 85–100. See also the 'British Labour Delegation to Russia, 1920: Report' in the University of Warwick Digital Collections, https://cdm21047.contentdm.oclc.org/digital/collection/russian/id/1874
6. George Riddell diary, 9 May 1920, quoted in Ullman, vol. 3, p. 48.
7. Isaac Babel diary, 14 July 1920, in Avins (ed.).
8. Ibid., 17 August 1920.
9. Ibid., 28 August 1920.
10. Ibid., 23 July 1920.
11. Churchill speech at the Cannon St Hotel, 4 November 1920, quoted in Gilbert, p. 464.
12. Henry Wilson diary, 15 January, 27 May and 23 July 1920, quoted in Ullman, vol. 3, p. 275.
13. Ibid., 18 and 23 August 1920, quoted in Ullman, vol. 3, p. 278 and Gilbert, p. 425.
14. Jocelyn Percy letter to Frederick Lister, 9 May 1920, Lister papers, LHCMA-KCL.

15. George Wood, 'Old, Unhappy Far-off Things: A Subaltern in South Russia 1919–20', p. 16, Wood papers, IWM.
16. Lever letter to his brother, undated, and diary pp. 117–18, LHCMA-KCL.
17. Lendon FitzPayne interview, recorded 1983, IWM.
18. Silverlight, p. 365.

Chapter 26: Aftermath

1. L. Duncan Porteous memoir, p. 134, IWM.
2. Lloyd George, *The Truth about the Peace Treaties*, vol. 2, pp. 324–5; Silverlight, pp. 286–7.
3. Churchill, *The Aftermath*, pp. 178, 255.
4. Charles Drage interview, recorded 1982, IWM.
5. See Weeks, pp. 192, 205, 213, 237–8.
6. MacDonell, pp. 318–19.

Select Bibliography

Quotations from the diaries of Lionel Dunsterville by kind permission of Han and Jane Dunsterville; of Maurice Howgrave-Graham by kind permission of Christopher Howgrave-Graham; of Edmund Ironside by kind permission of Charles, Lord Ironside; and of Zoya Mikhailova by kind permission of Sir Richard Onslow.

Books

Agar, Augustus, *Baltic Episode*, London, 1963

Albertson, Ralph, *Fighting Without a War: An Account of Military Intervention in North Russia*, New York, 1920

Astashkevich, Irina, *Gendered Violence: Jewish Women in the Pogroms of 1917–1921*, Boston, 2018

Avins, Carol J. (ed.), *Isaac Babel, 1920 Diary* (trans. H. T. Willetts), New Haven, 1995

Banine, *Days in the Caucasus* (trans. Anne Thompson-Ahmadova), London, 2018

Baron, Nick (ed.), *The King of Karelia: Col. P. J. Woods and the British Intervention in North Russia, 1918–19, a History and Memoir*, London, 2007

Bechhofer, C. E., *In Denikin's Russia and the Caucasus, 1919–1920*, London, 1921

Becvar, Gustav, *The Lost Legion: A Czechoslovakian Epic*, London, 1939

Beevor, Antony, *Russia: Revolution and Civil War, 1917–1921*, London, 2022

Bennett, Geoffrey, *Freeing the Baltic*, Edinburgh, 2002

Berg, A. Scott, *Wilson*, London, 2013

Berkman, Alexander, *The Bolshevik Myth: Diary 1920–22*, London, 2017

Bisher, Jamie, *White Terror: Cossack Warlords of the Trans-Siberian*, New York, 2005

Brandstrom, Elsa, *Among Prisoners of War in Russia and Siberia* (trans. C. Mabel Rickmers), London, 1929

Brogan, Hugh, *The Life of Arthur Ransome*, London, 1984

Bruce Lockhart, R. H., *Memoirs of a British Agent*, London, 1934

Budnitskii, Oleg, *Russian Jews Between the Reds and the Whites, 1917–1920* (trans. Timothy J. Portice), Philadelphia, 2012

Bunin, Ivan, *Cursed Days: A Diary of Revolution* (trans. Thomas Gaiton Marullo), London, 2000

Buxhoeveden, Baroness Sophie, *Left Behind: Fourteen Months in Siberia, December 1917–1919*, www.alexanderpalace.org/leftbehind/index.html

Bzhezinsky, L. V., *Vooruzhennaya interventsiya na Murmanye: Vospominaniya predsedatelya Tsentromura o sobytiyakh 1917–1918 gg.*, Murmansk, 2011

Capelotti, P. J., *Our Man in the Crimea: Commander Hugo Koehler and the Russian Civil War*, Columbia, 1991

Carey, Neil (ed.), *Fighting the Bolsheviks: The Russian War Memoir of Private First Class Donald E. Carey, US Army, 1918–1919*, Novato, 1997

Chamberlin, William Henry, *The Russian Revolution, 1917–1921* (2 vols), London, 1954

Churchill, Winston, *The Aftermath*, London, 1929

——, *Thoughts and Adventures*, London, 1932

Collishaw, Raymond, *Air Command: A Fighter Pilot's Story*, London, 1973

Costello, Harry J., *Why Did We Go to Russia?* Detroit, c.1920

Cudahy, John ('A Chronicler'), *Archangel: The American War with Russia*, Chicago, 1924

Dallas, Gregor, *At the Heart of a Tiger: Clemenceau and his World, 1841–1929*, London, 1993

Davies, Dido, *William Gerhardie: A Biography*, Oxford, 1991

Denikine [Denikin], A., *The White Army* (trans. Catherine Zvegintzov), London, 1930

Dobrovolsky, Sergei, *The Struggle for Russia's Revival in the Northern Region* (trans. Brian Dimler), lulu.com, 2018. (The original is included in Goldin, *Bely Sever*.)

Dobson, Christopher and John Miller, *The Day We Almost Bombed Moscow: The Allied War in Russia 1918–1920*, London, 1986

Dotsenko, Paul, *The Struggle for Democracy in Siberia, 1917–1920: Eyewitness Account of a Contemporary*, Stanford, 1983

Dunsterville, L. C., *The Adventures of Dunsterforce*, London, 1920

Egremont, Max, *The Glass Wall: Lives on the Baltic Frontier*, London, 2021

Ellis, C. H., *Transcaspian Episode, 1918–1919*, London, 1963

Farmborough, Florence, *Nurse at the Russian Front*, London, 1974

Fedotoff White, D., *Survival Through War and Revolution in Russia*, Philadelphia, 1939

Fen, Elisaveta, *Remember Russia, 1915–1925*, London, 1973

Ferguson, Harry, *Operation Kronstadt*, London, 2008

Figes, Orlando, *A People's Tragedy: The Russian Revolution, 1891–1924*, London, 1996

Fleming, Peter, *The Fate of Admiral Kolchak*, Edinburgh, 2001

Foglesong, David S., *America's Secret War against Bolshevism: US Intervention in the Russian Civil War, 1917–1920*, Chapel Hill, 1995

Francis, David R., *Russia from the American Embassy, April 1916–November 1918*, New York, 1921

Fraser, Eugenie, *The House by the Dvina: A Russian Childhood*, London, 1989

Gerhardie, William, *Futility*, London, 1922

——, *The Polyglots*, London, 1925

——, *Memoirs of a Polyglot: The Autobiography of William Gerhardie*, London, 1973

Gerwarth, Robert, *The Vanquished: Why the First World War Failed to End*, New York, 2016

—— and John Horne (eds), *War in Peace: Paramilitary Violence after the Great War*, Oxford, 2012

Gilbert, Martin, *World in Torment: Winston S. Churchill, 1917–1922*, London, 1990

Glenny, Michael and Norman Stone (eds), *The Other Russia*, London, 1990

Goldin, V. I., *Sever Rossii na puti k Grazhdanskoi Voinye, 1900–1920* (2 vols), Archangel, 2018

——, *Interventsiya na Russkom Severye, 1918–1920*, Archangel, 2018

—— (ed.), *Bely Sever, 1918–1920: memuary i dokumenty* (2 vols), Archangel, 1993

Goldman, Emma, *My Disillusionment in Russia*, London, 1925

Gough, Hubert, *Soldiering On*, London, 1954

Graves, William S., *America's Siberian Adventure, 1918–1920*, New York, 1941

Halliday, E. M., *The Ignorant Armies*, London, 1960

Halpern, Paul G. (ed.), *The Royal Navy and the Mediterranean, 1919–1929*, Farnham, 2011

Harris, John (ed.), *Farewell to the Don: The Russian Revolution in the Journals of Brigadier H. N. H. Williamson*, London, 1971

Hašek, Jaroslav, *Behind the Lines* (trans. Mark Corner), Prague, 2016

Hattersley, Roy, *The Great Outsider: David Lloyd George*, London, 2010

Heifetz, Elias, *The Slaughter of the Jews in the Ukraine in 1919*, New York, 1921

Hill, George Alexander, *Go Spy the Land*, London, 1932

Hodgson, John Ernest, *With Denikin's Armies: Being a Description of the Cossack Counter-Revolution in South Russia, 1918–1920*, London, 1932

Hopkirk, Peter, *On Secret Service East of Constantinople*, London, 1994

Horrocks, Brian, *A Full Life*, London, 1960

Ignatieff, Michael, *The Russian Album: A Family Saga of Revolution, Civil War and Exile*, London, 1987

Ilyin, Olga, *White Road: A Russian Odyssey, 1919–1923*, New York, 1984

Ironside, Edmund, *Archangel 1918–1919*, London, 1953

Ironside, Edmund [Field Marshal's son] with Andrew Bamford, *Ironside: The Authorised Biography of Field Marshal Lord Ironside*, Stroud, 2018

Isitt, Benjamin, *From Victoria to Vladivostok: Canada's Siberian Expedition, 1917–1919*, Vancouver, 2010

Janin, Maurice, *Ma Mission en Sibérie, 1918–1920*, Paris, 1933

Jeffreys, Keith, *Field Marshal Sir Henry Wilson: A Political Soldier*, Oxford, 2006

—— (ed.), *The Military Correspondence of Field Marshal Sir Henry Wilson, 1918–1922*, London, 1985

Jenkins, Roy, *Churchill*, London, 2001

Kadish, Sharman, *Bolsheviks and British Jews: The Anglo-Jewish Community, Britain and the Russian Revolution*, London, 1992

Kazemzadeh, Firuz, *The Struggle for Transcaucasia*, New York, 1951

Kearns, Gerry, *Geopolitics and Empire: The Legacy of Halford Mackinder*, Oxford, 2009

Kellogg, Michael, *The Russian Roots of Nazism: White Russians and the Making of National Socialism, 1917–1945*, Cambridge, 2005

Kenez, Peter, *Civil War in South Russia* (2 vols), Berkeley, 1971 and 1977

Kennan, George F., *The Decision to Intervene* (vol. 2 of *Soviet-American Relations, 1917–1920*), Princeton, 1958

Kettle, Michael, *Russia and the Allies*, vol. 1, *The Allies and the Russian Collapse: March 1917–March 1918*, London, 1981

——, *Russia and the Allies*, vol. 2, *The Road to Intervention: March–November 1918*, London, 1988

——, *Russia and the Allies*, vol. 3, *Churchill and the Archangel Fiasco: November 1918–July 1919*, London, 1992

Kinvig, Clifford, *Churchill's Crusade: The British Invasion of Russia 1918–1920*, London, 2006

Kiselyev, A. A. et al. (eds), *Grazhdanskaya voina na Murmanye: glazami uchast-nikov i ochevidtsyev*, Murmansk, 2006

Knox, Alfred, *With the Russian Army, 1914–17* (2 vols), London, 1921

Lansing, Robert, *War Memoirs of Robert Lansing, Secretary of State*, New York, 1935

Levene, Mark, *War, Jews and the New Europe: The Diplomacy of Lucien Wolf, 1914–1919*, Oxford, 1992

Lloyd George, David, *War Memoirs* (6 vols), London, 1933–6

——, *The Truth About the Peace Treaties* (2 vols), London, 1938

Lobanov-Rostovsky, Andrei, *The Grinding Mill: Reminiscences of War and Revolution in Russia, 1913–1920*, New York, 1935

Luckett, Richard, *The White Generals: An Account of the White Movement and the Russian Civil War*, London, 1971

McCullagh, Francis, *A Prisoner of the Reds: The Story of a British Officer Captured in Siberia*, London, 1921

MacDonell, Ranald, *And Nothing Long*, London, 1938

MacMillan, Margaret, *Peacemakers: Six Months that Changed the World*, London, 2002

McNamara, Kevin J., *Dreams of a Great Small Nation: The Mutinous Army that Threatened a Revolution, Destroyed an Empire, Founded a Republic and Remade the Map of Europe*, New York, 2016

Marushevsky, V. V., *God na Severye: Zapiski komanduyushchego voiskami Severnoi Oblasti*, Moscow, 2019

Mawdsley, Evan, *The Russian Civil War*, London, 2011

Maynard, C., *The Murmansk Venture*, London, 1928

Milton, Giles, *Russian Roulette: How British Spies Defeated Lenin*, London, 2014

Moore, Joel et al. (eds), *The History of the American Expedition Fighting the Bolsheviki, 1918–1919*, Detroit, 1920

Muirden, Bruce, *The Diggers Who Signed on for More: Australia's Part in the Russian Wars of Intervention, 1918–1919*, Adelaide, 1990

Nabokoff, C., *The Ordeal of a Diplomat*, London, 1921

Nicolson, Nigel, *Alex: The Life of Field Marshal Alexander of Tunis*, London, 1973

Novikova, Liudmilla, *An Anti-Bolshevik Alternative: The White Movement and the Civil War in the Russian North* (trans. Seth Bernstein), Madison, 2018

Ouspensky, P. D., *Letters from Russia, 1919*, London, 1991

Paustovsky, Konstantin, *In that Dawn* (trans. Manya Harari and Michael Duncan) (vol. 3 of *Story of a Life*), London, 1967

Phelps Hodges, Alexander, *Britmis: A Great Adventure of the War*, London, 1931

Philips Price, Morgan, *My Reminiscences of the Russian Revolution*, London, 1921

Pipes, Richard, *The Russian Revolution, 1899–1919*, London, 1990

——, *Russia Under the Bolshevik Regime, 1919–1924*, London, 1994

Pitcher, Harvey, *When Miss Emmie was in Russia: English Governesses Before, During and After the Russian Revolution*, London, 1977

Poole, DeWitt Clinton (ed. Lorraine Lees and William Rodner), *An American Diplomat in Bolshevik Russia*, Madison, 2014

Power, Rhoda, *Under Cossack and Bolshevik*, London, 1919

Ransome, Arthur, *Six Weeks in Russia in 1919*, London, 1919

Rappaport, Helen, *The Race to Save the Romanovs: The Truth Behind the Secret Plans to Rescue Russia's Imperial Family*, London, 2018

Richard, Carl J., *When the United States Invaded Russia: Woodrow Wilson's Siberian Disaster*, Washington DC, 2017

Roberts, Andrew, *Churchill*, London, 2018

Robien, Louis de, *The Diary of a Diplomat in Russia, 1917–1918* (trans. Camilla Sykes), New York, 1970

Rodzianko, Paul, *Tattered Banners: An Autobiography*, Philadelphia, 2018

Rothstein, Andrew, *When Britain Invaded Soviet Russia: The Consul Who Rebelled*, London, 1979

Ruhl, Arthur, *New Masters of the Baltic*, New York, 1921

Sadoul, Jacques, *Notes sur la révolution bolchévique*, Paris, 1919

Sakharow [Sakharov], Konstantin, *The Czechs [sic] Legions in Siberia*, Akron, Ohio, 1992 (first published in Berlin in 1936, as *Die tschechischen Legionen in Sibirien*)

Salomon, Ernst von, *The Outlaws* (trans. Ian Morrow), London, 1931

Schönpflug, Daniel, *A World on Edge: The End of the Great War and the Dawn of a New Age* (trans. Jefferson Chase), London, 2018

Sebestyen, Victor, *Lenin the Dictator: An Intimate Portrait*, London, 2017

Serge, Victor, *Conquered City* (trans. Richard Greeman), New York, 2011

Service, Robert, *Spies and Commissars: Bolshevik Russia and the West*, London, 2012

Shtif, Nokhem, *The Pogroms in Ukraine, 1918–1919: Prelude to the Holocaust* (trans. Maurice Wolfthal), Cambridge, 2019

Silverlight, John, *The Victors' Dilemma: Allied Intervention in the Russian Civil War*, London, 1970

Smele, Jonathan D., *Civil War in Siberia: The Anti-Bolshevik Government of Admiral Kolchak, 1918–1920*, Cambridge, 1996

——, *The Russian Revolution and Civil War, 1917–1921: An Annotated Bibliography*, London, 2003

——, *The 'Russian' Civil Wars, 1916–1926: Ten Years that Shook the World*, London, 2015

Smith, Douglas, *Former People: The Last Days of the Russian Aristocracy*, London, 2012

——, *The Russian Job: The Forgotten Story of How America Saved the Soviet Union from Famine*, London, 2019

Strakhovsky, Leonid, *Intervention at Archangel: The Story of Allied Intervention and Russian Counter-Revolution in North Russia, 1918–1920*, New York, 1971

Tallents, Stephen, *Man and Boy*, London, 1943

Teague-Jones, Reginald, *The Spy Who Disappeared: Diary of a Secret Mission to Russian Central Asia in 1918*, London, 1991

Teffi, *Memories: From Moscow to the Black Sea* (trans. Robert and Elizabeth Chandler, Anne Marie Jackson and Irina Steinberg), New York, 2016

Tooze, Adam, *The Deluge: The Great War and the Remaking of the Global Order, 1916–1931*, London, 2015

Ullman, Richard, *Anglo-Soviet Relations 1917–1921*, vol. 1, *Intervention and the War*, Princeton, 1961

——, *Anglo-Soviet Relations 1917–1921*, vol. 2, *Britain and the Russian Civil War*, Princeton, 1968

——, *Anglo-Soviet Relations 1917–1921*, vol. 3, *The Anglo-Soviet Accord*, Princeton, 1972

Unterberger, Betty M., *America's Siberian Expedition, 1918–1920: A Study of National Policy*, New York, 1969

Veidlinger, Jeffrey, *In the Midst of Civilised Europe: The 1918–1921 Pogroms in Ukraine and the Onset of the Holocaust*, London, 2022

Waal, Thomas de, *The Caucasus: An Introduction*, Oxford, 2019

Ward, John, *With the 'Die-Hards' in Siberia*, London, 1920

Weeks, Charles J., *An American Naval Diplomat in Revolutionary Russia: The Life and Times of Vice Admiral Newton A. McCully*, Annapolis, 1993

Welch, Frances, *The Russian Court at Sea: The Voyage of the HMS Marlborough, April 1919*, London, 2011

Wiart, Adrian Carton de, *Happy Odyssey*, London, 1950

Wieloch, Rupert, *Churchill's Abandoned Prisoners: The British Soldiers Deceived in the Russian Civil War*, Oxford, 2019

Wrangel, Pyotr, *The Memoirs of General Wrangel, the Last Commander-in-Chief of the Russian Army* (trans. Sophie Goulston), New York, 1929

Wright, Damien, *Churchill's Secret War with Lenin: British and Commonwealth Military Intervention in the Russian Civil War, 1918–1920*, Warwick, 2017

Young, E. Hilton, *By Sea and Land*, London, 1924

Zelenov, N. P., *Tragediya Severnoi Oblasti: Iz lichnykh vospominaniy*, Paris, 1922

Zobnin, Andrei, *Protivostoyaniye: Shenkurskiy uyezd Arkhangelskoi gubernii, 1918–1920 gody*, St Petersburg, 2018

Articles and Theses

Allen, Conrad, 'A Highly Disreputable Enterprise: Men-on-the-Spot and the Allied Intervention in the Russian Civil War, 1917–1920', Ohio State University, 2016

Bagni, Bruno, 'Lemnos, l'île aux Cosaques', *Cahiers du Monde Russe*, vol. 50, no. 1 (2009), pp. 187–230

Balbirnie, Steven, 'British Colonial Attitudes in the Arctic: The British Occupation of Archangel and Murmansk', University College Dublin, 2015

——, 'A Bad Business: British Responses to Mutinies among Local Forces in Northern Russia', *Revolutionary Russia*, vol. 29, no. 2 (2016), pp. 1–20

Beizer, Michael, 'Restoring Courage to Jewish Hearts: Frank Rosenblatt's Mission in Siberia in 1919', *East European Jewish Affairs*, vol. 39, no. 1 (2009), pp. 35–56

Bentinck, V. M., 'Mutiny in Murmansk: "The Hidden Shame": Royal Marines in North Russia, 1918/1919', Special Publication, no. 21, Royal Marines Historical Society, 1999

Boylan, Catherine, 'The North Russia Relief Force: A Study of Military Motivation in the Aftermath of the First World War', King's College London, 2016

Footman, David, 'The Civil War and the Baltic States: Von der Goltz and Bermondt-Avalov'; 'Civil War in the Baltic Area: The Northwestern Army', in David Footman, ed., *Soviet Affairs, Number Two*, St Antony's Papers, no. 6, Oxford, 1959

Goldin, Vladislav, 'New Views on the Allied Intervention', *Revolutionary Russia*, vol. 13, no. 1 (2000), pp. 88–95

Hatch McNeal, Robert, 'The Conference of Jassy: An Early Fiasco of the Anti-Bolshevik Movement', in John S. Curtiss (ed.), *Essays in Honor of Geroid Tanquary Robinson*, Leiden, 1963

Hope Carson, E., 'British Tanks in North-West Russia', *Royal Tank Corps Journal*, vol. 9, no. 98 (1927)

Horgan, John, 'The Great War Correspondent: Francis McCullagh, 1874–1956', *Irish Historical Studies*, vol. 36, no. 44 (2009), pp. 542–63

Irwin, Julia, 'The Great White Train: Typhus, Sanitation, and U.S. International Development During the Russian Civil War', *Endeavour*, vol. 35, no. 3 (2012), pp. 89–96

Jones, Simon, 'The Right Medicine for the Bolshevist: British Air-Dropped Chemical Weapons in North Russia, 1919', *Imperial War Museum Review*, no. 12 (1999), pp. 78–88

Kopisto, Lauri, 'The British Intervention in South Russia 1918–1920', University of Helsinki, 2011

Loftus, Jon, 'Major Collishaw's Bright Young Wings: Reconstructing the Experience of 47 Squadron Royal Air Force in the Russian Civil War, 1919–20', Leiden University, 2019

McGeever, Brendan, 'Red Antisemitism: Anti-Jewish Violence and Revolutionary Politics in Ukraine, 1919', in Elissa Bemporad and Thomas Chopard (ed.), 'The Pogroms of the Russian Civil War at 100: New Trends, New Sources', *Quest. Issues in Contemporary Jewish History*, no. 15 (2019), pp. 168–95

Millman, Brock, 'The Problem with Generals: Military Observers and the Origins of the Intervention in Russia and Persia, 1917–18', *Journal of Contemporary History*, vol. 33, no. 2 (1998), pp. 291–320

Munholland, Kim J., 'The French Army and Intervention in Southern Russia, 1918–1919', *Cahiers du Monde Russe*, vol. 22, no. 1 (1981), pp. 43–66

Noskov, Vladimir, 'David R. Francis, Ambassador to Four Russian Governments', *Journal of Russian American Studies*, vol. 2, no. 1 (2018), pp. 44–62

Novikova, Liudmilla, 'A Province of a Non-Existent State: The White Government in the Russian North and Political Power in the Russian Civil War, 1918–1920', *Revolutionary Russia*, vol. 18, no. 2 (2005), p. 121

——, 'Northerners Into Whites: Popular Participation in the Counter-Revolution in Arkhangelsk Province, Summer–Autumn 1918', *Europe–Asia Studies*, vol. 60, no. 2 (2008), pp. 277–93

——, 'Russia's Red Revolution and White Terror, 1917–1921: A Provincial Perspective', *Europe–Asia Studies*, vol. 65, no. 9 (2013), pp. 1,757–8

Petsalis-Diomidis, N., 'Hellenism in Southern Russia and the Ukrainian Campaign: Their Effect on the Pontus Question (1919)', *Balkan Studies*, vol. 13, no. 2 (1972), pp. 221–63

Polyakova, Tamara, 'The Memoirist and the Editor: Writing the History of the Civil War in Karelia', *Nordic and Baltic Studies Review*, no. 1 (2016), pp. 118–31

Prchal, Jan, 'The Myth of the Anabasis: The Czecho-Slovak Legions in Russia and Czechoslovakia, 1914–1928', University of British Columbia, 2018

Smele, Jonathan, 'White Gold: The Imperial Gold Reserve in the Anti-Bolshevik East, 1918–?', *Europe–Asia Studies*, vol. 46, no. 8 (1994), pp. 1317–47

Smith, Gaddis, 'Canada and the Siberian Intervention, 1918–1919', *American Historical Review*, vol. 64, no. 4 (1959), pp. 866–77

Winegard, Timothy, 'Dunsterforce: A Case Study of Coalition Warfare in the Middle East, 1918–1919', *Canadian Army Journal*, vol. 8, no. 3 (2005), pp. 93–109

Index

Index

Credit: Stacey Mutkin

Anna Reid was Kyiv correspondent for the *Economist* and the *Daily Telegraph* from 1993 to 1995, and has since written about Ukraine for *Foreign Affairs*, the *Observer*, and the *Times Literary Supplement*. She is the author of *Borderland*, *The Shaman's Coat*, and *Leningrad*, which was published in eighteen languages and short-listed for the Duff Cooper Prize. She lives in London.